TIME

LEGAL IMPLICATIONS OF PROJECT DELAY IN CONSTRUCTION

Matthew J. Ninneman, Editor

AMERICAN BAR ASSOCIATION
Forum on Construction Law

Cover design by Jill Tedhams/ABA Design

Printed in the United States of America.

30 29 28 27 26 5 4 3 2 1

A catalog record for this book is available from the Library of Congress.

CONTENTS

ABOUT THE EDITOR

Matthew J. Ninneman (Introduction/Editor) is a Partner and General Counsel of Hall & Evans, LLC and serves as it's Construction & Design Practice Co-Chair. Matthew litigates complex commercial and construction disputes in state and federal court and arbitration, representing public and private owners, developers, general contractors, design-builders, subcontractors, architects, engineers, and suppliers on private, public and hybrid projects. He focuses on resolving disputes over contract scope, payment, schedule/delay, construction and design defects, and performance claims for all types of vertical construction and infrastructure projects, and advises owners, designers and construction professionals on day-to-day risk management issues, drafting and negotiation of custom and form contracts. Matthew is also a construction arbitrator through the *American Arbitration Association's* National Panel of Construction Arbitrators. He has been recognized by Best Lawyers in America (Construction, Construction Law, Litigation—Insurance), SuperLawyers, 5280 Top Lawyers, and named Best Lawyers in America "Lawyer of the Year" in Denver for Construction in 2024.

ABOUT THE AUTHORS

Erin Fallon (Chapter 1) is a managing director with J.S. Held's Construction Advisory practice. She provides expert consulting services related to CPM schedule delay, disruption, and acceleration issues; construction cost; labor inefficiency; project controls and operational compliance; and project management standard of care. Erin has been a member of the American Bar Association Forum on Construction Law since 2007, is a board member of the Pittsburgh Section of the Association for the Advancement of Cost Engineering International (AACE International), and is a member of the American Society of Civil Engineers Schedule Delay Analysis Standard Committee. Erin also holds Planning and Scheduling Professional, and Certified Cost Professional certifications, both through AACE International.

Nicole Lentini (Chapter 1) is a partner in the construction group of Gordon Rees Scully Mansukhani in its Seattle and Denver offices. Nicole's practice focuses on litigation and arbitration of both public and private construction matters nationally. She is barred in state and federal court in Maryland, DC, Virginia, Colorado, and Washington. Nicole speaks nationally and has written on a variety of topics, including but not limited to insurance, contracts, sureties, and claim preservation. Nicole is the past chair of the Maryland Construction Law Division and is currently active in the ABA Forum on Construction Laws, serving as a Steering Committee member of Division 2 (Contracts), co-chair of the 2024 Regional Meetings, and a member of the Publications Committee. She has been recognized by The Maryland Daily Record, Superlawyers, and Best Lawyers.

Richard J. Tyler, FCIArb, (Chapter 2) is a lawyer, arbitrator, and mediator with Jones Walker LLP's nationally ranked Construction Practice, and is the former chair of the practice. With nearly 40 years' experience with complex, high-stakes construction disputes across the country, including multiple industrial megaprojects, he has been an advocate or a neutral with respect to claims having an aggregate value exceeding $750 million over the last decade. Rich is a fellow of the American College of Construction Lawyers and Chartered Institute of Arbitrators. He is a member of American Arbitration Association Commercial, Construction, Large

Complex Case, and International panels. He serves on the AAA-ICDR Council and co-chairs its National Construction Dispute Resolution Committee. He is experienced with AAA, ICDR, ICC, and UNCITRAL rule arbitrations. His ADR training includes AAA (commercial, construction, international), CIArb (international), Dispute Resolution Board Foundation, and Harvard Law School (mediation). Rich is a frequent writer and speaker on construction and ADR topics. He has been recognized by Chambers USA, Legal 500, Best Lawyers in America, and Who's Who Legal—Construction. Rich served as a member of the Forum on Construction Law Governing Committee and chaired the Division 3 Steering Committee. He received his undergraduate and law degrees from Georgetown University.

Matthew T. Arvin (Chapter 3) is a 2011 graduate from Ave Maria School of Law and is licensed to practice law in the state of Tennessee. Matthew has more than ten years of experience as a construction safety manager where he has worked in the commercial, industrial, and automotive sectors. He currently is a safety manager in Tennessee for Barton Malow, a large general contractor that has projects throughout the eastern part of the United States.

Shawn Paroline (Chapter 4) is a risk mitigation manager for Infrastructure and Capital Projects at Accenture's Santa Ana, California, office. Shawn has 31 years of professional experience in construction management, scheduling, risk management, and claims analysis. He has served as the construction manager, chief schedule engineer, and/or claims analyst on several major California public works civil infrastructure programs each in excess of $2 billion. Shawn has expertise in auditing the contract management protocols in place in the field office and providing strategic leadership to the owner's CM team in the areas of delay analysis, contemporaneous schedule review and monitoring, documentation for claims defense, and liaising with general counsel. He has prepared contract phasing language for complex projects, developed critical path method (CPM) scheduling specifications, turnaround of troubled projects, and real-time dispute management as a supplement to the agency's construction management field staff.

Kendall E. Woods (Chapter 4) is a shareholder at Buchalter in Chicago, Illinois. Kendall is a seasoned construction attorney regularly representing developers, contractors, and subcontractors in both contract negotiations and complex dispute resolution across both public and private projects. Kendall has extensive experience counseling clients on delay and lost productivity claims, design and construction defect claims, contract enforcement and breaches, lien issues, and insurance claims and coverage. Known for her strategic approach and deep understanding of construction law, Kendall regularly advises clients from project inception through dispute resolution. Kendall is also a frequent speaker and writer on construction risk management and emerging trends in the legal industry.

Susan Eccles (Chapter 5) serves as the partner in charge of the Adams & Reese Baton Rouge office, while maintaining a diverse legal practice centered on construction, state and federal procurement/government contracts, commercial litigation, environmental exposure/restoration, and insurance defense matters of all types. Susan stays abreast of the latest trends in the construction industry, including code changes, proactive tips to prevent construction defects, latest requirements on OSHA workplace inspections, and risk allocation strategies for design professionals, among other pressing topics. Susan is a published author, frequent speaker, and media source on construction industry trends, news, and legal changes. Since assuming her leadership role in the Baton Rouge office in 2022, Susan has helped double the size, developing incoming talent, mentoring younger attorneys, and instilling commitment to the community through volunteer service and fundraising. Susan is also a leading partner in the Adams & Reese ARROW program, mentoring rising female attorneys.

Wayne DeFlaminis (Chapter 6) is a partner with HKA based in Washington, DC. A mechanical engineer with more than 25 years of construction and government contracting claims experience, Wayne has provided litigation and arbitration testimony on CPM scheduling, delay analysis, lost productivity impacts, delay damages, construction management principles, and construction finance issues. Wayne has testified before U.S. federal and state courts, the ASBCA, and the AAA, and has provided opinions in international arbitration. Wayne is featured in the Lexology Index Construction Expert Witnesses and Public Projects & Procurement Guides. https://www.lexology.com/firms/hka/wayne_deflaminis.

Luke LaRocca (Chapter 6) is partner at Simon, Peragine, Smith & Redfearn in New Orleans, Louisiana. His practice focuses on construction litigation on behalf of owners, contractors, subcontractors, engineers, architects, and developers. He also negotiates general construction contracts, subcontracts, and professional services agreements. In addition to his construction practice, Luke advises clients on employment matters as they arise and counsels clients on day-to-day general business matters. Prior to his work as an attorney, Luke worked as a Human Resources Officer in the United States Navy where he was employed as the Enlisted Programs

Officer for Naval Recruiting District New Orleans. Luke is a native of Mobile, Alabama, and attended post-secondary education at Tulane University where he graduated with a bachelor's degree in management. During his time in the U.S. Navy, Luke received a master's degree in business administration with a concentration in human resources management from the University of New Orleans.

Laurie Choi (Chapter 7) is a partner and co-chair of the construction industry practice group at Snell & Wilmer, LLP's Denver office. Snell & Wilmer is a full-service law firm with offices in the United States and Mexico. Laurie is licensed to practice law in Colorado and California, and her practice is focused on construction law and construction litigation. Laurie's background in construction management, general contracting, and civil and environmental engineering allows her to provide clients with practical and strategic solutions for real-world construction issues. Laurie obtained a general contractor license in Nevada in 2009. Laurie counsels clients through construction contract drafting and negotiation, resolution of disputes arising from construction projects, legal advice for providing construction services, filing and bonding around mechanic's liens, and other construction concerns.

Brenda Radmacher (Chapter 8) is a partner with Seyfarth Shaw, LLP's Construction Practice Group based in the firm's downtown Los Angeles office. Brenda is also a mediator and arbitrator serving on the American Arbitration Association's panels. Her practice focuses on risk management, dispute resolution, and advice and counsel for national and international developers, owners, builders, and design professionals on issues including contract drafting and negotiation, delay and disruption claims, payment disputes, construction defects, indemnity and risk transfer, impacts of technology use in the construction industry, and negotiation and litigation strategies. She also has experience in complex disputes including building collapses, water-intrusion and building envelope problems, civil and highway construction, multifamily developments. Brenda has been recognized as "Lawyer of the Year—Construction (Los Angeles)" by Best Lawyers of America® for 2025–2026, a 2023 Leader of Influence by the Los Angeles Business Journal in 2023, and awarded as an Industry Veteran by Construction Dive in 2021, among other recognitions.

Jean M. Terry (Chapter 8) is a partner in the Louisville, Kentucky, office of Manion Stigger, LLP. Jean began working in the construction industry over 20 years ago, serving as an intern for a crane manufacturer in her native South Carolina. After earning her bachelor's degree in engineering from Vanderbilt University, Jean worked as a civil engineer on numerous projects throughout the public and private sectors for a multinational design and construction firm. She practices construction law throughout the country, zealously representing contractors and other construction professionals from project formation to litigation.

Sunu Pillai (Chapter 9) is a partner with Saul Ewing LLP in Pittsburgh, helping construction and energy industry clients on issues throughout the project life cycle, from contract formation through dispute resolution. He is also an arbitrator with the American Arbitration Association's construction panel and is certified as a fellow with the Chartered Institute of Arbitrators (FCIArb). Sunu worked in the construction and energy industries as an engineer, project management consultant, and expert witness consultant prior to his legal career.

Stephen R. Dowd, CPA/CFF, CVA, CMA/CFM, CFE, (Chapter 10) is a managing director in the Pittsburgh office of The Vertex Companies, LLC. Stephen has more than 30 years of experience in construction, damage claims, accounting, finance, forensic accounting, valuation, and litigation support. He has a bachelor of science in civil engineering from The Pennsylvania State University and a master of business administration from the University of Pittsburgh. In addition to holding a certified public accountant license in the state of Pennsylvania, Stephen also holds several other financial and valuation certifications. He has advised clients and assisted legal counsel in a variety of forums and has testified as an expert witness in federal court, several state courts, arbitrations, and the U.S. Court of Federal Claims.

Brian J. Schoolman (Chapter 10) is a construction attorney with Safran Law Offices in Raleigh, North Carolina. Brian is proud to represent owners, contractors, subcontractors, suppliers, and designers throughout North Carolina. Brian is happily active in the ABA Forum on Construction Law, and the North Carolina Bar Association Construction Law Section.

Buck S. Beltzer, P.E., Esq., (Chapter 11) is a founding partner of BBG Construction Law in Denver, Colorado. Buck is a professional engineer turned construction lawyer. He develops strategies to turn around troubled projects and, when disputes are unavoidable, steps in to help resolve them. Buck has successfully tried cases before juries, arbitration panels, and judges involving contract scope, schedule delays, project impacts, standards of care, and construction defects on commercial, infrastructure, and energy projects in both the private and public sectors. He has represented parties involved in various delivery method agreements and has resolved complex, multiparty, and multitier disputes involving significant financial damages. He is a fellow of the American College of Construction Lawyers and has been named Colorado's Lawyer of the Year three times by Best Lawyers for Construction Law and Construction Litigation.

John M. Neary (Chapter 12) is a partner at Akerman, LLP, in Washington, DC, and co-chair of Akerman's Construction practice. He represents owners, developers, contractors, subcontractors, and design professionals in civil litigation matters, focusing on, among other things, critical infrastructure projects, renewable and conventional power generation facilities, energy storage systems, as well as data centers and digital infrastructure. John also provides guidance on contract formation and administration on various project delivery systems for public and private construction contracts. In addition, John represents a wide variety of government contractors, including engineering, construction, and defense companies, with a focus on state and federal contract counseling and compliance. John's government contracts litigation experience includes claims litigation in federal courts and before boards of contract appeals and bid protests before various state and federal tribunals.

Daniel R. Miktus (Chapter 12) is a partner at Akerman, LLP, in Washington, DC. Daniel represents clients in the areas of construction contract drafting and negotiation, construction litigation, and government contract litigation. He has considerable experience representing clients in complex private and public construction and development disputes. Daniel's construction practice focuses on large-scale commercial, multifamily, energy (including renewable energy sources), hospitality/hotel, infrastructure/transportation, data centers, health/life science, and industrial, mixed-used, and warehouse/logistics developments. Daniel is licensed to practice in the state and federal courts of the District of Columbia, Virginia, and Maryland, and has also represented clients in the Civilian and Armed Forces Boards of Contract Appeals, Government Accountability Office Contract Appeals Board, as well as the District of Columbia Contract Appeals Board.

Daniel D. Rounds (Chapter 13) is a partner at Fox Rothschild, LLP, in Washington, DC, where he represents clients in construction and government contract matters. Daniel litigates complex federal contract and construction disputes, and he assists clients with change negotiations, requests for equitable adjustment, claim preparation, and termination settlement negotiations. Daniel also advises contractors on a wide range of federal and state procurement, regulatory compliance, and grant issues, particularly those relating to construction and to domestic preference regulations, including Buy American, Buy America, and Build America Buy America.

Daniel is a frequent speaker and contributor to construction and government contract law publications. He serves on the Board of Governors of the Virginia State Bar, Construction Law and Public Contracts Section. He is a contributing editor for the ABA Forum on Construction Law's publication The Construction Lawyer and a vice-chair on the Contract Claims and Disputes Resolutions Committee of the ABA Public Contract Law Section

John Marshall Cook (Chapter 13) is a partner at Fox Rothschild, LLP, in Washington, DC. He has practiced construction law for more than 30 years, handling projects in across the United States and internationally. John represents primarily contractors and engineering firms in disputes involving large, complex industrial and civil works projects. His list of representative projects includes all manner of power plants (nuclear, coal, gas, biomass, hydroelectric, wind, and solar), light rail transit systems, roadways, tunnels, bridges, dams, nuclear waste disposal facilities, space launch complexes, chemical demilitarization plants, ammunition factories, and food processing plants. He regularly works on matters involving cost and schedule analysis related to delay, disruption, inefficiency, and acceleration claims. John is active in the ABA Forum on Construction Law, having served as the Forum's chair in 2023 and 2024. John is also a fellow in the American College of Construction Lawyers and the Project Management College of Scheduling.

Michael Maroulis (Chapter 13) is an associate with Haynes Boone's Northern Virginia office, focusing his practice on the areas of government contracts and construction. He has experience in bid protests, contract drafting, alternative dispute resolution, litigation, regulatory compliance, mergers and acquisitions, and navigating government contract disputes. Before joining Haynes Boone, Michael served as a summer law clerk. Prior to attending law school, Michael was a project manager for a general contractor in the Mid-Atlantic area. Michael received his JD from the University of California, Berkeley, School of Law, where he served as an articles editor for the Berkeley Journal of International Law, and received a Business Law Certificate in 2022.

Greg Holness, P.E., Esq., (Chapter 14) is a managing director at FTI Consulting in New York City, where he performs forensic analysis of troubled projects and testifies in court and arbitration as an expert witness on construction disputes. For almost two decades of his career in the construction industry, Greg has worked as an attorney assisting clients resolve disputes. His focus is primarily on schedule delay, acceleration, and disruption, and the quantification of the resulting financial damages. He also works with owners and contractors, providing strategic advice on planned or ongoing projects to avoid claims and disputes. Greg has drafted and negotiated hundreds of construction and design contracts in his career, so he is intimately knowledgeable on the key terms that are often central to disputes. He also enjoys giving lectures on a wide variety of construction topics. The titles of his seminars include How Construction Problems Arise . . . And How to Avoid Them; Trips, Traps, and Ploys in Construction Scheduling; How Design Documents Can Prevent or Cause Claims; and Critical Construction Contract Clauses and the Disputes that Arise from Them, to name a few.

INTRODUCTION

The concept of "sempiternity" suggests time is infinite. Not so on a construction project. On a construction project, time is definite and, more importantly, time is money. A project's design and construction schedule, and the early completion or failure to meet the project's deadlines can and will have significant and potentially costly impacts to the project and the project participants. The schedule is one of the primary issues parties and their legal counsel work to negotiate when shifting risk under a design or construction contract, and often litigate when a project runs out of time.

For the owner of a project, failure to meet the required deadlines can cause actual and consequential damages, including loss of use, loss of income/profit, increased finance costs, and increased construction and construction management costs. Where actual costs due to delay are hard to quantify at the time of contracting, the parties will often consider liquidated damages whereby the parties agree to a set daily value that will be paid to the owner for each day the project is delayed beyond the defined completion deadline. Even when a project is completed early, time can equate to money. Some parties negotiate early completion savings provisions, where the owner and general contractor share some percentage of the savings. However, early completion can cause financial constraints on the owner, as it may be spending too quickly to keep up with the level or speed of its project financing.

Project delay is a major issue that is disputed and often litigated due to the measure of damages, the disputed facts relating to the delay, and the competing opinions of delay consultants. The parties will dispute whether delays are on the critical path, whether they are concurrent with other project delay for which it is not responsible, whether they actually caused any delay, and whether the designers and/or contractors are entitled to change orders for additional time, including compensation for the delay. Disputes often hinge on how the delay is quantified or measured, what delay model is used to determine the delay timeframe, whether liquidated damages are excessive or reasonable actual damages can be quantified, how the schedule was developed and updated, and how and whether the schedule can be recovered or accelerated to mitigate project impacts and costs.

This book is intended to serve as an essential tool to educate any party on a construction project, and the legal professionals who advise them, to understand the fundamental issues of delay and its impacts on a project, and the strategy and necessary elements of the claims and defenses that are relied on to maximize or mitigate the delay costs. In this book, Chapter 1 explores the basics of project delay, while Chapter 2 discusses the basics of project schedules and project scheduling methodologies. Chapter 3 focuses on the common causes of construction delay, and Chapter 4 discusses how contractors and owners handle time extension requests under the contract documents. Chapter 5 educates us on how the contractor delay claim develops, while Chapter 6 focuses on how the contractor proves the period of delay in order to establish its entitlement to damages. Chapter 7 discusses the owner's defenses to contractor delay claims. Chapters 8, 9 and 10 explain how damages are quantified and proven, including the contractor's delay damages in Chapter 8, the development and enforcement of liquidated damages in Chapter 9, and the categories and quantification of the owner's actual damages in Chapter 10. Chapter 11 dives into the procedures and strategies for analyzing the bases for contract termination for actual or prospective delayed completion. Conversely, Chapter 12 focuses on the impacts and benefits of early completion schedules and claims. Chapter 13 explains the fundamentals of acceleration claims and related cost impacts, and Chapter 14 explains how disruption claims are handled.

This book would not have been possible without the efforts of the ABA Forum's Governing and Publications Committee, including the former Publication Chairs, David Scotti and Tony Lehman, and the most recent Publications Chair, R. Thomas Dunn. Also, a special thank you to ABA Publishing, including specifically Sarah (Sam) Orwig, who has been instrumental in completing the book.

The drafting of this book began in 2021, and ironically, it too suffered from the implications of project delay. Since then, new authors came on board as well as a new editor. Special thanks to all of the authors who contributed so much time and effort in creating this fantastic resource for the project professionals and their legal advisors. Additional thanks are necessary for the multiple chapter editors and "cat herders" on this book, including Jayne Czik, Tony Lehman and Richard Tyler. Of course, a huge thanks must be extended to David Kirschbuam who served as the original editor of the book before I had the honor and privilege of bringing it to the finish line.

We all hope this book serves as a must-have resource to educate and strengthen the industry professionals who own, finance, design and construct any project, and assists them in understanding and realizing the risks and rewards of timely project completion. Scheduling will continue to advance and we are all excited to see what else the future holds in assisting the parties in bringing projects to successful, and hopefully, timely completion. Thanks again.

Matthew J. Ninneman, Editor
April 2026

CHAPTER 1

The Basics of Project Delays

Nicole Lentini and Erin Fallon

Introduction

Project delays are one of the most heavily disputed issues encountered during construction projects today. At its simplest, delay can be defined as the later-than-anticipated completion of a work task or a collection of work tasks necessary to progress and complete a construction project by the date required by the applicable construction contract. Late completion can be caused by a later-than-anticipated start, a longer-than-anticipated duration, or an interruption to work after the start. The quantum of delay is the variance between the actual completion date as compared to the planned or required completion date. Delays to the project can drive up costs for the owner, general contractor, and/or subcontractors and, as a result, can lead to disputes between the parties.

This chapter provides a general overview of basic principles for identifying and measuring project delays and determining delay responsibility and analyzes relevant contract provisions related to project delays.

Time Is of the Essence

Time is not ordinarily of the essence in a building or construction contract.[1] Therefore, many owners/developers specifically provide that "time is of the essence" in construction contracts. This language means that time of performance by the contractor is an important consideration and of primary importance, and that the completion date set forth in the construction contract is firm and not approximate. Where a construction contract does not expressly state that "time is of the essence," the law presumes that the parties intended performance to be completed within a

1. 15 Williston on Contracts § 46:7, Provision in Building Contracts (4th ed.).

reasonable time.[2] This presumption is valid, even where the parties have expressly agreed to a specific time of performance in their contract.[3] In any event, when an owner or developer incurs damages because of a delay, it may be in a position to recover those damages from a contractor to the extent allowed by the construction contract.[4]

Measuring Delay: The Significance of the Critical Path and Critical Delays

The Critical Path Method

The critical path method (CPM) of scheduling is a common, analytical scheduling tool used to plan the work tasks required to complete a construction project. CPM can be defined as network scheduling using activity durations and logic ties between activities to model the plan to execute the project work.[5] More specifically, a CPM schedule is developed by dividing the project scope into discrete work activities and designating the contractually responsible party for each activity; identifying the time, or duration, for each activity; and defining the logical relationships between those activities or the sequence in which activities are to be completed. The CPM algorithm is then used to determine the start and finish dates for each activity and how long the project will take to complete in the aggregate. A major advantage of CPM, and the reason for its name, is that it identifies the network of activities that determine the duration of the overall project, referred to as critical activities because if they fail to start and finish as scheduled, the entire project will be delayed.[6] Activities not on the critical path are known as "noncritical" activities and can, to some extent, be delayed without impacting the completion date of the overall project. The chain or string of critical activities is referred to as the critical path of the project, as further described later in the chapter.

A CPM schedule is often depicted as a network diagram, which is a graphical display of the discrete work activities that make up the project, the starting and

---

2. *Id.*

3. *Id.* (citing *In re* Zerodec Mega Corp., 54 B.R. 814, 42 U.C.C. Rep. Serv. 382 (Bankr. E.D. Pa. 1985) (even when the parties have expressly agreed to the time of performance in a building contract, time is not ordinarily of the essence); Empire Acquisition Grp., LLC v. Atlantic Mortg. Co., Inc., 35 A.3d 878 (R.I. 2012) (contract provisions relating to time do not by their mere presence in an agreement make time of the essence).

4. Deborah Mastin, *Damages in Construction Litigation*, Florida Civil Practice Damages ¶ 7.31 (2000).

5. AACE International Recommended Practice 10S-90, Cost Engineering Terminology (2013).

6. *Id.*

ending points of each activity,[7] and the relationships and dependencies among all of the activities that must be performed.[8] Activity durations are intended to reflect the scope and resources available to complete the work, such as labor, material, equipment, and so on.[9] The network diagram will also identify and distinguish activities considered to be on the critical path from those that are not.[10]

A major benefit of CPM is that it separates out the chain, or chains, of activities that drive the time it will take to finish the project from the activities that may slip without affecting the project's completion date. This allows the person(s) responsible for managing the project to focus resources on the activities that matter the most with respect to finishing the project on time and also to better predict the effect of individual activity schedule changes on the overall planned completion date. As a result, CPM schedules are suitable for managing all types and sizes of projects and are often required by contract. CPM schedule contract specifications may simply require that the CPM technique be used for scheduling, or may include more detailed requirements, such as the CPM scheduling software to be used on the project or the level of detailed information to be included in the CPM schedule (such as the scope of work or the maximum length of activity durations).

Identifying the Critical Path

CPM schedules are developed by breaking down the project into components of work, or activities, and then defining the relationships among these activities. The logical relationships and activity durations are programmed into the CPM network, and the algorithm calculates two sets of dates for each activity: the earliest it can start and finish (the early dates) and the latest it can start and finish without delaying a follow-on or successor activities (the late dates). The difference between an activity's early dates and its late dates determines the activity's total float value and assists with identifying whether an activity is critical. Critical activities are activities whose early dates match their late dates and have a total float value of zero.[11] The chain of critical activities from the beginning of the project to the end, referred to as the critical path, reflects a sequence of activities that will result in the earliest

---

7. Kenneth M. Cushman & Joyce K. Hakenbrach, *Advanced Construction Claims Workshop: The Law, Analysis, and Pricing of Delays and Disruptions*, 357 PLI/Real 11, 23 (1990).

8. *Id.*

9. Federal Contract Management ¶ 17.03, at 46 (2018).

10. *Id.* at 23.

11. While it is a common scheduling practice to strive to develop a schedule with a zero-float value critical path, it is possible that a critical path schedule will have a float value greater than zero. In this instance, the critical path will be defined as the string of activities with the least amount of total float in the schedule.

final completion date for the project.[12] If any critical path activity is delayed, the succeeding critical activity will be similarly delayed.[13] Consequently, delay to any critical activity will result in a corresponding delay to project completion.

Projects do not necessarily have only one critical path. It is entirely possible to have two or more sets of critical activities which, if delayed, would delay project completion. The activity chains that make up alternative critical path(s) of the project may be totally separate or they may share activities.

A simple example of the existence of multiple critical paths in a schedule is a building project where structural steel erection is critical. In this case, the foundation work needs to be complete, and the steel must be on-site to allow erection to begin. If the expected time it takes for steel procurement equals the planned time for completing foundation work, then both foundation and steel procurement would be on separate critical paths, and a delay in either would cause the start of structural steel erection and the overall project to be delayed.

When identifying a schedule's critical path, one should be aware of the various ways CPM scheduling software may manipulate or modify the critical path. Many CPM scheduling software packages have the ability to assign interim constraints to activities that dictate when activities must start or finish, which force the system to calculate the late dates for an activity based on the internal constraints as opposed to the overall completion date. When the constraint dates require an activity to start or finish earlier than what would be otherwise necessary to meet the project completion date, the constraint dates will override the late date calculation and reset the late dates, decreasing the activity's float value and making the activity appear to be more critical than it would be without the application of the constraint.[14]

Also, as the CPM scheduling software has the ability to define multiple working calendars, the variations associated with multiple calendars can make discerning the true critical path for a project more difficult than simply finding the path with the least amount of float. While most work activities may be on a five-day-per-week calendar with holidays, procurement, administrative, and concrete curing activities may be on a seven-day-per-week calendar with no holidays. In this example, seven days of float for an activity on a seven-day calendar is only one week, whereas seven days of float for an activity on a five-day calendar would be one week plus two more workdays. These discrepancies can affect float values.[15] Some scheduling systems therefore provide a feature that defines the longest

12. *Id.*
13. *Id.*
14. AACE International Recommended Practice 49R-06, Identifying the Critical Path (2010).
15. *Id.*

path to completion of the project without referring to the float values, in order to address these concerns.

The Concept of Total Float

The concept of float represents flexibility. To fully understand the concept of float, it is important to understand how a CPM schedule is calculated. Once the CPM network is developed—meaning all schedule activities and their respective durations are defined, the activities are arranged in a sequential order, and the logic relationships between activities are set—the schedule activity network is ready for calculation.[16] The first step in the calculation, known as the forward pass, is the calculation of the early start and early finish dates for each activity in the project and for the overall project duration, commencing with the first activity in the project.[17] Absent changes in logic or activity durations, the early dates represent the soonest an activity can begin and the earliest it can finish. The second step is the backward pass, which is the calculation of the late start and late finish dates for each activity and for the overall project duration. As its name implies, the backwards pass calculation begins with the last activity in the schedule and proceeds backward through the schedule. Absent changes to the network, the late dates represent the latest an activity can start or end without delaying the overall project.[18]

The number of days an activity can be delayed before delaying the overall project is referred to as the total float value of such activity. Generally speaking, activities with a total float of zero are typically on the schedule's critical path, and those activities that contain total float, or a total float value greater than zero, are generally not on the critical path.[19] The total float of an activity is the difference between the activity's late start date and early start date, or its late finish date and early finish date.

Another type of float, referred to as free float, is also calculated for each schedule activity in a CPM network. Free float represents the amount of time an activity can be delayed before any successor activity will be delayed, as distinct from the overall project duration.[20] Free float is calculated by determining the number of days between the early finish date of an activity and the early start date of the next activity. It is important to distinguish between total float and free float when

---

16. S.W. Kramer & J.L. Jenkins *Understanding the Basics of CPM Calculations: What Is Scheduling Software Really Telling You?*, Paper presented at PMI® Global Congress 2006 – EMEA, Madrid, Spain. Newtown Square, PA: Project Management Institute.

17. *Id.*

18. *Id.*

19. Joseph E. Bennett, GSBCA 2362, 72-1 BCA 9364 (1972).

20. *Id.*

analyzing and measuring critical delay to a project. A noncritical path activity will have a total float value that is greater than its free float value, meaning that a delay in a noncritical path activity that results in delay to a successor activity will not necessarily delay the overall project completion. However, a critical path activity's free float and total float values are equal, and any delay to a critical activity will result in a corresponding delay to its successor activity and project completion.

Identifying and Measuring Critical Delay

An activity's total float value can be an indicator of critical delay. In a "pure" CPM network, which does not incorporate any activity or project constraints that would require an activity or the activity network to finish by a certain date, the backward pass calculation is started at the early project completion date that was calculated by the forward pass. In this scenario, all activities will have positive or zero float. This is because the forward pass calculated how long the project will take to complete, and the late dates are based upon the network achieving that calculated completion date. The total float along the critical path will be zero, and the float for any activity not on the critical path will be a positive number. And if a critical path activity is delayed, the total float along the critical path will maintain a value of zero when the CPM network is rescheduled due to the lack of activity or project constraints.

Construction contracts almost always specify a required project completion date. The starting time for the backward pass is therefore typically constrained in the CPM schedule to be the completion date designated by the contract, and not the date calculated in the forward pass. If the forward and backwards pass calculations allow the network to complete on the required or constrained completion date, then the critical path will have zero days of total float. If the calculation allows the project to complete prior to the required completion date, all activities will have positive float, and the critical path will be identified by the path of activities with the least amount of positive float. If the calculation requires the project to complete after the required completion date, the critical path will have negative float, and some noncritical activities may also have negative float. Positive float will still be an indicator that an activity is noncritical; however, negative float, or a float value of less than zero, typically indicates how many days the critical network of activities will finish beyond the required completion date. If a schedule has negative float, it cannot be completed by the required completion date, and the parties must alter work methods on the critical path activities to eliminate the negative float if they expect the project to complete by the contractual date. If the contract schedule has zero float, it can be completed by the contractual completion date, but if any activity on the critical path is delayed, the contractual completion date will be delayed to the same extent, and the difference between the updated project completion date calculated by the schedule and the completion date required by the contract will be the measurement of critical delay.

A variety of schedule analysis methodologies exist for analyzing critical delay during the course of an entire project. The schedule analysis methodology selected is dependent upon a variety of factors, including the availability and quality of the schedule data. Several industry publications exist that provide guidance and insight for selecting a schedule analysis methodology for the purposes of measuring critical delay. Some of the most commonly referenced include the Association for the Advancement of Cost Engineering (AACE) International's Forensic Schedule Analysis Recommended Practice, the Society of Construction Law's Delay and Disruption Protocol, and the American Society of Civil Engineers Schedule Delay Analysis Standard.

Assessing Responsibility for Delays

Delays on a project are either excusable or not excusable. Excusable delays entitle the contractor to a time extension, and, depending on the cause and contract provisions, may entitle the contractor to additional compensation. Non-excusable delays are the responsibility of the contractor and do not result in an extension of the project completion date or additional compensation.

Excusable Delays

Generally, delays are excusable when caused either by matters within the owner's control or matters controlled by neither party.[21] An excusable delay usually is defined in the construction contract. Excusable delays caused by the owner, or those for whom the owner is responsible, entitle the contractor to an extension of the completion date and additional compensation for the costs resulting from the delay (unless the contract states otherwise). Excusable delays caused by neither the contractor nor the owner, typically identified as force majeure delays, entitle the contractor to an extension of contract time but may not entitle the contractor to additional compensation, as neither the owner nor the contractor can control this type of delay. A force majeure event is often defined in the contract; however, examples include government action, unusually severe weather, unforeseeable site conditions, unanticipated labor strikes, war, riot, earthquake,[22] and given

21. *See* O. William Faison & Timothy C. Barber, *Delay Damages: The Claims You Didn't Bargain For*, 26 Tort & Ins. L.J. 856, 1 (1991).

22. *Id.* at 2.

the circumstances of the recent COVID-19 pandemic, epidemics and pandemics. Delays of a similar nature are considered excusable in the American Institute of Architects (AIA) General Conditions (AIA Form A201), section 8.3.1, which provides as follows:

> If the Contractor is delayed at any time in progress of the work by an act or neglect of the Owner or Architect, or of an employee of either, or of a separate contractor employed by the Owner, or by changes ordered in the work, or by labor disputes, fire, unusual delay in deliveries, unavoidable casualties or other causes beyond the Contractor's control, or by delay authorized by the Owner pending arbitration, or by other causes which the Architect determines may justify delay, then the Contract Time shall be extended by Change Order for such reasonable time as the Architect may determine.

In contrast, under Federal Acquisition Regulation (FAR) 52.249-14 (1984), government contracts define excusable delays as follows:

> (a) Except for defaults of subcontractors at any tier, the Contractor shall not be in default because of any failure to perform this contract under its terms if the failure arises from causes beyond the control and without the fault or negligence of the Contractor. Examples of these causes are (1) acts of God or of the public enemy, (2) acts of the Government in either its sovereign or contractual capacity, (3) fires, (4) floods, (5) epidemics, (6) quarantine restrictions, (7) strikes, (8) freight embargoes, and (9) unusually severe weather. In each instance, the failure to perform must be beyond the control and without the fault or negligence of the Contractor. "Default" includes failure to make progress in the work so as to endanger performance.
>
> (b) If the failure to perform is caused by the failure of a subcontractor at any tier to perform or make progress, and if the cause of the failure was beyond the control of both the Contractor and subcontractor, and without the fault or negligence of either, the Contractor shall not be deemed to be in default,- unless- (1) The subcontracted supplies or services were obtainable from other sources; (2) The Contracting Officer ordered the Contractor in writing to purchase these supplies or services from the other source; and (3) The Contractor failed to comply reasonably with this order.

Accordingly, under government contracts, to the extent the cause of the contractor's failure to perform is a force majeure event (as defined in the contract), the contractor is relieved of performing its obligations under the contract. Thus, for example, if a force majeure event prevents the contractor from proceeding with its work for one week, and assuming no follow-on delays and that all conditions as may be set forth in the contract are satisfied (e.g., notice to the owner), the contractor will be excused from performance during that one week of delay. That is not to suggest, however, that the contractor will be entitled to a one-week extension of the completion date as a result of that one-week excusable delay. Generally speaking, in a well-drafted contract, to obtain an extension of the completion date, the one-week excusable delay must have impacted the critical path. If the delay did not impact the critical path, the contractor would (typically) not be entitled to any extension of the project completion date.

The most effective way for a contractor to protect itself from bearing the risk of delays that may be typically considered excusable is to include specific language in the contract relating to the circumstances that result in excusable delay.[23] Even when the contract includes such language, the contractor must still perform its duties under the contract reasonably. Where a court finds that a contractor acted unreasonably by failing to mitigate damages or otherwise, it may reject that contractor's claim of excusable delay, notwithstanding the contract's language.[24]

Inexcusable Delays

Inexcusable delays are typically those that are within the contractor's control. They are delays caused by the contractor's team, which can include subcontractors or suppliers. As a result of an inexcusable delay, a contractor is not excused from performance during such delay or entitled to receive additional time to complete the project or compensation for any related delay damages. Examples of this type of delay include the failure to provide sufficient labor or late delivery of equipment or materials. Under many contracts, inexcusable delays may entitle the owner to recover damages from the contractor or to direct the contractor to accelerate work at the contractor's own expense to recover lost time.[25]

It should be noted that while any remedy for inexcusable delays cannot be recovered from the owner, the contractor may have a claim for damages against a subcontractor, supplier, or other party whether or not the delay is on the project critical path.

Compensable Delays

A compensable delay includes any delay that, under the contract, is the basis for additional compensation to the contractor.[26] These delays are generally limited to

---

23. *Id.*

24. *See, e.g.*, Roger Johnson Constr. Co., Inc. v. Bossier City, 330 So. 2d 338, 85 A.L.R. 3d 1080 (La. App. 2d Cir. 1976) (rejecting contractor's claim of entitlement to an extension of the completion date due to abnormal weather where court found that the contractor could have avoided the delay by working with sufficient crews at all times during good weather).

25. James G. Zack, Jr. & Peter V. Badala, Pricing Contractor Delay Costs 3 (2016).

26. Enforcement of these clauses varies depending on the jurisdiction.

excusable delays that are caused by the owner and/or by parties retained by the owner, such as the owner's architect or construction manager, and do not include delays caused by force majeure events. Examples of possible compensable delays include failure to grant site access, provision of defective plans and specifications, unforeseen site conditions on the project, delays in owner supplied material or equipment, or other improper acts or omissions of the owner that delay work on the critical path.[27] When a compensable delay arises, contractors may look to the project owner to compensate them for direct and indirect delay damages, as described in the construction contract.[28] Such damages sought by the contractor may include additional field general condition costs, costs to accelerate and recover the delay time, additional equipment costs, or additional home office overhead costs. Contractors are entitled to both a time extension and compensation for related damages for compensable delays unless the contract indicates otherwise.[29]

In order to recover for an alleged compensable delay, a contractor must typically demonstrate (1) the delay caused a resultant delay to the project critical path; (2) the extent of the delay; (3) that the delay was proximately caused by the owner's actions; and (4) that the delay caused specific, quantifiable injury to the contractor.[30] If the contractor can show these factors, it will be entitled to both an extension of time within which to perform, and recovery of excess costs associated with the delay.[31] Furthermore, the contractor must show that the owner was the sole proximate cause of the delay and that no concurrent cause (delay that is not caused by the owner occurring at the same time) would have equally delayed the project, regardless of the owner's action or inaction.[32] In the event concurrent delay does exist, the contractor is barred from recovering delay damages to the extent that concurrent contractor-caused delays offset owner-caused delays, and similarly,

27. Victor F. Luke, Who Has the Burden of Proving Delay and How Do They Prove It? 24 (2016).

28. *Id.* at 2.

29. *See, e.g.*, Weaver-Bailey Contractors, Inc. v. United States, 19 Cl. Ct. 474 (1990); Jonathan P. Cohen & Elizabeth Rivera, *Methods of Analyzing the Critical Path for Proving Delay Damages and Courts' Preferences*, Fid. & Sur. L. Comm. Newsl. 9, 31 (2019); Wendy Kennedy Venoit & Kenji Hoshino, *Follow the Money: Interpretation and Evaluation in a Forensic Schedule Analysis*, Constr. Law. 1 (Winter 2019); Gibbs, Hunt California Construction Law § 6.07(A), at 224 (16th ed. 2000).

30. *See* Servidone Constr. Corp. v. United States, 931 F.2d 861 (Fed. Cir. 1984); Blinderman Constr. Co. v. United States, 695 F.2d 552, 559 (Fed. Cir. 1982).

31. Weaver-Baily Contractors, Inc. v. United States, 19 Cl. Ct. 474, 476 (1990) (citing G.M. Shupe, Inc. v. United States, 5 Cl. Ct. 662, 700 (1984)).

32. Merritt-Chapman & Scott Corp. v. United States, 15 Cl. Ct. at 653, 659 (recovery denied "because concurrent delays rendered the [owner-caused] delay . . . irrelevant").

the owner is barred from recovering delay damages to the extent that concurrent owner-caused delays offset contractor-caused delays.

Despite the contractor's entitlement to recover additional time and cost as a result of owner-caused delays to the project, many contracts incorporate a "no damages for delay" clause in an attempt to award solely an extension of time to the contractor for owner-caused delays and bar the recovery of any delay-related damages. Contractual limitations on the right to recover damages for excusable delays are generally enforceable with certain exceptions, although many states have enacted legislation limiting or prohibiting the enforcement of such clauses.

The Concept of Concurrent Delay

Concurrent Delay Defined

Concurrent delay is one of the most important concepts in the field of schedule delay—and one of the most poorly understood. While there are many definitions, concurrent delay essentially means multiple independent delays to the project caused by different parties that occur at the same time. This concept has been defined by the courts as denoting a "period of project overrun which is caused by two or more effective causes of delays which are of approximately equal causative potency."[33] Concurrent delay has five main characteristics:[34]

- Two or more delays that are unrelated and independent;
- Each of which would have delayed the project even if the other delay did not exist;
- The delays are the contractual responsibility of different parties, but one may be a force majeure event;
- The delays must be involuntary; and
- The delayed work must be substantial and not easily curable.

As with all construction disputes, the first thing to consider is what the contract provides: whether it defines concurrent delays and, if so, whether it specifies a remedy for the contractor.[35] If the contract specifically addresses concurrent delays, that provision will govern the analysis. Otherwise, principles that are generally recognized in the construction industry will govern. Generally speaking, when otherwise compensable delays overlap with noncompensable delays, or are

33. William Haydt, Dueling Delays: How to Combat Concurrently Claims (2019).

34. K. Hoshino, C. Carson & J. Livengood, et al., Recommended Practice 29R-03, Forensic Schedule Analysis, at 101 (2011).

35. William Haydt, Dueling Delays: How to Combat Concurrently Claims (2019).

so entwined with noncompensable delays that they cannot be reasonably separated or apportioned, neither the owner nor the contractor will be entitled to compensation. However, a more recent trend expressed by courts and other tribunals is to attempt to apportion the damages suffered by the contractor and award such damages as can be attributed to the compensable delay.[36] Accurate apportionment is difficult, however, when concurrent delays occur that include non-excusable, excusable/noncompensable, and excusable/compensable delays, these combinations can produce a variety of results regarding the excusability and compensability of the concurrent delays.[37]

Identifying Concurrent Delay and Related Challenges

As with any project delay, when evaluating concurrent delays, one needs to confirm that the delaying events are on the critical path, as only delays to the critical path of the project can delay the project. In fact, if only one of the concurrent delays is a critical path delay, then it may not be considered a concurrent delay.[38] For example, in *Santa Fe, Inc.*, the board found that the claimed concurrent delays were not on the critical path because they did not extend the completion of the project:

> In terms of the concurrent delay rule, the concurrent delay must pertain to activities whose completion was critical to the completion of the project itself. . . . Relief from the imposition of liquidated damages must depend upon showing concurrent delay in respect to activities on the critical path.[39]

However, if a project contains a secondary noncritical path that is within only a few days of being critical, often referred to as a near-critical path,[40] it might be reasonable to consider the critical path and near-critical path to be concurrently critical and, thus, if they are both delayed, they may be concurrent delays.[41]

Additionally, if the owner causes a delay to an activity on the critical path, but the contractor simultaneously delays the same work, the contractor will not be entitled to any compensation.[42] The reasoning for this result is that the owner's

---

36. John Livengood, Daniel S. Brennan, *Approaches to Concurrent Delay*, CONSTR. LAW., Winter 2019, at 27.

37. *Id.*

38. *Id.*

39. *Santa Fe, Inc.*, ABCA Nos. 1943–1946, 84-2 BCA 17,341 (1984).

40. Near-critical delays have the greatest potential of becoming concurrent delays. This is because a near-critical delay, upon consumption of relative float against the critical path delay, will become critical.

41. *Id.*

42. VICTOR F. LUKE, WHO HAS THE BURDEN OF PROVING DELAY AND HOW DO THEY PROVE IT? 22 (2016).

concurrent delay is immaterial, because those same critical activities would have been delayed by the contractor.[43] There are also occasions when there are concurrent delays, but the delays of the owner and the delays of the contractor are of different, though perhaps overlapping, durations.[44] A CPM schedule analysis can determine which party is responsible for the longer delay, and that party should bear the expense of that delay beyond the other party's shorter, concurrent delay.[45]

It is necessary to distinguish between cases involving truly concurrent causes of delay and cases that involve sequential or separate aspects of delay attributable to various competing causes.[46] True concurrency occurs when multiple events cause delay and project overrun at the same time and for the same duration. Stated another way, these two or more effective causes of delay are of approximately equal causative potency.[47] The distinction between sequential and simultaneous delays has occasionally been specifically addressed by the courts. These courts have come to the conclusion that CPM analysis can distinguish between simultaneous, or concurrent, and non-simultaneous delays, and that sequential or non-simultaneous delays should not be treated as anything but separate delays. In *R.P. Wallace, Inc. v. U.S.*,[48] the court defined "sequential delays" as two or more different delays occurring over time, not necessarily connected or in exact sequence. The court then proceeded to discuss the evolution of how sequential delays should be evaluated for purposes of assessing liquidated damages. The court opted for an approach that allocated responsibility for such delays. For those delays for which the contractor was solely responsible, the government was entitled to assess liquidated damages.

The case of *Fischbach & Moore International Corp.* is often cited for the proposition that nonsimultaneous delays along the critical path can create concurrency.[49] Yet, in this case there was no late completion due to recovery efforts implemented by the prime contractor. Therefore, the court only considered the amount of delay caused by the government prior to the contractor's subsequent acceleration to determine if the contractor could recover delay damages. The court concluded that sequential delays of the government reduced the alleged concurrency, stating:

> With regard to the alleged intertwining of Government-caused and concurrent delays in this case, we have found, in the critical path analysis offered by appellant, a ready and reasonable basis for segregating the delays. If the delays can be

43. *Id.*
44. *Id.*
45. *Id.*
46. *Id.*
47. *Id.*
48. R.P. Wallace, Inc. v. U.S., 63 Fed. Cl. 402, 410 (2004).
49. B. Bramble & M. Callahan, Construction Delay Claims, para 11.09[A] (3d ed. Supp. 2010).

> segregated, responsibility therefor [sic] may be allocated to the parties. . . . As will be seen in the discussion that follows, we have no such difficulty in [segregating delays in] the present case.[50]

Therefore, the court found that delays, alleged to be concurrent and critical, were in fact sequential and could be apportioned.[51] In U.S. courts, the typical method for evaluating nonsimultaneous delays is to look to the CPM delay analysis presented at trial. For example, in *Tyger Construction Co. v. U.S.*,[52] the U.S. Court of Federal Claims was able to apportion responsibility related to potentially simultaneous delaying events on the project based on the delay analysis testimony presented by the contractor's expert.

While there appears to be general agreement among courts regarding the basic rules of concurrency, there is little consistency in how courts have approached the issue:

> [T]he uneven application of [concurrency] rules to recurring fact patterns has given rise to inconsistent precedent and a lack of predictable guidance for parties seeking to avoid future disputes.[53]

This uncertainty of application is reflected in the courts themselves, one of which observed that concurrency is "at best murky and confusing."[54] A recent major case that cogently summarized the current status of delay analysis and the law states:

> The exact definition of concurrent delay is not readily apparent from its use in contract law, although it is a term which has both temporal and causation aspects. Concurrent delays affect the same "delay period."[55]

The identification of different evaluative theories in concurrency is made more difficult and complicated because the term "apportionment" is used in two separate ways. "Apportionment" is used to describe the process in which the court looks at the detailed factual basis, particularly a forensic CPM delay analysis, and concludes that the events are not actually concurrent—the events do not both fall on

---

50. Fischbach & Moore Int'l Corp., ASBCA 14216, 71-1 BCA 8775, 59244.

51. *See also* Essex Electro Eng'rs v. Danzig, 224 F.3d 1283 1295 (Fed Cir. 2000), where the court was able to apportion alleged concurrent delays that occurred sequentially (footnotes excluded).

52. 31 Fed. Cl. 177 (1994), *on reconsideration* (May 4, 1994).

53. C. Brasco & C. Anzidei, *Concurrent Delay and the Critical Path: Views from the Bench*, Cost Eng'g J. 18 (Feb. 2010).

54. Sterling Millwrights, Inc. v. U.S., 26 Cl. Ct. 49 (1992).

55. George Sollitt Constr. Co. v. U.S., 64 Fed. Cl. 229, n.8 (2005).

the critical path.[56] "Apportionment" is also sometimes used in cases to allocate the delays based on the significance of each of the concurrent events on the project as a whole. The distinction between these understandings is often confused. First, the historical record of the facts and basis of previous court decisions is murky. Second, an admonition by courts that "allocation" is not preferred is often directly contradicted by a process by the same courts that parses the delays based on a fact-based CPM analysis—that is, allocation.[57]

The courts' treatment of concurrent delay can make a contractor's decisions regarding the contemporaneous management and mitigation of project delays challenging. It is prudent for a contractor to adjust the schedule as the project progresses, to account for changes in the plan that are often made to account for unanticipated circumstances, to mitigate project risk, and to keep the project moving forward. As a result, the project critical path may shift and evolve throughout the project. If the court applies a methodology in which it only looks to the critical path at the completion of the project, as was done in *Santa Fe*, the result may be different than what was contemporaneously represented when the delay was actually incurred.[58]

Conclusion

During contract negotiations special attention should be provided to delay-related clauses. Identifying and negotiating delay risks is critical as delays are a common and frequently litigated project risk, which can result in catastrophic loss or bankruptcy. Delay or No Damages for Delay clauses allow the parties to understand the financial and economic risks associated with delays and attempt to mitigate those risks with different risk management tools.

---

56. *Santa Fe, Inc.*, VABCA Nos. 1943–1946, 84-2 BCA 17,341 (1984); Williams Enters., Inc. v. Strait Mfg. & Welding, Inc., 728 F. Supp. 12 (D.D.C. 1990); *Utley James, Inc.*, GSBCA No. 5370, 85-1 BCA 17,816 (1994); Tyger Constr. Co. v. U.S., 31 Fed. Cl. 177 (1994).

57. Sauer Inc. v. Danzig, 244 F.3d 1340 (Fed. Cir. 2000).

58. *Santa Fe, Inc.*, VABCA Nos. 1943–1946, 84-2 BCA 17,341 (1984).

CHAPTER 2

Understanding Project Schedules and Scheduling Concepts

Richard J. Tyler

The concept that "time is money" is an old one.[1] Notwithstanding, time of performance historically was not deemed a material component of a construction contract because delays were foreseeable.[2] In the early 1900s, a mechanical engineer named Henry Gantt developed a methodology for tracking industrial production using a bar graph to show scheduled and actual progress.[3] In the graph, project time is shown horizontally along the x-axis, and activities are listed in roughly reverse chronological order up the y-axis. The activities are depicted in bars with the left edge indicating the start date and the right edge indicating the completion date. Thus, each bar shows the start, finish, and duration of the associated activity, and the chart as a whole depicts the time sequence of activities needed to complete the project.

The so-called Gantt chart was adopted on large construction projects, like the Hoover Dam, beginning in the 1930s. Bar charts, however, have a number of drawbacks: First, physical constraints—paper size for one—limited the data that

1. In *Advice to a Young Tradesman*, published in 1748, Benjamin Franklin wrote:

> Remember that Time is Money. He that can earn Ten Shillings a Day by his Labour, and goes abroad, or sits idle one half of that Day, tho' he spends but Sixpence during his Diversion or Idleness, ought not to reckon That the only Expence; he has really spent or rather thrown away Five Shillings besides.

Available at Founders Online, https://founders.archives.gov/documents/Franklin/01-03-02-0130 (last visited Nov. 19, 2023).

2. *E.g.*, Melville Lumber Co. v. Welpton Lumber Co., 121 Neb. 370, 371–72, 236 N.W. 438, 439 (1931) ("Time is not generally considered as the essence of a contract, unless it is expressly provided or it appears that it was the intention of the parties that it should be of the essence thereof.").

3. *See generally* WALLACE CLARK, THE GANTT CHART, A WORKING TOOL OF MANAGEMENT (1922).

could be graphicly presented.[4] Second, the chart could only show the interrelationship between activities in simplistic terms. Third, they had limited utility showing the impact of the delay on one activity over other activities. Fourth, charts require frequent updating to remain accurate and useful, but the process could be time-consuming.

With the advent of computers in the mid-1950s, engineers at E.I. Dupont began work to improve the planning and control of chemical plant maintenance and construction projects.[5] The result of that effort was the creation of the critical path method (CPM) schedule, sometimes referred to as a "network diagram." A CPM schedule is typically a computer-generated graphical representation of project activities, their durations, and the logical connections between the activities to assist with the management of construction projects, particularly those having long durations or technical complexity. In simple terms, a CPM schedule is a tool that allows project participants to monitor progress and identify and manage potential sources of project delay.

This chapter reviews the basic elements of, and the terminology employed in connection with, construction project scheduling, particularly CPM scheduling.

Introduction to Project Scheduling

Certain commonplace events exhibit characteristics that lend themselves to depiction of scheduling concepts. A holiday dinner, such as Thanksgiving, is one such event. There is a project (a full meal ready to eat), a completion time (somewhere in the gap between football games), and multiple tasks (activities) that must be accomplished in order to achieve timely completion. These activities must be sequenced in the proper order, but some activities are critical to the meal being served on time and others are not. Applying these concepts to the main course, the turkey, a schedule of activities emerges as does the existence of relationships between the activities:

4. For example, as the number of tasks increases, the chart can become cluttered and difficult to read. Likewise, on complex projects of long duration the chart might need to be split across multiple pages to accommodate both the project duration and the number of activities.

5. *See generally* Jon Wickwire et al., Construction Scheduling: Preparation, Liability and Claims § 2.02 (3d ed. 2010).

Activity ID	Activity Description	Depends On Activity	Time
1	buy turkey		
2	thaw turkey	1	6 hours
3	prepare turkey	2	1 hour
4	cook turkey	3	5 hours
5	make gravy	4	30 minutes

Under this scenario, the frozen turkey must be purchased and in the kitchen no later than 12½ hours before the appointed time the meal is to be served. There are other activities associated with the meal—potatoes, stuffing, cranberry sauce, pies—but these activities can be performed in parallel with the turkey (assuming no resource limitations such as a single oven), or, in the case of cranberry sauce and pies, performed the day before. The longest sequence of dependent tasks—that is, the "critical path"—for getting the meal served is the turkey. Delay any task in its sequence and the whole dinner is delayed.

Construction Project Scheduling

As the introductory section suggests, scheduling involves taking a construction project, identifying the individual activities required to build it, and then sequencing those activities in a logical fashion to achieve the end result in the time required. A construction schedule, however, does not spring fully grown from the brow of the scheduler.[6] The scheduling process starts with the development of a strategic plan for effective project delivery that defines the scope of work; identifies major activities to be performed and their sequence; develops a general plan for executing the scope of work; and identifies the cost, resources, and time constraints for the scope of work.[7] This plan is derived from multiple sources. The contract for the project will often supply various key dates—milestones and completion—that will drive the schedule, as well as contractual requirements for the schedule itself. Project design basis documents, plans, and specifications define the scope of work. In

6. In Greek mythology, Athena, the goddess of wisdom and war, is said to have been born fully grown and in battle armor from the forehead (brow) of Zeus, the king of the gods. E. Hamilton, Mythology 29 (1942).

7. *See generally* AACE International Recommended Practice 14R-90, Required Skills and Knowledge of Planning and Scheduling (rev. Aug. 30, 2022).

many complex projects it is common to prepare a construction execution plan that describes how the construction team envisions performing the work.[8]

Armed with this information, the scheduler then implements the plan by identifying the specific activities or tasks required and the sequencing of those activities, and determining the length of time it will take to perform the activities and thus the length of time it will take to complete the overall project. Whether formally or informally, schedulers will document how they converted the planning documents into the schedule, including assumptions, exclusions, exceptions, interpretations, and other matters that provided the basis for the schedule.[9]

Over the years, standardized nomenclature has been adopted with respect to scheduling. The basic terminology is as follows:

Activity

An activity is an element of work that must be performed in order to complete a project.[10] Depending on the needs of the project, an activity may be described generally, for example, install foundation, or it may be broken down into tasks, that is, discrete items of work that are components of the general activity, for example, form footers, install rebar, pour concrete.[11] Generally speaking, activities consume resources, such as labor hours and time.

Each schedule activity is assigned a unique identification number (Activity ID). In addition, an activity is usually named in a fashion that is unique, descriptive of the work being performed, and understandable in isolation. This can be achieved by assigning a name that incorporates a work function (e.g., pour, review, excavate), a subject (e.g., wall, HVAC, submittal), and a specific location (e.g., floor, room, component). For example:

Activity ID	Activity Name
837	Fabricate Rebar for Cooling Tower Foundation #31

While it is common to think about activities in terms of physical construction work in the field, effective scheduling requires the inclusion of other activities and events that could affect project completion. These include but are not limited to design deliverables; procurement of long lead items; permitting; submittal development, review, and approval; inspections; and test periods.

8. See AACE International Recommended Practice 39R-06, Project Planning (Dec. 8, 2011) for more detailed information of project planning.

9. AACE International Recommended Practice 38R-06, Documenting the Schedule Basis (June 18, 2009).

10. AACE International Recommended Practice 10S-90, Cost Engineering Terminology (rev. July 24, 2024) [hereinafter Cost Terminology] at 10.

11. Cost Terminology, *supra* note 10, at 129 (Task).

Activity Sequencing

Sequencing is the determination of the logical order in which activities will occur in relation to other activities.[12] For example, the building foundation must be completed before the building frame can be erected on that foundation. Likewise, the building foundation must be formed, reinforced, poured, cured, and inspected before it is ready to accept the building frame.

Dependencies

Closely allied to sequencing is the concept of dependencies, that is, an interrelationship between activities or tasks. An activity may be a "predecessor activity," one that necessarily must be completed before other activities may start, or it may be a "successor activity," an activity that cannot begin until the completion, in whole or in part, of another activity.[13] The typical relationship types are:

- **Finish-to-Start (FS).** In this relationship, the start of the successor activity depends on the completion of the predecessor activity, that is, Task B cannot start until Task A finishes. Using a concrete foundation wall as an example, the formwork for the wall needs to be finished and the rebar installed before the start of the concrete pour for the wall. Therefore, the activity "forming of the concrete foundation" would be linked as a finish-to-start relationship to the activity "pouring of the concrete foundation." Finish-to-start relationships are the most common dependencies seen in project schedules.
- **Finish-to-Finish (FF).** In this relationship, the start and finish dates of the successor activity depend on the finish of the predecessor activity, that is, Task B finishes when Task A finishes. For example, the taping and floating of drywall cannot finish until the associated drywall installation is complete. The finishing crew can begin working on installed sections of drywall, but they can't complete the drywall finishing work until all drywall is installed.
- **Start-to-Start (SS).** In this relationship, the successor activity can begin once the predecessor activity begins, that is, Task B can start when Task A starts, but they do not necessarily start at the same time. Using the concrete foundation wall as an example again, rebar work cannot start until the formwork starts, but the rebar work can begin once the formwork has progressed to a certain point even though it is not fully complete.

12. *Id.* at 11 (Activity Sequencing) and 120 (Sequence).
13. *Id.* at 95 (Predecessor Activity) and 127 (Successor Activity).

- **Start-to-Finish (SF).** The completion of the successor activity depends on the start of the predecessor work, that is, Task B finishes when Task A starts. This type of relationship is most often seen where there is a continuous operation that must be maintained, and an existing system cannot be shutdown until a temporary system is in place. An example would be a damaged natural gas pipeline where delivery must be maintained; the temporary bypass must be finished before the damaged section can be replaced. Start-to-Finish relationships are very rare because, in most instances, the relationship is better modeled by one of the other dependencies.

These relationships, sometimes called "constraints," "restraints," "ties," or "logic ties," are how dependent activities are logically linked to each other in the schedule. These activity relationships are what the software uses to identify dependencies and to calculate a critical path through the schedule from the first activity to the last activity.

An activity can have multiple predecessor activities, each having a different relationship to the activity. An activity likewise can have multiple successor activities, each having a different relationship to its predecessor.

Duration

"Duration" is the amount of time estimated to complete an activity, usually measured in days for land-based construction.[14] Stated differently, duration is the answer to the question "how fast can you do this work?" The answer to this question, however, is complicated because duration is a function of the activity being performed, the resources devoted to the activity, and planned production rates. By way of example, a single worker who can manually dig at a rate of 2 feet per hour will take 50 hours to complete a 100-foot trench; that same worker operating an excavator that digs at a rate of 20 feet per hour will take 5 hours to complete that same trench. In some industries there are commercially available guides that are resources for determining production rates. For example, in mechanical construction "Page & Nation" is a well-known source for production rates with respect to the fabrication and erection of industrial piping and associated fittings.[15] In addition, sophisticated contractors frequently maintain production data from past projects as reference materials for creating estimates and schedules for new projects. Because duration is a function of production rates, a scheduler must be cognizant of the project-specific factors that might affect productivity. These factors include crew size, working days per week and hours per day, weather (will the

14. *Id.* at 50.
15. John S. Page, Estimator's Piping Man-Hour Manual (5th ed. 1999).

work be performed in extreme cold or heat), and the location of the work (will it be performed in a shop, on the ground, or at elevation).[16] As might be suspected, a scheduler must work in close coordination with the construction team to convert the project plan into a usable schedule that reflects the execution of the planned scope of work.

Work Breakdown Structure

A Work Breakdown Structure (WBS) is a framework for organizing the activities of a construction project into groupings that can be planned and managed effectively. For example, on a building construction project it can be useful to "decompose" the project scope into different components such as preconstruction (design and permitting), sitework, foundations, framing and roofing, building envelope, MEP (mechanical, electrical, and plumbing), interior, and finish work.[17] On complex construction projects, for example, industrial and petrochemical facilities where the scope, scale, and technical complexity are immense, the WBS serves as a framework for planning, scheduling, and managing the different components, which may be projects in and of themselves.[18] For example, a new steel mill may have separate WBS for raw material receiving areas, raw material storage facilities, electrical substations, water supply, melt shops, one or more rolling mills, storage for finished goods, and transportation facilities for those goods. Each WBS may have its own activities for the civil, structural, mechanical, piping, electrical, and instrumentation disciplines.

Project Scheduling and the Critical Path

Once the demographic information is developed, a schedule can be created. While a scheduler may be able to create one manually on a small project, the data is typically input into commercially available scheduling software. Such software is available as a standalone program or as a component of a project management suite, such as Procore. Currently, the most commonly used programs are Oracle Primavera (now in its sixth version, P6) and Microsoft Project.

---

16. Productivity is the measure of output relative to input (e.g., pounds of ductwork installed per hour). While productivity affects durations in the project schedule, it is a separate field of study with a significant body on factors that affect productivity. *E.g.*, AACE International Recommended Practice No. 25R-03, Estimating Lost Labor Productivity in Construction Claims (2004). The topic of productivity is beyond the scope of this chapter.

17. AACE International Recommended Practice 33R-15, Developing the Project Work Breakdown Structure (Mar. 1, 2016).

18. In large industrial "megaprojects," it is not unusual to see schedules that are dozens of pages in length and contain 10,000 activities, or more.

Following data input the software can perform a number of calculations, including:

Forward Pass (Early Start/Early Finish)

The software performs a so-called "forward pass" by calculating the earliest time an activity can begin, based on its predecessors (the Early Start, or ES), and then the earliest date the activity can conclude based on its duration (the Early Finish, or EF).[19] The forward pass establishes the critical path for the project.

Backward Pass (Late Start/Late Finish)

After the forward pass, the software performs a "backward pass" starting with the last activity (typically project completion) and moves backward through the activities to calculate the latest date an activity can finish (Late Finish, or LF), and then the latest date that activity can start (Late Start, or LS) while still maintaining the overall project duration calculated by the forward pass.[20] The backward pass determines the amount of time an activity may slip in its start and completion without delaying completion of the project, an amount of time known as "float" or "slack."[21] For example, if an activity has an Early Finish date of September 5, and a Late Finish date of September 17, it has 12 days of total float.

Critical Path

Based on the input data, scheduling software is able to calculate the "critical path" for the project. The critical path is described as the longest sequence of dependent activities in the schedule that establishes the minimum overall project duration.[22] The defined path is "critical" because there is no schedule flexibility and a slippage or delay to any of the activities on the critical path, such as a late start or increase in duration, will delay the project completion date accordingly. "By definition, the critical path has no float."[23]

While people commonly refer to "*the* critical path," this singular reference is often erroneous for at least two reasons. First, it fails to recognize that construction projects are dynamic, events are unpredictable, and circumstances can change over

---

19. Cost Technology, *supra* note 10, at 6.
20. *Id.* at 17.
21. *Id.* at 60.
22. *Id.* at 40 (Critical Path) and 77 (Longest Path). *Accord*, A Guide to the Project Management Body of Knowledge (PMBOK Guide) 536 (5th ed. 2013) (defining CPM as "A method used to estimate the minimum project duration and determine the amount of scheduling flexibility on the logical network paths within the schedule model").
23. Construction Law 316 (Am. Bar Ass'n. 2010). Most schedule software designates the critical path with the color red.

the life of the project.[24] Therefore the critical path of a construction project can shift over the course of the project as a result of changed conditions, the addition or deletion of work, resequencing of work, delayed delivery of materials or equipment, or resource availability (e.g., skilled workers). At project commencement, the critical path might run through site preparation and foundation work, but as those activities are completed, the path could run through other activities such as vertical construction or equipment installation. Delays to an activity that was originally noncritical can consume float, causing that series of activities to become critical. Procurement delays, design revisions, weather impacts, or labor shortages can also cause changes in activity durations or dependencies, creating one or more new critical paths.

Second, complex industrial construction projects, such as the steel mill discussed earlier, can have multiple critical paths. This occurs because the project consists of several major subsystems, such as raw material receiving areas, melt shops, electrical substations, rolling mills, and transportation infrastructure—each with its own sequence of activities and dependencies. Overall completion of the mill involves concurrent construction of interdependent systems that must be operational in sequence or in parallel. For example, electrical substations must be completed to power the melt shop and rolling mill, the melt shop needs to be operational to feed material to the rolling mill, and transportation facilities must be ready to handle finished goods once manufacturing begins. When the longest activity sequence within two or more of these subsystems have similar durations, each sequence constitutes a critical path, and any delay along one path will directly affect the overall project completion. This scenario requires monitoring and managing multiple critical sequences simultaneously and making adjustments to maintain schedule integrity and ensure timely project delivery.

---

24. As one court noted:

> [E]xcept in the middle of a battlefield, nowhere must men coordinate the movement of other men and all materials in the midst of such chaos and with such limited certainty of present facts and future occurrences as in a huge construction project such as the building of this 100 million dollar hospital. Even the most painstaking planning frequently turns out to be mere conjecture and accommodation to changes must necessarily be of the rough, quick and ad hoc sort, analogous to ever-changing commands on the battlefield.

Blake Constr. Co. v. C. J. Coakley Co., Inc., 431 A.2d 569, 575 (D.C. 1981).

Beyond the Basics

Types of Schedules

Baseline and Updates

A baseline schedule is the original approved project schedule that serves as a reference point throughout the project's lifecycle. It outlines the planned start and finish dates for all project activities, milestones, and key deliverables based on the scope, budget, and resources known at the time of planning. The baseline schedule provides a framework for measuring progress and evaluating performance.

As the project progresses, the schedule needs to be updated to reflect current reality. Almost every project will inevitably experience changes during the life of the project. Changes that affect the schedule can come from a variety of sources: work can progress more quickly or slowly than planned; there may be changes to the scope of work that alter the planned activities, sequencing, or durations; there may be delays in material or equipment delays; or unforeseen conditions. In order for the schedule to remain a useful management tool, the schedule needs to be updated. The update process begins with the collection of data on the actual status of the work, such as actual start and finish dates and for activities in progress the amount of work performed, and the time needed to complete the remaining work. Data also needs to be collected on any changes in the durations of future activities. If the schedule is resource or cost loaded, information on resource utilization and incurred costs needs to be collected.

Once the data is collected it needs to be input into the schedule to determine the impact on the schedule and cost so that any variances can be reviewed and managed. In addition, any changes resulting from approved change orders need to be addressed in the schedule so that it accurately reflects the scope of the work as of the update. Regular updates are essential for accurate forecasting, identifying schedule risks, and enabling proactive project management.

Levels

Construction project schedules are typically classified by a numeric level that is based on the amount of detail reported, which, in turn, is driven by the information needs of the target audience.[25] Schedules are commonly categorized into four levels:

Level 1. A milestone schedule, providing a high-level overview with only key components, deliverables, or milestones depicted. A Level 1 schedule is typically

---

25. AACE International Recommended Practice 37R-06, Schedule Levels of Detail—As Applied in Engineering, Procurement, and Construction (Mar. 20, 2010).

prepared during the early stages of a project, such as the conceptual, feasibility, or proposal phase, when limited detail is available. This schedule is usually intended for executives, project sponsors, or external stakeholders who need a broad understanding of the project's scope and timeframe without being burdened by detailed task-level data.

Level 2. A summary schedule, showing major project phases or work packages, often used for senior management reporting. A Level 2 schedule is typically prepared after project approval but before detailed planning begins, often during the preconstruction or early planning phase, providing more detail than a Level 1 schedule but still at a summary level. This type of schedule is useful for senior management, project sponsors, and owners who need to track progress across major project segments but who do not need task-level detail.

Level 3. A project control schedule in which a meaningful critical path can be shown and used for project monitoring and management. A Level 3 schedule is typically prepared after the contract is awarded and detailed project planning begins, often during the preconstruction or early execution phase. It provides a comprehensive view of the entire project, including all major activities, milestones, and interfaces necessary to manage, monitor, and control the work. This schedule is detailed enough to support monthly progress reporting, critical path analysis, and risk management, and is usually the baseline schedule submitted for approval by the owner or client.

Level 4. Typically, a working schedule used by project teams to manage day-to-day activities, including specific tasks, resource assignments, and crew workflows. These schedules are prepared during detailed planning and execution phases, once the Level 3 project schedule is approved and the focus shifts to managing day-to-day activities. This schedule is commonly a short-term look-ahead that provides a high level of detail as to the tasks, crew assignments, and resources needed to perform the work. It is used primarily by project managers, superintendents, and foremen to coordinate field work and activities.[26]

Each level builds on the one above it, offering increasing detail. The baseline schedule, typically created at Level 3 serves as the original plan against which project performance is measured. As work progresses, schedule updates are issued to reflect actual performance, changes, and forecasts, allowing stakeholders to assess deviations from the baseline and make informed decisions.

---

26. Some industry literature references schedules higher than a Level 4—e.g., AACEI RP 37R-06 discusses a Level 5 Schedule—but these schedules are typically developed for specific trades or specific tasks occurring in a discrete time period.

Resource Loading and Cost Loading

"Resource Loading" refers to the process of assigning to each schedule activity the resources, distributed over time, required to perform the activity.[27] Resource loading allows project managers to evaluate the demand for resources over the life of the project and take appropriate action to ensure that planned activities are supported by the appropriate quantity and type of resources in a timely fashion. Resource loading is particularly important on complex projects with tight deadlines and limited resource availability.

Resource loading involves quantifying the amount of each resource required per activity, spreading that usage over the activity's duration, and analyzing the cumulative demand across the project timeline. It helps identify periods of overallocation, where resource demands exceed availability, or underutilization, where resources are idle, enabling corrective actions such as resource reallocation or adjusting activity sequencing. Accurate resource loading supports better cost forecasting, improves productivity planning, and enhances communication between the scheduling and field management teams. Schedule programs such as Primavera P6 and Microsoft Project support resource-loaded schedules.

"Cost Loading" refers to assigning an estimated or actual cost to an activity. Cost loading provides important cost management information to project managers. First, a cost-loaded schedule permits the forecasting of cash flow requirements over the duration of the project. By assigning costs to activities, stakeholders can visualize when expenditures will occur and ensure that funds are available to meet payment obligations. Second, cost-loading permits a more objective basis for supporting payment applications that are required to be based on earned value or completed work because the schedule of values its tied directly to the CPM schedule. Third, cost-loaded schedules allow implementation of Earned Value Management, an assessment of project performance that compares Earned Value (the budgeted cost of work performed), Planned Value (the budgeted cost of work scheduled), and Actual Value (actual cost of work performed). Comparison of these items can reveal schedule and cost variances that require action.[28]

It is important to note that software resourcing capabilities allow resources to be leveled when calculating critical path. This simply means that a restriction is

---

27. A "Resource" is "any consumable required to accomplish an activity," and includes labor, equipment, and materials. Cost Terminology, *supra* note 10, at 108.

28. For example, an Earned Value less than the Planned Value suggests that the project is behind schedule. Similarly, an Earned Value that less than the Actual Cost may indicate that the project is over budget. Earned Value Management is discussed in detail in the PMBOK Guide. *See also* AACE International Recommended Practice 86R-14, Variance Analysis and Reporting (Oct. 19, 2015).

placed on the sequencing of the work based on the number of resources identified for a particular subset of work. For example, a concrete placement subcontractor might have at most two crews allotted for this project. If concrete pouring activities are delayed, the schedule would automatically calculate float paths based on a maximum of two crews performing work. This ensures that resources are not duplicated in other activities.

Types of Float

As discussed, some activity durations can contain "float" or "slack," which is generally defined as "the amount of time that an activity may slip in its start and completion before becoming critical."[29] One measure of float is the difference between the activity's Early Finish and late Finish Dates (or the Early Start and Late Start dates).[30] This period, if any, is known as "Total Float" an refers to the amount of time the activity can be delayed without having an impact on the project completion time. The other type of float, "Free Float," is the total amount of time an activity can be delayed without impacting another activity, usually a successor activity. The two concepts differ in that an activity that exhausts its float may not affect project completion if successor activities have available float.

Float is typically referred to as "positive" (there is slack time in the schedule), "zero" (there is no slack time available), or "negative" (the activity has exceeded its estimated duration and is now affecting successor activities and, potentially, the overall project). If negative float adversely affects the calculated project completion date in the schedule, actions to "recover the schedule" must be undertaken. Such actions could include changes in work methods, resequencing activities, and modifying resources and their allocation (e.g., adding workers, working longer shifts, adding a night shift, or work more days per week) in order to complete the project on time.

Where there is positive float in the schedule, disputes can arise over who owns the float, the owner or the contractor. The issue is not often addressed in the contract documents for the project, but if it is, the contract will obviously control. In the absence of a contractual provision, industry practice is that float "is a shared commodity between the owner and the contractor. In such a case float must be shared in the interest of the project rather than to the sole benefit of one of the parties to the contract."[31]

---

29. Cost Terminology, *supra* note 10, at 60.

30. PMI Practice Standard for Scheduling 31 (2d ed. 2011).

31. AACE International Recommended Practice No. 29R-03, Forensic Schedule Analysis (rev. Apr. 25, 2011), at 18.

Use of the CPM Schedule in Practice

CPM as a Contractual Requirement

While they generally do not require CPM schedules by name, standard form industry contracts require contractors to prepare schedules that contain the constituent elements. For example, the AIA General Conditions provide:

> The Contractor, promptly after being awarded the Contract, shall submit for the Owner's and Architect's information a Contractor's construction schedule for the Work. The schedule shall contain detail appropriate for the Project, including (1) the date of commencement of the Work, interim schedule milestone dates, and the date of Substantial Completion; (2) an apportionment of the Work by construction activity; and (3) the time required for completion of each portion of the Work. The schedule shall provide for the orderly progression of the Work to completion and shall not exceed time limits current under the Contract Documents. The schedule shall be revised at appropriate intervals as required by the conditions of the Work and Project.[32]

Similarly, the ConsensusDocs 200 Standard Agreement and General Conditions Between Owner and Constructor originally imposed on the contractor the obligation to prepare and maintain a schedule of the work "showing the dates on which the Constructor plans to commence and complete various parts of the Work, including dates on which information and approvals are required from the Owner." More recent versions of the document have added language stating, "Unless otherwise agreed, the Schedule of the Work shall be formatted in a detailed precedence-style CPM that (a) provides a graphic representation of all activities and events, including float values that will affect the critical path of the Work, and (b) identifies dates that are critical to ensure timely and orderly completion of the Work. Constructor shall update the Schedule of the Work monthly or as mutually agreed by the Parties."[33]

Likewise, EJCDC C-700 (2018), Standard General Conditions of the Construction Contract, requires a contractor to prepare a "Progress Schedule" which is defined as "[a] schedule, prepared and maintained by Contractor, describing the sequence and duration of the activities comprising Contractor's plan to accomplish the Work within the Contract Times."

Beyond these generic references, it is quite common for private and public owners to explicitly impose stringent CPM scheduling requirements. For example, the Standard Specifications of the California State Transportation Agency

32. AIA A201 (2017), § 3.10.1.
33. ConsensusDocs 200, § 6.2.1 (revised Feb. 2024).

(Caltrans) prescribes three levels of CPM schedule requirements based on cost and duration of the project:[34] a Level 1 CPM Schedule for contracts with a total bid less than $1 million and less than 100 original working days;[35] a Level 2 CPM Schedule for contracts with (1) a total bid less than $1 million and 100 or more original working days, (2) a total bid from $1 to $5 million, or (3) a total bid over $5 million and less than 100 original working days; [36] and a Level 3 CPM Schedule for contracts with a total bid over $5 million and 100 or more original working days.[37] As might be suspected, as the cost and time of contract performance increase, the Caltrans specification impose greater requirements on the contractor with respect to submission, updating, format, number of activities, minimum and maximum durations, and constraints.[38]

With respect to federal government contracting, the Federal Acquisition Regulations (FAR) do not explicitly require the use of CPM scheduling, but FAR 52.236-15, Schedules for Construction Contracts, states that:

> (a) The Contractor shall, within five days after the work commences on the contract or another period of time determined by the Contracting Officer, prepare and submit to the Contracting Officer for approval three copies of a practicable schedule showing the order in which the Contractor proposes to perform the work, and the dates on which the Contractor contemplates starting and completing the several salient features of the work (including acquiring materials, plant, and equipment). The schedule shall be in the form of a progress chart of suitable scale to indicate appropriately the percentage of work scheduled for completion by any given date during the period[.]

Individual agencies, however, are free to require the use of CPM scheduling on projects and impose detailed requirements for those schedules. For example, the Unified Facilities Guide Specifications (UFGS)[39] contain requirements regarding project scheduler qualifications and the scheduling software used.[40] The UFGS

---

34. Section 8. The Caltrans Standard Specification, https://dot.ca.gov/-/media/dot-media/programs/design/documents/f00203402018stdspecs-a11y.pdf (last visited June 27, 2025).

35. Section 8-1.02B.

36. Section 8-1.02C.

37. Section 8-1.02D.

38. E.g., a Level 3 schedule must show at least 50 but not more than 500 activities; department-owned float as the predecessor activity to the scheduled completion date; and activities with identification codes for responsibility, stage, work shifts, location, and bid items. Section 8-1.02D(2).

39. The UFGS are jointly promulgated by the U.S. Army Corps of Engineers, the Naval Facilities Engineering Systems Command, and the Air Force Civil Engineer Center for use in construction of real property facilities for the military services. https://www.wbdg.org/dod (last accessed July 31, 2025).

40. UFGS 01 32 01.00 10, ¶ 1.3 and pt. 2, respectively.

further provides for the use of the CPM of network calculation to generate all project schedules.[41] The specifications also contain detailed requirements regarding cost loading, durations, design and permitting activities, procurement activities, submittals, testing, inspections, punch lists, and government and other agency activities that could impact progress.[42]

In private sector contracting CPM schedules are often required, particularly on so-called megaprojects.[43] One publicly reported EPC contract for an LNG facility contained the obligation to produce a CPM schedule detailing all activities to be completed in a logical sequence and being in sufficient detail to identify key activities and restraints, interdependencies, interrelationships, and resources required to control the project. The schedule specification required a level of detail sufficient for the contractor to plan, organize, direct, coordinate, perform, and execute the work and services of the contract, including separate activities for engineering, procurement, construction and precommissioning; the duration, start dates, and finish dates for each activity; logical relationships between activities that depicted an uninterrupted critical path from notice to proceed through anticipated dates for acceptance of various systems; and progress updating.

In sum, the use of CPM scheduling has become ubiquitous in the construction industry, and owners have the ability to dictate parameters that best suit their project management needs.

CPM as a Management Tool

The greatest utility of a properly developed and maintained CPM schedule is in the planning, coordination, and management of construction projects. Among the benefits are the following:

- **Time Management and Planning.** By calculating Early Start, Late Start, Early Finish, and Late Finish dates, a CPM schedule helps to identify flexibility (float or slack) in noncritical activities that potentially can be used to ameliorate the impact of issues affecting critical activities.

41. *Id.* ¶ 3.1.

42. *Id.* ¶¶ 3.2, 3.3.

43. "Megaprojects" are generally defined as large-scale, complex ventures that typically cost more than $1 billion, take many years to build, involve multiple public and private stakeholders, are transformational, and impact millions of people. Bent Flyvbjerg, *What You Should Know About Megaprojects and Why: An Overview*, Project Mgmt. Inst. (Oct. 2014), https://www.pmi.org/learning/library/what-you-should-know-megaprojects-11656.

- **Resource Allocation.** When resources are loaded into a CPM schedule, it can be used to optimize resource use, identify and avoid potential bottlenecks, and manage costs more effectively. For example, the CPM schedule can help identify overallocated resources (workers) and move the excess to other areas or resequence activities to facilitate the efficient use of resources and control costs.
- **Risk Management.** The critical path allows stakeholders to identify what could jeopardize the schedule and develop contingency plans or mitigation strategies with respect to those risks.
- **Progress Monitoring and Control.** During project execution, the CPM schedule depicts actual versus planned progress to allow identification and assessment of variances, potential delays to project completion, and potential added costs.
- **Communication and Documentation.** A CPM schedule provides a clear, standardized means for sharing information among the stakeholders so that everyone is speaking the same language when addressing issues.
- **Claims and Dispute Resolution.** CPM schedules are often used in forensic schedule analysis to demonstrate cause-and-effect relationships between events and schedule impacts.

CPM as a Claim Tool

In the event of claims, the CPM schedule can serve a vital role in analyzing the claim. As is discussed elsewhere, there are multiple standardized techniques whereby CPM schedules can be used to examine delays, which can be categorized as follows:

- **As-Planned Versus As-Built Analysis.** This methodology compares the original (as-planned) CPM schedule against the actual (as-built) project progression.
- **Windows Analysis.** This methodology divides the schedule into time segments (windows) and analyzes delays within each segment to determine impacts and responsibility.
- **Time-Impact Analysis (TIA).** This methodology adds delay events to the CPM schedule to model their effect on critical path and overall project completion.
- **Collapsed As-Built.** This methodology removes delays attributable to one party (e.g., the contractor) from the actual schedule and then recalculates completion.

As a general rule each of these methodologies can have sub-methodologies,[44] and there is a substantial body of industry and legal writing on which methodologies are appropriate under particular circumstances.[45]

CPM Jurisprudence

It is axiomatic that the burden of proof is on the claimant to establish the elements of a claim for breach of contract, that is, "the existence of a contract, a party's breach thereof, and damages."[46] In the context of a construction delay claim the claimant must prove that the counterparty breached the construction contract by delaying the claimant's performance of the work and resulting damages.[47] In *Mega Construction Company, Inc. v. The United States*,[48] the court held that a contractor failed to establish entitlement to adjustment for government-caused delay because it failed to show how government delays affected the critical path. The court began by noting the challenges of proving a delay claim:

> Not only must plaintiff disentangle its delays from those allegedly caused by the government, but the delays must have affected activities on the critical path. It is not enough that an activity is delayed: there must be delay of an activity on the critical path for there to be project, or compensable, delay. An interruption in one phase of the work . . . does not always result in an increase in the time necessary for total performance. In such a case, the absence of any delay would obviously preclude recovery[.][49]

The court then concluded that a critical path analysis was essential to establishing a right of recovery: "In order for the court to be able to award damages to plaintiff for government caused project delay along the critical path, the court must have before it evidence that establishes the critical path of plaintiff's project."[50] While the federal courts have not required CPM-based delay analysis in all cases,[51] they have expressed a strong preference for such analysis.[52]

---

44. *See generally* S. Dale & R. D'Onofrio, Construction Schedule Delays (2023).

45. *See, e.g., id.*; AACEI Recommended Practice 29R-03, Forensic Schedule Analysis (rev. 2011); ASCE Standard 67-17, Schedule Delay Analysis; and Society of Construction Law Delay and Disruption Protocol (2d ed. 2017).

46. JMF Med., LLC v. Team Health, LLC, 490 F. Supp. 3d 947, 973 (M.D. La. 2020) (citing Favrot v. Favrot, 2010-0986 (La. App. 4 Cir. 2/9/11), 68 So. 3d 1099, 1108–09); IberiaBank v. Broussard, 907 F.3d 826, 835 (5th Cir. 2018).

47. Dale & D'Onofrio, *supra* note 44, § 3.2 and n.2 (citing cases).

48. 29 Fed. Cl. 396 (1993).

49. *Id.* at 424–25.

50. *Id.* at 425–26.

51. Dale & D'Onofrio, *supra* note 44, § 3.2 and nn.5–7 (citing cases).

52. *Id.* § 3.2 and n.3 (citing cases). See also note 9 citing cases where alternative methods of proving delay were rejected by courts.

The jurisprudence is not so well-developed at the state court level. Most states have not addressed the issue, and those that have generally adopt the approach that analyses that do not use a computerized network diagram are acceptable provided that the alternative methodology shows a delay to the critical path.[53]

Conclusion

The CPM has become widely accepted both as a tool for project management and a valid means for presenting (and defending) damage claims based on delays. In both instances, however, it must be recognized that the validity and accuracy of the schedule depend on a variety of factors: the skill of the scheduling professional, the reasonableness of assumptions (e.g., durations and logic ties) underlying the schedule, the accuracy of data input into the schedule, and the timeliness of schedule updates. The phrase "garbage in, garbage out" (GIGO) originated in the early days of computer science and data processing and embodies the principle that computers will process whatever inputs they are given, regardless of quality. The adage also holds true for CPM scheduling. The end product is only as good as the inputs used to create (and maintain) it.

53. Howard Contracting, Inc. v. G. A. MacDonald Constr. Co., 83 Cal. Rptr. 2d 590 (1998) (computer-generated network diagram schedule not required to prove construction delay damages; bar chart that identified the project's critical path and demonstrated critical path delays sufficient).

CHAPTER 3

Common Causes of Construction Delay

Matthew T. Arvin

Introduction

There are many different causes of delays in the construction industry. This chapter discusses several of these causes, divided into three different categories: namely, early delays on the job site; delays caused by legal actions; and delays throughout the project due to issues with tools, materials, work forces, safety, and natural forces.

Sometimes, such as in the case of *Kiewit v. Iowa Southern Utilities*,[1] many different small delays will add up throughout the entire project to create one large problem, often referred to as a "cumulative impact." Power-generating company Iowa Southern began constructing a new coal-driven power-generating station in May of 1966 in Burlington, Iowa. Kiewit was awarded the mechanical and electrical contract for the new plant. Another contractor, Havens, was supposed to set the steel for Iowa Southern before Kiewit was to do any of its work. However, Havens was delayed when much of the steel did not arrive on schedule. Havens did not run a night shift "because of the dangers involved in working at heights at night" and "the lack of additional qualified iron workers as a result of other major construction taking place in the Burlington area."[2]

In addition to the steel work delaying Kiewit, the boiler was delayed three months when there was a strike at the plant that was constructing the boiler. In February, "a large pipe fell from some considerable height when the cable supporting it snapped. The pipe created extensive damage to some of the structural steel

1. Peter Kiewit Sons & Co. v. Iowa S. Utilities Co., 355 F. Supp. 376 (S.D. Iowa 1973).
2. *Id.* at 386.

members, and these members had to be replaced."[3] Finally, Kiewit wasted time by continually moving Havens' material out of Kiewit's work areas, and Kiewit had to stop work on some occasions "because of the danger of falling objects dropped by Havens worker[s] because of the impracticability of erecting netting or other devices to restrain the falling objects."[4] Many of these issues addressed in the *Kiewit* case are discussed throughout this chapter.

Early Delays on the Job

Licensing, Insurance, Bonding, and Permits

States all have their own form of general contractor licensing requirements, and these requirements may vary greatly from state to state. If a contractor is not properly licensed, it could delay the project until the contractor is properly licensed. However, licenses may also be trade specific. For example, New Jersey has a regulation that outlines how an electrician can become licensed. New Jersey states that "no person shall be granted an electrical contractor's license unless he shall first establish his qualifications [four years as an apprentice and one year as a journeyman in a program approved by the United States Department of Labor] and shall take and pass the examination for electrical contractors."[5] Other trades that generally need special licensing include HVAC installation contractors, plumbers, asbestos abatement contractors, and radon measurement contractors.

Most clients require proof of insurance before the contractor starts the project. Common types of construction coverage include workers' compensation and employee's liability (which usually covers legal fees while workers' compensation does not), automobile liability, professional liability, builder's risk (which protects the building, equipment, and material from property damage, theft, vandalism, fire, and acts of God while the project is under construction), pollution liability, and commercial general liability (which provides coverage to contractors involving third party claims).[6] The client may decide to delay awarding a contract to a contractor if a particular type of insurance coverage is lacking from the contractor. However, only getting the right type of coverage, by itself, is not enough. The coverage should also be of an appropriate amount before work begins with both an

3. *Id.*

4. *Id.* at 387 (alteration in citation).

5. N.J. Stat. Ann. § 45:5A-9 (2019) (alteration in citation).

6. The American Institute of Architect's sample draft for Commercial General Liability includes (1) damages because of bodily injury, sickness, or disease and death of any person; (2) personal injury and advertising injury; (3) physical damages to tangible property; and (4) bodily injury or property damages arising out of completed operations, American Institute of Architects, AIA Document A101-2017, Insurance and Bonds § A.3.2 (2017).

adequate per-occurrence limit and an aggregate limit amount. The client may shut down the contractor in the middle of the project if the contractor has lapsed coverage. Because of this, prudent contractors will regularly audit their policies to ensure that their policies remain current.

States may also require proof of insurance before issuing a contractor license. For example, to obtain a roofing license in Oklahoma,

> a copy of the roofing contractor's certificate of liability insurance shall be filed with the application and shall be not less than Five Hundred Thousand Dollars ($500,000.00) for residential roofing contractor work and shall not be less than One Million Dollars ($1,000,000.00) for commercial roofing contractor work.[7]

In 1935, the United States Miller Act was passed into law. This law requires contractors to have payment bonds[8] and performance bonds[9] for any government construction project over $100,000.[10] Subsequently, most states passed what are called Little Miller Acts, which are laws that, at least in part, mimic their federal counterpart. Generally, most states do not require contractors in private construction projects to require bonds. However, some states have addressed payment bonds for private construction cases. For example,

> Texas is one of relatively few states with a statutory form of payment bond for private construction projects. This form of bond provides an alternative means of dealing with potential lien claims on real property. Under the state's statutory regime, an owner can require his general contractor to obtain a payment bond for the protection of those furnishing labor or materials to the project.[11]

City, state, and federal governments also have their own respective permitting systems for construction. A contractor lacking the proper permits could end up delaying the project. Most municipalities, before a construction project begins, require both building permits and trades permits (to allow construction on specific trades such as electrical, plumbing, boilers, civil excavations, elevators, and fire protection). Many municipalities will have a building permit reviewed by other

---

7. Okla. Stat. tit. 59, § 1151.5 (2018).

8. Generally, a payment bond is a surety satisfaction for payment from contractors "to all persons furnishing services, equipment or supplies to Contractor for the performance of work." STATE EX REL. OWS v. United Pacific, 18 P.3d 491, 492 (Or. App. 2001).

9. "The purpose of a performance bond is to guarantee the completion of the contract upon default by the contractor. Ordinarily a performance bond only ensures the completion of the contract. The surety agrees to complete the construction or to pay the obligee the reasonable costs of completion if the contractor defaults." Am. Home Assur. Co. v. Larkin Gen. Hosp., Ltd., 593 So. 2d 195, 198 (Fla. 1992).

10. The Miller Act, 40 U.S.C. § 3131(b).

11. Laughlin Env'l v. Premier Towers, 126 S.W.3d 668, 671 (Tex. App. 2004).

agencies, which could delay the permitting process significantly.[12] Washington DC, also has permits for the occupation of public space, public right of way, and public structure in which "the mayor may revoke any permit at any time."[13] It is common for a municipality to have an occupancy permit requirement. For example, in Washington, DC, a Certificate of Occupancy "verifies that the use of a building, structure, or land in Washington, DC complies with the Zoning Regulations (DCMR Title 11), DC Construction Codes, and the Green Building Act, ensuring adherence to legal and safety standards."[14] And finally, it is also not uncommon for states to have a slew of environmental permits that construction projects may have to obtain. For example, construction projects in Tennessee may require environmental permits such as air pollution control permits, mining permits, wastewater discharge permits, oil and gas permits, and stormwater discharge permits.[15]

Bid Delays in Private Projects and Mobilization

After a solicitation to bid goes out to contractors, there may be several bid meetings depending on the size of the project. After a contractor's estimator looks at the bid package and estimates the cost to complete the project along with gathering bids from subcontractors, the contractor will then submit a bid to the client. Generally, there is a cut-off time and date to submit bids. If no one submits a bid before that cut-off date, then the client may either extend the bid submission date or invite new contractors to bid on the project. This obviously could delay the startup time. Likewise, if no one submits an amount that the client finds appropriate, then the project could go out to bid again, potentially delaying the project.

After a contractor is awarded the project, mobilization issues could delay the project. A client may delay a contractor's access to a project. For example, if there are delays in the client purchasing the land for the project, this will delay the start of the project.

---

12. For example, building permits in Washington, DC, may be reviewed by "DC Water (if there are new water connections), the District Department of Transportation (for impact of public alleys, sidewalks or streets), the Historical Preservation Review Board and Commission of Fine Arts (for properties located within a historically designated area or deemed an area commissioned by the fine arts), the Washington Metropolitan Area Transit Authority (to ensure metro operations and riders are not negatively impacted), the Department of Health (regarding food establishments or hygiene facilities), and the Department of Energy and the Environment (for projects involving soil disturbance, flood plains, and lead abatement)." DC Dep't of Building, How to Obtain a Permit, https://dob.dc.gov/page/get-permit (last visited Oct. 4, 2024).

13. D.C. Code § 10-1141.03(c).

14. How to Obtain a Permit, *supra* note 12.

15. Tenn. Dep't of Env'l & Conservation, Permits, https://www.tn.gov/environment/permit-permits-home.html (last visited Oct. 21, 2024).

However, a contractor may or may not already be mobilized on-site. This type of delay is well illustrated when dealing with industrial construction projects. There are two basic types of industrial construction projects: greenfield projects and projects within an existing facility.

Greenfield industrial projects are construction projects where, on the first day of the project, there is nothing but a plot of land. Earth is moved, a foundation is constructed, a building is erected, and new equipment is installed inside the facility. However, many industrial projects exist within an already operating facility. Some delays can occur in both types of construction. However, certain types of delay are unique to either greenfield or existing facility construction.

When a greenfield project begins, a general contractor must bring its own office trailers, office supplies and equipment, washroom facilities, tools, mobilized equipment, and safety supplies to the site. Slow mobilization could delay the start of the project and subsequently delay the finish of the project.

On construction projects within an existing facility, the contractor may or may not already be on-site. Often, larger clients with many different types of projects will keep several general contractors on-site. These contractors are already mobilized with an office trailer in "trailer city," with mobilized equipment on-site, and with a workforce already trained and ready for work at the project site. Contractors that are not already on-site may face the same mobilization issues that contractors face on greenfield projects. Thus, they could be at a disadvantage compared to contractors already on-site.

There are many advantages of greenfield construction that can expedite construction. For example, a contractor does not have to co-exist with manufacturing production while installing equipment. Contractors are freer to move about the facility and work when and where they wish. However, there are also some distinct disadvantages. On some greenfield projects, there may be several "general" contractors who have contracted directly with the owner to construct different components of the overall project. For example, one general contractor may have the contract to construct the building, but another general contractor may have the contract to install the process equipment inside the building. A delay by one general contractor could very easily delay another general contractor. Likewise, one contractor's mistake could result in delay for all the other contractors. For example, it is very important for concrete to be poured correctly. There are two distinct ways a concrete pour can go wrong. The first is that the concrete is poured unevenly, which can cause a delay for weeks or even months while the problem is remediated. The second is if the contractor uses the wrong grade for the project. Concrete has various grades and strengths; if a lower compressive strength is used than what is required, the entire project could be compromised for all contractors.

Delays from Legal Actions and Lawsuits

Disputes certainly have a way of creating delay. This is particularly true when dealing with delays caused by environmental, historical, and cultural legislation and regulations.

Endangered Species Act Lawsuits

Lawsuits from concerned citizens protecting local wildlife and vegetation could considerably delay projects. In 2008, NextLight Renewable Power requested a right of way from the Bureau of Land Management (BLM) to use federal government land in southern Clark County, Nevada, to install solar energy panels. The project was divided into two adjacent facilities named Silver State South Solar Project and Silver State North Solar Project.

In October 2010, the BLM approved the application for Silver State North but deferred approval of the application for Silver State South. The BLM explained that "the deferral of Silver State South was in part due to the 'higher density of [desert] tortoise that reside in that portion of the project area' which 'requires additional wildlife consideration and potentially further consultation with the U.S. Fish and Wildlife Service (FWS).'"[16] The desert tortoise is native to the Mojave Desert region where the solar panels were proposed to be installed, and in 1990, the FWS determined "the Mojave population of the desert tortoise (*Gopherus agassizii*) to be a threatened species pursuant to the Endangered Species Act of 1973."[17] Therefore, on September 30, 2013, the FWS issued their Biological Opinion (BiOp) which reviewed the BLM's course of actions.

> The BiOp made several conclusions including: (1) Silver State South would be not likely to adversely affect the critical habitat of the desert tortoise, because the proposed actions would not occur within the boundaries of critical habitat of the desert tortoise or directly or indirectly affect the primary constituent elements of critical habitat, (2) Silver State South was unlikely to appreciably diminish the reproduction numbers, or distribution of the desert tortoise in action areas, (3) few tortoises would be harmed or killed because of the proposed translocation of tortoises found in the project site and fencing to be built around Silver State South, and (4) while the habitat loss of 2,388 acres will reduce connectivity between the southern and northern ends of the Ivanpah Valley, the proposed

16. Defenders of Wildlife v. Zinke, 856 F.3d 1248, 1254 (9th Cir. 2017).

17. Endangered and Threatened Wildlife and Plants; Determination of Threatened Status for the Mojave Population of the Desert Tortoise, 5 Fed. Reg. 63, 12178 (Apr. 2, 1990).

> mitigation measures would offset, to some degree, the decrease in the width of the linkage.[18]

In February 2014, the BLM, relying on the BiOp, issued the right of way for Silver State South. On March 6, 2014, Defenders of Wildlife (DOW) sued the federal defendants to enjoin construction of Silver State South. The district court denied DOW's request for a preliminary injunction, concluding that DOW could "not show a likelihood of success on the merits of their claim that the Biological Opinion's 'no jeopardy' determination was arbitrary or capricious."[19]

By that September, construction began on Silver State South, and was completed in December 2016. In 2017, the Ninth Circuit affirmed the district court's decision "because the BiOp was neither legally nor factually flawed, the BLM permissibly relied upon the BiOp in approving of the right-of-way for Silver State South."[20]

Environmental Lawsuits and the Tar Sands Pipeline Cases

The Keystone XL pipeline reached national news in 2015 when President Obama effectively blocked the building of the pipeline. However, what President Obama blocked was just the fourth and final phase of the Keystone project. Phase I was completed in 2010. This pipeline went east from Hardisty, Alberta, Canada, to southern Manitoba. From Manitoba, it went south through both Dakotas and Nebraska before heading east at Steele City, Nebraska. The pipe then traveled through southeast Nebraska, northeast Kansas, and all of Missouri before eventually ending in south central Illinois. Phase II, which went from Steele City to Cushing, Oklahoma, was completed in early 2011. Phase III, which traveled from Cushing to Freeport, Texas, a town on the coast of the Gulf of Mexico, was completed in 2014. It was only Phase IV, scheduled to be completed in late 2015, that was vetoed by President Obama. This pipeline would have gone more directly from Hardisty to Steele City by cutting through Saskatchewan, Montana, South Dakota, and Nebraska.

Another large, international tar sands pipeline that remained separate from the Keystone project was the Alberta Clipper Pipeline, which was completed in 2010. This pipeline stretched from Hardisty across Canada into northern Minnesota before ending in Superior, Wisconsin. Just before the pipeline was set to be

18. *Zinke*, 856 F.3d at 1255.

19. Defenders of Wildlife v. Jewell, No. CV 14-1656-MWF, 2014 WL 1364452, at *14 (C.D. Cal. Apr. 2, 2014).

20. *Zinke*, 856 F.3d at 1265.

completed, a group of environmentalists led by the Sierra Club filed suit in the U.S. District Court of Minnesota in *Sierra Club v. Clinton*.[21] In this case, the court ruled against the plaintiff and allowed the project to be completed. The court considered two distinct issues: (1) whether the presidential permit issued for the AC Pipeline was constitutional; and (2) whether the government violated the National Environmental Protection Act (NEPA) and the Clean Water Act.

The plaintiffs first claimed that "the President has no constitutional or statutory authority to issue Presidential permits for international tar sands crude oil pipelines and that international oil pipelines are a matter of foreign commerce and, therefore, the power to regulate these pipelines is under the exclusive and plenary constitutional authority of Congress to 'regulate commerce with foreign nations.'"[22] The Court disagreed, ruling that, "[g]iven the history of the President's issuance of permits for border crossings, the congressional silence on the issue of such border crossings, and the involvement of several agencies in the regulation of the pipeline, the Court, at this stage in the litigation, determines that Plaintiffs have not established a substantial probability that they can demonstrate that the issuance of the Permit was unconstitutional."[23]

The court also looked to see if the federal government violated the NEPA when it published its environmental impact study (EIS).[24] Plaintiffs claimed that the government did not look at the cumulative impact of the project, did not state a defined purpose, and did not adequately consider the reasonable alternatives. However, the court found that the defendants did not violate the NEPA because they did take the requisite look at the impact and all alternatives before making their decision.[25]

---

21. Sierra Club v. Clinton, 689 F. Supp. 2d 1123 (D. Minn. 2010).

22. *Id.* at 1130.

23. *Id.* at 1131 (alteration in citation).

24. The NEPA requires an environmental impact statement to contain: "(1) A statement of the purpose and need for the action; (2) A description of the proposed action; (3) The environmental impact of the proposed action; (4) A brief description of the affected environment; (5) Any adverse environmental effects which cannot be avoided should the proposal be implemented; (6) Alternatives to the proposed action; (7) The relationship between local short-term uses of the human environment and the maintenance and enhancement of long-term productivity; (8) Any irreversible or irretrievable commitments of resources which would be involved in the proposed action should it be implemented; and (9) The process used to coordinate with other Federal agencies, State, tribal and local governments, and persons or organizations who may be interested or affected, and the results thereof." National Environmental Policy Act of 1969, 43 C.F.R. § 46.415 (2019).

25. Under the Administrative Procedures Act, the reviewing court must affirm an agency decision unless it is "arbitrary, capricious, an abuse of discretion, or otherwise not in accordance with law." Administrative Procedures Act, 5 U.S.C. § 706(2)(A). The courts found that "neither the statute nor its legislative history contemplates that a court should substitute its judgment for that of the

Two years later, in *Sierra Club v. Bostick*,[26] the Sierra Club filed suit claiming that Nationwide Permit 12 issued by the federal government to construct Phase III of the Keystone pipeline system violated the Clean Water Act and the NEPA. Here, the government did not even write an EIS. Instead, the government only wrote an Environmental Assessment (EA), which is "a concise public document . . . that serves to . . . briefly provide sufficient evidence and analysis for determining whether to prepare an environmental impact statement[.]"[27] When the government uses an EA, there are still requirements that must be met: "An EA must, at a minimum, include discussion of the need for the proposal, alternatives, the environmental impacts of the proposed action and the alternatives, and the agencies and persons consulted."[28] The court found that the EA, in this case, met the minimum requirements because it discussed alternatives and the impact of the proposed action, and offered mitigation options to offset certain environmental impacts.[29] Because the requirements of the EA were satisfied, the court found that the government did take the requisite hard look at the environmental consequences and did not act arbitrarily and capriciously even though a full EIS was never drafted. On appeal, the Tenth Circuit affirmed the finding that the district court did not show an abuse of discretion. The pipeline was completed in 2014.

Throughout this time, President Obama never gave a presidential permit for construction of Keystone XL Phase IV. In light of the President's silence, Congress in 2015 passed approval to start construction of Phase IV. However, President Obama vetoed Congress's bill, and the Senate did not override the president with a two-thirds supermajority.

After President Trump became President, he issued a Presidential Memorandum inviting TransCanada Keystone Pipeline, L.P., "to promptly re-submit its application to the Department of State for a Presidential permit for the construction and operation of the Keystone XL Pipeline."[30] A few months later, a presidential permit was granted to TransCanada. In 2018, the Indigenous Environmental Network sued the Department of State in the U.S. District Court of Montana. Here,

---

agency as to the environmental consequences of its actions." Scenic Hudson Preservation Conference v. FPC, 453 F.2d 463, 481 (2d Cir. 1971). And that the "only role for a court is to ensure that the agency has taken a 'hard look' at environmental consequences; it cannot 'interject itself within the area of discretion of the executive as to the choice of the action to be taken.'" Nat. Res. Def. Council v. Morton, 458 F.2d 827, 838 (D.C. Cir. 1972).

26. Sierra Club, Inc. v. Bostick CASE NO CIV-12-742-R (W.D. Okla. Aug. 5, 2012).

27. *Id.* at 11.

28. *Id.* at 12.

29. *Id.*

30. Presidential Memorandum on Construction of the Keystone XL Pipeline, 82 Fed. Reg. 18, 8663 (Jan. 24, 2017).

the court sided with the plaintiff, again blocking construction on several grounds including:

> the effect of current oil prices on the viability of Keystone, the cumulative effects of greenhouse gas emissions from the Alberta Clipper expansion and the Keystone, a survey of potential cultural resources contained in the 1,038 acres not addressed in the SEIS, [and] an updated modeling of potential oil spills and recommended mitigation measures.[31]

However, in 2019, the Ninth Circuit "granted TransCanada's motion to vacate the district court's 2018 judgment, dissolved the district court's permanent injunction orders, and remanded with instructions to dismiss the district court actions as moot."[32] On President Biden's first day in office on January 20, 2021, he revoked the presidential permit that President Trump granted to TransCanada in 2018. His executive order stated that "the Keystone XL pipeline disserves the U.S. national interest."[33] In June of 2021, TransCanada officially stated that it would permanently be terminating the Keystone XL project.[34]

Historical and Archeological Preservation

Construction projects may get delayed because of archeological or historical finds within the construction zone. For example, if human remains are found on a project site in Illinois, "the coroner has to make the initial determination if [the bones] are over 100 years old. If so, they then call the Illinois Historic Preservation Agency. If the find is not deemed to be culturally significant, coroners usually take what they need for further examination and, in many cases, let crews get back to work. The process will not move quickly if it looks like a recent crime may have been committed on the site."[35]

Lawsuits against federal construction projects may arise to ensure violations of the National Historic Preservation Act (NHPA) or the archeological clause of the Department of Transportation Act of 1966 are prevented or remedied. Under the

---

31. Indigenous Env't Network v. U.S. Dep't of State, 347 F. Supp. 3d 561, 590 (D. Mont. 2018) (alteration in citation).

32. Indigenous Env't Network v. U.S. Dep't of State, No. CV 18-36068, at *4 (9th Cir. 2019).

33. Exec. Order No. 13990 on Protecting Public Health and the Environment and Restoring Science to Tackle the Climate Crisis, 86 Fed. Reg. 7037, 7041 (Jan. 25, 2021).

34. *Developer Officially Cancels Keystone XL Pipeline Project Blocked by Biden*, Reuters (June 10, 2021), https://www.reuters.com/business/energy/tc-energy-terminates-keystone-xl-pipeline-project-2021-06-09/.

35. Kim Slowey, *Digging Up Delays: How to Handle Unexpected Archaeological Finds on the Job Site*, Construction Dive (Feb. 2017), https://www.constructiondive.com/news/digging-up-delays-how-to-handle-unexpected-archaeological-finds-on-the-job/435756/.

NHPA, a federal agency: "must (1) make a reasonable and good faith effort to identify historic properties; (2) determine whether identified properties are eligible for listing on the National Register based on criteria in 36 C.F.R. § 60.4; (3) assess the effects of the undertaking on any eligible historic properties found; (4) determine whether the effect will be adverse; and (5) avoid or mitigate any adverse effects."[36]

A building need not be registered in the National Register to qualify for NHPA protections. Instead, the building or location merely needs to qualify for inclusion for protection to be allowed.[37] For example, in *Friends of St. Frances Xavier Cabrini Church v. Paulson*,[38] even though Cabrini Church was not listed in the National Register, it was eligible for listing "for its innovative and complex structural design, exemplifying an exceptional singular design for a house of worship in New Orleans erected during the post-World War II period, and because the Church represents the work of the preeminent Modern local architecture firm of Curtis and Davis."[39]

For any federal agency to be able to determine the effect, it will need to seek out and obtain the views of the State Historic Preservation Officer (SHPO) of the state. If the agency "determines that either there are no historic properties or that there is no effect on any such properties that were identified, and there is no timely objection to that determination, then the project may proceed."[40] However, if the agency determines there is an adverse effect, then it must notify the Advisory Council on Historical Preservation (ACHP)[41] so that it can "comment on the effects and consult with the State Historic Preservation Officer (SHPO) to seek ways to reduce or

---

36. Neighborhood Ass'n, Back Bay v. Fed. Transit, 407 F. Supp. 2d 323, 332 (D. Mass. 2005).

37. The criteria for eligibility as outlined to become a national historic place includes four broad categories: "(A) That are associated with events that have made a significant contribution to the broad patterns of our history; or (B) That are associated with the lives of persons significant in our past; or (C) That embody the distinctive characteristics of a type, period, or method of construction, or that represent the work of a master, or that possess high artistic values, or that represent a significant and distinguishable entity whose components may lack individual distinction; or (D) That have yielded, or may be likely to yield, information important in prehistory or history." National Register of Historic Places, 36 C.F.R. § 60.4 (2012).

38. Friends of St. Frances Xavier Cabrini Church v. Paulson, 728 F. Supp. 2d 820 (E.D. La. 2010).

39. *Id.* at 824.

40. Walsh v. U.S. Army Corps of Eng'rs, 757 F. Supp. 781, 788 (W.D. Tex. 1990).

41. "The Advisory Council on Historic Preservation (ACHP) is an independent federal agency that promotes the preservation, enhancement, and sustainable use of our nation's diverse historic resources, and advises the President and the Congress on national historic preservation policy. The goal of the National Historic Preservation Act (NHPA), which established the ACHP in 1966, is to have federal agencies act as responsible stewards of our nation's resources when their actions affect historic properties. The ACHP is the only entity with the legal responsibility to encourage federal agencies to factor historic preservation into their decision making." Notice of Advisory Council on Historic Preservation Quarterly Business Meeting, 85 Fed. Reg. 47, 13909 (Mar. 10, 2020).

avoid the effects of the undertaking on the historic properties."[42] That agency must give the ACHP reasonable opportunity to respond before starting the project. Even if the project is not blocked entirely on historical preservation grounds, unforeseeable administrative complications and burdensome compliance requirements, such as installing shoring underneath wooden floors or placing protective tarps over walls to protect the historical integrity of the building, could slow down projects.

However, the effects may end up being disputed in court. For example, in 2013, Virginia Electric and Power Company (Dominion) was to construct "a new electrical switching station and two transmission lines supported by seventeen 250-or-so-foot steel lattice transmission towers."[43] Electrical lines would "traverse over the James River for four miles and cut through the middle of the historic district encompassing Jamestown and other historic resources."[44] The U.S. Army Corps of Engineers (USACE) claimed that the structures from Dominion did not physically stand on the historic grounds; therefore, there could not be a violation of the Preservation Act. The court disagreed with USACE. In so doing, it held that, while the act clearly encompasses physical effect, the statute does not limit its reach to just physical effects. Instead, all effects are encompassed into the law. The court reasoned, "had Congress wished to restrict the reach merely to physical impacts, it could have easily done so by using the word physically."[45]

Plaintiffs may potentially sue to preserve historical properties under the Transportation Act of 1966. Under section 4(f) of the Transportation Act, "a transportation project that impacts a historic site cannot be implemented unless the agency shows that there is no feasible and prudent alternative to the use of the site, and that it has done all possible planning to minimize harm to the site."[46]

However, there are some statutory exceptions to section 4(f). For example, 23 C.F.R. § 774.13 (b)(1) provides for such an exception "if the Administration, after consultation with the State Historic Preservation Officer and the Advisory Council on Historic Preservation, determines that the archeological resource is important chiefly because of what can be learned by data recovery and has minimal value for preservation in place."[47]

In another archaeological preservation case, *Belmont v. Dole*, the First Circuit found that the exception would not apply "if the archeological items give a particular site a special 'in place' historical or archeological significance. (Consider, for example, the Civil War battle artifacts at Gettysburg.) The regulation also would

42. *Walsh*, 757 F. Supp. at 789.
43. Nat'l Parks Conservation Ass'n v. Semonite, 916 F.3d 1075, 1078 (D.C. Cir. 2019).
44. *Id.*
45. *Id.* at 1088.
46. Preservation Coal. v. Fed. Transit Admin., 129 F. Supp. 2d 538, 541 (W.D.N.Y. 2000).
47. Town of Belmont v. Dole, 766 F.2d 28, 29 (1st Cir. 1985).

not apply if it turns out that the related agencies cannot develop a 'resource recovery plan' that would remove and preserve the significant items."[48]

Other Preservation Interests

Citizens may bring a state lawsuit to stop construction to preserve the integrity of an area or a particular building. For example, in 2018 concerned citizens sued the City of Nashville, Tennessee, relating to the city's decision to allow a soccer stadium to be built at the state fairgrounds. In 2011, Nashville's Metro Charter was amended to ensure that any existing activities at the fairgrounds would be able to continue to use the fairgrounds despite any changes that may occur there. In 2017, Metro Council passed a resolution approving the construction of a Major League Soccer stadium on the fairground property. The plaintiffs sued, claiming that the new stadium would violate the Metro Charter by prohibiting the existing activities adequate use of the fairgrounds. For its part, the city claimed that "building brand new, modern facilities for the existing activities does not violate the right for these activities to continue."[49] Eventually, the city's position was successful. The stadium was built and, two full years behind schedule, Nashville's Major League soccer team played its first game in May of 2022 at Geodis Park.

Native American Rights

Native Americans may bring suit to stop construction to either protect their cultural lands or their religious practices. In 2016, the Standing Rock Sioux Tribe brought a lawsuit against the United States government. In this case, the tribe sued USACE to block construction of the Dakota Access Pipeline (DAPL). The pipe traveled across private land, and only a fraction of the pipe came within a half mile of the federal lands designated for the Standing Rock Reservation. The tribe claimed that the pipe construction violated the National Historic Preservation Act because of "the likelihood that the Dakota Access Pipeline's ongoing construction activities—specifically, grading and clearing of land—might damage or destroy sites of great cultural or historical significance to the tribe."[50] However, the court ruled that "no federal agency had the ability to prevent DAPL's construction from proceeding on these private lands. At most, the Corps could only have stopped these activities at the banks of a navigable U.S. waterway. An injunction of any unlawful permitting now can, at most, do the same."[51]

---

48. *Id.* at 33.

49. Save Our Fairgrounds v. Metro Gov't of Nashville & Davidson Cnty., No. M2019-00724-COA-R3-CV, at *5 (Tenn. Ct. App. July 30, 2019).

50. Standing Rock Sioux Tribe v. U.S. Army Corps of Eng'rs, 205 F. Supp. 3d 4, 33 (D.D.C. 2016).

51. *Id.* at 34.

A year later, the Cheyenne River Sioux Tribe brought suit in the District Court of Washington, DC. Fearing that the presence of oil in the pipeline under Lake Oahe would cause irreparable harm to its members' religious exercise, the Cheyenne River Sioux sought an injunction under the Religious Freedom Restoration Act (RFRA).[52] USACE did not dispute that the lake, which much of the Tribe's reservation adjoins, had religious and ceremonial importance to the Tribe.

> The Tribe elaborated their position in front of the District Court of Washington D.C. claiming that the Lakota people believe that the mere existence of a crude oil pipeline under the waters of Lake Oahe will desecrate those waters and render them unsuitable for use in their religious sacraments. . . . The Lakota people believe that the pipeline correlates with a terrible Black Snake prophesied to come into the Lakota homeland and cause destruction. . . . The Lakota believe that the very existence of the Black Snake under their sacred waters in Lake Oahe will unbalance and desecrate the water and render it impossible for the Lakota to use that water in their Inipi ceremony.[53]

In the end, however, the Court found that USACE's grant of an easement would only incidentally affect the Lakota people's exercise of their religious practices.[54] Thus, the easement was not likely to impose a substantial burden on religious exercise, as is required to establish a violation of the RFRA.

Delays Throughout the Project

Overlapping Work, Change in Scope, and Schedule Changes

As mentioned in the introduction, the *Kiewit* case shows how projects can become delayed when schedules with different contractors overlap. If there is an overlap, one contractor will usually get priority over the other from the project owner. There are a few options that the contractors can try to stay on schedule. One contractor can start a night shift to continue work while the other contractor works during the day. A contractor can also downsize its manpower until it has control

52. Standing Rock Sioux Tribe v. U.S. Army Corps of Eng'rs, 239 F. Supp. 3d 77, 80 (D.D.C. 2017).

53. *Id.* at 82.

54. In *Lyng v. Northwest Indian Cemetery Protective Ass'n*, a collective group of Native Americans brought suit to enjoin the federal government from harvesting timber and upgrading federal highways because it would damage sacred religious areas for the Tribes. The Supreme Court rejected their Free Exercise argument claiming that these harms were not the kind protected under the Free Exercise Clause because they were "incidental effects of government programs, which may make it more difficult to practice certain religions but which have no tendency to coerce individuals into acting contrary to their religious beliefs." Lyng v. Northwest Indian Cemetery Protective Ass'n, 485 U.S. 439, 465 (1988).

of the work area, then hire up and work premium hours after it regains control of the work zone.

Certainly, delays can be caused by either poor workmanship by the contractor or by property damage to the product before final buyoff from the client. This could result in an extensive rework period leading to an extension of the project. There could also be a dispute between the general contractor and a subcontractor as to whether rework is actually needed and who will be paying for it.

However, schedule delays can be caused by a plethora of other reasons. For example, the scope of work can change within the project. A well-constructed industrial project bid package will have clear, concise, and detailed language on the tasks that the contractor is to perform. However, ambiguities in the contract could result in delays. Arguments and disputes over those ambiguities could slow down progress until clarity is provided. And any unanticipated additional work thrust upon the contractor in the middle of the project because of these ambiguities could change the scope of the project and cause delays.

The addition of several change orders to the existing contract could also extend the project. For example, if the contract with the client calls for the installation of an assembly line but does not explicitly call for the installation of permanent overhead lighting or the installation of an overhead crane system, these projects are likely to be considered an "add-on." The contractor would then create a field order or change order with the cost of completing these items and submit it to the client before work begins. These "add-ons" certainly could delay the project—especially if manpower needs to be spread thinner or if existing tasks are pushed back on the schedule to accommodate the change orders. Understanding potential add-ons at the front end of the project and accounting for them in a contractor's schedule could prevent these costly delays.

Financial and budgeting issues also could cause a delay. First, the project owner can become insolvent. If that is the case, the project would most likely become suspended indefinitely. However, even with a solvent owner, contractors could have difficulty getting paid. To combat this, Prompt Pay Acts have been enacted by several states "to ensure that contractors and subcontractors on construction work are timely paid the full amount they are due."[55] Despite these measures, if the general contractor or the subcontractors are not getting paid in a timely manner, there could be a contractual breach, and the contractor may walk off the site. If this happens, a new contractor will need to be found, or the owner must wait until

55. Tennessee Courts, *Tennessee Supreme Court Holds Contractor Potentially Liable for $300-Per-Day Penalty* (June 30, 2021), https://www.tncourts.gov/press/2021/06/30/tennessee-supreme-court-holds-contractor-potentially-liable-300-day-penalty#:~:text=The%20Prompt%20Pay%20Act%20was,full%20amount%20they%20are%20due.

the contractor returns to the project. This could create considerable delays in the project.

There may be a situation where the general contractor is so bogged down with additional and unexpected expenses, that they may just cut their losses and leave. If the general contractor breaches the contract, they may be on the hook for any additional costs incurred to the client in finding a new contractor.

Finally, there may be geopolitical issues (such as waiting for an outcome of a presidential election) or world economy issues that could create a delay. For example, in December 2008, Toyota "delayed the construction of their Mississippi facility when about 90% completed because of a downturn in the economy. Toyota reported its auto sales in the U.S. fell 34 percent in November, while sales across the industry sank 37 percent; the company's sales are down 13 percent for the first 11 months of the year compared with the same period in 2007."[56]

It is often said by construction workers that if you give them the right tools, information, and materials, they can get any project completed. However, if any one of these three is missing, it can cause considerable delays.

A Lack of Information

Information can be lacking from either (1) a slow chain of command where the project is waiting on information or (2) from incorrect information given to the project manager. Information for projects may be provided in many different forms including Gantt charts, shop drawings, blueprint plans, electrical panel schedules, or piping and instrumentation diagrams. As found in *Cameo Homes v. Kraus-Anderson Construction Co.*,[57] faulty blueprints can be devastating to a project. In *Cameo Homes*, "errors in the architectural plans provided by the City complicated Cameo's performance on the City Hall contract. According to Cameo, mistakes in the City's blueprints required it to remove and re-pour substantial amounts of concrete. This resulted in added delays and costs, and as a result, Kraus-Anderson said it would have to verify the proper placement of concrete before Cameo did any future pours."[58]

A Lack of Tools

Projects can be delayed while contractors are waiting for tools and mobilized equipment to arrive on-site. Tools and equipment such as forklifts and propane

56. *Toyota Delays Mississippi Assembly Plant*, The Meridian Star (Dec. 15, 2008), https://www.meridianstar.com/news/local_news/toyota-delays-mississippi-assembly-plant/article_069a9bc8-35df-58b0-af40-e1222975b631.html.

57. Cameo Homes v. Kraus-Anderson Constr. Co., 394 F.3d 1084 (8th Cir. 2005).

58. *Id.* at 1086.

welders could potentially break down on-site. If the contractor owns its equipment and it breaks down on-site, it could cause a delay in the work until repairs are made, or a replacement is either bought or transferred from another project. Often, contractors rent their mobile equipment from a local rental company. If demand locally for a piece of equipment is higher than what the rental company can supply, there could be a delay until the piece of equipment is provided.

The need for specialty equipment that was not anticipated to be required during the project may slow down work. For example, if it is discovered that a contractor can only cut fine details with a water jet saw or needs to access an area with scaffolding or an all-terrain aerial lift, that equipment will have to be ordered and sent to the site. Work may slow down or even stop until that piece of equipment arrives.

The savvy project manager will see the need for these tools well before the time they are needed and get them on-site while not causing any delays. However, if this does not happen, delays in the project may occur.

A Lack of Materials

Contractors cannot install what they do not have to install. Materials may be lacking for a few different reasons. There could be a delay in the shipping of the material, such as the steel to Havens in the *Kiewit* case. The material could be shipped on time, but it could turn out to be initially defective or nonconforming. Finally, the material could be the correct material and timely installed, but then recalled later by the manufacturer. For example, "between 2004 and 2007, an estimated 100,000 homes in more than 20 states were built with toxic drywall imported from China."[59]

Common features of the reports submitted to the United States Consumer Product Safety Commission from homes believed to contain problem drywall have been: "(1) Consumers have reported a 'rotten egg' smell within their homes, (2) Consumers have reported health concerns such as irritated and itchy eyes and skin, difficulty in breathing, persistent cough, bloody noses, runny noses, recurrent headaches, sinus infection, and asthma attacks, and (3) Consumers have reported blackened and corroded metal components in their homes and the frequent replacement of components in air conditioning units."[60]

59. Greg Allen, *Toxic Chinese Drywall Creates a Housing Disaster*, NPR (Oct. 27, 2009), https://www.npr.org/2009/10/27/114182073/toxic-chinese-drywall-creates-a-housing-disaster.

60. U.S. Consumer Product Safety Comm'n, *Where Has Problem Drywall Been Reported?*, https://www.cpsc.gov/safety-education/safety-education-centers/drywall-information-center/where-has-problem-drywall-been-reported#:~:text=To%20date%2C%20the%20CPSC%20has,of%20drywall%20produced%20in%20China (last visited Oct. 27, 2024).

Many home builders such as Maimi-based Lennar Homes "worked to remedy the situation, in some cases removing and replacing the drywall and relocating homeowners during the process."[61]

Some companies do fabricate their own materials. However, most of the time, a third-party supplier manufactures the piece of industrial equipment being installed. If these suppliers are behind schedule, delivery of the equipment could be delayed. This could result in an installation delay, which was the case of Combustion Engineering who was late in supplying the boiler in the *Kiewit* case.

Equipment could be shipped from outside the United States especially if the owner of the project is an international company. If that is the case, then equipment could be delayed at the international border while it sits at customs. Sometimes material can sit at the border for weeks or even months at a time before it passes customs. For example, shipping boats from October 2020 to November of 2022 had difficulty docking in Los Angeles Port as there was a constant backup of ships waiting to dock. The backup peaked "in January of 2022 with over 100 ships waiting at any given time. After January, the backlog steadily declined until there were zero ships waiting to dock in November of 2022."[62]

Other supply chain issues occurred frequently in the early part of the 2020s; they were caused by "the perfect storm-a combination of the pandemic, global economy and events in Eastern Europe."[63] These supply chain issues led to greater lead time. It was reported by manufacturers that lead times from suppliers was the longest since 1987.[64]

Notably, the semiconductor shortage that began in 2020 and continued throughout the next several years impacted construction schedules, especially in the automobile industry. Vehicle production schedules began being altered in the first quarter of 2021 due to the semiconductor shortage.[65] Because of the

---

61. Teresa Burney, *Lennar Files Suit Over Chinese Drywall: Defective Drywall Is Being Blamed for Copper Corrosion and Odors*, Builder Online (Feb. 4, 2009), https://www.builderonline.com/building/regulation-policy/lennar-files-suit-over-chinese-drywall_o#:~:text=By%20Teresa%20Burney,of%20product%20liability%20and%20negligence.

62. Paul Berger, *Southern California's Container Ship Backup Ends*, Wall St. J. (Nov. 22, 2022), https://www.wsj.com/articles/southern-californias-container-ship-backup-ends-11669162514.

63. Diana Kightlinger, *Building Material Lead Times Are a Major Problem Right Now. Here's Why*, Bluebeam (Jan. 13, 2023), http://blog.bluebeam.com/construction-materials-lead-times-2023/.

64. Gigi Wood, *Manufacturers Report Longest Supplier Lead Time Since 1987*, For Construction Pros.com (June 1, 2021), https://www.forconstructionpros.com/business/article/21452407/institute-for-supply-management-ism-manufacturers-report-longest-supplier-lead-time-since-1987.

65. Jamie L. LaReau, *GM Extends Production Shutdown into April Due to Semiconductor Chip Shortage*, The Detroit Free Press (Mar. 3, 2021), https://www.freep.com/story/money/cars/general-motors/2021/03/03/gm-production-shutdown-semiconductor-chip-shortage/6903746002/.

unexpected production shut down in early 2021,[66] companies scrambled to keep up with production later in the year when more semiconductors became available. The result was vehicle production being pushed into scheduled downtime that was planned for construction shutdowns and weekend construction work, ultimately delaying construction projects.

In addition to the vehicle industry being impacted by the semiconductor shortage, electrical equipment to be installed by electrical contractors that had semiconductors in them were also impacted. In 2023, "switchgear and switch panel lead times continued to be at 70 to 80 weeks and are expected to increase due to demand from the data center, industrial, healthcare, education and semiconductor sectors."[67]

And it wasn't just the semiconductor industry in the early 2020s that had massive shortages. In November 2022, there were concrete supply shortages that delayed construction projects across the country. At the time, there were

> 43 states experiencing a concrete shortage due to a limited supply of cementitious materials (cement, slag cement and fly ash) available to produce concrete. Due in large part to favorable weather conditions and high demand over the summer, the supply of cementitious material that is usually stored in large volumes in terminals across the country has diminished leading to limits being placed on the amount of those materials available for purchase. In an effort to provide service to all concrete producers and paving contractors, the amount each receives has also been limited.[68]

The sudden rise of the cost of goods can also impact a construction schedule. In the early 2020s, inflation resulted in budget and scheduling issues. It became very difficult to budget a project with inflation quickly soaring "from 1.7% to 5.4% between February and June of 2021, and eventually reaching over 9% in June of

---

66. General Motors kept two of its assembly plants shuttered until at least mid-April, another until the end of March, and will idle a fourth. Ford Motor Co. has had to either shut down or cancel shifts in January and February at a half-dozen of its North American plants, including its F-150 pickup plants because of parts shortages. Stellantis, formerly Fiat Chrysler Automobiles, shuttered plants in Mexico and Canada, building the Jeep, Chrysler and Dodge vehicles, through the end of January. *Id.*

67. Katie Kuehner-Hebert, *Report Predicts Mixed News on Construction Price Inflation, Supply Chain*, Elec. Contractor Mag. (Mar. 22, 2023), https://www.ecmag.com/magazine/articles/article-detail/report-predicts-mixed-news-on-construction-price-inflation-supply-chain.

68. *Plan Ahead to Mitigate the Impact of Nationwide Concrete Shortage,* UHY (Nov. 17, 2022), https://uhy-us.com/insights/2022/november/plan-ahead-to-mitigate-impact-of-nationwide-concrete-shortage.

2022."[69] Sometimes, projects are budgeted for months, if not years, in advance. And if the monetary surplus suddenly evaporates due to an unexpected rise of costs, it can slow down or even stop a project. Additionally, gas prices during this time period soared from an average price of $2.56 a gallon in December 2019 to $4.93 a gallon in June 2022,[70] causing both an increase in prices of goods and slower shipping times.

And finally, the risks of strikes in the common carrier industry can threaten transportation of goods in a timely manner. In March 2022, the Burlington North Santa Fe Railway implemented a new attendance policy. By that summer, labor began considering striking unless the new policy was changed. Under the Railway Labor Act of 1926, the federal agency that oversees railroad and airline labor relations is the National Mediation Board. If there is a dispute between labor and management, the Board "tries to bring the two sides together. It sets up a series of limits and cooling off periods during which the unions cannot strike and management cannot lock out the workers. And if all those efforts fail, then Congress can step in and impose a contract under which both sides will have to operate."[71] In 1917, the Supreme Court, in *Wilson v. New*, ruled that under the interstate commerce clause found in Article I, Section 8, of the Constitution, Congress has the authority to remedy strikes found in common carrier industries.[72] And this is exactly what Congress did in December 2022. After remedial efforts by the National Mediation Board failed, a strike was avoided when both the House and the Senate passed a law that rendered a final decision that both parties had to follow. President Biden signed the law on December 2, 2022.

---

69. Alicia Wallace, *Annual Inflation Cooled Last Month to the Lowest Level Since April 2021*, CNN Bus. (May 10, 2023), https://www.cnn.com/2023/05/10/economy/cpi-consumer-inflation-april/index.html.

70. *Id.*

71. Chris Isidore, *How an Arcane 96-Year-Old Law Stopped the Rail Strike*, CNN Bus. (Dec. 2, 2022), https://www.cnn.com/2022/12/02/business/railway-labor-act-freight-railroad-strike/index.html.

72. In *Wilson v. New*, the Court found that "in the dispute between employers and employees, their failure to agree, resulting absence of such standard, the entire interruption of interstate commerce which was threatened and the infinite injury to the public interest which was imminent, it would seem inevitably to result that the power to regulate necessarily obtained and was subject to be applied to the extent necessary to provide a remedy for the situation, which included the power to deal with the dispute, to provide by appropriate action. . .and to give effect by appropriate legislation to the regulations thus adopted." Wilson v. New, 243 U.S. 332, 348 (1917).

Issues with the Workforce

Delays Caused by Organizing Labor

Generally, union workers will not cross a picket line to work. This could considerably delay construction projects. For example, on September 15th of 2019, the United Auto Workers at all General Motors facilities decided to go on strike. The next day, the Teamsters General President James P. Hoffa said in a statement, "Teamsters and the UAW have a decades-long relationship of having each other's back. And that continues with the UAW's notification that it will go out on strike against General Motors at midnight. Our 1.4 million members stand in solidarity with the UAW and will honor their picket lines."[73] As the month-long strike continued, various trade leaders and union workers in construction debated if they were going to cross the picket line to participate in construction projects on General Motors property.

Sometimes picketers will actively block access into the manufacturer's facility. This could slow down construction projects on the site. For example, General Motors on September 23, 2019, filed a motion for a temporary restraining order against the United Auto Workers protesting outside the Spring Hill General Motors.

> The Court found that under the guise of a lawful protest, defendants have: (1) prevented ingress and egress to the Spring Hill facility by obstructing public roadway; (2) stopped traffic around the facility for extended periods to unlawfully detain motorist; (3) placed screws and nails on the roadway leading to the facility; (4) menaced and threatened motorists, including non-union GM employees, contractors, and unwitting members of the public; and (5) damaged vehicles being driven on public roads en route to and from the facility.[74]

The court continued, finding that the First Amendment, while it does allow protestors to peaceably voice their opinions, it "does not embrace lawlessness."[75] The restraining order declared that the defendants were "committing illegal acts that violate Tennessee law and that are not protected by the First Amendment."[76]

In *Kennedy & Co. v. International Brotherhood of Teamsters*,[77] the Teamsters of Local 90 were picketing a labor dispute with a ready-mix concrete company at the

73. Press Release, Int'l Bhd. of Teamsters, Hoffa: Teamsters Stand in Solidarity with Striking GM UAW Members (Sep. 15, 2019), https://teamster.org/news/2019/09/hoffa-teamsters-stand-solidarity-striking-gm-uaw-members.

74. Gen. Motors v. United Auto. Workers of Am., No. CV 19-496, at *1 (Tenn. Cir. 2019).

75. *Id.* at 8.

76. *Id.* at 9.

77. Kennedy & Co., Inc. v. Int'l Bhd. of Teamsters, 315 F. Supp. 2d 992 (S.D. Iowa 2004).

plaintiff's construction sites. Defendants were not picketing any issues with plaintiff; they were only picketing at its site. Plaintiff contended that, "as a result of the Union's actions, plaintiff employees who were union members in trades other than those represented by Local 90 refused to cross the picket to work at the Wells Fargo and Iowa Blood Center construction sites, even though there was productive work for them to do."[78] Work on the Wells Fargo and Iowa Blood Center sites was shut down for the day as a result.

Here, the court ruled that "under the National Labor Relations act 'NLRA,' all secondary picketing is illegal . . . which is defined as picketing which is calculated to involved neutral employers and employees in a union's dispute with the primary employer."[79] The court also found that to prevail, plaintiffs must "prove that Union members engaged in coercive activity with the intent of disrupting the plaintiffs' business, and that it is not enough to show that picketing of a primary employer incidentally, albeit foreseeably affects secondary employers; rather, plaintiff must show the union intended to disrupt the secondary employer's business."[80] Thus, if a group is picketing outside a construction site they are not striking against and that group in effect delays construction projects on-site, they may be allowed to continue to picket so long as the union didn't picket with the purpose to stop construction.

Union organizers sometimes might come onto site merely trying to organize labor, which may cause delays and disruptions. In *Robert Lloyd Sheet Metal v. Sheet Metal Workers International Association, Local Union 16*,[81] "employees on three different job sites complained to employer's senior project manager about Anderson's 'harassing' behaving, and they asked the project manager to stop Anderson from delaying or interfering with their work."[82]

Using both union and non-union workers on the same construction site may cause conflict between the two sides. The perception between these two groups could be that of one side taking work away from the other side. This conflict may potentially manifest itself into delays if the conflict is severe enough for one group to walk off the project. Because of this, some clients are generally hesitant to bring both union and non-union companies on the project at the same time.

---

78. *Id.* at 996.

79. *Id.* at 1000.

80. *Id.*

81. Robert Lloyd Sheet Metal, Inc. v. Sheet Metal Workers Int'l Ass'n, Local Union 16, 940 P.2d 1214 (Or. 1997).

82. *Id.* at 1216.

Delays from a Lack of Manpower

Contractors may have difficulty filling manpower to stay on schedule. Some reasons for this may include a high number of construction projects ongoing in the region, a lack of construction workers in the region, the size and magnitude of the project, high turnover rate, and a lack of interest in the project. Some reasons that could cause a lack of interest from the workers include wrong hours or wrong time of day; not enough hours; a lack of premium time; lower per diem rates; a contractor with a reputation for poor treatment; and work that is unsanitary, unpleasant, or dangerous.

Delays from Cultural and Regional Differences in the Workforce

There may also be some delays due to failed expectations of the workforce. For example, unanticipated delays may occur due to the decision to use either union or non-union labor. Economist Steven G. Allen, through his empirical studies published in *The Quarterly Journal of Economics*, found that "union productivity, measured by value added per employee, is 44 to 52 percent higher than nonunion; the estimate declines to 17 to 22 percent when estimates of inter-area construction price differences are used to delete value added."[83] Allen explained why unionism led to higher productivity: "The most likely factors, based upon the discussion of the case study evidence, were (1) better training at the journeyman level through joint apprenticeship programs, (2) changes in the occupational mix (including reduced use of unskilled labor and lower foreman to journeyman ratios), (3) reduced recruiting and screening costs for contractors, and (4) greater managerial ability."[84]

Further, there are regional differences in productivity levels in construction. According to Ronald L. Moomaw and his research published in the *Southern Economics Journal*, "regional labor productivity variations exist and are large enough to influence regional disparities in economic growth and change."[85] Moomaw continues with "labor productivity in a region is related to capital intensity and total factor productivity henceforth called productive efficiency. Both capital intensity and productive efficiency may vary over industries and over city size, resulting in variations in labor productivity."[86] Moomaw, after inputting his empirical data, claims that "the picture that now emerges is one with the North Central and West

83. Steven G. Allen, *Unionized Construction Workers Are More Productive*, 99(2) Q. J. Econ. 251 (May 1984).

84. *Id.* at 269.

85. Ronald L. Moomaw, *Productive Efficiency and Region*, S. Econ. J. 345 (Oct. 1981).

86. *Id.* at 346.

somewhat more productive than the Northeast with all three regions more productive than the South."[87] Therefore, if project management does not account for these differences, it could delay the project and cost the general contractor money if not fully anticipated and accounted for at contract formation.

According to the Department of Labor in 2021, construction was the second highest occupation (at nearly 10 percent) for all foreign-born persons over the age of 16 in the United States.[88] During the first Trump administration, the country saw an increase of raids on workplaces by U.S. Immigration and Customs Enforcement (ICE). In fact, "there were 300–750% increases in FY18 relating to worksite investigations, Form I-9 audits, criminal arrests and administrative arrests."[89] The result was the possibility of a reduction in a construction project's workforce if one such raid did occur. However, the Biden administration pushed to change that. In September 2021, Alejandro Mayorkas, the director of the Department of Homeland Security, issued a statement that the Biden administration felt that "the fact an individual is a removeable noncitizen therefore should not alone be the basis of an enforcement action against them. We [the Biden Administration] will use our discretion and focus our enforcement resources in a more targeted ways."[90] However, application of the Mayorkas Memorandum was suspended after the U.S. District Court of the Southern District of Texas found the memorandum to be arbitrary and capricious, contrary to law, and failing to observe procedure under the Administrative Procedure Act.[91] After the Fifth Circuit denied appeal, the Supreme Court, in June 2023, overturned the district court's ruling. The Court held that the state of Texas did not have Article III standing because the executive branch traditionally had "discretion over whether to take enforcement actions against violations of federal law. And this case raises only the narrow Article III standing question of whether the Federal Judiciary may in effect order the Executive Branch to take enforcement actions against violators of federal law-here, by making more arrests."[92] No doubt, as those in political power continue to fight over immigration issues, the decisions by those policymakers will continue to affect the workforce of future construction projects and could cause delays in the future.

87. *Id.* at 354.

88. News Release, Bureau of Lab. Statistics, U.S. Dep't of Lab., Foreign-Born Workers: Labor Force Characteristics-2022 (May 18, 2023), https://www.bls.gov/news.release/pdf/forbrn.pdf.

89. Paul Allen, *The ICEman Cometh*, 21(1) ABA's UNDER CONSTR. (July 1, 2019).

90. Department of Homeland Security, Guideline for the Enforcement of Civil Immigration Law (Sep. 30, 2021), https://www.ice.gov/doclib/news/guidelines-civilimmigrationlaw.pdf.

91. State v. United States, Civil Action 6:21-cv-00016 (S.D. Tex. June 10, 2022).

92. United States v. Texas, 599 U.S. 670, 685 (2023).

Safety Issues Causing Delays

Safety is a significant concern on construction sites. According to the Occupational Safety and Health Agency (OSHA), over 20 percent of work-related fatalities each year are in the construction field. Many construction jobs are extremely dangerous, such as those that work in highly explosive environments, at heights, or underwater. Avoiding accidents is the best way to avoid delays. But if an accident occurs, the delays will come as well, starting with an accident investigation that will take time away from jobsite productivity. The smaller the incident, the shorter the delay. More serious injuries often lead to longer delays. For more serious incidents, clients may wish to shut down work until corrective actions are fully in place which may include engineering out the hazard, buying new personal protective equipment, or creating new administrative controls such as safety stand downs or retraining employees.

OSHA Investigations

OSHA may investigate a construction site for one of the following reasons: an imminently dangerous situation that could cause death, severe injuries and illnesses that have already occurred, worker complaints, targeted inspections at high-hazard workplace situations, or follow up inspections to check for abatement of violations.

If an OSHA officer does arrive on-site, a representative from the company will stop their task and tour the site with the officer. Production by the crew may slow down or even stop while the officer is on-site due to the fear of conducting a safety violation in front of the OSHA officer. If a citation is issued, all citations must be abated within a defined period, which may cost the jobsite time and money to abate. Contesting a citation is also a very expensive and time-consuming process that could delay the project. The contest of a federal OSHA citation will first be heard in a hearing by an Administrative Law Judge (ALJ) off-site in a public place close to the contestant's place of business. There are also several appeal levels, including: in front of the Occupational Safety and Health Review Commission (OSHRC) or the Federal Court of Appeals in the district where the case arose, and, while unlikely, the citation contest could even be heard by the United States Supreme Court.

Hazardous Materials

For buildings constructed before the 1970s, the existence of asbestos in some form—whether as insulation for pipes, caulking for windows and roofs, or as plaster—is a distinct possibility. Asbestos is especially dangerous because, if inhaled, it can cause asbestosis, fibrosis, and even mesothelioma. Asbestos fibers, when airborne, cannot be seen with the naked eye. If a contractor must interact with asbestos, it is safest if an abatement team comes in and removes the asbestos. The abatement team should be trained and licensed to be able to remove asbestos.

The abatement team will first have to find and evaluate the asbestos. Then, "the asbestos-abatement-services provider prepares the worksite to ensure that asbestos fibers are contained within that area. Many precautions, including the placement of warning signs at the worksite, the use of respirators, and the wearing of protective suits, are taken to ensure worker and public safety. As soon as the asbestos is removed from the structure, it is placed in bags marked with warning tape. While some workers are continuously cleaning the worksite, others are removing the material from the structure. The bags are then hauled to an authorized landfill."[93] As one can see, this is a process that takes some time. If needed on a jobsite, this could cause some delays to the overall schedule of the project.

The presence of lead, in either the form of paints or piping systems, may also need abatement. If lead is not identified in advance, it could likewise result in project delays. There are four major abatement measures for lead paint. Those measures include encapsulation (coating with a sealant), enclosure (covering with a solid physical barrier), removal of the paint, and replacement (removing the component and replacing it with a new one). "Encapsulation and enclosure render the lead paint hazard inaccessible, whereas chemical stripping, abrasive removal, hand-scraping and component replacement permanently remove lead-based paints."[94] Abatement measures vary from each other in time and cost; however, encapsulation is generally considered the simplest and cheapest abatement measure.

Lead pipes may also be a concern during construction projects. In October 2024, the Environmental Protection Agency (EPA) published the National Primary Drinking Water Regulations for Lead and Copper: Improvements (LCRI) in the *Federal Register* stating that the EPA "is requiring the water systems to replace all lead and certain galvanized service lines under their control no later than 10 years after the compliance date."[95] And while the LCRI does not require private homeowners to take any action, the additional requirement of removing lead piping on public construction projects could potentially significantly delay projects.

---

93. Rylander v. Associated Technics Co., Inc., 987 S.W.2d 947, 948 (Tex. App. 1999).

94. David O'Connor et al., *Lead-Based Paint Remains a Major Public Health Concern: A Critical Review of Global Production, Trade, Use, Exposure, Health Risk, and Implications*, 121(pt. 1) Env'l Int'l 85 (Dec. 2018).

95. National Primary Drinking Water Regulations for Lead and Copper: Improvements (LCRI), 89 Fed. Reg. 86418, 86419 (Oct. 30, 2024).

Kingston Fossil Fuel Power Station Disaster

Delays in industrial projects could come from environmental cleanups and the subsequent lawsuits from those accidents. The Kingston Fossil Plant, a TVA run coal-fired power-generating station in eastern Tennessee, began using nearby Swan Pond to deposit their fly ash shortly after the plant was constructed in 1951. Fly ash is the byproduct of coal being burned in the power plant's boiler. Coal is brought into the facility and stored in bunkers until coal is crushed in what is called a pulverizer. This fine coal dust is blown into the coal burners at the corners of the boiler where the dust is burned. The fires then heat up water in the tubes of the walls of the boiler. That water is turned into steam, which powers the turbines that create electricity. The byproduct dust of this process either falls to the bottom of the boiler (which is called bottom ash) or floats away in the exhaust gas. The portion that floats away is called fly ash. Fly ash is pulled out of the gas along with other impurities in a series of cleansing procedures through the use of baghouses, electrostatic precipitators, and wet scrubbers. By the time the gas reaches the smokestack, almost all impurities are removed from the gas. The fly ash that has been removed is then collected and stored nearby. Often, it is stored in a retention pond. The TVA at Kingston Fossil Plant stored fly ash at its designated retention pond, Swan Pond.

On December 22, 2008, one of the coal ash containment dikes at the Swan Pond facilities failed. "As a result of the dike failure, approximately 5.4 million cubic yards of coal ash sludge spilled from the 84-acre containment area of the Swan Pond facilities to an adjacent area of about 300 acres, consisting of primarily the Watts Bar Reservoir, the Clinch and Emory Rivers, and government and privately owned shoreline properties."[96]

In 2009, property owners affected by the spillage brought suit in the U.S. Eastern District Court of Tennessee. Plaintiffs asserted "causes of action based on tort law-negligence, negligence per se, gross negligence, trespass, nuisance, and strict liability."[97] At issue in this case was (1) whether the Federal Torts Claims Act (FTCA), which allows private persons to sue a federal agency based the actions of their employees, applied to the TVA, and (2) if the FTCA did apply, whether TVA's actions fell under the statutory discretionary function exception of the FTCA.[98]

96. Mays v. Tennessee Valley Auth., 699 F. Supp. 2d 991, 998 (E.D. Tenn. 2010).

97. *Id.* at 1000.

98. *See* the Federal Torts Claims Act, which claims that "the United States shall be liable, respecting the provisions of this title relating to tort claims, in the same manner and to the same extent as a private individual under like circumstances, but shall not be liable for interest prior to judgment or for punitive damages." Federal Torts Claims Act, 28 U.S.C. § 2674 (1946). *See also* Nonliability of Federal Government, 42 U.S.C. § 5148 (1974) ("the Federal Government shall not be liable for any

After four years of litigation, the court found in favor of the property owners, ruling that the TVA was a governmental agency under the umbrella of the FTCA, and its actions were nondiscretionary in that "once TVA determined and implemented the policy decision to have a coal ash storage facility at Swan Pond, TVA had an obligation to continue and pursue that policy decision in a nonnegligent manner,"[99] and that "the specific nondiscretionary conduct on the part of TVA caused the failure of the coal ash containment dike at TVA's KIF plant on December 22, 2008 and that, but for the nondiscretionary conduct described above, the dike failure would not have occurred. TVA is therefore liable for damages to each plaintiff."[100] In August 2014, "U.S. District Court Judge Thomas Varlan approved a $27.8 million settlement from the Tennessee Valley Authority to more than 800 people affected by a Kingston Fossil Plant's spill."[101] In addition to legal costs and settlement costs, the cleanup costs were also significant. Between December of 2008 and the end of 2014, the TVA spent over $1.1 billion on cleaning up the coal ash from the Kingston Power Generating Station.[102] With time, resources, and money being concentrated into the spill, construction projects were either delayed or cancelled entirely.

The biggest hit was within TVA's nuclear division. Three TVA nuclear stations, either fully operational or in the construction phase, were completely abandoned between 1985 and 1988. These nuclear stations were (1) Browns Ferry, approximately 40 miles west of Huntsville, Alabama; (2) Watts Bar, approximately 60 miles west of Knoxville; and (3) Bellefonte, about 50 miles southwest of Chattanooga. During the turn of the century, TVA began a nuclear renaissance to bring these plants online. In 2002, construction on the first unit of Browns Ferry commenced, with the unit coming online in 2007. The same year that Browns Ferry I came online, the TVA re-commenced construction on the second unit of Watts Bar (the first Watts Bar unit was completed in 1996). Also in 2007, the TVA had plans to finish the two existing Bellefonte units and "filed applications with the Nuclear

---

claim based upon the exercise or performance of or the failure to exercise or perform a discretionary function or duty on the part of a Federal agency or an employee of the Federal Government.").

99. *In re* Tennessee Valley Auth. Ash Spill Litigation 3:09-CV-582 at 110 (E.D. Tenn. Aug. 23, 2012).

100. *Id.* at 130.

101. Jessica Dye, *U.S. Court Approves $27.8 Million Deal for Toxic Tennessee Spill*, Reuters (Aug. 5, 2014), https://www.reuters.com/article/us-spill-tva-settlement/u-s-court-approves-27-8-million-deal-for-toxic-tennessee-spill-idUSKBN0G51ZA20140805.

102. U.S. Environmental Protection Agency and Tennessee Valley Authority Kingston Coal Ash Release Site, Project Completion Fact Sheet (Dec. 2014), https://semspub.epa.gov/work/04/11015836.pdf.

Regulatory Commission to build two AP 1000 pressurized water reactors at Bellefonte to be known as Units 3 and 4."[103]

However, the Kingston Fossil Plant disaster in 2008 effectively ended TVA's nuclear renaissance. During the summer of 2010, the Bellefonte plans shrunk from constructing four potential units to one.[104] At that time, the initial plan was for the TVA to begin construction on Bellefonte's first unit near the completion of Watts Bar II.[105]

With the lawsuits and cleanup efforts in full effect, "the TVA moved the completion date of Watts Bar II back from 2012 to 2015 and added a further $1.5 to $2 billion to its cost estimate."[106] Watts Bar II did not go online until 2016, and the Bellefonte project never commenced with the TVA ultimately putting the power plant up for sale.[107]

In September of 2021,

> the Tennessee Valley Authority gave up its construction permit abandoning any plans to complete the twin-reactor facility. TVA notified the U.S. Nuclear Regulatory Commission that month that it would not renew its regulatory permit at Bellefonte after a federal court agreed to cancel the proposed sale of the nuclear plant to an investment group that had hoped to complete the two pressurized water reactors and operate the nuclear facility. Former Chattanooga developer Franklin L. Haney, whose Nuclear Development LLC agreed to buy the Bellefonte plant five years ago, was unable to transfer the construction permit from TVA and a federal judge ruled last month that TVA could cancel the sale of Bellefonte to Haney's group.[108]

---

103. Tennessee Valley Authority, Combined License Application for Bellefonte Nuclear Plant Units 3 & 4, ADAMS Accession No. ML073110527 (U.S. Nuclear Regulatory Commission, filed Oct. 30, 2007).

104. *Id.*

105. Josh Flory, *TVA Approves Completion of Bellefonte Nuclear Plant, Rate Increase*, Knox News (Aug. 18, 2011), https://archive.knoxnews.com/business/tva-approves-completion-of-bellefonte-nuclear-plant-rate-increase-ep-403394784-357602141.html/.

106. Don Safer & Sara Barczak, *Watts Bar Unit 2, Last Old Reactor of the 20th Century: A Cautionary Tale,* Bull. Atomic Scientists (Oct. 8, 2015), https://thebulletin.org/2015/10/watts-bar-unit-2-last-old-reactor-of-the-20th-century-a-cautionary-tale/.

107. Jay Reeves, *Tennessee Valley Authority to Sell Nuclear Plant at Fraction of Cost*, The Tennessean (Sep. 12, 2016), https://www.tennessean.com/story/news/2016/09/12/tennessee-valley-authority-sale-nuclear-plan-fraction-cost/90259420/.

108. Dave Flessner, *The End of an Era: TVA Gives Up Construction Permit for Bellefonte Nuclear Plant after 47 Years* (Sep. 17, 2021), https://www.timesfreepress.com/news/2021/sep/17/end-eratvgives-constructipermit-bellefonte-nu/.

Novel Coronavirus

On January 21, 2020, "a Washington state resident became the first person in the United States with a confirmed case of the 2019 novel coronavirus, having returned from Wuhan, China, on January 15."[109] On March 11, the World Health Organization (WHO) declared coronavirus a pandemic[110] and two days later President Trump declared the pandemic a national emergency.[111] From there, the virus spread quickly, with more than one million cases contracted in the United States by April 27, 2020.[112]

Throughout March and April, governors and mayors began issuing "stay at home" directives in which many governments shut down non-essential activities. Each state made its own determination whether construction was deemed essential or not. Because of this, many construction projects across the country were shut down entirely because of these mandates. For example, on March 16, 2020, Martin Walsh, Mayor of Boston, enacted a very progressive governmental order becoming one of the first major metropolitan areas to shut down citywide construction.[113] Soon afterwards, on March 30th, New York City issued an order shutting down all non-essential construction.[114]

---

109. Michelle L. Holshue et al., *First Case of 2019 Novel Coronavirus in the United States*, New Eng. J. Med. (Mar. 5, 2020), https://www.nejm.org/doi/10.1056/NEJMoa2001191#article_citing_articles.

110. Jamey Keaten et al., *WHO Declares Coronavirus a Pandemic, Urges Aggressive Action* (Mar. 11, 2022), https://apnews.com/article/united-nations-michael-pence-religion-travel-virus-outbreak-52e12ca90c55b6e0c398d134a2cc286e.

111. Proclamation on Declaring a National Emergency Concern the Novel Coronavirus Disease (COVID-19) Outbreak (Mar. 13, 2020), https://trumpwhitehouse.archives.gov/presidential-actions/proclamation-declaring-national-emergency-concerning-novel-coronavirus-disease-covid-19-outbreak/.

112. World Health Organization, https://covid19.who.int/region/amro/country/us (last visited May 21, 2023).

113. Mayor Walsh's order stated, "Effective tomorrow, Tuesday, March 17, 2020, the City is suspending all regular activity at construction sites in Boston. Employers should maintain the necessary crews to keep their sites safe and secure, keep any materials from blowing away, and prevent trespassing. This work needs to be completed in the next week, by Monday, March 23, 2020. After sites have been secured, skeleton crews will be permitted for the remainder of this suspension to ensure safety. The only work that will be permitted moving forward will be emergency work, which will need to be approved by the City of Boston's Inspectional Services Department. That essential work includes: (1) Emergency utility, road or building work, such as gas leaks, water leaks and sinkholes, (2) New utility connections to occupied buildings, (3) Mandated building or utility work, (4) Work at public health facilities, healthcare facilities, shelters, including temporary shelters and other facilities that support vulnerable populations, (5) Work which ensures the reliability of the transportation network, and (6) Other work necessary to render occupied residential buildings fully habitable." Mayor Order, Construction Activity to be Suspended in the City (Mar. 16, 2020), https://www.boston.gov/news/construction-activity-be-suspended-city-library-locations-bcyf-centers-close.

114. The Empire State Development on March 20, 2020, gave a definitive and controlling definition on what was to be considered essential construction work. "Essential construction includes:

Many of the construction projects that stayed open throughout March and April saw delays for a myriad of reasons. For example, there were delays in materials being shipped. With international borders being closed, suppliers being shut down, and transportation means being slowed, construction projects slowed down drastically. Issues with the workforce were also a concern. People stopped coming to work and contractors did their best to replace those workers with new hires. However, many contractors could not keep up with their schedules due to difficulty getting workers on the project. And many workers that did come to work had low morale and concerns about the virus, which affected productivity.

The pandemic continued throughout the early 2020s seeing several different variants such as the Delta variant during the summer of 2021 and the Omicron variant during the winter of 2021–2022. From January 2020 to January 2023, over 100 million Covid cases in the United States were contracted, resulting in more than a million deaths.[115] Many general contractors did their best to try to keep the virus from spreading to their project sites. They limited the hours worked per day or cut out premium time days. They took extra time out of the day to gauge the health of workers or to give extra toolbox talks on the virus. For many contractors, it took longer to mobilize in the morning, as shuttle buses and elevators were not used to maintain social distancing. And finally, cleaning efforts were increased. Many project managers pulled workers from a construction task to dedicate their time to cleaning tools and equipment that may have become infected with the virus. All of these additional precautions resulted in delays to construction.

Weather, Fires, Geological Issues, and Evacuations

Rain often creates "rainouts"—situations where construction work cannot be done because of the weather on one day. In greenfield industrial construction, if the construction of the building is delayed, then the start of utilities and equipment

(1) construction for, or your business provides necessary support for construction projects involving, roads, bridges, transit facilities, utilities, hospitals or healthcare facilities, homeless shelters, or public or private schools; (2) construction for affordable housing, as defined as construction work where either (i) a minimum of 20% of the residential units are or will be deemed affordable and are or will be subject to a regulatory agreement and/or a declaration from a local, state, or federal government agency or (ii) where the project is being undertaken by, or on behalf of, a public housing authority; (3) construction necessary to protect the health and safety of occupants of a structure; (4) construction necessary to continue a project if allowing the project to remain undone would be unsafe, provided that the construction must be shut down when it is safe to do so; (5) construction for existing (i.e. currently underway) projects of an essential business; or (6) construction work that is being completed by a single worker who is the sole employee/worker on the job site." Guidance for Determining Whether a Business Enterprise Is Subject to a Workforce Reduction Under Recent Executive Orders (Mar. 30, 2020), https://esd.ny.gov/guidance-executive-order-2026.

115. World Health Organization, *supra* note 112.

installation will be pushed back until the building is completed. In November 2018, a car manufacturing company broke ground for a new automobile manufacturing facility in northern Alabama. "Rainfall records for the month of February were observed in Huntsville Alabama (13.63 inches), with widespread flooding occurring along rivers and tributaries as well as mudslides impacting travel for May. That meteorological winter between December of 2018 and February of 2019 was the wettest on record in Huntsville recording 30.67 inches of rain at Huntsville International Airport,"[116] which created issues for the contractors to work around the weather to stay on schedule.

In certain rare cases, rain can also adversely affect construction work in an existing facility. During May 2016, an unprecedented amount of rainfall for San Antonio occurred, resulting in up to 4 inches of water "causing a roof cave-in of an automobile manufacturing facility in south Texas."[117] While this was not a construction project per se, both nonconstruction activities and construction projects were delayed for several days until power was returned and the plant was deemed safe for workers to return to work.

If consistently dangerous winds and lightning persist on a project, it could delay operations. For most projects, it is not considered safe to stand on a scaffold, use an aerial lift, or use a crane outside when wind speeds are more than 20 or 25 miles per hour. Winds can also cause extensive property damage on a construction site. For example, during September 2017, "a construction crane collapsed onto a high-rise building in Miami as wind from Hurricane Irma intensified across the city, bringing significant flooding and storm surges."[118] For property damaged by wind, it will take time to reorder and reinstall the material. If material was blown out of designated laydown areas, it could take time finding and re-staging the material. And if unsecured material is being blown off a roof due to high winds, safety delays may occur to protect the people below. Further, lightning could delay outside projects if strikes occur within proximity to the workers. Generally, outdoor construction should stop if lighting strikes within 10 miles of the jobsite.

Finally, extreme outdoor temperatures can be a factor. For example, construction companies that install solar panels in deserts may have to give workers breaks

116. *Wettest Winter on Record for the Contiguous United States* (Mar. 6, 2019), https://www.ncei.noaa.gov/news/national-climate-201902#:~:text=Rainfall%20records%20for%20the%20month,mudslides%20impacting%20travel%20for%20many.

117. Jim Forsyth, *Toyota Suspends Output at Texas Truck Plant Due to Storm Damage*, Reuters (May 18, 2016), https://www.reuters.com/article/world/us/toyota-suspends-output-at-texas-truck-plant-due-to-storm-damage-idUSKCN0Y9271/.

118. Thomas Franck, *Hurricane Irma Topples a Miami Crane, and Floods Part of the City*, CNBC (Sep. 10, 2017), https://www.cnbc.com/2017/09/10/hurricane-irma-nearly-topples-a-miami-construction-crane-and-floods-parts-of-the-city.html.

every 15 or 30 minutes to avoid heat-related illnesses on very hot days. Delays can also occur due to extreme cold. For example, it takes time to remove ice or snow from parking lots, roofs, or scaffolds before workers are allowed access to these areas. And power outages, such as the outages that plagued much of the state of Texas in February 2021 after a series of unexpectedly harsh winter storms, can delay construction projects.

Concrete pours can be affected by both extreme heat[119] and extreme cold[120] resulting in cracking or decreased compression strength. Contractors can use several different control measures to combat cold temperatures including ground thaws, mixing with hot water, heaters inside enclosures, admixtures, and covering the concrete with straw or concrete blankets. And conversely, to maintain proper temperatures on hot days, contractors can mix the concrete with colder water, use liquid nitrogen to keep the concrete cool, water the ground with cold water before pouring, and pour on night shifts.

Fire is another situation that could delay construction. For example, at a North American automobile manufacturing facility a fire that broke out during the construction of the new paint shop in May 2019.[121] If a fire does happen on a construction site, it will not only take time to find out what equipment or structures are damaged after the fire subsides, but it will also take time to order, ship, and install new equipment to replace the damaged equipment or facilities.

Geological issues can also cause delays. Construction on fault lines could end up causing massive property damage and delays to construction projects, and Los Angeles County even has a building code stating, "No building or structure shall be constructed over or upon the trace of a known active earthquake fault"[122] In certain geographical areas throughout the country, underground limestone and bedrock are predominant. These underground rock formations can cause delays in civil projects on construction sites due to the difficulty in foreseeing these formations under the topsoil, and then taking the time to break apart these rock formations. Bedrock can potentially require the ordering and using of rock trenchers and or

---

119. "For concrete mixtures with a specified strength of less than 6000 psi, temperatures should not reach over 80 degrees Fahrenheit during the initial curing. For concrete mixtures with a specified strength of 6000 psi or greater, temperatures should not exceed 78 degrees Fahrenheit." AM. SOC'Y FOR TESTING & MATERIALS, STANDARD PRACTICE FOR MAKING AND CURING CONCRETE TEST SPECIMENS IN THE FIELD 4 (2019).

120. "Two assumptions commonly used during modeling of cold weather placement are: (1) Early-age concrete hydration is negligible below a concrete temperature of 40°F (5°C), and (2) Freezing damage may take place when the concrete temperature drops below 32°F (0°C)." William J. Lyons III et al., Guide to Cold Weather Concreting, AM. CONCRETE INST. 14 (2016).

121. *Fire Breaks Out at Georgetown Toyota Plant*, WKYT NEWS (May 22, 2019), https://www.wkyt.com/content/news/Fire-breaks-out-at-Georgetown-Toyota-Plant-510261581.html.

122. Los Angeles County Building Code, § 113.5 (1995).

explosives to effectively break up the rocks. If the company needs to wait for these tactics to commence on-site, delays may be inevitable. Further, in areas with large underground rock formations, sink holes may emerge due to underground water slowly eroding the underground rock. Sink holes, such as the 25-foot deep hole that emerged at the General Motors facility in Bowling Green, Kentucky, in 2014, could seriously delay construction. In addition to unforeseeable underground rock issues, there are hundreds of subterranean streams underneath the United States that could likewise cause construction delays. Modern technology such as proton magnetic resonance[123] and ground penetration radar systems[124] can now effectively find subterranean waterflow from the surface level. This technology, if used early and effectively, may prevent delays later in the project.

Construction sites, in the unfortunate event of a chemical spill, active shooter, or a bomb threat, may have to evacuate the premises. It may take days or even weeks for a chemical spill to be fully cleaned up by a trained and properly protected hazmat team. In the event of a bomb threat, if the construction site is expansive, it may take an entire day for a bomb squad to clear the premises. Generally, dogs are used to sniff for explosive devices. But not every jurisdiction has a bomb squad; so, it may take some time for the team to mobilize on-site. Depending on temperature and humidity conditions, dogs may be able to work only about 20 minutes before they need a rest.[125] Because of this, the bomb search may be slow and meticulous, causing delays in the schedule.

Conclusion

There are many ways a project can become delayed, whether during the preconstruction period, through legal actions, or throughout the course of the project. Savvy project management teams and attorneys will be able to identify potential causes of delays on a project well before they become problematic. If these road bumps are not identified early enough, it could result in lost profits on the project, possible future legal actions with the client or subcontractors, or diminished faith in the contractor by the client resulting in fewer awarded contracts in the future.

---

123. Anatoly Legchenko & Pierre Valla, *A Review of the Basic Principles for Proton Magnetic Resonance Sounding Measurements*, 50(1–2) J. Applied Geophysics 3 (May 2002).

124. Dalia N. Elsheakh & Esmat A. Abdallah, *Detection of Underground Water by Using GPR, in* Groundwater: Resource Characterization and Management Aspects 1–20 (Modrek Gomo ed., 2019).

125. Technology Against Terrorism: Structuring Security, Appendix B, Explosives Detection: Dogs 105 (1991), https://www.google.com/books/edition/Technology_Against_Terrorism/JHdEVifANs8C?hl=en&gbpv=1&printsec=frontcover.

CHAPTER 4

Time Extension Requests

Kendall E. Woods and Shawn Paroline

The Time Extension Request Defined

Time, provisions in a construction contract, are some of the most important provisions, because time is a critical resource for a construction project. Initially, construction contracts set forth the contract time,[1] that is, the number of days to complete the project. Project delays or schedule extensions will inevitably impact the contract time and schedule.[2]

Changes in scope or unanticipated circumstances arising on a project often result in delay, and require a time extension for performance of the work and/or an increase in price to compensate for the impact of the change. Construction contracts typically include various provisions that address project delays and define what circumstances constitute an excusable delay, that is, a delay warrantying an extension to perform the work (a "time extension"). These provisions set out the process the parties must comply with when requesting any adjustments to the contract time or the contract sum[3] due to the delay. Further, these provisions establish the process for the contracting parties to address liability for any delay and/or impacts to the contract time (or contract duration) or contract sum. Generally, time extension provisions provide the process for the contractor to obtain relief from contract time obligations when performance has been delayed and the contractor is not at fault.

1. "Contract time" is generally a defined term in construction contracts that establishes the time the contractor has to complete its work on a project.

2. "Schedule" is generally a defined term in construction contracts that refers to the timeline for every task and event in a construction project.

3. "Contract sum" is generally a defined term in construction contracts that establishes the amount of money the contractor will be paid for its work on a project.

Time Extension Request Substance: The Underlying Basis, Grounds, or Justification

Common Law Concepts: Allocation of the Risk of Time

The construction industry has adopted specific provisions in standard construction contracts to allocate risk related to contract time between the owner and the contractor.[4] These common contractual provisions regarding delay in construction contracts are generally based on common law allocation of the risk.

The contractor's obligation to complete the contract work[5] within a specified period or by a specific completion date creates a risk for the contractor if the construction is not completed in the allocated time. Time of performance is considered a material condition of the contract. As such, during contract negotiations, "contract time/duration" is a critical term that should be negotiated. If time is not specified in the contract, a reasonable time is implied based on the facts, circumstances, or scope.[6]

The risk of time generally belongs to the contractor; however, the law has developed to include various legal doctrines and/or implied contract provisions to more fairly allocate risk between the parties. The overriding consideration when apportioning risk is the level of control each party has over the delay. In circumstances where the delay resulted from events outside of the contractor's control, legal principles have developed that excuse the contractor from its obligation to perform the work in the time allocated in the contract. Some examples of common law principles that serve to balance the risk include:

- **Impossibility/Impracticability.** Excuses performance when events subsequent to contract execution occur, without any fault of the contractor, that render the contractor's performance either impossible or impracticable.[7]

4. In this chapter, we use "owner" and "contractor" as the contracting parties, but "subcontracts" and "contracts between the contractor and subcontractors" have similar provisions and considerations.

5. " Contract work" is generally a defined term in construction contracts that establishes the scope of work the contractor has to complete a project.

6. *See, e.g.*, Teramo & Co. v. O'Brien-Sheipe Funeral Home, Inc., 283 A.D.2d 635, 636, 725 N.Y.S.2d 87, 89 (2001) ("Where a contract fails to state a date for the completion of a construction project, a reasonable time is implied."); Coulter & Smith, Ltd. v. Russell, 966 P.2d 852, 858 (Utah 1998); Deer Creek Constr. Co. v. Peterson, 412 So. 2d 1169, 1172 (Miss. 1982).

7. *See generally* Restatement (Second) of Contracts § 261, Discharge by Supervening Impracticability; 102 Am. Jur. Proof of Facts 3d § 6, at 401 (Westlaw, database updated Apr. 2022).

- **Force Majeure.**[8] Excuses performance to the extent that performance is prohibited by a force majeure event.[9]
- **Doctrine of Mitigation.** Requires the owner and/or contractor to make a reasonable effort to mitigate any damages arising from a contractor's failure to perform by the completion date.[10]
- **Foreseeability/Assumption of Risk.**[11] If the event causing the delay was not foreseeable by the contractor when it entered into the contract, the event could give rise to an excusable delay. Conversely, if the event was foreseeable, the contractor is generally deemed to have assumed the risk.

Application of these principles works as a practical matter to excuse or relax the contractor's obligation to perform by a certain date or within a certain duration to the extent the cause of the delay fell outside the contractor's control. Notably, the jurisprudence surrounding the application of these principles focuses on the general view that strict, absolute liability should give way to common sense and fairness.

Additionally, understanding the various implied warranties in all construction contracts is imperative when analyzing who bears the risk of a particular delay event. An "implied warranty" is a contract term for assurances that are presumed in contracts arising from operation of the common law. These conditions can impact a party's obligations under a contract absent a specific contractual provision governing the specific issue. Certain implied warranties that arise in the context of delay include:

- **Implied Warranty of Specifications.** If the contractor is bound to build according to plans and specifications prepared by the owner, the contractor

8. A force majeure event is an unforeseen and unavoidable event that impacts the ability to complete the contract. These events are generally defined in the contract and cover both natural disasters, for example, hurricanes, tornadoes, floods, and earthquakes, and man-made catastrophes such as war, invasion, civil unrest, and labor strikes.

9. *Force majeure risks*, 2A Bruner & O'Connor Construction Law § 7:320. "The doctrine of force majeure or impossibility is an equitable principle that excuses nonperformance under situations where events are beyond the control of the parties and no agreement has been reached with respect to who is to bear the risk for such events." *Id.*

10. Restatement (Second) of Contracts § 350 (1981) ("damages are not recoverable for loss that the injured party could have avoided without undue risk, burden or humiliation"); 6 Bruner & O'Connor Construction Law § 19:21 (2021).

11. Fru-Con Constr. Corp. v. United States, 44 Fed. Cl. 298, 314 (1999) (discussing the concepts of foreseeability and assumption of risk as it applies to delay events).

will not be responsible for the consequences of defects in the plans and specifications, including delays arising from such defects.[12]

- **Implied Duty Not to Hinder.** The owner has an implied duty to cooperate and not hinder the work of the contractor.[13]
- **Implied Duty to Manage/Coordinate Work.** The owner has a duty to manage or coordinate the work of separate contractors hired by the owner such that the contractors do not impede or delay the work of other contractors.[14]

When engaging in a delay analysis, control and foreseeability are foremost considerations in determining which party bears the risk of a delay. If the event falls outside the contractor's control, the likelihood of the event warranting an extension of the contract time increases. Similarly, whether the event was foreseeable by the contractor at the time it entered into the contract will be a critical factor of any evaluation of the contractor's right to an extension of time to perform, because if it was foreseeable, the contractor will likely not get an extension of time. If the contract has provisions governing delay, knowledge of the concepts that gave rise to the standard provisions will assist in determining whether an event entitles the contractor to an extension to the contract time or an increase in the contract sum. If there are no provisions governing delay in the contract, these common law principles will guide the analysis of whether a delay event warrants and extension to the contract time or contract sum.

The construction industry has worked to reduce much of the ambiguity regarding responsibility for potential time impacts and delays through the proactive use of express contract provisions. Currently, standardized form contracts that include these provisions are regularly used. Some examples of standardized forms include the American Institute of Architects (AIA) A201, ConsensusDocs® 200, Engineers Joint Contract Documents Committee (EJCDC®), and federal contracts.

---

12. United States v. Spearin, 248 U.S. 132, 136, 39 S. Ct. 59, 61, 63 L. Ed. 166 (1918). This is commonly referred to as the *Spearin* doctrine.

13. Restatement (Second) of Contracts § 245 (1981); generally 13 Williston on Contracts § 39:3 (4th ed.); *see also* H.N. Wood Prod., Inc. v. United States, 59 Fed. Cl. 479, 486 (2003) ("The implied duty to cooperate and not to hinder the other party's performance is an obligation that exists in every Government contract."); Mega Constr. Co. v. United States, 29 Fed. Cl. 396, 423 (1993) ("every contract with the government contains an implied obligation that neither party will do anything to prevent, hinder, or delay performance").

14. 5 Bruner & O'Connor Construction Law § 15:55 ("Delay to the critical path caused by an owner's failure to coordinate and manage the work of multiple prime contractors is 'compensable.'").

Time Impact or Delay Classifications

To properly evaluate the classification of delays two threshold questions must be considered: (1) who had control over the delay event and (2) did the event cause a delay to the critical path. The answers to these questions ultimately will guide the determination of any "time extension," for example, an adjustment to the contract time to provide the contractor with additional time to complete the project. Accordingly, we must touch on the importance of critical path analysis and an explanation of the common law classifications related to delay and time extensions; however, these concepts are discussed in detail in Chapters 6 and 7, respectively.

Time extension requests will likely only be successful if there is an actual effect or impact on the project schedule. The most widely utilized methodology for determining whether a delay event impacted the project schedule is the critical path method (CPM) (discussed in Chapter 6). Generally, only events that cause impact to the project's critical path can legitimately serve as grounds for a time extension request.

Once it is determined that a delay event impacted the project schedule, the next step is to determine the classification of the delay event. Delay events typically fall within four categories of delays: inexcusable delays, excusable and compensable delays, excusable but not compensable delays, and concurrent delays.

- **Inexcusable Delay.** Delay caused by the contractor or any of its subcontractors or caused by events within the control of the contractor and/or any tier of its subcontractor/suppliers constitute delays for which the contractor bears responsibility. Such contractor-caused delay typically results in no time extension or extension recovery of delay costs for the contractor.
- **Excusable and Compensable Delay.** Delay caused solely by the owner and/or the owner's consultants, separate contractors or agents; or delay caused by an event within the control of the owner and not within the control of the contractor. The typical remedy for compensable delay is an adjustment to both contract time and the contract sum.
- **Excusable but Not Compensable Delay.** Delay that is beyond the control of both the owner and the contractor, resulting from an event for which neither party bears fault or responsibility and which was not foreseeable by either party. As such delay is not foreseeable or within the control of either party, the result is typically a no-cost time extension to the project schedule, with both parties bearing their own financial losses. This type of delay is often set out in the contract documents.
- **Concurrent Delay.** Where concurrent owner and contractor delay has occurred, the typical result is to limit any time extension to an adjustment

> in contract time only with no adjustment to the contract sum, despite the increased costs resulting from the extended performance. The contractor, however, may recover a portion of its added costs or delay damages if it is able to apportion the concurrent critical path delay. Apportionment of the delay is the process, through detailed critical path or schedule analysis of the delay or segregating the contractor—caused delay from the concurrent owner-caused delays.

Construction delays arise from many and varied causes—for example, weather, scope changes, poor planning, resource limits, and differing site conditions. Recognizing the diverse underlying causes of delays, the importance of control when considering the cause of the delay, and the resulting time impacts is essential to understanding if the contractor has a valid basis for seeking an extension of time and/or additional compensation for the delay and the extent to which the contractor may be so entitled.

Construction Contract Time Extension Remedy Granting Clauses

Standard construction industry construction contracts contain provisions to address events that commonly occur that give rise to a project delay. How a delay event is treated generally depends on the cause of the delay. The concept of control of the cause of the delay is central to any request for a contract time extension, as the liability for a delay flows from the party to the contractor who is responsible for or has control of the underlying event.

The three main categories of delays include owner-caused delays, contractor-caused delays, and third-party delays, which are delays not attributable to either contracting parties. In many instances, third-party delays are considered "excusable" but not "compensable," for example, delays caused by utility providers. This general concept is illustrated by a review of standard time extension provisions.[15] Standard industry contracts, such as AIA A201-2017, ConsensusDocs® 200, Engineers Joint Contract Documents Committee (EJCDC®), and federal contracts, contain provisions that identify categories of common delay events, such as an act

15. As already noted, commercial construction contracts include multiple provisions addressing schedule and time, including the "Changes" and "Claims" provisions as well as specific sections of the specifications. The authors counsel that many of these provisions may impact the basis or grounds for which a time extension is due and will most certainly address the procedure and level of proof/support needed. For example, the following provisions in the Standard AIA A201-2017 General Conditions touch on aspects of the Time Extension Request: §§ 7.2, 7.3, 8.3, 15.1.5. As such, a full reading and evaluation of the Contract Documents is always a prudent and recommended course of action when confronting a delay and evaluating obligations and potential remedies.

of owner, architect, or contractor; changes in the work; weather conditions; force majeure; dispute resolution; and other causes.[16]

Typical time extension provisions in common standardized contracts state that if an event falls outside the reasonable control of the contractor it will likely qualify as an excusable delay (discussed earlier in the chapter) and entitle the contractor to extensions to the contract time (and possibly contract sum). Common contractual provisions allow extensions for owner changes; delays outside the control of the contractor; unforeseeable labor problems; government acts, changes of law; Acts of God, epidemics, abnormal weather; site access issues; late owner-furnished materials/equipment; defective specifications; and unforeseen or differing site conditions.

In contrast, events that fall within the contractor's control or that were reasonably foreseeable to contractor when the parties executed the contract will likely qualify as an inexcusable delay (discussed earlier) and do not generally give rise to an extension of contract time. Examples of time impacts that fall within the contractor's control or that were reasonably foreseeable include delays caused by anticipated weather conditions (e.g., normal seasonal weather), improper scheduling by contractor, insufficient labor or staffing, poor supervision, or delays caused due to resolving defective work.

Time Extension Request Procedure

Notice of Delay

When there is any event that occurs that will or may cause a delay, the first step is to provide the owner notice of the delay. Construction contracts invariably have provisions governing the process and timing to properly provide notice to the owner of any delay event as a procedural hurdle to request an extension of time. It is critical that the contractor review and understand these provisions as failure to comply with the contract requirements to provide proper notice can result in the owner denying the contractor's claim for additional time and/or compensation. Most notice provisions have three key elements: timeliness of the notice, content of the notice, and, if applicable, reservations of rights.

Timelines for Providing Notice of Time Extension Request

Construction contracts often set out timelines for contractors to provide notice of an instance that gives rise to a claim for delay and a request for an extension of contract time. The time to give notice is generally outlined in each contract, but

16. *See, e.g.*, AIA A201-2017 § 8.3; ConsensusDocs, Article 6.3; EJCDC, Section 4.05; Federal Acquisition Regulation (FAR) 52.242-17(a), 52.249-10(b); Code of Federal Regulations (C.F.R.) 48 C.F.R. § 52.249-14(a).

generally the contractor must give the owner notice of delay and any claim for a time extension within 21 days or less after the occurrence giving rise to the claim. If there are no provisions governing notice in the contract, a "reasonable time" to provide notice would be implied. Notice requirements are intended to afford the owner the opportunity to evaluate the potential causes of the delay and to mitigate the impact of the claimed delaying occurrence in a timely fashion.

If a contractor fails to provide notice within the contract notice period, or if there is no provision governing notice, a reasonable time, the contractor can be deemed to have waived any potential claim for an extension of time arising from that event.[17] Legal arguments to help overcome a contractor's failure to comply with the contractual notice requirements include waiver, actual notice, and lack of prejudice. When arguing waiver, a contractor will generally argue that the course of conduct between the parties was such that the owner waived any right to strict compliance with the notice requirements in the contract.[18] To establish a valid waiver of a contractor's obligation to adhere to the timing requirements in the notice provisions of the contract, the contractor must show an intentional relinquishment of a known right.[19]

Another often-argued basis to excuse failure to comply with contract notice provisions is that the owner had actual notice.[20] This argument often fails if the

17. *E.g.* Buchman Plumbing Co. v. Regents of the Univ. of Minn., 298 Minn. 328, 339, 215 N.W.2d 479, 486 (1974) (Court held that written notice was a condition precedent to the contractual claim. "The law in this area is that, in the absence of a waiver, conditions of this type are valid and for the protection of the party for whom the work is done. A notice provision of this type is designed to inform a party of delay and afford it an opportunity to eliminate the cause of the delay); Am. Nat'l Elec. Corp. v. Poythress Com. Contractors, Inc., 167 N.C. App. 97, 100, 604 S.E.2d 315, 317 (2004) (contractor waived claim by failing to provide timely notice of claim); MLB Constr. Servs., LLC v. Dormitory Auth., 194 A.D.3d 1140, 1142, 149 N.Y.S.3d 271, 276, *leave to appeal dismissed*, 37 N.Y.3d 1046, 176 N.E.3d 305 (2021); TSI Constr., Inc. v. Louisville & Jefferson Cnty. Metro. Sewer Dist., 2020 WL 6538758 (Ky. Ct. App. 2020) (denying claim for failure to comply with timing requirements) *but cf. Ace Constructors, Inc. v. United States*, 70 Fed. Cl. 253, 272 (2006), *aff'd*, 499 F.3d 1357 (Fed. Cir. 2007) ("Because the purpose of the notice requirement is to allow the government to mitigate costs that might result from the differing site condition, a contractor that fails to provide adequate notice will not be barred from recovery unless the government is prejudiced by the lack of notice.").

18. Alstom Power, Inc. v. RMF Indus. Contracting, Inc., 418 F. Supp. 2d 766 (W.D. Pa. 2006) (issue of fact as to whether strict compliance with the notice provisions was waived by course of conduct).

19. MLB Constr. Servs., LLC v. Dormitory Auth., 194 A.D.3d 1140, 1142, 149 N.Y.S.3d 271, 276, *leave to appeal dismissed*, 37 N.Y.3d 1046, 176 N.E.3d 305 (2021) ("A waiver is an intentional relinquishment of a known right and, as such, must be 'explicit, unmistakable, and unambiguous.' It cannot be inferred by a doubtful or equivocal act, and the discussion of disputed items in an attempt to resolve them does not evince a waiver of the requirements.").

20. *E.g.*, Brinderson Corp. v. Hampton Roads Sanitation Dist., 825 F.2d 41, 45 (4th Cir. 1987) ("A more liberal approach, focusing on the purpose of the clause, has been adopted. Generally, when the owner has actual or constructive notice of the conditions underlying the claim and an opportunity to investigate, that is sufficient."); Just Wood Indus., Inc. v. Centex Constr. Co., 1999 WL 606859, at

court determines that notice is a condition precedent to a claim. Finally, prejudice can be a factor the courts consider when determining whether to bar a claim based on the contractor's failure to provide timely notice.[21] Again, this argument will fail if the court finds that notice is a condition precedent to a claim. Absent evidence of a legitimate basis to overlook the contractor's failure to follow the contract's requirements, the contractor is at risk of losing its claim due to its failure to provide timely notice. It is also important to note that different defenses might prevail in some jurisdictions and fail in others. It is critical to be familiar with the law where the construction project is located and if any litigation or alternative dispute proceedings are pending.[22]

Procedures and Support

What to Include in a Time Extension Request

The contractor should make a diligent effort to provide the owner with all relevant and supporting documentation so that the owner has all the facts and data supporting the contractor's claim. In almost every instance, the contractor is bound by a duty to mitigate[23] damages, and act in the best interests of the project. This duty usually includes acting in good faith to timely assess the potential impact and inform the owner so that the owner is afforded an opportunity to mitigate. This duty usually excludes incurring any additional costs without just cause. In its notice of delay or time extension request, the contractor should provide the following: (1) diligent research and management of the issue for the best interest of the project; (2) notice of delay within the number of days provided by the contract; (3) prompt notice to the owner of the duration and impact of the delay; (4) identification of alternative procurement strategies, means and methods, and any associated order of magnitude cost, if readily available; and (5) sufficient analysis and supporting documentation to allow the owner to quickly evaluate both entitlement and quantum.

---

*8–9 (4th Cir.); Travelers Cas. & Sur. Co. v. Dormitory Authority-State of New York, 735 F. Supp. 2d 42 (S.D.N.Y. 2010); Boone Coleman Constr., Inc. v. Village of Piketon, 2014-Ohio-2377, 13 N.E.3d 1190 (Ohio Ct. App. 4th Dist. Pike Cnty. 2014), *appeal allowed*, 140 Ohio St. 3d 1451, 2014-Ohio-4414, 17 N.E.3d 598 (2014) *and judgment vacated*, 145 Ohio St. 3d 450, 2016-Ohio-628, 50 N.E.3d 502 (2016).

21. Ace Constructors, Inc. v. United States, 70 Fed. Cl. 253, 272 (2006), *aff'd*, 499 F.3d 1357 (Fed. Cir. 2007) ("Because the purpose of the notice requirement is to allow the government to mitigate costs that might result from the differing site condition, a contractor that fails to provide adequate notice will not be barred from recovery unless the government is prejudiced by the lack of notice.").

22. *See, e.g.*, AIA A201, § 15.1.1 and § 15.1.3; Consensus Docs, Article 6.3.3, 6.4, Article 8; Federal Acquisition Regulation (FAR) 52.249-10(b)(2).

23. Bruner & O'Connor Construction Law, *supra* note 14, § 15.27.

Time Extension Support—Information and Documentation

Most contracts require that time extension requests are accompanied by a schedule analysis demonstrating how the event impacted the forecasted completion date. There are situations where several interrelated issues may be analyzed in one time impact analysis; however, most owners mandate that each delay (e.g., dispute issue) be analyzed independently using a prospective methodology, such as time impact analysis (described in Chapter 6). Though not always specifically cited by the contract, common elements and supporting documents for a time extension request include the following: issue narrative; causation, that is, how the excusable event influenced the sequence of construction; contractual entitlement argument, that is, why the delay was out of the contractor's control; account for minor-cost and no-cost mitigation, such as easy re-sequencing; chronology of events; fragnet[24] plot; tabular list of added activities and durations representing the delay; tabular list of added interactivity relationships representing the sequence of the delay and how it prevented progress of succeeding base (unimpacted) schedule activities; criteria for selecting the base (unimpacted) schedule used by the contractor for the analysis; criteria for modifying the baseline (unimpacted) schedule, for example, updating the schedule to just prior the date that the delay issue became known to one or both of the parties; electronic CPM schedule export file for the baseline (unimpacted) schedule; and electronic CPM schedule export file for impacted schedule.

Related Issues and Responses: Other Options for Managing a Delay

Usually, the contractor must continue performance while a time extension or additional compensation claim is pending. Further, a contractor's claim for a time extension might be denied or disputed by the owner or there might be circumstances that render additional time impossible, for example, a school being completed in time for classes to commence. In these instances, the contractor must consider alternative means to manage the delay while continuing performance of the work. Initially, the contractor must take reasonable steps to mitigate the impact of the delay event and any damages arising therefrom. Ultimately, the contractor may have no other option but to accelerate construction to attempt to meet the original completion date. These two options are discussed next.

24. This is a scheduling term of art indicating only a portion or fragment of the overall schedule which demonstrates the delaying impact without having to analyze and resubmit the entire project schedule.

Duty to Prevent and/or the Duty to Mitigate Time Impacts and Delay

Taking steps to prevent and/or mitigate project delay is generally required as a matter of implied legal duty[25] or contract obligations.[26] This duty to mitigate means that project participants are required to take all reasonable steps to mitigate delays and additional costs, regardless of who is responsible for the delay. As a practical matter, mitigation efforts should be evaluated on a cost-benefit basis (cost of extended time versus mitigation cost impact) with priority given to initial mitigation efforts that involve the least cost.

Some examples of mitigation strategies to be considered when increased costs, prolonged duration, and potential quality reductions as a result of the delay occur or are imminent include: remobilizing controlling operation crew to an unaffected section of the project; proceeding contrary to preferred sequence (for instance, proceeding with framing and drywall before exterior envelope is dried-in); expediting critical path submittal reviews; purchasing in-plant priority for fabricated elements; accepting alternate manufacturer for a long-lead item; accepting foreign-made equipment (in lieu of domestically produced); expediting shipment methods for materials; working premium labor time; adding crews; adding construction equipment; deleting scope; accepting partial credit for noncompliant work (in lieu of demo and replacement); seeking permit variances (such as working through moratorium periods); and value engineering to alternative construction materials and methods.

Transparency and communication by all interested parties—the owner, contractor, architect, subcontractors, and suppliers—will further help to prevent or mitigate the impact of a delay event.

Mitigation will likely involve additional costs that should be borne by the party responsible for the underlying delay. Although a party is required to undertake reasonable mitigation efforts, a party does not have to undertake inordinate or unreasonable measures.[27]

---

25. Even where the duty to mitigate is not specifically expressed or required by contract, the common law as applied in a particular jurisdiction generally implies duties to all parties to mitigate damages (to include delay) on a project. *See* Rockingham Cnty. v. Luten Bridge Co., 35 F.2d 301, 307 (4th Cir. 1929); Restatement (Second) of Contracts § 350 (1981) ("damages are not recoverable for loss that the injured party could have avoided without undue risk, burden or humiliation."); Bruner & O'Connor Construction Law, *supra* note 14.

26. Construction contracts often place an express obligation on the contractor to mitigate the effects of delay.

27. Fair v. Red Lion Inn, 943 P.2d 431, 437 (Colo. 1997) ("A plaintiff's failure to mitigate damages is excused, however, if mitigation would require inordinate or unreasonable measures or if there were reasonable grounds for the failure to mitigate."

Acceleration and the Recovery Plan

Acceleration in the context of construction occurs when the contractor performs the original scope of work in a shorter period and/or performs a modified scope of the work in the original unadjusted time period. Acceleration is sometimes described as a subset of mitigation.[28] By increasing or adding resources, the goal is to increase the rate of production and progress to "catch up" or "make up" time. Acceleration typically involves adding labor, in the form of adding extra crews, additional shifts, authorizing overtime, additional equipment, or modifying the process and work sequences to increase the rate of performance. Increasing the work force, re-sequencing, and working overtime all have attendant cost increases. Contractors must evaluate the cost-benefit of such acceleration efforts as well as who bears the ultimate responsibility for these extra, additional, and unplanned costs. When possible, the best practice is for the parties to agree as to who was responsible for the delay and/or the need to accelerate, and the resulting costs, before acceleration efforts commence.

Among the most common ways to accelerate is to increase crew sizes, add crews, or work crews longer using overtime. Another approach is to work during a previously idle period, such as evenings/nights or weekends, by adding a second or third shift to the work plan. The contractor can also re-sequence the scheduled work or sequence the work so as to perform two separate activities at the project concurrently when the activities were originally planned to be performed sequentially.

Acceleration efforts usually are a combination of many different approaches with those that are least effective, typically giving way to those that are more effective. The effectiveness of any accelerative effect is often an evaluation of the net benefit or gain as acceleration efforts often come with both direct and indirect costs (in the form of productivity impacts).

Most standard industry construction contracts do not require or obligate the contractor to remedy delay through acceleration. The typical remedy for delay is addressed through a contract time extension for the contractor and delay damages, either actual damages for the contractor or liquidated damages for the owner, as discussed in Chapter 13. Acceleration by the contractor often follows a directive from the owner[29] (directed acceleration) or the owner's denial of a time

---

28. Acceleration is more fully discussed at Chapter 13. The limited discussion here is to address the potential use and effect of acceleration measures as a response to a project delay.

29. It is somewhat more common for standard industry contracts to provide a party the right to direct acceleration, either generally through the changes clause or through a more specific directed acceleration provision.

extension request. Acceleration then becomes a mitigation strategy (constructive acceleration).

A current industry trend is the inclusion of either a "scheduling" provision within the contract or a separate "scheduling" specification within general and supplementary conditions of the contract specifications. These provisions often address details, for example the type of scheduling to be used (even the software requirements), the frequency of schedule updates, and various specific requirements related to time extension requests. Moreover, it is becoming common for these provisions to address acceleration obligations in various ways.

Scheduling provisions often require the contractor to proactively address project delays by specifying that the contractor is required to implement acceleration efforts and/or prepare, submit, and adhere to a recovery plan or recovery schedule. The Code of Federal Regulations (C.F.R.) provides a good example of requirements for contractors to provide a recovery plan.[30]

The Owner's Response

The Owner's Role and Obligations

The owner has an obligation to review all notices of delay and delay claims submitted by the contractor. The owner must determine whether the claimed delay is an excusable delay, compensable delay, an inexcusable delay, or a concurrent delay, and to what extent the delay impacts the contract date. Under the implied covenant of good faith and fair dealing, the owner is obliged to timely evaluate the merit and quantum of the contractor's time extension request, and approve or deny time extensions so that the contractor may adjust its planned use of resources and prosecute the work in the most efficient manner.[31] The owner should relieve the contractor from the burden of the threat of liquidated damages as soon as it determines a time extension is warranted and the amount of the delay can be reasonably measured by schedule analysis.

The owner may choose to perform its own delay analysis and determine if a time extension is warranted and make a determination as to the number of days of

30. *See, e.g.*, 48 C.F.R. § 52.236-15.

31. Restatement (Second) of Contracts § 245 (1981) ("Every contract imposes upon each party a duty of good faith and fair dealing in its performance and its enforcement"); Generally, 13 Williston on Contracts § 39:3 (4th ed.); *see also* H.N. Wood Prod., Inc. v. United States, 59 Fed. Cl. 479, 486 (2003) ("The implied duty to cooperate and not to hinder the other party's performance is an obligation that exists in every Government contract."); Mega Constr. Co. v. United States, 29 Fed. Cl. 396, 423 (1993) ("every contract with the government contains an implied obligation that neither party will do anything to prevent, hinder, or delay performance").

extension. The owner may defer compensation issues for items such as extended general conditions and time-related overhead for later analysis and possible settlement in a future change order. The owner may include a reasonable estimate of these additional costs in a proposed change order that addresses both delay days and additional cost for the contractor's consideration. If the contractor refuses to bilaterally accept and execute the proposed change order for the owner's estimate of allowable time extension for the disputed change or group of issues at hand, the owner may choose to execute the time extension unilaterally so that the contractor is relieved from the threat of liquidated damages and the owner may circumvent a claim for constructive acceleration.

In practice, even with an excused delay event, an owner might be compelled to withhold its response to a time extension request due to its perception of the existence of concurrent contractor-caused, inexcusable delay. Such apprehension is risky since most contracts recognize that an inexcusable delay to completion occurring within the same time period as an excusable delay results in an excusable delay for the period where the respective completion date slippage overlaps. Although most contracts do not require that the contractor's time extension request include an analysis of concurrency with other delays, evaluation of concurrent delay is typically considered by the owner when reviewing a time extension request.

Courts have repeatedly ruled in favor of contractors, and returned liquidated damages withheld from a contractor, when concurrent delays exist, and the associated cost cannot be apportioned between the parties.[32] In summary, an owner is required to evaluate a request for a time extension resulting from on an owner-responsible or third-party delay whether or not it perceives that the contractor's own delay is a contributing or concurrent factor.[33]

Procedural Response

The owner should evaluate the time extension request and accompanying package for completeness and proper methodology, such as a time impact analysis. If the contractor's request doesn't meet the contract requirements, the owner should return written correspondence (either a formal letter or submittal review

32. Blinderman Constr. Co., Inc. v. U.S., 695 F.2d 552 (1982) ("Where both parties contribute to the delay 'neither can recover damage, unless there is in the proof a clear apportionment of the delay and the expense attributable to each party.'") quoting Coath & Goss, Inc. v. United States, 101 Ct. Cl. 702, 714–15 (1944); Com. Int'l Co. v. United States, 338 F.2d 81, 90, 167 Ct. Cl. 529 (1964).

33. *Utley-James, Inc.*, GSBCA No. 5370 (1984); Fischbach & Moore Int'l Corp., ASBCA No. 18146, 77-1 B.C.A. (CCH), 12,300 (1977); *Hammond Construction Inc.*, NASABCA No. 06-0290 (1992).

comments) enumerating the missing information, disputed elements of the quantum analysis, and a due date to return a revised response. A common response states:

> The Owner is returning the Contractor's [*select notice of delay, request for time extension*] because it is either incomplete, unreviewable, or objectionable on the following grounds [*select only applicable categories and briefly summarize objections in Attachment A*]:
>
> If the Contractor elects to continue to contest this matter, please promptly re-submit.

The owner's procedural response should list both objections that prejudice the owner or flaws that impair the owner's review. Typical grounds include: dispute issue or differing site condition is not sufficiently described to permit the owner to act to mitigate; untimeliness, for example, the issue is past and the owner was not afforded the opportunity to address or mitigate the delay; time request is not explicitly stated; missing schedule analysis; schedule analysis does not support stated time request; improper delay analysis methodology; methodology not recognized by the contract or good practice; missing chronology of events; missing narrative; missing causation, for example, how did the excusable delay event actually influence the sequence of construction?; missing contractual entitlement argument, for example, how was the delay not the contractor's responsibility?; missing plot or list of fragnet activities; missing electronic CPM schedule export file for the base (unimpacted) schedule used by the contractor for the analysis; improper selection of the "unimpacted" schedule used by the contractor as the basis for the analysis; improper modification of the base (unimpacted) schedule; and/or missing electronic CPM schedule export file for impacted schedule.

Unless the disputed issue is abundantly clear in the contract documents, the owner's response should avoid rejecting based on merit until the contractor has satisfied all of the missing elements required by contract that prevent the owner's review or acceptance of the time extension request.

Substantive Response

After receipt of the contractor's notice of delay or request for time extension, the owner should respond by actively managing delay events that have merit (e.g., not within the contractor's control) in order to mitigate both the cost and time impact. For instance, if the contractor provides notice of a differing site condition, the owner's architect or engineer should immediately visit the construction site to evaluate the potential differing site condition, since the owner is usually entitled or obligated to select the remedial method when a differing site condition is encountered, especially if it must be designed by a professional engineer. For example, the owner might decide to direct the contractor to emergency backfill the excavation, procure and install additional shoring, demobilize to another area, or completely omit the work in question from the contract. The owner's maintenance of issue files and issuance of written correspondence demonstrating its timeliness addressing the contractor's notice is important for the owner's own delay analysis and possible later claim defense. In the case of a differing site condition, it may be prudent to respond to the contractor's notice of delay with a date that the design engineer will visit the site and a date when the owner expects to issue direction for its preferred remedial measure. Such correspondence signals the owner's substantive response to the contractor's notice.

In cases where the owner determines that the contractor's notice of delay or request for time extension is not only procedurally flawed but also entirely without merit (e.g., the delay issue in question is determined to be an inexcusable delay under the provisions of the contract), the owner may respond to the contractor's time extension request with a request for a recovery schedule demonstrating the contractor's plan to recover the contractor's delay.

Significance of and Risks Associated with Contractor Response

As stated in the preceding section, the owner's response should avoid rejecting based on merit unless the disputed issue is abundantly clear in the contract documents. The owner is well served to perform its own schedule analysis and extend the contract time for the undisputed amount of time owed while the owner formulates a thorough list of objections to the contractor's request and the contractor is able to address and possibly remedy its entitlement arguments and quantum analysis. If the owner either fails to grant a proper time extension within a reasonable time before the contract time expires or prematurely denies the merit of a proper request for time extension, the owner might constructively accelerate the contractor. The contractor might incur costs to add resources and perform work inefficiently to hurry to achieve milestones earlier than it would have been obligated had the owner properly allowed the time extension. The contractor may elect to pursue the owner to recover such costs of its acceleration. The Army Corp of Engineers sets forth possible acceleration and/or recovery plan obligations.[34]

---

34. U.S. Army Corp. of Engineers, Specifications, Section 01 32 01.00 10, § 3.9 Failure to Achieve Progress.

CHAPTER 5

Contractor Delay Claims: Proving Entitlement and Addressing Concurrent Delay Arguments

Susan Eccles

Was a construction project delay caused by an owner or a contractor? Or both, concurrently? One of the biggest issues in construction contract language is that there is often a lack of specific, or any, direction in the parties' agreement of what happens when there is a concurrent delay—meaning a situation in which a project is delayed by two concurring, overlapping events during a specific window of time within a project. These delays frequently occur in complex construction projects, and there is a question as to what extent each party contributed to the delay.

There are many challenging layers of complexity to concurrent delay instances, resulting in contention between parties within construction claims. Contract language and provisions alluding to concurrent delays minimize these kinds of related disputes in construction projects, assigning the responsibility and assessing compensability when delays are concurrent. There are two parts of a contractor delay claim—entitlement, then calculation of damages. Without proving entitlement, you don't get to the calculation of damages. Concurrent delays could either be a defense by an owner to a contractor's entitlement to compensation, or a contractor's strategy to offset liquidated damages. Typically, concurrent delays are noncompensable.

First, some definitions of need-to-know terms and phrases. There are several tier levels of schedule delay classification types on a construction project: critical versus noncritical, excusable versus non-excusable, and compensable versus noncompensable. Critical delays affect the completion date; noncritical delays do not. "Compensable delays," also known as non-excusable, often occur when the negligence responsibility falls on the owner, causing a delay to the completion of the project's work beyond the expiration date of the contract time. Contractors can file for time extension, compensation, or both. Noncompensable delays, or excusable, can occur when the contractor is at fault or weather occurs. Under non-compensable delays, the contractor is not given a time extension or compensation for the delay.

The Requisite Elements for the Contractor to Prove Entitlement to a Compensable Time Extension

While there is no perfect construction project, if the parties contractually agreed that time is of the essence in performing and completing the project, then delayed performance may provide a contractual basis for a cause of action by the delayed party. It is important to verify that the contract is free from no-damages-for-delay clauses, which seek to insulate the owner from liability.[1] In the absence of such limitations, or with an exception thereto, the contractor may be entitled to recover damages from the owner, attributable to the owner's delay.[2]

In seeking a compensable time extension, the contractor must prove entitlement to damages, and the amount of damages. The contractor satisfies its burden of proof by a reasonable degree of certainty or preponderance of the evidence.[3] The contractor need not prove its damages with mathematical precision.[4] Further, "specific proof of actual damages is not required for breach of contract claims because nominal damages may also be awarded."[5] Shouldering the burden of proof prior to prevailing on a compensable time extension claim is the same regardless of whether the contractor is seeking recovery on a public or private project. The only difference is a slight tweak in the language of the government versus private project test. For example, on a government project, the contractor must show: "(1) that the delays or extra expenses were *directly* caused by the actions of the government; (2) that the delay was for an *unreasonable* period of time; and (3) that the injury was occasioned by injury to the contractor in the form of additional expense or loss."[6]

1. *See* Chapter 7 for discussion of no-damages-for-delay clauses and exceptions thereto.
2. JMR Constr. Corp. v. Env'l Assessment & Remediation Mgmt., 243 Cal. App. 4th 571, 198 Cal. Rptr. 3d 47 (2015).
3. Wilner v. United States, 24 F.3d 1397, 1401 (Fed. Cir. 1994); Tolliver Grp., Inc. v. U.S., 146 F. Cl. 475, 26 Fed. Cir. 2020); John Spearly Constr., Inc. v. Penns Valley Area School Dist., 121 A.3d 593,602 (Pa. Cmmw. 2015); Allegheny Intermediate Unit v. East Allegheny Sch. Dist., 203 A.3d 371 (Pa. Cmmw. 2019); Clearwater Constructors, Inc. v. U.S., 71 Fed. Cl. 25 (2006); Kirby v. Chrysler Corp., 554 F. Supp. 743, 752 (D. Md. 1982); Servidone Constr. Corp. v. U.S., 931 F.2d 860, 861 (Fed. Cir. 1991); George Sollitt Constr. Co. v. U.S., 64 Fed. Cl. 229, 238 (2005); Shintech Inc. v. Grp. Constructors, Inc., 688 S.W.2d 144, (Tex. Civ. App.-Houston [14th Dist.] 1985).
4. Kirby v. Chrysler Corp., 554 F. Supp. 743, 752 (D. Md. 1982).
5. Zip Designs, LLC v. Glowzone Las Vegas, Civ. No. CCB-17-1327 (D. Md. 2019).
6. Beauchamp Constr. Co., Inc. v. United States, 14 Cl. Ct. 430, 437 (1988).

In establishing its claim for a compensable delay on private projects it is imperative that the contractor establish:

1. that there is a delay to the critical path of the project thereby extending the overall project duration;
2. that the delay is compensable;
3. whether and to what extent the contractor's work was unreasonably delayed by the owner's action;
4. whether any unreasonable delays caused by the owner were concurrent with or separate from delays charged to the contractor; and
5. whether the contractor is entitled to a time extension and/or recovery of damages and, if so, how much.[7]

In such delay litigation, the contractor bears the burden of establishing the extent of the delay, that the delay was caused by the owner, and that the contractor was damaged by the actions of the other party.[8] It is essential that the contractor also demonstrate that the owner's caused delays impacted the project's critical path[9] and, specifically, the contractor's performance.[10] A contractor will likely not be entitled to recover monetary damages for delays unless work impacted the time in which the project was completed. Specifically, the delay at issue caused the extension of the contract completion date.[11] In supporting its claim, the contractor must present evidence of scheduling impacts. Failure to do so may impact its ability to recover at trial.[12]

It is often not enough to merely claim that a project delay is critical. Rather, the contractor must prove it to the court. This can be done by identifying which project elements were critical activities on the schedule. The contractor cannot depend on the award of a time extension from the owner as the sole support for establishing the critical nature of the delay, as the owner may argue that the delays claimed by the contractor were not critical to the project. Further,

---

7. Fieldcrest Builders, Inc. v. Antonucci, 311 Ill. App. 3d 597, 243 Ill. Dec. 740, 724 N.E.2d 49 (1st Dist. 1999); Mid-State Precast Systems Inc. v. Corbetta Constr. Co. Inc., 608 N.Y.S.2d 546, 202 A.D. 702, 704; Plato Gen. Constr. Corp. et al. v. Dormitory of the State, 932 N.Y.S. 504, 89 A.D.3d 819, 825–36; Aetna Cas. & Sur. Co. v. Chapel Hill Independent Sch. Dist., 860 S.W.2d 667, 671 (Tex. Civ. App.—Tyler 1993).

8. Wilner v. U.S., 24 F.3d 1397 (Fed. Cir. 1994); City of Beaumont v. Excavators & Constructors, Inc., 870 S.W.2d 123 (Tex. App. Beaumont 1993).

9. See Chapter 2 for a detailed discussion about the critical path of a project schedule.

10. Allstate Interiors & Exteriors, Inc. v. Stonestreet Constr., LLC, 907 F. Supp. 2d 216 (D.R.I. 2012).

11. Brinderson Corp. v. Hamilton Roads Sanitation Dist., 825 F.2d 41 (4th Cir. 1987); CCM Corp. v. U.S., 20 Cl. Ct. 649 (1990).

12. Oasis Int'l Waters, Inc. v. U.S., 135 Fed. Cl. 230 (2017).

the interconnected nature of the delays or a lack of documentation to support the party's position may make apportionment of delays nearly impossible. Such impossibility can be used as a successful defense when litigating a claim for delay damages. Instead of addressing the individual delays head on, the defending party asserts a claim for concurrency. The result often forces the claimant to undertake a complicated and expensive delay study that may lead the court to include that the delays are so intertwined that apportionment is impossible.

Entitlement as a Result of Owner-Caused Delays

Generally speaking, when analyzing delay claims, any critical path delays proven to be caused solely by the owner are not attributable to the contractor. Even when not specifically stated in the contract, the owner may not interfere with the contractor's performance of the work. Despite a contractual obligation to complete a project by a certain date, the contractor's delayed performance will be excused if the contractor is prevented by the owner from timely performing its work. For example, owners are generally responsible for delays resulting from:

1. Failure of the owner to provide contractually promised equipment and materials;
2. Differing site conditions;
3. Coordination of other contractors/subcontractors hired by the owner;[13]
4. Delayed site availability, restricted site access, or failure to clear right of ways;[14]
5. Defective plans, specifications, and excessive change orders;[15]
6. Suspensions/stoppage of work or payment.[16]

Owner Delays Attributable to Delayed Site Availability, Materials, and Failed Coordination Efforts

When evaluating an owner's performance with respect to project delays, one must first review the owner's obligation under the contract. For example, what are the owner's contractual obligations related to providing the contractor access to the site? Specifically, did the owner warrant or represent that the site would be available by a specific day? If a date for substantial completion is included in the contract such that work must be finished within a certain number of days, or by a specific

13. Ultimate Concrete, LLC v. U.S., 141 Fed. Cl. 463, 480 (2019).

14. Sergent Mech. Sys., Inc. v. U.S., 34 Fed. Cl. 505 (1995); North Star Alaska Hous. Corp. v. U.S., 76 Fed. Cl. 158 (2007).

15. Alley Constr. Co. v. State, 300 Minn. 356, 360; 219 N.W.2d 922 (1974).

16. Gilchrist Constr. Co., LLC v. State Dep't of Transp. & Dev., 166 So. 3d 1045 (La. 1 Cir. 2015).

date, initial and ongoing site access to the contractor is critical. While some courts recognize an implied warranty of unfettered site access, others will examine the contract to determine if the owner was contractually obligated to provide access by a certain date. Regardless of the contractual requirements, in every construction contract there is an implied duty of cooperation and to not negatively impact or hinder the performance of the other party.[17]

In addition to site access provisions, courts will also examine whether, and to what extent, the owner agreed to provide materials, supplies, or equipment to the site that are critical to the project's completion. If so, delays in delivery and access may directly impact the contractor's critical path and cause an overall project delay for which it will not be responsible and for which it may be compensated.

It is also important to evaluate whether the contractor was awaiting performance by another contractor before it could begin or perform its work. An owner may be responsible for delays when it awards another contract that interferes with the original contractor's work.[18] Although a contractor may be able to mobilize its team, it may not be able to start, continue, or complete its work due to a sequencing problem caused by the owner and its additional contractors. While the owner may attempt to blame its contractors for the delay, this delay will not be a defense afforded to the owner for delays caused by other respective contractors.

Owners should be mindful that the contractor may be owed compensatory damages for project delays caused by the actions, inactions, or interference by the owner's contract representative, the owner's architect/consultant, and the government's contracting officers.[19] Furthermore, in addition to proving that it is entitled to compensatory damages for delay, the contractor must also prove that there were no concurrent delays that would block compensation for delay. Specifically, even assuming the government/owner caused the delay, in order for the contractor "to prevail on this issue, it must demonstrate that any such government caused delays were not concurrent (i.e. offsetting) or intertwined with other delays, for which the government was not responsible. Thus, a contractor asserting a delay claim against the government must prove not only that it incurred additional costs making up its claim, but also that such costs would not have been incurred but for some government action."[20]

17. Glassman Constr. Co. v. Md. City Plaza, Inc., 371 F. Supp. 1154, 1161 (D. Md. 1974).

18. Calvert Gen. Contractors Corp., MDOTBCA 1004, 1 MSBCA ¶ 5 (1981).

19. E.C. Ernst, Inc. v. Manhattan Constr. Co. of Texas, 551 F.2d 1026 (5th Cir. 1977); Coyle Constr. Co. v. Skagit Cnty., 177 Wash. 520, 43 P.2d 106 (1934); H.E. Crook Co. v. U.S., 270 U.S. 4, 46 S. Ct. 184, 70 L. Ed. 438 (1934); John Weil Plumbing Corp. v. State, 267 A.D. 247, 45 N.Y.S.2d 456 (3d Dep't 1943).

20. Arntz Contracting Co. v. Beacon Constr. Co. et al., EBCA NO. 187-12-81, 84-3 BCA ¶ 17,604 (1984); Merritt-Chapman & Scott Corp. v. U.S., 208 Ct. Cl. 639, 650, 528 F.2d 1392 (1976).

Owner Delays Attributable to Defective Plans, Defective Specifications, and Excess Change Orders

It is generally accepted that all construction projects will have design changes resulting in change orders. While a reasonable number of changes are expected on construction projects, courts have awarded delay damages for a significant increase in the scope of work.[21] A time extension to the overall project duration may be appropriate regardless of whether the revision is incorporated prior to or during construction.[22] Courts recognize that such increased scope increases the burden on the contractor and likewise should result in additional time/compensation.

While most contracts include clauses addressing revisions for project changes, others do not. Additionally, even if the contract addresses changes, and the owner's representative fails to respond to the contractor's pricing or fails to provide a notice to proceed with the changed work in a reasonable amount of time, damages may also be awarded. Such damages can be attributable to delayed approval of plan revisions or project materials.[23]

In evaluating a delay claim for defective plans and specifications, it is important to note that a majority of jurisdictions recognize that under the design-bid-build project delivery method, wherein the owner contracts directly with the designers, the owner guarantees the sufficiency of the specifications,[24] essentially adopting what has become known as the *Spearin* doctrine. The *Spearin* doctrine, named after the U.S. Supreme Court case, *U.S. v. Spearin*, recognizes that the owner warrants that the design plans and specifications are free from defects and, if followed, will result in the construction of the desired structure.[25] Consequently, if the plans and specifications contain defects that result in project delays, then the owner is liable to the contractor for the costs of the delay.[26] The *Spearin* Court noted that the responsibility "of the owner is not overcome by the usual clauses requiring builders to visit the site, to check the plans, and to inform themselves of the requirements of the work."[27] However, to fall within this doctrine, the defect must be in the owner's design specifications, which were provided to the contractor. Courts have found that design specifications are those that specifically detail the manner in

---

21. Axthelm & Swett Constr., Inc. v. Caudill, 86 Wash. App. 1002, 1997 WL 241575 (Div. 1 1997).
22. *Id.*
23. Plato v. U.S., 86 Ct. Cl. 665, 1938 WL 3963 (1938); Spitcaufsky v. State Highway Comm'n of Missouri, 349 Mo. 117, 159 S.W.2d 647 (1941); Martin Constr., Inc. v. U.S., 102 Fed. Cl. 562 (2011); Frelund v. De Rosa, 309 A.D.2d 1287, 765 N.Y.S.2d 395 (4th Dep't 2003).
24. Alamo Cmty. College Dis. v. Browning Constr. Co., 131 S.W.3d 146, 156 (Tex. Civ. App.—San Antonio 2004).
25. U.S. v. Spearin, 39 S. Ct. 59, 248 U.S. 132 (1918).
26. Metric Constr. Co., Inc. v. U.S., 80 Fed. Cl. 178 (2008).
27. U.S. v. Spearin, 39 S. Ct. 59, 61, 248 U.S. 132, 136 (1918).

which work is to be performed.[28] Further, *Spearin* has been found to exclude performance specifications that merely set forth the project's objective and allow the contractor freedom to achieve it.[29] In evaluating whether an objective is a design or performance objective, contractors should examine whether the "contractor has no discretion to deviate from the specifications, but is 'required to follow them as a road map.'"[30]

Stop-Work Orders: Who's Responsible for the Delay?

Responsibility in a stop-work order or project suspension situation may depend on the reason for the suspension or on the contract language itself. A contractor seeking damages due to a stop-work order or suspension of work should first review the contract. The contract may contain limitations restricting the owner's liability. However, if such damages are not contractually prohibited then the contractor may seek recovery for delays attributable to the unreasonable suspension or stop-work order.[31]

Addressing Concurrent Delay

In seeking recovery for owner-caused delay, a contractor must evaluate the owner's potential defense of concurrent delay. A reminder that concurrent delay is defined as a delay "which has both temporal and causation aspects. Concurrent delays affect the same 'delay period.' A concurrent delay is also independently sufficient to cause the delay days attributable to that source of delay."[32] In attempting to explain the concept of concurrent delays, the Armed Services Board of Contract Appeals wrote, "strictly speaking, there can be but a single delay over a given period of time, and when that delay has multiple, indivisible causes, it is attributable not to either party but to both. Hence it would probably be more accurate to speak not of concurrent delays but of a single delay with concurrent causes."[33]

If the actions or inactions of both the owner and the contractor concurrently contribute to the delay of the project's critical path, then neither party may have a claim for compensation (increased contract amount or assessment of liquidated

28. Williamette Crushing Co. v. State By & Through Dep't of Transp., 188 Ariz. 79, 932 P.2d 1350 (Ct. App. Div. 1 1997).

29. *Id.*

30. P.R. Burke v. U.S., 277 F.3d 1346 (Fed. Cir. 2002), citing Blake Constr. Co. v. U.S., 987 F.2d 743 (Fed. Cir. 1993).

31. JMR Constr. Corp. v. U.S., 117 Fed. Cl. 436 (2014).

32. George Sollitt Constr. Co. v. U.S., 64 Fed. Cl. 229, 239 (2005).

33. Appeal of Utley-James, Inc., G.S.B.C.A. No. 5370, 85-1 B.C.A. (CCH) ¶ 17816,89109, 1984 WL 13874.

damages), however, a time extension may be awarded.[34] The reason for the denial of compensation is simply that both parties contributed to the delay and should be prohibited from financially benefiting from the delay. Thus, instead, the contractor may be granted additional time on the schedule but may not be compensated for its extended overhead associated with those additional days. As such, it is considered an excusable delay but not a compensable delay.

In certain cases, a more modern approach has been taken, which results in the apportionment of the delay and consequently the expense attributable to the actions of both parties. When attempting to apportion delays between parties, it is important to recognize that there are several different scenarios in which concurrent delays may occur:

1. Cases in which there are two separate delays such as when the owner and the contractor simultaneously delay the critical path activity;
2. Cases in which one party is delayed by the other party in two separate situations at the same time and both delays impact the critical path; and
3. Cases in which multiple contractors cause delays that occur at the same time, and each delay impacts the project completion date.

When seeking to recover for delay, the contractor bears the burden of separating its delays from the delays it alleges were caused by the other parties. Such examination is factually intensive and can be extremely complicated given the nature of the project. In fact, under certain circumstances it may be impossible to allocate the cause of the delays. In cases in which responsibility cannot be apportioned, concurrent delay generally excuses the contractor from liquidated damages. In undertaking a concurrent delay analysis, the contractor must first clear the initial hurdle of determining whether there are at least two separate and independent causes of the delay. If "two or more parties contribute to a single delay to the project and the causation is linked or related, the event is not considered to have two concurrent causes."[35] Once it is established that the delay is concurrent, then it must be determined if the delay was on the critical path and impacted the project completion date.

In examining impacts to the critical path, it is important to determine whether the delay occurred at the same time. If not, the delay may be sequential and not concurrent. In cases in which a delay may be classified as sequential, the award

34. Weaver-Bailey Contractors, Inc. v. U.S., 19 Cl. Ct. 474, 476 (1990), 1990 WL 10845; R.P. Wallace, Inc. v. U.S., 63 Fed. Cl. 402, 410 (2004); Essex Electro Eng'rs v. Danzig, 224 F.3d 1283, 1295 (Fed. Cir. 2000).

35. Association for the Advancement of Cost Engineering International, Inc., Recommended Practice on Forensic Schedule Analysis (AACE RP29R-03-2011).

of compensation, whether to the contractor or the owner, may be in play. While non-simultaneous delays can still impact the critical path to the extent to establish concurrency, it is through the detailed examination of the critical path that such impacts will be proven.[36] A contractor must show that the government or owner "was the sole proximate cause of the delay and that no concurrent cause would have equally delayed the contract . . . . 'Only if the delay was caused solely by the government [owner] will the contractor be entitled to . . . recovery of excess costs associated with the delay.'"[37]

Additionally, a contractor should be mindful that the examination of concurrent delays may also involve the review of the performance of the contractor's subcontractors and suppliers. Specifically, the contractor will be barred from recovering delay damages from the owner when the contractor's own subcontractor or supplier caused a concurrent delay. This additional layer of examination adds further complexity to an extremely difficult undertaking. This undertaking is often best left to a forensic scheduling expert who can perform the post-construction analysis of the parties' performance and testify at trial.

36. Williams Enters., Inc. v. Strait Mfg. & Welding, Inc., 728 F. Supp. 12 (D.D.C. 1990); E.C. Ernst, Inc. v. Manhattan Constr. Co., 387 F. Supp. 1001 (S.D. Ala. 1974); U.S. v. William F. Klingensmith, Inc., 670 F.2d 1227 (Cl. Ct. 1982).

37. Wayne Knorr, Inc. v. Dep't of Transp., 973 A.2d 1061, 1082 (Pa. Cmmw. 2009), citing Weaver-Bailey Contractors, Inc. v. U.S., 19 Cl. Ct. 474, 476 (1990).

CHAPTER 6

Proving the Period of Delay

Wayne DeFaminis and Luke LaRocca

Introduction

When a construction project becomes delayed, proving entitlement for additional contract time or delay damages typically requires the preparation of a "delay analysis." A delay analysis may be presented as a detailed report, short memorandum, or a graphical presentation. Regardless of its format, the delay analysis should present the results of a principled analysis of the contemporaneous schedule information and project records and credibly answer these deceptively simple questions:

- Which activities caused the project to be delayed?
- How did they impact the project's critical path?
- When did the delays occur?
- How long did the activities delay the project?

Alternatively stated, the delay analysis must *identify* and *quantify* the project's critical delays in a reasoned and objective way.

This chapter covers key issues for preparing a delay analysis and the process for getting that information introduced into evidence. It provides the construction lawyer with an overview of key differences between commonly used delay analysis methods and important considerations that the construction lawyer and delay expert must make during the delay claim preparation and litigation.

Why the Controversy?

Arguably, there are few areas of construction law more controversial than the evaluation and disposition of delay claims. During the past three decades, the once specialized field of forensic schedule analysis has grown rapidly within the U.S. economy. But this fact alone does not explain why assessing and dispositioning delay claims remains so controversial.

To begin with, time is a readily quantifiable resource (a day, an hour, etc.). However, "lost time" (i.e., a project delay) is much less easily quantified. This is because delays may be mitigated if not fully recovered by accelerating critical work, working activities in parallel, resequencing future work, or some combination of these measures. The process for depicting these changes can be quite arduous, especially for large projects. Next, the important distinction between a *contemporaneous delay event* (cause) and a *future impact event* (effect) is often blurred or nonexistent when delays are presented. This makes objective assessment of project delay more difficult.

Though we now live in the age of big data, the truth is that delay analysis remains both art and science. Even the most scrupulously prepared delay analysis cannot, by itself, eliminate schedule uncertainty, account for faulty input data, or satisfy crucial information gaps. These circumstances require the schedule expert to make assumptions and apply subjective reasoning to arrive at a conclusion. There "will always be some subjectivity in schedule delay analysis due to factual and project complexity and limitations in information."[1]

No delay analysis is truly exact no matter how detailed it may appear to be. This is because the accuracy of any delay analysis directly depends on the quality of the input schedule information. All forecast schedules contain some degree of uncertainty, precisely because they are models of how a project *should* progress based on metrics, assumptions, and information that may or may not reflect actual project circumstances. Hence, it is often difficult, if not impossible, for the delay expert to remove all uncertainty from the delay analysis results without making further subjective assumptions.

To the inexperienced, there are a dizzying number of delay analysis methodologies and schedule techniques, each with particular strengths and weaknesses. There is also no universally approved or accepted delay analysis method. Notwithstanding these challenges, recent years have seen a growing consensus among scheduling professionals and legal authorities that certain delay analysis methods and scheduling techniques are more reliable than others when applied under specific circumstances. This chapter serves to assist the reader in discerning when and how commonly used delay analysis methods should be applied—and how they may be misapplied—based on the reliability and frequency of the input data and the analytical techniques employed.

As described in this chapter, choosing a delay analysis method should be performed after careful consideration of the contract requirements, quality of the baseline schedule and updates, if available, other available contemporaneous

1. W. Stephen Dale, Esq. & Robert M. D'Onofrio, P.E., Construction Schedule Delays 624 (2015).

records, and project-specific facts and circumstances. In addition, careful thought must be placed on expert selection to ensure that the expert will survive challenges to their qualifications, methodology, and opinions.

In recent years, there has been a profusion of techniques, junk science, and "voodoo" analysis that has further clouded the picture. It is not unusual for opposing experts claiming to have followed the same delay analysis method to produce wildly divergent results, even before assessing entitlement and responsibility.

Fortunately, there are resources available to the construction lawyer that describe best practices and sound guiding principles to help minimize controversy. The following recent publications differ in scope and content, but each provides the practitioner with helpful guidance for preparing a delay analysis that will be perceived as reasonably objective, legally defensible, and technically sound.

This chapter begins with a discussion related to the Association for the Advancement of Cost Engineering International (AACE) recommended practice and other delay analysis standards. Next, the chapter examines expert selection and engaging a forensic schedule analysis into evidence. Finally, the chapter examines preparation of a delay analysis from the viewpoint of a seasoned expert in preparation of delay analysis.

AACE Recommended Practice and Other Delay Analysis Standards

Technical White Paper, Forensic Schedule Analysis, Recommended Practice 29R-03 from AACE International, © 2011

AACE RP 29R-03 was first released by AACE in 2009 and later updated in 2011. Initial criticism of the AACE RP centered chiefly on what the publication, by its own admission, *did not* provide: a prescriptive recommendation for analyzing schedule delays, the establishment of detailed standard of practice, and legal analysis of the various delay analysis methods covered.[2] Nevertheless, the AACE RP remains one of the most detailed sources of technical information available to practitioners for the objective evaluation of numerous, distinct delay analysis methods. The AACE RP covers some 14 distinct delay analysis methods and provides useful insights regarding delay analysis taxonomy, nomenclature, and best practices for the objective evaluation of schedule delays. The AACE RP groups the various delay analysis methods into two "basic methods": observational and modeled. Observational methods utilize the contemporaneous schedule updates "without the analyst

2. AACE International, *Forensic Schedule Analysis*, AACE International Recommended Practice No. 29 29R-03 (2011).

making any changes to the schedule to simulate any specific scenario."[3] Modeled methods call "for intervention by the analyst beyond mere observation. In preparing a modeled analysis the analyst inserts or extracts activities representing delay events into or from a CPM network and compares the calculated results of the 'before' and 'after' states."[4] These two primary categories are further subdivided by the particular schedule techniques employed in each method. A graphical depiction of the delay analysis method taxonomy shown in the AACE RP is displayed in Figure 6.1.

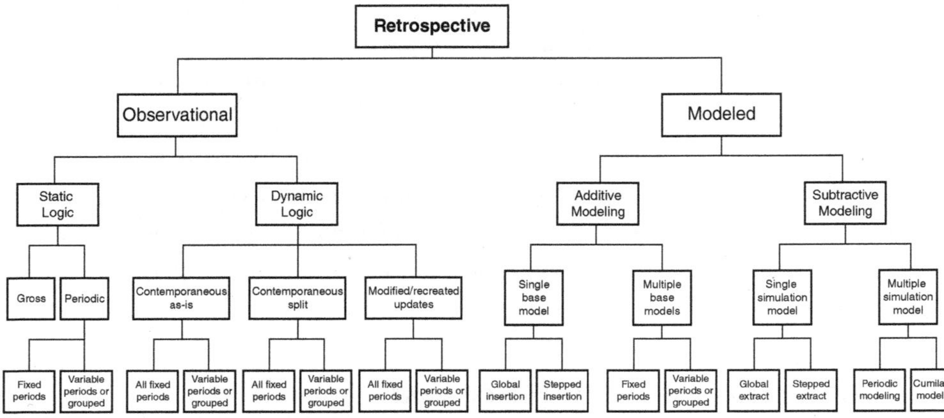

FIGURE 6.1 AACE RP 29R-03 Delay Analysis Taxonomy[5]

Despite the statement that it is not a prescriptive document to be followed in every circumstance, the AACE RP remains a "go-to guide" for lawyers and delay experts alike when evaluating the technical merits of delay claims or other critical path method (CPM) analyses.[6]

Reference Standard 67-17, Schedule Delay Analysis, from the American Society of Civil Engineering (ASCE), © 2017

ASCE 67-17 is a reference standard published by the ASCE and developed in conformance with a consensus standards development process accredited by the American National Standards Institute (ANSI). ASCE 67-17 presents a set of 35

3. *Id.* at 13.
4. *Id.* at 13–14.
5. *Id.* at 12.
6. At the time of this writing, AACE RP 29R-03 is being updated and is undergoing AACE committee evaluation and peer reviews by the forensic schedule analysis community.

guidelines that "any [delay analysis] method used should follow" that "generally reflect the best engineering principles associated with schedule delay analysis and standard of practice in the United States construction industry."[7] The ASCE guidelines enable practitioners to identify delays to a project completion date or to intermediary milestones utilizing CPM schedule techniques that are consistent with prevailing CPM theory and practice. The reference standard covers the following general topics:

- The critical path;
- Schedule float;
- Early project completion schedules;
- Delay chronology;
- Concurrent delay;
- Evaluating responsibility for delay;
- Changing schedules after the fact; and
- Acceleration measures.

It is important to note that ASCE 67-17 *does not* address specific delay analysis methods. This is not a limitation of the application or usefulness of this standard because it provides a reliable framework for preparing an objective, credible, and defensible delay analysis.

While the delay analysis for an individual case may not follow all of the general guidelines detailed in ASCE 67-17, departures should be supported by the contract and case facts, and should be adequately explained to prevent insinuations of subjectivity or impropriety. In short, a delay analysis should comply with ASCE 67-17 general standards as closely as possible.

Construction Schedule Delays, by W. Stephen Dale, Esq. and Robert M. D'Onofrio, PE, © 2022

Construction Schedule Delays is a recent and comprehensive treatise dealing with the topic of schedule delays and delay analysis methods.[8] Part I presents the foundation for delay analysis: frameworks for analyzing project delays, legal issues, delay damages, and no-damages-for-delay issues. Part II is devoted to each of five generalized delay analysis method categories:

7. American Society of Civil Engineers, *Schedule Delay Analysis*, Reference Standard No. 67-17, at 1 (2017).

8. W. Stephen Dale, Esq. & Robert M. D'Onofrio, PE, Construction Schedule Delays (2022).

- Time impact analysis;
- Collapsed as-built;
- As-built critical path;
- Impacted as planned; and
- As planned/as-built or total time.

Although the organization of the various delay analysis methods differs slightly from the AACE RP, *Construction Schedule Delays* also covers 14 distinct delay analysis methods. The 14 delay analysis methods comprise the five generalized delay analysis method categories shown in Table 6.1.[9]

TABLE 6.1 *Construction Schedule Delays*—Delay Analysis Method Categories

Category	Method
Time impact analysis (TIA)	Adjusted TIA
	Unadjusted TIA (windows)
	Prospective TIA
	Windows (wide periods)
Collapsed as-built	Multiple period using updates
	Collapsed stepped removal
	Remove owner delays
	Remove contractor delays
As-built critical path	Critical path using updates
	As-built path
Impacted as-planned	Stepped insertion
	Global insertion
	Compare owner/contractor
Total time	As-planned vs. as-built

9. *Id.* at 284.

In the chapter entitled "Method Comparison Study," *Construction Schedule Delays* presents the results of an evaluation of each of the distinct delay analysis methods based on the same fact pattern.[10] The exercise is revealing and highlights that delay analysis methods can produce differing results even when based on the same input information. According to this study, of all the delay analysis methods, the time impact analysis (adjusted) method "will most often constitute the optimum way to evaluate delays for criticality, concurrency, and excusability."[11]

On both a technical and legal basis, *Construction Schedule Delays* concludes that "all variations of the time impact analysis [method] are preferred over other methodologies."[12] The delay analysis methods ranked by preference are shown in Table 6.2.

TABLE 6.2 *Construction Schedule Delays*—Methods Ranked by Preference

Preference	Category
1	Time impact analysis (adjusted)
2	Windows (unadjusted)
3	Prospective time impact analysis
4	Collapsed as-built
5	As-built critical path
6	Impacted as-planned
7	Total time / as-planned vs. as-built

Construction Schedule Delays also summarizes the decisions of 179 U.S. court delay cases between 1968 and 2022 pertaining to the acceptance or rejection of a delay analysis method identified therein.[13] The study notes that nearly every delay method has been both accepted and not accepted by courts and boards. In support of the preference ranking previously indicated, the time impact analysis (adjusted) has been the most accepted method followed by the windows (unadjusted) method. The decision study results are summarized in Table 6.3.

10. *Id.* chs. X to Y.
11. *Id. at* 627.
12. *Id. at* 624.
13. *Id.* at 628.

TABLE 6.3 *Construction Schedule Delays*—Summary of U.S. Cases Referencing Schedule Delay Methods

Delay Analysis Method	No. Cases Evaluated	% Accepted vs. Not Accepted or Rejected	% Not Accepted or Rejected vs. Accepted
Adjusted TIA	20	85%	15%
Windows	20	50%	50%
Prospective TIA	12	50%	50%
Windows (wide periods)	4	25%	75%
Collapsed as-built	11	27%	73%
As-built critical path	28	18%	82%
Impacted as-planned	25	20%	80%
As-planned vs. as-built	59	14%	86%
Total	**179**		

The practitioner should consider the relative rates of court acceptance and rejection for any delay analysis method being used to assert or defend against delay claims they are involved in. Beyond the delay analysis method that has been chosen that particular project or claim, and how the chosen method has been implemented, the practitioner must also be aware that the most common reasons for the court's rejection or lack of acceptance are:

- Failure to consider actual project events;
- Bias or failure to consider each party's delays;
- Schedule defects or the improper recreation of the project's schedules;
- Failure to address concurrent delay or to segregate and apportion delay as in a "total time" approach;
- Failure to consider contemporaneously prepared schedules; and
- Other calculation errors or methodology deficiencies.

The best practices in the three references described here provide an abundance of information to prevent against and avoid such failure.

Getting a Forensic Schedule Analysis into Evidence (Expert Challenges)

An important consideration at the outset and throughout the preparation of a delay analysis is selection of an expert and getting the expert as well as his or her analysis through an in-court challenge. Furthermore, opposing counsel should consider and strategize from the outset of a dispute whether a pretrial challenge to the admissibility of expert testimony is proper under the circumstances. This section discusses the current state of the courts relating to expert requirements and challenges to experts, and examines several decisions related to expert challenges decided in courts throughout the country.

Two Main Standards

Daubert: Federal Courts and 41 States

The majority of state courts and all federal courts throughout the country subscribe to the expert standard espoused in *Daubert v. Merrell Dow Pharmaceuticals, Inc.* and its progeny or some modified form of *Daubert.*[14] The standard, based on Rule 702 of the Federal Rules of Evidence, asks the trial judge to utilize his or her role as "gatekeeper" and to determine whether the reasoning and methodology of an expert is reliable and relevant.[15]

As an additional matter, the Civilian Board of Contract Appeals and the Armed Services Board of Contract Appeals, while not bound by the Federal Rules of Civil Procedure, often look to the Federal Rules in making evidentiary rulings.[16] There are a number of decisions from both the Civilian Board of Contract Appeals and the Armed Services Board of Contract Appeals that utilized *Daubert* and Federal Rule of Evidence 702 in determining expert testimony admissibility.[17]

Frye: Used in Seven U.S. States and the District of Columbia

Seven states and the District of Columbia use the standard that preceded *Daubert* and that was espoused in *Frye v. United States.*[18] In short, this standard requires that the opinions espoused by the expert are based on scientific analysis or data that is considered to be "generally accepted" by others in the expert's discipline.[19]

---

14. *See* Daubert v. Merrell Pharm., Inc., 509 U.S. 579, 113 S. Ct. 2786 (1993); Gen. Electric Co. v. Joiner, 522 U.S. 127 (1997); Kumho Tire Co. Ltd v. Carmichael, 526 U.S. 137, 113 S. Ct. 1167 (1999) (expanding *Daubert* to all expert testimony).

15. *Kumho Tire*, 113 S. Ct. at 1173.

16. Rule 10 of the Armed Services Board of Contract Appeals provides "The parties may offer such evidence as they deem appropriate and as would be admissible under the Federal Rules of Evidence or in the sound discretion of the presiding Administrative Judge or examiner." Rules of Armed Services Board of Contract Appeals, Rule 10, 48 C.F.R. 2, app. A, pt. 2.

17. *See, e.g., In re* Universal Yacht Servs., Inc. ASBCA No 53951, 04-2 B.C.A. (CCH) ¶ 32648 (May 24, 2004).

18. Frye v. United States, 293 F. 1013 (D.C. Cir. 1923).

19. *Id.*

Challenges to Expert Testimony

Expert Qualifications Under *Daubert* (Rule 702)

Rule 702 of the Federal Rules of Evidence is the basis for admissibility of expert testimony in those courts where *Daubert* is utilized. Rule 702 of the Federal Rules of Evidence provides:

> A witness who is qualified as an expert by knowledge, skill, experience, training, or education may testify in the form of an opinion or otherwise if:
> (a) the expert's scientific, technical, or other specialized knowledge will help the trier of fact to understand the evidence or to determine a fact in issue;
> (b) the testimony is based on sufficient facts or data;
> (c) the testimony is the product of reliable principles and methods; and
> (d) the expert has reliably applied the principles and methods to the facts of the case.[20]

Rule 702 takes a "flexible" approach to admissibility of expert testimony, and courts utilize Rule 702, which has incorporated various Supreme Court precedents in determining whether to exclude expert testimony.[21]

Is the Witness Sufficiently Qualified as an Expert by Knowledge, Skill, Experience, Training, and Education?

The first consideration in determining expert admissibility is whether the expert is sufficiently qualified to testify about the particular topic. The particular expert put forth must be qualified to testify regarding the specific claim at issue.[22] In determining whether the expert is qualified, the court will examine whether the scope of the expert's testimony does not exceed the scope of the expert's experience and qualifications.[23] Several courts that have examined whether a particular expert was qualified to render certain opinions have ruled that lack of experience in one certain area of testimony should go to the weight of the expert's testimony and not its admissibility.[24]

Scientific, Technical, or Other Specialized Knowledge Will Help the Trier of Fact to Understand the Evidence or Determine a Fact at Issue

The second consideration of the court in determining expert admissibility is whether the testimony will aid the trier of fact in understanding the evidence of

20. Fed. R. Evid. 702.

21. *See, e.g., Kumho*, 119 S. Ct. 1167, 1176 ("[W]e conclude that the trial judge must have considerable leeway in deciding in a particular case[.]").

22. *See, e.g., In re* Paoli R.R. Yard PCb Litigation, 35 F.3d 717 (3d Cir. 1994).

23. *See, e.g.,* Wheeling Pittsburgh Steel Corp. v. Beelman River Terminals, Inc., 254 F.3d 706 (8th Cir. 2001).

24. U.S. v. Wen Chyu Liu, 716 F.3d 159 (5th Cir. 2013).

determining a fact at issue.[25] Thus, the expert's testimony must be considered relevant to be admissible. Often an expert's testimony is considered inadmissible if the testimony is considered common knowledge, is considered common sense, or espouses legal conclusions.[26] Furthermore, the expert's testimony must not rely on unsupported assumptions that are not supported by evidence.[27]

The Testimony Is Based on Sufficient Facts or Data (Sufficiency)

The third consideration of the court in determining expert admissibility is whether the testimony of the expert is based on sufficient facts or data. The consideration is "quantitative rather than qualitative in nature."[28] Challenges to the quality of the facts or data do not necessarily render the expert's opinion insufficient; rather those challenges often go to the weight to be given to the testimony—a question to be resolved by the jury.[29]

The Testimony Is a Product of Reliable Principles and Methods

When evaluating an expert opinion's reliability, the Supreme Court had originally instructed gatekeepers to "focus . . . solely on principles and methodology, not on the conclusions that they generate."[30] However, Rule 702 was revised in 2000 to make clear that the testimony most be both a product of reliable principles and methods as well as reliably applied to the principles and methods. As it relates to examining whether the principles and methods are reliable, the court may include the following factors: (1) whether the theory or technique has been, or can be, tested; (2) the method's known or potential rate of error; (3) whether the theory or technique has been subjected to peer review and publication; (4) the existence and maintenance of standards and controls; and (5) the degree to which it has been accepted—or not—by members of the relevant scientific community.[31] However, the U.S. Supreme Court has made clear that this list of factors is nonexclusive and, in line with the instruction that the Rule 702 analysis should be "flexible," likewise instructs courts to maintain flexibility in their analysis and that the list of factors is nonexclusive and is not required to be applied to every expert in every circumstance.[32]

25. Fed. R. Evid. 702.
26. *See, e.g.*, Rosenfield v. Oceania Cruises, Inc., 682 F.3d 1320 (11th Cir. 2012).
27. *See, e.g.*, Elock v. Kmart Corp., 233 F.3d 734 (11th Cir. 2000).
28. Fed. R. Evid. 702, Advisory Committee Notes on 2000 Amendment.
29. *Id.*
30. *Daubert*, 509 U.S. at 595.
31. *Id.*
32. Kumho Tire Co. Ltd. v. Carmichael, 113 S. Ct. 1167, 1175–76 (1999).

The Expert Has Reliably Applied the Relevant Principles and Methods to the Facts of the Case

The last inquiry a court will undertake in determining expert admissibility asks whether the expert has reliably applied the relevant principles and methods to the facts of the case.[33] The court will ask whether the methodology fits the legal and factual context of the case.[34] This includes insuring that the expert is not "cherry-picking" facts in formulating opinions.[35]

To Challenge or Not to Challenge

Once a case is underway and expert selection has begun, an important step for the construction lawyer is to undertake an analysis and strategize whether and when to make a potential expert challenge. This analysis and strategy will likely need to be revisited throughout the course of litigation as parties identify additional experts, discovery is exchanged, and expert opinions are provided.

In considering whether to challenge an expert, the construction lawyer should take into account the following considerations:

- What is the applicable law? Given that applicable law does vary, especially in those states that do not utilize FRE 702 and *Daubert*, it is important to understand and consider how the applicable law will impact an expert challenge.
- Case management leading up to challenge. Often, challenges are lodged at the close of expert discovery. However, counsel should consider the time the particular court could take to rule on its motion. For example, one study conducted in 2015 determined that, on average, federal courts take 84 days to rule on a *Daubert* motion.[36]
- Is the expert unqualified? Research the expert to determine the expert's background, experience, publications, and previous testimony. Keep a particular eye out for previous disqualification as well as conflicting testimony or ideas.
- Do the expert's opinions contain flaws in methodology/foundation?
- Does the jurisdiction require or favor a particular delay analysis methodology?
- Has the expert failed to follow/use accepted methodology?
- Has the expert chosen a method that cannot be tested or replicated?

---

33. Fed. R. Evid. 702.

34. *See, e.g.*, Lees v. Carthage Coll., 714 F.3d 516 (7th Cir. 2013).

35. *See, e.g.*, Barber v. United Airlines, Inc., 17 Fed. Appx 433 (7th Cir. 2001).

36. James C. Cooper, Timing and Disposition of Daubert Motions in Federal District Court: An Empirical Examination (George Mason University School of Law 2015).

- Has the expert relied on anecdotal evidence (and more)?
- Are there jurisdictional considerations? Research your judge and district to determine previous outcomes in similar cases and what, if any, particular arguments have impacted particular outcomes.
- What is the timing of the challenge?

In addition to strategizing and performing analysis as to whether to make a challenge against an expert, and when, the following are some considerations to take into account, which may counsel against making an expert challenge:

- Will the challenge expose our strategy prematurely?
- What are my client's resources, and how will making the challenge impact them?
- Would this be more impactful or better left for cross-examination? Often, especially in those courts that tend to not exclude expert evidentiary challenges, it may be more beneficial to save the argument for cross-examination. Making an expert challenge that is unsuccessful will certainly expose strategy for attacking an expert at trial and give opposing counsel opportunity to prepare its expert well in advance of trial on those issues.
- Is this type of expert generally accepted in the court or jurisdiction?
- Are there other jurisdictional considerations? After performing research on the judge or venue, you may determine that expert challenges are rarely granted. As such, if the chances of success are particularly low, it may be better to save the arguments for trial.

Case Law Examining Delay Experts

A number of cases have examined and/or undertaken challenges to scheduling experts. As previously discussed, performing a delay analysis is a mix of science, experience, and knowledge. This section reviews jurisprudence from a number of venues where there have been specific challenges to delay experts and/or their analyses.

Qualification Challenges[37]

In *Mactec, Inc. v. Bechtel Jacobs Co., LLC*, the district court considered a challenge to the qualifications of the defense damages expert.[38] In that case, defendant's damages expert had also expressed an opinion regarding the CPM analysis performed

37. *See, e.g.*, Handex of Maryland, Inc. v. Waste Mgmt. Disposal Servs. of Maryland, Nos. AW-05-1044, AW-05-2584, 2018 WL 11363273 (S.D. Md. Feb. 11, 2008); Weitz Co., LLC v. MacKenzie House, LLC, No. 07-0103-CV-W-ODS, 2009 WL 4030756 (W.D. Mo. Nov. 19, 2009).

38. Mactec, Inc. v. Bechtel Jacobs Co., LLC, Nos. 3:05-CV-255; 3:06-CV-265 2008 WL 250518, at *1 (E.D. Tenn. Jan. 28, 2008).

by plaintiff's delay expert.[39] Specifically, defendant's expert opined that plaintiff's expert failed "to properly perform a CPM analysis by failing to properly determine whether delays in construction were critical and by failing to determine the cause of the delays."[40] Plaintiff argued defendant's expert lacked qualifications to make the opinions related to the CPM analysis.[41] In denying plaintiff's motion to exclude defendant's expert, the district court explained that while defendant's expert admittedly was not a CPM expert, he "has sufficient knowledge, experience, and training in working with construction claims and other CPM experts to offer the limited analysis represented in his opinions."[42]

In *United States of America for the Use and Benefit of M.L. Young Construction Corp. v. The Austin Company*, the district court considered a challenge to the qualifications of plaintiff's scheduling and damage expert.[43] Defendant argued that the plaintiff's expert was not qualified to opine relating to delay, causes of delay, and associated damage because he had not authored any articles relating to delay damages or scheduling and because he lacked experience related to "the type involved in [the] case."[44] The court first analyzed the expert's resume and determined that he had 30 years of on-site construction experience, including government contract experience (the subject of the suit related to a government project).[45] It further determined the expert had experience related to developing work schedules and had "analyzed construction projects involving construction schedules and delays."[46] Third, the court commented that the expert in question was a licensed professional engineer and had degrees in civil engineering and business administration.[47] Finally, the court explained that the expert's experience as a "litigation consultant or expert witness has involved numerous disputes involving construction projects."[48] The court then reasoned that just because the expert had not been published was not alone a basis for disqualifying the expert from testifying. Further, the court held that the expert had the necessary qualifications to testify.[49]

---

39. *Id.*
40. *Id.* at *2.
41. *Id.*
42. *Id.*
43. *U.S. for the Use and Benefit of M.L. Young Constr. Corp. v. The Austin Co.*, No. CIV-04-0078-T, 2005 WL 60000505, at *1 (W.D. Okla. Sep. 29, 2005).
44. *Id.* at *2.
45. *Id.*
46. *Id.*
47. *Id.*
48. *Id.* at *2.
49. *Id.* at *3.

Relevancy and Reliability[50]

In *E. Allen Reeves, Inc. v. Michael Graves & Associates, Inc.*, the district court addressed plaintiff's arguments that defendant's expert's opinions relating to project delays were unreliable. Plaintiff argued the expert failed to prepare his own schedule analysis and primarily relied upon material contained in the report prepared by plaintiff's expert.[51] The district court, in denying plaintiff's motion to the extent it sought to exclude the testimony, explained that the testimony and opinions were admissible and that the expert's report "is not inherently unreliable simply because he look[ed] to another expert's opinion and primarily refuted that opinion using other materials typically relied upon by experts in the field."[52]

In *GLF v. Fedcon Joint Venture*, the district court addressed a *Daubert* challenge asserted by plaintiff that argued that defendant's scheduling expert's opinions were unreliable because she had "impermissibly base[d] her opinions on inapplicable schedules that plaintiff was not bound to follow."[53] Plaintiff argued that the schedules the expert relied upon in formulating her opinions were early completion schedules and were not applicable to the plaintiff.[54] As such, plaintiff argued the expert's methodology was unreliable and her testimony would not assist the trier of fact.[55] In opposing the motion, defendants argued the schedule analyzed was the project schedule and that plaintiff's motion was merely raising a factual dispute over which schedules on the project were applicable.[56] In denying plaintiff's motion, the district court agreed and explained that the motion "mainly represents a factual dispute between the parties that implicates the weight of the evidence and testimony."[57]

In *Hutton Contracting Co., Inc. v. City of Coffeyville*, the court examined whether to exclude plaintiff's expert's opinion. Relating to the opinions expressed by plaintiff's expert regarding weather-related extensions and extensions for inability to provide certain materials, the expert's opinion was based on custom and the

50. *See also* Petrobas America, Inc. v. Vicinay Cadenas, S.A., No. H-12-888, 202 WL 11192911 (S.D. Tex. Apr. 30, 2020); RLI Ins. Co. v. Indian River Sch. Dist., No. 05-858-JJF, 2007 WL 4292109 (D. Del. Dec. 4, 2007).

51. E. Allen Reeves, Inc. v. Michael Graves & Assoc., Inc., No. 10-1393-MAS-TJB, 2015 WK 105825, at *1 (D.N.J. Jan. 7, 2015).

52. *Id.* at *6.

53. GLF Constr. Corp. v. Fedcon JV et al., No. 8:17-cv-1932-T-36AAS, 2019 WL 7423552, at *1 (M.D. Fla. Oct. 15, 2019).

54. *Id.* at *4.

55. *Id.*

56. *Id.*

57. *Id.*

expert's own experience rather than on the language in the contract.[58] As such, the court found the testimony and opinions were not relevant and contained legal conclusions that were inadmissible.[59]

Preparing the Delay Analysis: A Three-Stage Process

This section focuses on the delay expert's preparation of the delay analysis and three general stages that are typically undertaken: (1) source validation; (2) method selection; and (3) delay analysis and report preparation. Following are best practices and potential pitfalls to avoid in each of these three stages.

Stage 1: Source Validation

An important first step in the preparation of a delay analysis is the process of source validation, which the AACE RP states is to provide guidance in the process of assuring the validity of the source input data that forms the foundation of the schedule analysis.[60] To avoid against such "garbage in, garbage out" errors, it is essential for the delay expert to review and validate at least the following input information alongside other contemporaneous project records:

- Baseline schedule;
- Contemporaneous schedule updates; and
- As-built schedule.

The goal of the source validation step is to objectively conclude that the input project schedule information is suitable for analysis. Once source validation has been performed, the delay expert should be able to confirm that the input schedules, at a minimum:

- Are reasonably complete and representative of the entire project scope;
- Generally conform with the contract milestones and substantial completion date;
- Generally conform with other relevant contract requirements, including the scheduling provisions;
- Contain clear and reasonable critical and near-critical paths of work;
- Are sufficiently detailed based on the size and complexity of the project;
- Contain reasonable schedule logic, work sequences, and activity durations;

58. Hutton Contracting Co., Inc. v. City of Coffeyville, No. 02-4130-JAR, 2004 WL 2203449, at *11 (D. Kan. Sep. 24, 2004).

59. *Id.* at *12–16.

60. AACE RP 29R-03 (2011), at 18.

- Contain complete and accurate as-built information for completed activities; and
- Represent the contractor's best understanding of the project's requirements and its means and methods for delivering the project.

Throughout the project, the number of schedule activities may increase as the contractor's understanding of the project requirements improves and the project schedule becomes further detailed or refined. Source validation is an iterative process: It should be performed at each stage of the delay analysis to ensure the delay analysis results are consistent to actual project events.

If the delay expert suspects that the schedules are flawed, then under reasonable circumstances it is advisable for the delay expert to make corrections or modifications to the schedules rather than rejecting them altogether[61] or performing an analysis using a less preferred method.[62] In such cases, the delay expert should not only clearly describe the specific modifications made to the schedules but also their effects on the project's critical path and schedule float for relevant work activities. On the other hand, if the delay expert concludes that the project schedules are manipulated, incomplete, or contain irreparable flaws, then it may not be possible to perform a complete CPM delay analysis relying on the project schedules. In such cases, the expert may choose to perform or supplement the delay analysis using one of the following:

- As-built summation based on information in the daily field reports and other contemporaneously prepared source records;
- Detailed bar chart or as-planned/as-built delay analysis; or
- Total time or high-level project milestone analysis.

Before undertaking a less-preferred option, the expert should consult with counsel to ensure that such a delay analysis will meet the standard of proof required.

In summary, there is no "perfect" schedule. After performing source validation, the expert should conclude that the schedules are reasonably accurate, objectively updated, contemporaneously reviewed, and reflect the best understanding and intentions of the parties throughout construction.

Stage 2: Delay Analysis Method Selection

When the delay expert has reviewed the input data and determined it to be suitable for analysis, she then must select a delay analysis method. Counsel should be aware that *not all delay analysis methods are the same* and should thoroughly examine the

61. ASCE 67-17, at 10.
62. Dale & D'Onofrio, *supra* note 7, § 12:2, at 632.

delay expert's reasoning for selecting a particular delay analysis method. Selecting the appropriate delay analysis method is a deliberate and informed process that should consider relevant information such as:

- Contract provisions;
- Stage of the project (in-progress or completed);
- Scheduling software requirements;
- Availability of other contemporaneous project records;
- Nature of delays and issues in dispute;
- Stage of dispute; and
- Time (or budget) available.

After considering this information, the delay expert should select the delay analysis method that is the most preferred *and* suitable for the given project. Table 6.4 references the preferential ranking of the delay analysis methods indicated in *Construction Schedule Delays.*[63]

TABLE 6.4 Delay Analysis Methods Ranked by Order of Preference

1	Time impact analysis (TIA)
2	Windows (unadjusted)
3	Prospective time impact analysis
4	Collapsed as-built
5	As-built critical path
6	Impacted as-planned
7	Total time / as-planned vs. as-built

When the delay expert has selected the delay analysis method, it may be helpful for counsel and expert to discuss underlying reasons for the decision:

- What observations has the delay expert made relative to the applicable contract provisions?
- What observations has the delay expert made relative to the input project schedules?
- Why, specifically, has the delay expert chosen the particular delay analysis method over other delay analysis methods?

63. *Id.*

- How does the delay expert intend to identify criticality and measure project delays?
- Might the particular delay analysis method selected affect counsel's negotiations or legal strategy?

Stage 3: Delay Analysis and Report Preparation

The remainder of this chapter is devoted to discussing five common delay methods, their various strengths and other qualities as indicated in prevailing literature:

- Time impact analysis
- Contemporaneous analysis using "windows"
- Collapsed as-built
- Impacted as-planned analysis
- Total time or as-planned as-built analysis

Method 1: Time Impact Analysis

Although the specific steps for preparing a delay analysis using the TIA method may vary, it is generally the method most accepted by U.S. courts and boards as described previously. As with any delay analysis, when presented with a TIA, counsel should become familiar with the general procedure used to prepare the delay analysis and consult with the schedule expert to understand if the procedure conforms with best practices. Counsel should also consider the following when asserting or defending against delay claims reliant on the TIA method:

Strengths and Weaknesses of the TIA Method

The TIA's greatest strength is that it takes into consideration changes to the critical path as they occur on the project through its periodic-analysis approach. A properly prepared TIA using regularly scheduled updates logically should minimize delay measurement errors. The method also will account for critical path shifts and accurately quantify concurrent delays and acceleration—schedule delay types that other analysis methods are unsuitable to reliably evaluate.

A "properly adjusted" TIA, the most widely accepted by U.S. courts and boards, is one that contemporaneously accounts for excusable delays.[64] TIAs are extremely sensitive to the order in which the fragnets are inserted into the schedule. For instance, two events that cause delays to a tracked milestone, insertion of the first fragnet can create float for the other fragnet when it is inserted and may mask some or all of the second inserted fragnet's effects.[65]

64. *Id.* at 627.
65. AACE CDR-3567, The Law of Forensic Delay Analysis, Derauf & Livengood, at 24.

The TIA is known as a "cause and effect" analysis as it begins with an assumption of the cause of the delay—the delay event itself or fragnet. Equally important however are the delay events that may not be modeled and thus sidestep proper evaluation. Does the TIA analysis reasonably include all noteworthy delay events? If not, which events were left out and why? These are fundamental questions the TIA must address.

Key Considerations

Counsel should understand the assumptions underpinning the TIA analysis and question the expert who prepared the analysis. While not an exhaustive list, counsel should consider the following:

- Are the TIA's delay events calculated before and after the delays occurred, or as of the data date of each schedule update? Would the distinction cause a difference to the delays calculated?
- Is the TIA prepared in conformance with contract requirements and industry best practices?
- Does the TIA rely on "hindsight" or "blindsight" durations?
- Does the analysis include all noteworthy delay events?
- Which other noteworthy delay events were not modeled into the TIA analysis?
- Is the analysis replicable? Given the same set of schedules and assumptions, would another expert produce the same results?
- Is the analysis, called a TIA, actually an impacted as-planned, similar but less rigorous and less favored delay method?

Method 2: Contemporaneous "Windows" Analysis

Though not the most preferred method, contemporaneous windows analysis is generally considered among the most preferred delay analysis methods.[66] However, the term "windows" is a vague descriptor and can be used to hide analysis shortcomings. A windows analysis can include most any study that subdivides the construction period into smaller periods of time. Because not all windows analyses are created equal, as with any delay analysis, counsel should be familiar with the specific procedure used and understand if it was prepared using best practices.

Strengths and Weaknesses of the Contemporaneous Windows Method

The contemporaneous windows analysis is known as an "effect and cause" analysis because delays are first measured in the project schedule and the causes of the delays are later determined. Like the TIA, the contemporaneous windows analysis

66. Dale & D'Onofrio, *supra* note 7, at 632, method ranking table.

is reliant on CPM schedule logic. In fact, the only difference between the TIA method and the contemporaneous windows method is that "the windows method typically uses the schedule updates as they were submitted and does not adjust the requirement contract completion date to reflect excusable delay as it occurs. As a result, the float values on the work may often become inaccurate and make it difficult to determine which work was critical. Consequently, users of this method typically only acknowledge delay that falls on the longest path as opposed to any critical path. This method sometimes is referred to as a contemporaneous period analysis."[67]

The contemporaneous windows method is among the more reliable delay analysis methods because it considers *dynamic* changes to the project's critical path. Critical path shifts can occur when revisions are made to the project schedule through the normal updating process, when critical work is delayed, or when other changes are realized in the schedule. A schedule update reflecting significant project revisions or changed construction methods, often called a "rebaseline schedule," logically becomes the starting point in the next period of focus.

An important distinction of the contemporaneous windows method is that, unlike the TIA method, it is retrospective only: It cannot be used to forecast the effects of ongoing delays or project changes like the TIA method. Additionally, when many changes are made to the project schedules and frequent critical path shifts occur, the contemporaneous windows can produce "mathematically correct" but convoluted results that are difficult to explain. As with any delay analysis, corroboration by other contemporaneous project records that describe what actually happened is essential.

Key Considerations

Counsel should understand the assumptions underpinning the contemporaneous windows analysis. While not an exhaustive list, counsel should consider the following:

- Were all of the schedule updates used in the analysis? If not, why were some schedules omitted?
- Do the windows cover all of the delays in dispute?
- Specifically, how was criticality determined? Was the rationale followed consistently throughout the analysis?
- Does the analysis clearly distinguish and account for *contemporaneous schedule delays* and *forecasted schedule impacts to future critical work activities*?

---

67. *Id.* at 284–85.

Method 3: Collapsed As-Built

The collapsed as-built (CAB), also known as a "but for" analysis, takes the project as it was actually built and subtracts impacts to show what would have happened if those impacts had not occurred. The analysis begins with, and is reliant on, an accurate as-built schedule. Using this, the analyst creates a CPM model through insertion of identified logic connections. The resulting schedule is intended to reflect, as closely as possible, the CPM logic and durations that were used to build the project. The analyst then removes selected delay activities identified as being delay activities that are the responsibility of the opposing party and recalculates the schedule to show what would have happened "but for" the delaying event.[68]

The CAB analysis method may be used on a builder's risk insurance claim for which an incomplete project experiences an insured loss due to delay. In such an instance, the builder's risk expert will review the pre-loss and post-loss schedules to determine when the project or event "would have finished had the loss not occurred. In this review, they may find the project was already delayed due to factors unrelated to the loss prior to the loss occurring."[69]

Strengths and Weaknesses of the CAB Method

The "but for" schedule analysis may be effective in situations where contemporaneous updates or a baseline schedule does not exist. Other schedule analysis models rely heavily on schedule data, so when it is not available the collapsed as-built approach provides a path forward.[70]

The CAB method is well suited for the identification of concurrency. Because the CPM model, based on the as-built schedule, contains all delays and events that occurred on the project, the post-extraction schedule will show the impact of all delays that were left in the model, thereby accounting for possible concurrency.[71]

The CAB method is less suited for dealing with acceleration or delay mitigation. Because acceleration or mitigation that *actually occurred* is built into the as-built CPM model, the resulting schedule will still retain their effects once the delay events are removed. However, it may be possible, if sufficient contemporaneous detail exists, to correct the CAB model or address acceleration and mitigation efforts separately.

---

68. AACE CDR-3567, The Law of Forensic Delay Analysis, Derauf & Livengood, at 26.

69. Diane Zimmer & Chaz Mello, *How Do Builder's Risk Claims Differ from Property Damage Claims?*, JS Held 4 (2020).

70. Andrew Sargent, *But-For Construction Delay Analysis—The Collapsed As-Built Method*, Vertex (Jan. 13, 2021), https://vertexeng.com/insights/but-for-construction-delay-analysis-the-collapsed-as-built-method/.

71. AACE CDR-3567, The Law of Forensic Delay Analysis, Derauf & Livengood, at 27.

Key Considerations

Counsel should understand the assumptions underpinning the CAB model. While not an exhaustive list, counsel should consider the following:

- Are the purported delay events removed from the schedule in the CAB analysis single activities or "fragnets" (multiple activities)?
- Which logic relationships are assumed both before and after the activities are removed?
- In which order are delay events removed from the CAB model?
- Has the analysis stated and applied consistent rules for establishing preferential logic in each period?

Method 4: Impacted As-Planned Analysis

The impacted as-planned analysis (IAP) method can be used both prospectively and after-the-fact. The IAP method is considered a "static" approach that does not consider the dynamic effects of a changed critical path.[72] This is because the IAP method relies on only one baseline or planned schedule. In the IAP method, known delay events (fragnets) are modeled as one or more schedule activities and inserted into the schedule. The resulting "impact" to the project's completion date is attributed to the known events.

Strengths and Weaknesses of the IAP Method

The IAP is often preferred by contractors because it is simple to prepare relative to more rigorous delay methods. Also, unlike other analysis methods, the IAP does not require an as-built schedule or contemporaneous schedule updates. Results based on the IAP method are highly dependent on the accuracy of the baseline schedule and the order in which impacts are inserted. The IAP method frequently is not accepted by U.S. courts and boards because it fails to consider:[73]

- Own party's delays and impacts;
- Actual progress, project events, and information;
- Shifts in the critical path; and
- Concurrent delays.

The IAP method is also faulted for the relative ease that delays can be exaggerated.

---

72. AACE RP 29R-03 (2011), at 13.
73. Dale & D'Onofrio, *supra* note 1, at 528.

Key Considerations

- How much time elapsed between the date of the schedule used in the IAP analysis and when the purported delay events occurred? (Generally, the less time, the better.)
- How much time elapsed between the start of the delay event and the completion of the delay event?
- Does the IAP rely on "hindsight" or "blindsight" duration assumptions?
- Which other activities were performed and completed during the IAP's impact period? Do they have relevance?

Method 5: Total Time or As-Planned As-Built Analysis

The total time, or as-planned as-built (APAB), analysis is perhaps the original delay analysis method. This method compares the project's as-planned schedule with its actual, or as-built schedule. The method doesn't rely on CPM logic and can merely be a study of the variance of activity start and finish dates.[74] Like the IAP method, the total time method is considered a "static" approach that does not consider the dynamic effects of a changed critical path.[75] Such changes must be determined by the analyst, which can raise questions of subjectivity. This is because the method only relies on a single baseline or as-planned schedule that does not incorporate changed logic or project conditions that were realized later in time.

Strengths and Weaknesses of the APAB Method

The total time method may be relatively straightforward to prepare and easy to explain. However, it is not suitable for projects where acceleration, concurrent delays, or pacing delays are at issue. The total time method is generally disfavored because it is not reliant on CPM logic and it "does not involve any investigation of the delay period or efforts to allocate concurrent or overlapping delays. Instead, causation for delay is generally assumed with little analysis of responsibility for delay causing events. As a result, use of the total time approach can run afoul of a claimant's obligation to prove causation."[76]

Still, the APAB, or total time, method may be the only option when schedule updates do not exist or when they do not include important changes, project events, or revised construction means and methods. As the method least accepted by U.S. courts and boards, the practitioner must carefully weigh the risks involved with asserting or defending against delay claims using this method.

---

74. AACE RP 29R-03 (2011), p. 39.
75. *Id.* at 13.
76. Dale & D'Onofrio, *supra* note 1, at 582.

Key Considerations

- Has the correct, complete, and approved as-planned schedule been used?
- Was the project built in a substantially different manner than planned?
- Are there concurrent delays, acceleration, or pacing delays at issue?
- What are the specific reasons for using this approach?
- Do the delays or quality of available schedule information make it impossible or highly impracticable to use another delay analysis method?

CHAPTER 7

Owner Defenses to Contractor Delay Claims

Laurie Choi

Project delays can present numerous and significant problems for developers of construction projects. Owners may suffer unrealized lost revenue and profits while a project remains incomplete, be at risk of being in breach of separate agreements, such as lease agreements with the property owner, and face issues with project lenders when a project is not completed on time, to name of few of these potential issues. Additionally, contractor claims for delay may create further exposure of delay damages.

The first lines of defense include making sure construction contracts appropriately incentivize timely completion and protect the owner from exposure for contractor claims for delay and to manage the contractor and schedule proactively during the project. However, at the end of the day, most owner-contractor agreements leave open the possibility and risk of contractor delay claims. This chapter addresses strategies for owners' defenses in such situations.

Failure to Comply with Contractual Notice Requirements

Most commercial construction contracts require the contractor to provide the owner with notice of delays and delay claims. Such notice provisions typically require the notice to be in writing, in a certain form, and provided to the owner and/or another specifically designated person or party, within a defined time period. Notice provisions often provide that the failure to provide notice will result in a waiver or forfeiture of any claim for delay damages. Notice requirements may be set forth in the contract itself or, in the case of federal projects, by regulation.[1]

The legal ramifications of a lack of notice, or the failure to adhere to or comply with the contract notice requirements, vary across jurisdictions. Some jurisdictions

1. *See* 48 C.F.R. § 52.243-4.

remain strict in their interpretation and enforcement of contractual notice provisions, while others adopt the more flexible or equitable approach taken by courts and boards having jurisdiction over federal contracts, which tend to find that delay claims are barred only when the government or owner is materially prejudiced as a result of the lack of notice.

Strict Interpretation and Enforcement

A minority of jurisdictions strictly interpret and enforce notice provisions, particularly those provisions that explicitly state that compliance with the notice requirement is a "condition precedent" to bringing a delay claim, or explicitly set forth the consequences of a failure to strictly comply with the notice requirements.[2] A few jurisdictions have held that actual notice is not an exception to a failure to comply with contractual notice requirements.[3]

Exceptions to Strict Compliance

"Substantial" Compliance with Notice Requirements Is Sufficient

Where a contractual notice provision does not clearly and unambiguously make compliance a "condition precedent" to the contractor's right to assert a delay claim, some courts allow the claim on the grounds that the contractor had "substantially" complied with the contractual notice requirements. In *Balfour Beatty Rail Inc. v. Kansas City S. Ry. Co.*, Balfour Beatty Rail, Inc. (BBRI) sought to recover delay damages from the owner, The Kansas City Southern Railway Company (KCSR), for delays experienced on a Texas railway project.[4] KCSR filed a motion for partial summary judgment on the ground that BBRI was not entitled to claim delay

---

2. *See, e.g.*, Tuttle/White Constructors, Inc. v. State, Dep't of General Services, 371 So. 2d 1096 (Fla. 1st DCA 1979) (enforcing notice provision stating that failure to submit claim within 20 days after the occurrence of the event giving rise to the claim "shall be waived or deemed invalid"); *American Mfrs. Mut. Ins. Co. v. Payton Lane Nursing Home, Inc.*, 2010 WL 144426, at *15 (E.D.N.Y. Jan. 11, 2010) (discussing cases in which courts have required strict compliance with notice provisions where such provisions specifically state that a claim is waived if the notice requirements are not followed); Kingsley Arms, Inc. v. Sano Rubin Constr. Co., 16 A.D.3d 813, 791 N.Y.S.2d 196, 197–98 (2005) (finding contractor waived delay claim due to failure to strictly comply with notice provisions that expressly stated that compliance with notice requirements was a condition precedent to asserting such a claim); F. Garofalo Elec. Co. v. New York Univ., 270 A.D.2d 76, 705 N.Y.S.2d 327 (2000) (finding contract's notice and documentation requirements for delay damages were condition precedents to contractor's recovery and failure to strictly comply waived such claims).

3. *See, e.g.*, Commonwealth v. AMEC Civil, LLC, 699 S.E.2d 499, 506 (Va. 2010) (holding that actual notice is not sufficient to satisfy the written claim notice requirement in statute); Mike M. Johnson, Inc. v. Cnty. of Spokane, 150 Wash. 2d 375, 78 P.3d 161, 167–68 (2003) (holding that actual notice is not an exception to compliance with mandatory contractual claim provisions).

4. Balfour Beatty Rail, Inc. v. Kansas City S. Ry. Co., 2012 WL 3100833 (N.D. Tex. July 31, 2012).

damages since it failed to notify KCSR of "delay days," failed to maintain records of "delay days," and failed to meet with KCSR to discuss and agree on "delay days" in accordance with the contract.[5] The U.S. District Court for the Northern District of Texas, applying Texas law, determined that the contract language did not expressly condition BBRI's right to recover delay damages on compliance with the notice requirements.[6] The court also stated that "substantial" compliance with the notice requirements is sufficient where the contract does not specifically require strict compliance as a condition precedent to the contractor's right to recover delay damages:

> [B]ecause the Contract does not expressly require strict compliance in providing notice of project delays, maintaining records, or participating in periodic meetings to discuss delays, the court disagrees that absolute literal compliance was required. In situations where the parties' contract does not expressly require strict compliance with the contract's terms, substantial compliance is sufficient.[7]

The court held that BBRI's letters, emails, and daily reports exchanged during the project kept KCSR apprised of BBRI's potential delays so that KCSR could "monitor progress and address issues during the progress," thereby raising a genuine issue of material fact as to whether BBRI substantially complied with the contractual notice provisions.[8]

Owner Must Be Materially Prejudiced by Lack of Notice

The U.S. Court of Federal Claims and some states have taken a more flexible approach to interpreting notice requirements. These jurisdictions have embraced the premise espoused in *Hoel-Steffen Construction Co. v. United States*,[9] which is that adopting a narrow application of the notice requirements "would be out of tune with the language and purpose of the notice provisions, as well as with this court's wholesome concern that notice provisions in contract-adjustment clauses not be applied too technically and illiberally where the Government is quite aware of the operative facts."[10] The analysis of whether the government or owner was prejudiced

5. *Id.* at *4. The contract stated, in part: "If such failure by the Company prevents Contractor's crews from working more than 4 hours during a day (each such occurrence referred to as a 'Delay Day'), then Contractor shall notify railroad of such delay and reason therefore." *Id.* The contract also contained a detailed provision on the required form and means of providing notice under the contract. *Id.* at *6.

6. *Id.* at *6.

7. *Id.* at 8.

8. *Id.* at *8–9.

9. 456 F.2d 760, 767–68 (Ct. Cl. 1972).

10. *See also* K-Con Bldg. Sys., Inc. v. United States, 131 Fed. Cl. 275, 321 (2017) (declining to apply notice requirement strictly, stating, "binding precedent suggests that courts should apply a contract's notice clauses with a certain measure of flexibility").

by the lack of compliance with the contractual notice requirements often turns on evidence that the government or owner had actual or imputed knowledge of the facts giving rise to the contractor's delay claim, such as was the case in *Hoel-Steffen* and its progeny. In *Seaboard Lumber Co. v. United States*,[11] the Court of Federal Claims succinctly explained the rationale behind the liberal approach to enforcing notice requirements in government construction contracts:

> The purpose of notice in these cases was to permit the government to resolve, for example, differing site conditions short of the necessity of a claim, or to mitigate costs to the contractor of a government-caused delay. What they have in common is the government's independent ability to react to knowledge of facts. Whether notice is constructive or written, therefore, is not critical. Instead, the question is whether the lack of notice caused any real prejudice to the government's ability either to defend against the contractor's claim, or to limit damages.

In *James Corp. v. North Allegheny School District*, the Pennsylvania Commonwealth Court cited *Hoel-Steffen* in finding that the contractor's acceleration claim was not barred as a result of its failure to make a timely claim because the school district "knew of the operative facts giving rise to the construction delays."[12] Similarly, in *American Electric Co., LLC v. Parsons RCI, Inc.*, the U.S. District Court for the District of Hawaii predicted that Hawaii courts would adopt what it viewed to be the "purpose-based" interpretation of contract notice requirements, which does not strictly enforce notice provisions "absent evidence that the party claiming no notice was materially prejudiced by not receiving it," as opposed to the "more literal or formalistic approach to notice provisions" that requires strict compliance.[13]

Waiver of Lack of Notice Defense: Owner Considered Merits of Delay Claim

Negotiating a claim on its merits without raising the defense of lack of notice can, in some circumstances, operate as a waiver of the owner's defense. This principle is

11. 45 Fed. Cl. 404, 407 (1999).

12. James Corp. v. North Allegheny Sch. Dist., 938 A.2d 474, 485–87 (Pa. Commw. Ct. 2007); *see also* John Spearly Constr., Inc. v. Penns Valley Area Sch. Dist., 121 A.3d 593 (Pa. Commw. Ct. 2015); *but see* Allgood Elec. Co., Inc. v. Martin K. Eby Constr. Co., 959 F. Supp. 1573 (M.D. Ga. 1997) (finding that even though subcontractor's letters may have qualified as "adequate" notices under the notice provisions to alert contractor of the delays, subcontractor's notices were untimely since they were not submitted until six months had elapsed, which was long after the time periods specified in the notice provisions).

13. American Elec. Co., LLC v. Parsons RCI, Inc., 2014 WL 12573012, at *5–6 (D. Haw. June 4, 2014).

particularly true in federal contracts[14] and has some support in state law as well.[15] The Arizona case of *Chaney Building Co. v. Sunnyside School District No. 12* articulates this principle.[16] There, Chaney Building Co. sought to recover contract payments withheld for performance delay. Chaney was required to provide seven days' written notice at the beginning of any delay but there was no evidence that Chaney had done so. Despite the lack of notice, Sunnyside considered the delay, ultimately to its detriment. In reversing the trial court, the appellate court stated:

> No request for an extension of time was made within the 7-day written notice provision, and Sunnyside might have decided to reject the entire claim for a 90-day extension based on this reason alone. But once Sunnyside undertook to determine and decide the merits of the claim supporting the request for the 90-day extension, as shown by the evidence in exhibits listed above, a jury could infer they waived strict compliance with the 7-day written notice provision.[17]

Cause of Delay Is Contractor's Responsibility

Generally, a contractor seeking to recover delay damages has the burden to prove that the owner is the proximate cause of the delay that allegedly produced the damages that the contractor is seeking to recover. In *PCL Construction Services, Inc.*, the Court of Federal Claims articulated the contractor's burden of proof as follows:

> In order to recover for an alleged compensable delay, whether or not the delay is caused by hindrance, a contractor must demonstrate: (1) the extent of the delay with a reasonable degree of accuracy; (2) that the delay proximately was caused solely by the government's actions; and (3) that the delay caused specific,

14. *Appeal of Korshoj Constr. Co.*, 1963 B.C.A. (CCH) ¶ 3848 (Aug. 27, 1963) (finding that failure to strictly adhere to notice requirement will not be fatal when contracting officer actually considered the contractor's claim on its merits without invoking the protest or notice requirement); *Appeal of James Hamilton Constr. Co.*, 68-2 B.C.A. (CCH) ¶ 7127 (July 18, 1968) (stating "even if appellant unreasonably delayed in giving formal notice of its claim, prompt notice is unnecessary where, as here, the contracting officer, in fact knew of the circumstances that form the basis of the claim, actually considered the claim on its merits without protesting appellant's lack of timeliness").

15. Metropolitan Paving Co. v. City of Aurora, Colo., 449 F.2d 177 (10th Cir. 1971) (owner considered claim on the merits and therefore could not later raise a notice defense); *but see* Mike M. Johnson, Inc. v. Cnty. of Spokane, 78 P.3d 161 (2003) (County did not waive contractual claim procedures by corresponding and attending negotiations with contractor concerning problems contractor had when County correspondence repeatedly informed contractor that County did not waive claims, defenses or other remedies or contract provisions.); Dan Nelson Constr., Inc. v. Nodland & Dickson, 608 N.W.2d 267, 276 (under Wyoming law active settlement negotiations with the government are insufficient to estop the government from defending on the basis of the failure to timely file a claim).

16. Chaney Bldg. Co., Inc. v. Sunnyside Sch. Dist., No. 12, 709 P.2d 904 (Ariz. Ct. App. 1985).

17. *Id.* at 907.

> quantifiable injury to the contractor. The burden of establishing these factors falls squarely upon the contractor. Moreover, "[o]nly if the delay was caused *solely* by the government will the contractor be entitled to both an extension of time within which to perform, and recovery of excess costs associated with the delay."[18]

Given the contractor's burden of proving the owner is the sole cause of the delay that gave rise to the claimed damages, the owner, in defense, may be able to defeat the contractor's claim by challenging the sufficiency of the evidence proffered by the contractor regarding who or what caused the delay in question,[19] or by proffering its own evidence that the contractor in fact was responsible, in whole or in part, for the delay.

In *Prestex, Inc. v. United States*,[20] for example, the court found that a government procurement agent's promise to extend the delivery schedule was invalid and unenforceable because the procurement agent lacked the authority to make such promise and because it conflicted with the subsequent written contract. The court also held that the contractor was responsible for the delays caused by its suppliers even though the delays were caused by extensive government textile buying and the government price controls existing at the time of the contract.[21]

Concurrent Delays

Concept of Concurrent Delay

A concurrent delay is when two or more delays to the critical path—delays that extend the completion date—occur in the same general time period as a result of independent causes.[22] Concurrent delays arise, for example, when the owner and

---

18. 47 Fed. Cl. 745, 801 (2000) (citations omitted). *See also* George Sollitt Constr. Co. v. U.S., 64 Fed. Cl. 229, 238 (2005) ("For the government to be found to have caused compensable delay, the general rule is that the government must have been the *sole* proximate cause of the contractor's additional loss, and the contractor would not have been delayed for *any other reason* during that period.") (citing Triax-Pacific v. Stone, 958 F.2d 351, 354 (Fed. Cir. 1992) (quotations omitted)).

19. *See, e.g.*, ADP Marshall, Inc. v. Noresco, LLC, 710 F. Supp. 2d 197, 226–27 (D.R.I. 2010) (finding that subcontractor's expert failed to support delay claim against general contractor as testimony neither shed light on the cause of the delays nor ascribed responsibility for delays to a particular party); *see also* Blinderman Constr. Co., Inc. v. U.S., 39 Fed. Cl. 529, 544 (1997) (plaintiff failure to timely submit contractually required CQC plan cast doubt as to whether government was sole cause of the delay).

20. 3 Cl. Ct. 373 (1983).

21. Prestex, Inc. v. United States, 3 Cl. Ct. at 382.

22. As one decision states:

> The exact definition of concurrent delay is not readily apparent from its use in contract law, although it is a term which has both temporal and causation aspects. Concurrent delays affect the same "delay period." *See* Tyger Constr. Co. v. United States, 31 Fed. Cl. 177, 259 (1994) ("In cases of concurrent delay, where both parties contributed significantly to the delay period by separate and distinct actions, justice requires that the

the contractor are each responsible for a critical-path delay during the same time period and one or both parties assert a claim for delay damages against the other. The owner may take the position that the contractor is also responsible for an independent critical-path delay, meaning that the contractor's delay is not compensable. Often, the relevant agreement will include a specific waiver of the contractor's right to relief where excusable delays run concurrently with contractor-caused delays. The following subsections address how courts view such claims in the absence of express contract language.

Traditional Approach—Neither Party Recovers

Historically, courts faced with concurrent delays concluded that neither party could recover delay damages if they both contributed to the delay.[23] This approach eliminated the need for the courts to engage in the more difficult analysis as to whether and to what extent the claimed delays could be apportioned between the parties.

Modern Approach—Apportionment

As the concept of concurrent delay developed, some courts allowed claimants the opportunity to prove that the concurrent delays were capable of being apportioned between the responsible parties. In *Blinderman Construction Co., Inc. v. U.S.*, the Court of Federal Claims articulated the modern approach to concurrent delay:

> Where both parties contribute to the delay neither can recover damage, unless there is in the proof a clear apportionment of the delay and the expense attributable to each party[.] Generally, courts will deny recovery where the delays are concurrent or intertwined and the contractor has not met its burden of separating its delays from those chargeable to the Government.[24]

---

cost of the delay be allocated between the two parties proportionally."). A concurrent delay is also independently sufficient to cause the delay days attributed to that source of delay. *See* Beauchamp Constr. Co. v. United States, 14 Cl. Ct. 430, 437 (1988) (noting that a concurrent action "would have independently generated the delay during the same time period even if it does not predominate over the government's action as the cause of the delay" (citations omitted)).

George Sollitt, 64 Fed. Cl. at 238 n.8.

23. *See, e.g.*, CCM Corp. v. U.S., 20 Cl. Ct. 649, 659 (1990) ("The basic rule for concurrent delays is when each party is responsible for a concurrent cause of delay, neither party can recover money from the other party."); Commerce Int'l Co., Inc. v. U.S., 167 Ct. Cl. 529, 542–43 (1964) ("we must apply the rule that there can be no recovery where the defendant's delay is concurrent or intertwined with other delays"); Newport News Shipbuilding & Dry Dock Co. v. U.S., 79 Ct. Cl. 25, 34–37 (1934) (same).

24. Blinderman Constr. Co., Inc. v. United States, 695 F.2d 552, 559 (Fed. Cir. 1982) (citations and quotations omitted).

In *Calumet Construction Corp. v. Metropolitan Sanitary District of Greater Chicago*, the Illinois Appellate Court observed that the "older rule of non-apportionment . . . is now being abandoned by a growing number of courts in favor of the more modern rule of apportionment" for several reasons, including the "harshness" of the older rule's application.[25] Other state courts have followed suit in adopting the modern rule of apportionment.[26]

In these cases, the burden is on the contractor asserting the compensable delay claim to apportion delays between it and the owner.[27] "To prove the resultant injury to the contractor from the government-caused unreasonable delay, the contractor must prove the extent of the delay attributable to the government, and that the delay caused the contractors to incur additional costs."[28] With respect to apportionment, the contractor has the burden of establishing "clear apportionment" of the delay attributable to each party.[29] In federal projects, owners can defend against such delay claims by showing that contractor did not utilize a critical path method (CPM) analysis to establish the portion of delay attributable to the owner.[30]

The challenges of apportionment are illustrated clearly in *T. Brown Constructors, Inc. v. Peña*.[31] Brown, a road-construction contractor, alleged that the government was responsible for delays resulting from imposition of an overly stringent subgrade tolerance, differing site conditions, and a change to the traffic-control requirements.[32] The court, however, found that weather and equipment problems caused a five-week delay in starting the project and the government could only be responsible for a delay of approximately one week.[33] Accordingly, the court concluded that the government was not the proximate cause of the contractor's damages and, at a minimum, the two parties' delays were inseparable.[34] As a result, denial of the delay claim was proper.

---

25. 533 N.E.2d 453, 419–20 (Ill. App. Ct. 1988) (citing Robinson v. U.S., 261 U.S. 486, 43 S. Ct. 420, 67 L.Ed. 760 (1923)). The court in *Calumet Construction* adopted the exception to apportionment in circumstances where the owner has acted in bad faith and stated another exception for situations where the owner "has substantially contributed to the delay, *i.e.*, where the owner has made it practically impossible for the contractor to work as scheduled." *Id.* at 420–22.

26. *See, e.g.*, Cleveland Constr., Inc. v. Ellis-Don Constr., Inc., 709 S.E.2d 512, 525 (N.C. App. 2011) (allowing subcontractor recovery despite concurrent delays).

27. *George Sollitt*, 64 Fed. Cl. at 238.

28. *Id.* at 239 (citations omitted) (quotations omitted).

29. *Id.* at 238 (citing T. Brown Constructors, Inc. v. Pena, 132 F.3d 724, 734 (Fed. Cir. 1997)).

30. Phillip L. Bruner & Patrick J. O'Connor, Jr., 6 Bruner & O'Conner on Construction Law § 15:69 n.3; *In re* Appeal of Fed. Ins. Co., IBCA No. 3236, 96-2 B.C.A. (CCH) (July 2, 1996).

31. 132 F.3d 724 (Fed. Cir. 1997).

32. *Id.* at 734.

33. *Id.*

34. *Id.*

Concurrent Delays—Functional Versus Literal Concurrency and the Critical Path

The Association for Advancement of Cost Engineering (AACE) International Recommended Practice sets forth two methods of measuring concurrency—functional concurrency and literal concurrency.[35] With functional concurrency, concurrent delays are present when the delays occur within the same analysis period. A delay-analysis period is usually one month, or it may also be the time between schedule updates. A theory of literal concurrency, as its name suggests, requires that delays occur at the exact same time, meaning the delays start on the same date and remain concurrent until one ends.

Regardless of which method is being utilized to measure concurrency, only delays to the critical path are truly concurrent. In other words, concurrent delays must be concurrently critical.[36] Courts have recognized that maintaining and keeping current CPM schedules during a project to reflect delays as they occur is an "established way" to prove critical path delays.[37]

Delays Are Excusable and Not Compensable

While the definition of "excusable" delay is controlled by the terms of the specific agreement, the concept is generally viewed in treatises as follows:

> "Excusable" delay is delay to the critical path outside of the "control" of both the contracting parties. The parties share this risk by bearing their respective costs incurred because of such delay but granting each other time extensions to cover the extended duration resulting from the delay. In other words, one receives "time but not money" for excusable delays.[38]

In the absence of contract language defining "excusable" delay and the relief therefor, an owner may try to limit a contractor's cost relief if the delay is one that is traditionally viewed as "excusable" rather than "compensable"—for example,

35. Forensic Schedule Analysis, AACE International Recommended Practice No. 29R-03 (2011).

36. A "critical path" is a way of grouping interrelated activities in a construction project. A delay to an activity that is on the critical path usually results in a corresponding delay to the completion of the project. The reason that the determination of the critical path is crucial to the calculation of delay damages is that only construction work on the critical path had an impact upon the time in which the project was completed. Wilner v. United States, 24 F.3d 1397, 1399 n.5 (Fed. Cir. 1994) (citing G.M. Shupe, Inc. v. United States, 5 Cl. Ct. 662, 728 (1984)).

37. *PCL Constr. Servs.*, 47 Fed. Cl. at 801; *see also Preston-Brady, Co., Inc.*, V.A.B.C.A. Nos. 1892, 1991, 2555, 87-1 B.C.A. (CCH) ¶ 19,649 at 99,520 (1987) ("A general statement that disruption or impact occurred, absent any showing through use of update CPM schedules, Logs or credible and specific data or testimony, will not suffice to meet the plaintiff's burden.").

38. Bruner & O'Connor, *supra* note 30, § 15:43.

unusually severe weather conditions. Since abnormal or unusually severe weather is widely recognized to be an event beyond the control of the owner and the contractor, it is considered to be an "excusable delay."[39] When faced with such a claim, the owner, in defense, can argue that the weather delay from which the contractor's damages arises is "excusable," therefore the contractor is not entitled to compensation.[40] An owner can extend the excusable delay defense to a contractor's claim from delay damages to any delay-causing event that the owner can prove was beyond its control,[41] or that was permissible under the contract.[42]

Contract Terms Determining Excusable Delays

Construction contracts often contain provisions intended to allocate the risks of delay. For example, depending on the language of the relevant owner-contractor agreement, some types of delay may provide a contractor to time but not cost relief. Often in agreements, excusable delays such as force majeure and other delays caused by events outside the contractor's control are defined as "excusable" and contractor's relief is limited to an extension of time whereas owner-caused (including its consultants and separate contractors) delays, often referred to as "compensable" delays, are defined separately from "excusable" delays and entitle the contractor to time and money.

---

39. Fru-Con Constr. Corp. v. U.S., 44 Fed. Cl. 298, 314 (1999). "Federal regulations provide for extensions of *time* for excusable delays (e.g., unusually severe weather), but do not provide for equitable adjustments for such delays." Edge Constr. Co., Inc. v. U.S., 95 Fed. Cl. 407, 420 (2010) (citing FAR 52.249-10).

40. *See, e.g.*, *Edge Constr.*, 95 Fed. Cl. at 420 (holding that "because the delays [the contractor] experienced from unusually severe weather conditions were not caused by the Government, [the contractor] is not entitled to an equitable adjustment for lost productivity due to severe conditions").

41. Zafer Taahhut Insaat Ve Ticaret, A.S. v. U.S., 120 Fed. Cl. 604, 610–11 (2015) (holding contractor not entitled to equitable adjustment for delays caused by Government of Pakistan's decision to close its border since such delay was excusable in that it was beyond the control of the U.S. government); *J. W. Bateson Company, Inc.*, B-162868 (Comp. Gen.), 1969 WL 4572 (Jan. 9, 1969) (contractor not entitled to delay damages as GSA was not at fault for delay resulting from misaligned steel by steel subcontractor and the subsequent investigation by GSA and others into problem even though such investigation and resolution lasted three months); Sloane v. United States, 196 F. Supp. 643 (E.D.S.C. 1961) (holding government not liable to contactor for delay damages due to site availability due to default of separate contractor performing predecessor work because government not responsible for delay and contractor received a time extension under provisions for "acts of the government" or "unforeseeable causes").

42. *See, e.g.*, Kent v. U.S., 228 F. Supp. 929, 934–35 (S.D.N.Y. 1964) (holding that contractor not entitled to equitable adjustment for delay costs resulting from delayed issuance by the Government of the Notice to Proceed where contract imposed no obligation on the Government to issue the Notice to Proceed by any particular time); Chicora Constr. Co. v. U.S., 252 F. Supp. 910, 912–13 (E.D.N.C. 1965) ("If . . . the delay is occasioned by another contractor, or the delay is authorized or unavoidable even though occurring without the intervention of another contractor, the United States will not be liable.").

In the absence of a contractual definition otherwise, force majeure is generally viewed as follows:[43]

> "Force majeure" is a term that describes a particular type of event which may excuse performance under the contract. To determine whether a certain event excuses performance, a court should look to the language that the parties specifically bargained for in the contract to determine the parties' intent, rather than resorting to any traditional definition of the term. Contractual terms are controlling regarding force majeure with common law rules merely filling in gaps left by the document. In other words, when the parties have themselves defined the contours of force majeure in their agreement, those contours dictate the application, effect, and scope of force majeure.[44]

A delay caused by force majeure will only be excusable where the force majeure provision in the contract specifically identifies as a force majeure event, the event that in fact caused the delay at issue.[45] Some force majeure provisions include broad "catch-all" language[46] that enables a party to argue that the delay-causing event falls within the force majeure provision and is therefore excusable. Other force majeure provisions may limit the force majeure events to those specifically identified in the contract.

Where a contract defines force majeure events in terms of a nonexhaustive, categorical list of events, or includes catch-all language, courts often employ the doctrine of *ejusdem generis*, that is, general words in a contract are limited by particular words to things of the same kind or class, to determine whether the delay-causing event at issue falls within the force majeure provision.[47] Interpretation of a

---

43. "A force majeure excusing event, by its very nature, must be unforeseeable to some extent at the time of contracting." Roost Project, LLC v. Andersen Constr. Co., 437 F. Supp. 3d 808, 821 (D. Idaho 2020).

44. R & B Falcon Drilling Co. v. Amer. Exploration Co., 154 F. Supp. 2d 969, 973 (S.D. Tex. 2001).

45. *See* Kel Kim Corp. v. Central Markets, Inc., 519 N.E.2d 295 (N.Y. 1987).

46. By way of example, the following broad, open-ended phrase is considered "catch-all language" in a force majeure provision: "strikes or acts of Labor Union, fires, floods, earthquakes, *or other conditions or contingencies beyond its control.*" *See, e.g.*, Seitz v. Mark-O-Lite Sign Contractors, Inc., 510 A.2d 319, 321 (N.J. Super. Ct. App. Div. 1986); *Roost Project, LLC*, 437 F. Supp. 3d at 822 ("The catch-all sentence of the clause refers to event beyond the reasonable control of the Contractor 'despite prudent and diligent efforts to prevent, avoid, delay, or mitigate[.]'").

47. *See, e.g.*, Austin Co. v. U.S., 314 F.2d 518, (Ct. Cl. 1963); TEC Olmos, LLC v. ConocoPhillips Co., 555 S.W.3d 176, 185 (Tex. App. 2018) (applying *ejusdem generis* in determining that an economic downturn was not like the other events specified in the contract's force majeure clause); *Kel Kim Corp.*, 519 N.E.2d 295 at 385–86 (finding plaintiff's inability to procure and maintain insurance was neither listed as a force majeure event in the contract nor fell "within the catchall 'or other similar causes beyond the control of such party'" as the inability to procure insurance was not within the kind of events listed in the force majeure clause which pertained "to a party's ability to conduct day-to-day commercial operations on the premises").

force majeure provision in the context of *ejusdem generis* serves to limit the provision to excusing delays "due to the kind or class of extraneous contingencies enumerated" in the provision, whatever they may be:[48]

> Under [the rule of *ejusdem generis*], the catch-all language of the force *majeure* clause relied upon by defendant is not to be construed to its widest extent; rather, such language is to be narrowly interpreted as contemplating only events or things of the same general nature or class as those specifically enumerated.[49]

The question of whether the delay-causing event at issue in a given case was foreseeable,[50] and/or in fact within the nonperforming (i.e., delayed) party's control,[51] often becomes an integral part of the court's application of *ejusdem generis* in the context of force majeure provisions.[52] In sum, in the context of a

48. *See Austin Co.*, 161 Ct. Cl. at 80.

49. *Mark-O-Lite Sign Contractors*, 510 A.2d at 321.

50. "Even where . . . a contract's force majeure clause does not expressly use the word 'foreseeability,' courts consider foreseeability when determining whether the event qualifies as force majeure." *Roost Project, LLC*, 437 F. Supp. 3d at 821 (citing Burns Concrete, Inc. v. Teton Cnty., 384 P.3d 364 (Idaho 2016)); *In re* Flying Cow Ranch HC, LLC, Case No. 18-12681-BKC-MAM, 2018 WL 7500475, at *3 (Bankr. S.D. Fla. June 22, 2018). Issue of fact existed regarding whether the contractor "could have foreseen at the time of contracting or had reasonable control over" the winter weather and labor shortage, precluded summary judgment on issue of whether those events qualify as force majeure under the contract. *Roost Project, LLC*, 437 F. Supp. 3d at 822; *Seitz*, 510 A.2d at 321–22 (sheet metal worker-employee's foot amputation, which was a foreseeable result of the progressive aggravation of his diabetes, a pre-existing condition, did not fall within the same class of force majeure events as those identified in the contract, i.e., "labor strikes, fires, floods, earthquakes or war," all of which are "sudden" events).

51. Murdock & Sons Constr., Inc. v. Goheen Gen. Constr., Inc., 461 F.3d 837, 841 (7th Cir. 2006) (holding that masonry contractor's union masons failure to meet labor production rate used when estimating labor costs was not an excusable delay under force majeure provision of contract, which included "labor disputes . . . or causes beyond the Contractor's control" as categories of force majeure events, where contractor failed to prove that "the slower-than-anticipated pace of the masons was due to either a labor dispute or a cause beyond its control"); Rohm & Haas Co. v. Crompton Corp., 2002 WL 1023435, at *4–5 (Pa. Com. Pl. Apr. 29, 2002) (holding that plaintiff's voluntary decision to shut down its plant due to financial considerations resulting from compliance with a Consent Decree that it negotiated and entered into with the Environmental Protection Agency prior to the contract from which it sought to be excused from performance, was not an event beyond its control for which it was entitled to be excused from under the force majeure clause in the contract).

52. *See, e.g.*, Carnegie Steel Co. v. U.S., 36 S. Ct. 342, 60 L. Ed. 576, 240 U.S. 156 (1916) (holding that a delay in performance of a contract due to ignorance of the scientific process necessary to face-harness 18-inch armor plate to meet certain specifications, was not of the same character or kind of "unavoidable causes" described in the contract, which included "fires, storms, labor strikes, action of the United States, etc.," because, although unforeseeable, the inability to make a product due to a lack of knowledge was avoidable since it was discoverable prior to entering the contract and is not an extraneous cause of the kind enumerated in the contract); *Austin Co.*, 314 F.2d at 520 ("[I]f plaintiff's failure of performance was due to the absolute impossibility of performance inherent in the subject matter of the contract itself, and which impossibility already existed at the time the contract was

claim for delay damages, the owner may be able to avoid liability on the grounds that the claim arises from an excusable delay. It is therefore noncompensable to the extent that the owner can prove that the delay-causing event falls within the force majeure provision in the contract, was a foreseeable event, or was an event within the contractor's control.

No-Damages-for-Delay Provisions

Owners frequently try to shield themselves from liability to contractors for damages resulting from delays within the owner's control or sphere of responsibility through a no-damages-for-delay clause:

> [No-damages-for-delay] provisions recognize that among the most obvious and common risks in the construction industry is the risk of delay. . . . The parties to construction contracts vie to shift the risk of delay onto the other. Subcontractors, in general, want to minimize their delay risk so they can accurately assess a bid low enough to be competitive, while owners and general contractors attempt to minimize the economically devastating effect of delay damages affecting all tiers of a project.[53]

A no-damages-for-delay clause is, in essence, the owner's attempt to convert a delay for which they would otherwise be liable, that is, a "compensable delay," into an "excusable delay."[54] A no-damages-for-delay clause accomplishes this by expressly providing that an extension of time shall be the contractor's sole remedy for certain delays that would otherwise be compensable.[55]

---

entered into, plaintiff's failure would not be excused" under the force majeure clause which excuses non-performance that "arises out of causes beyond the control and without the fault or negligence of the Contractor [and] include, but are not restricted to, acts of God or the public enemy, acts of the Government, fires, floods, epidemics, quarantine restrictions, strikes, freight embargoes, unusually severe weather," etc.); Hutton Contracting Co., Inc. v. City of Coffeyville, 487 F.3d 772, 778 (10th Cir. 2007) (finding delay caused by contractor's supplier was not a force majeure event where force majeure provision excused a delay "which is due exclusively to causes beyond the control and without the fault of [Hutton], including Acts of God, fires, floods, and acts or omissions of [the City] with respect to matters for which [the City] is solely responsible").

53. Macomb Mechanical, Inc. v. LaSalle Grp., Inc., 2015 WL 1880189, at *3 (Mich. Ct. App. Apr. 23, 2015) (citing Beattie, *Apportioning the Risk of Delay in Construction Projects: A Proposed Alternative to the Inadequate "No Damages for Delay" Clause*, 46 Wm & Mary L. Rev. 1857, 1857 (2005)) (quotations omitted).

54. Bruner & O'Connor, *supra* note 30, § 15:76.

55. Section 8.3.3 of the American Institute of Architects (AIA) Document A201–2017, *General Conditions of the Contract for Construction*, is an example of a "no damages for delay" clause in a contract between an owner and a contractor:

> an extension in the Contract Time, to the extent permitted under this paragraph 8.3, shall be the sole remedy of the Contractor against Owner or Architect for (1) delay in

Most courts have held that no-damages-for-delay clauses are enforceable exculpatory clauses in light of freedom of contract principles. In *Wells Brothers Co. of New York v. U.S.*, the U.S. Supreme Court upheld a "no damages for delay" clause in the context of a government construction project stating:

> Men who take $1,000,000 contracts for government buildings are neither unsophisticated nor careless. Inexperience and inattention are more likely to be found in other parties to such contracts than the contractors, and the presumption obvious and strong that the men signing such a contract as we have here protected themselves against such delays as are complained of by the higher price exacted for the work.[56]

Most state and federal jurisdictions have also found no-damages-for-delay clauses to be enforceable.[57] Despite their general enforceability, courts usually construe these clauses strictly against the owner as exculpatory clauses.[58] In strictly construing these clauses, courts across various jurisdictions also recognize certain exceptions to their enforceability.

Owner Fraud, Misrepresentation, or Bad Faith

Fraud, misrepresentation, or bad faith on the part of the owner is a widely recognized exception to the enforceability of no-damages-for-delay clauses.[59] This

---

> the commencement, prosecution or completion of the Work; (2) hindrance or obstruction in the performance of the Work; (3) loss of productivity; or (4) other similar claims (collectively referred to in this subparagraph as delays) whether or not such delays are foreseeable[.]

56. 41 S. Ct. 34, 65 L. Ed. 148, 254 U.S. 83, 87 (1920).

57. *See, e.g.*, W.C. James, Inc. v. Phillips Petroleum Co., 485 F.2d 22, 25 (10th Cir. 1973); U.S. v. Travelers Casualty, 2015 WL 5634607, at *9 (N.D.W. Va. Sep. 24, 2015); Tricon Kent Co. v. LaFarge North America, Inc., 186 P.3d 155, 159 (Colo. App. 2008); Guy M. Cooper, Inc. v. E. Penn. Sch. Dist., 903 A.2d 608, 613 (Pa. Commw. Ct. 2006); L & B Constr. Co. v. Ragan Enters., Inc., 482 S.E.2d 279, 280 (Ga. 1997); Phoenix Contractors, Inc. v. Gen. Motors Corp., 135 Mich. App. 787, 355 N.W.2d 673, 676 (1984); Kalisch-Jarcho, Inc. v. City of New York, 58 N.Y.2d 377, 448 N.E.2d 413, 461 N.Y.S.2d 746, 749 (1983); Broadway Maintenance Corp. v. Rutgers, State Univ., 447 A.2d 906, 914 (N.J. 1982); Owen Constr. Co. v. Iowa State Dep't of Transp., 274 N.W.2d 304, 306 (Iowa 1979).

58. *Tricon Kent Co.*, 186 P.3d 155, 159 ("'[N]o damages for delay' clauses have been strictly construed against owners or contractees because of the harsh results that may flow from the enforcement of such clauses") (citing John E. Green Plumbing & Heating Co. v, Turner Constr. Co., 742 F.2d 965, 966 (6th Cir. 1984) (applying Michigan law); E.C. Ernst, Inc. v. Manhattan Constr. Co., 551 F.2d 1026, 1029 (5th Cir. 1977) (applying Alabama law); Cunningham Bros., Inc. v. City of Waterloo, 254 Iowa 659, 664, 117 N.W.2d 46, 49 (1962); John Spearly Constr., Inc. v. Penns Valley Area Sch. Dist., 121 A.3d 593, 604 (Pa. Commw. Ct. 2015); *Macomb Mechanical, Inc.*, 2015 WL 1880189, at *3 (citing several other jurisdictions that strictly construe "no damages for delay" clauses); Forward Industries, Inc. v. Rolm of New York Corp., 123 A.D.2d 374, 506 N.Y.S.2d 453, 454 (1986).

59. "Of those cases addressing this exception, it appears to have been adopted in all but one jurisdiction." U.S. for the Use and Benefit of Williams Elec. Co., Inc. v. Metric Constructors, Inc., 325

exception is "rooted in the duty of good faith and fair dealing implied in every contract and [is] intended to avoid the otherwise draconian results that might flow from strict enforcement—namely, excusing the owner for harm to the contractor caused by the owner's egregious and unfair conduct."[60]

Active Interference

Active interference is another widely recognized exception to the enforceability of no-damages-for-delay clauses. This exception applies when the owner commits an affirmative, willful act that interferes directly with the contractor's work or ability to comply with the contract. This exception also arises out of the implied duty of good faith and fair dealing in contracts. The active interference exception does not require the contractor to show bad faith on the part of the owner in interfering with the contractor's work.[61] However, the owner's interference must have some level of intentionality in order to constitute "active interference." The term "active" is significant and qualifies the type of "interference" that falls within the exception. The term "active":

> clearly implies that more than a simple mistake, error in judgment, lack of total effort, or lack of complete diligence is needed for plaintiff to prove the "active interference" necessary to render unenforceable an otherwise clear and unambiguous "no damage" clause.[62]

In addition to adopting the common definition of "active interference"—an affirmative or positive interference by the owner with the contractor's work—Pennsylvania courts have also defined "active interference" as including owner *inaction* and situations where "there is a failure on the part of the owner to act [in] some essential manner necessary to the prosecution of the work."[63] Active interference

---

S.C. 129, 480 S.E.2d 447, 449 (1997) (citing jurisdictions that have adopted the bad faith exception). Massachusetts is the one jurisdiction that refused to adopt a fraud exception. *Id.* (citing Marsch v. Southern N.E.R. Corp., 230 Mass. 483, 120 N.E. 120 (1918)). *See also Macomb Mechanical, Inc.*, 2015 WL 1880189, at *3; *Tricon Kent Co.*, 186 P.3d 155, 159–60; J.A. Jones Constr. Co. v. Lehrer McGovern Bovis, Inc., 120 Nev. 277, 89 P.3d 1009, 1015 (2004); Triple R Paving, Inc. v. Broward Cnty., 774 So. 2d 50, 54 (Fla. 4th DCA 2000); Mississippi Transp. Comm'n v. SCI, Inc., 717 So. 2d 332, 339 (Miss. 1998) (all recognizing fraud or bad faith exception).

60. *Macomb Mechanical, Inc.*, 2015 WL 1880189, at *3 (citing C & H Electric, Inc. v. Town of Bethel, 312 Conn. 843, 854–55, 96 A.3d 477 (2014)).

61. *Tricon Kent Co.*, 186 P.3d at 161 ("the bad faith component of [the definition of 'active interference'] has all but been eviscerated due to the recognition of a separate 'bad faith' exemption from a no-damage-for-delay clause") (citing Steven B. Lesser & Daniel L. Wallach, *Risky Business: The "Active Interference" Exception to No Damage-For Delay Clauses*, 23 Constr. Law 26 (Winter 2003)).

62. Peter Kiewit Sons' Co. v. Iowa S. Utilities Co., 355 F. Supp. 376, 399 (S.D. Iowa 1973) (relying on Cunningham Brothers, Inc. v. City of Waterloo, 254 Iowa 659, 664, 117 N.W.2d 46 (1962)).

63. *James Corp.*, 938 A.2d at 484 (citing Coatesville Contractors & Eng'rs, Inc. v. Borough of Ridley Park, 509 Pa. 553, 506 A.2d 862 (1986)).

by the owner may involve "availability, access or design problems that pre-existed the bidding process and were known by the owner but not by the contractor."[64] A classic example of active interference is a directive by the owner to the contractor to proceed with its work despite a lack of access to, or availability of, the work site.[65]

Unreasonable Delay Justifying Abandonment of Contract

Some states have recognized an exception to enforcement of "no damages for delay" clauses in situations where the delays are so unreasonable in length or duration that they constitute an abandonment of the contract by the owner.[66] For example, in *Abax Inc. v. New York City Housing Authority*,[67] the plaintiff demonstrated that there were over 600 days of delays. The court reasoned that the 600 days of delays "is sufficiently indicative of delays beyond the contemplation of the contracting parties or of an abandonment by the contractee."[68] Therefore, the court held that there was a meritorious cause of action for delay damages even with the exculpatory contract provision.[69]

Delays Not Contemplated by the Parties

Courts have also refused to enforce "no damages for delay" clauses where the delays, or the causes of the delays, were not contemplated by the parties at the time they entered into the contract. The Court of Appeals of New York explained the rationale behind this exception:

> It has been settled for some time that exculpatory clauses will not bar claims resulting from delays caused by the contractee if the delays or their causes were not within the contemplation of the parties at the time they entered into the contract. The exception is based on the concept of mutual assent. Having agreed to the exculpatory clause when he entered into the contract, it is presumed that the contractor intended to be bound by its terms. It can hardly be presumed, however, that the contractor bargained away his right to bring a claim for damages resulting from delays which the parties did not contemplate at the time. Thus,

---

64. *Id.*

65. *See, e.g.*, Gasparini Excavating Co. v. Pa. Tpk. Comm'n, 409 Pa. 465, 476, 187 A.2d 157, 162 (1963) (finding that Pennsylvania Turnpike Commission actively interfered with contractor when it gave contractor formal notice to proceed despite knowing site would not be available to contractor due to delays by other contractors).

66. *See, e.g.*, Framan Mechanical, Inc. v. State Univ. Constr. Fund, 182 A.D.3d 947, 123 N.Y.S.3d 256, 260 (2020); *Metric Constructors, Inc.*, 480 S.E.2d at 449–50; Western Eng'rs, Inc. v. State By & Through Road Commission, 20 Utah 2d 294, 437 P.2d 216, 218 (1968).

67. 282 A.D.2d 372, 373, 723 N.Y.S.2d 490, 492 (2001).

68. *Id.*

69. *Id.*

> even broadly worded exculpatory clauses . . . are generally held to encompass only those delays which are reasonably foreseeable, arise from the contractor's work during performance, or which are mentioned in the contract.[70]

The failure by an owner to fulfill an obligation or duty, or to perform an act that only it can perform, and which is essential to the contractor's ability to perform its work, can result in a delay not contemplated by the parties. Likewise, the Supreme Court of Idaho affirmed a lower court's finding that the State Board of Highway Directors' failure to make timely arrangements with the owners of utility poles to relocate such poles so that highway construction could proceed as planned and scheduled, caused delays and obstructions not contemplated by the parties when they entered into the contract.[71] Therefore, the contractor's claim for additional costs was not barred by the "no damages for delay" clause.[72]

Delays Caused by Gross Negligence

Some states have even noted an exception to a no-damages-for-delay clause for gross negligence by the owner.[73] The rationale behind this exception is that the willful, wanton, or reckless conduct by an owner rising to the level of gross negligence constitutes a breach of the implied obligation of good faith and fair dealing.[74]

70. Corinno Civetta Constr. Corp. v. City of New York, 67 N.Y.2d 297, 309–10, 493 N.E.2d 905, 910 (1986) (citations omitted). *But see* John E. Gregory & Son, Inc. v. A. Guenther & Sons Co., Inc., 147 Wis. 2d 298, 432 N.W.2d 584, 586 (1988) (holding that delays not contemplated by the parties is not an exception to the enforceability of a "no damages for delay" clause).

71. Grant Constr. Co. v. Burns, 92 Idaho 408, 443 P.2d 1005, 1011–12 (1968). In *Grant Construction Co.*, the trial court found that the owner's failure to schedule the utility pole relocation was not contemplated by the parties and the owner's act of "ordering the contractor to proceed with construction in the face of the [owner's] failure to schedule the relocation, constituted active interference on the part of the [owner]." *Id.* at 1012.

72. *Id.*

73. *See, e.g.*, North Star Contracting Corp. v. City of New York, 203 A.D.2d 214, 611 N.Y.S.2d 11, 12 (1994) ("No-damages-for-delay" clause "will not preclude recovery for damages resulting from the City's intentional wrongdoing, gross negligence or willful misconduct."); White Oak Corp. v. Dep't of Transp., 217 Conn. 281, 585 A.2d 1199, 1203–04 (1991) (recognizing exception for "contractee's bad faith or its willful, malicious, or grossly negligent conduct"); State Highway Admin. v. Greiner Eng'g Sciences, Inc., 83 Md. App. 621, 577 A.2d 363, 372 (1990) (recognizing exception under Maryland law for "intentional wrongdoing or gross negligence"); John E. Gregory & Son, Inc. v. A. Guenther & Sons Co., Inc., 147 Wis. 2d 298, 432 N.W.2d 584, 586 (1988) (under Wisconsin law "no damages for delay" clause is not enforceable in cases where there is intentional wrongdoing or gross negligence); Gust K. Newberg, Inc. v. Illinois State Toll Highway Auth., 153 Ill. App. 3d 918, 106 Ill. Dec. 858, 506 N.E.2d 658, 664 (1987) ("The only recognized exception to the enforceability of a non-damages-for-delay clause occurs where there is an allegation of bad faith or gross negligence.").

74. *U.S. for the Use and Benefit of Williams Elec. Co.*, 480 S.E.2d at 450–51.

Failure to Mitigate Delay or Delay Costs

The duty to mitigate damages is not unique to construction contracts, nor to delay costs. The doctrine of avoidable consequences, also known as the duty to mitigate damages, prevents a nonbreaching party from recovering losses that could have been avoided by reasonable effort and without risk of substantial loss or injury.[75] Stated another way, "the law does not permit an injured party to stand idly by, accumulating damages."[76] However, the duty to mitigate damages is not applicable in all circumstances, for example:

> Where both the plaintiff and the defendant have had equal opportunity to reduce the damages by the same act and it is equally reasonable to expect the defendant to minimize damages, the defendant is in no position to contend that the plaintiff failed to mitigate. Nor will the award be reduced on account of damages the defendant could have avoided as easily as the plaintiff. *The duty to mitigate damages is not applicable where the party whose duty it is primarily to perform a contract has equal opportunity for performance and equal knowledge of the consequences of nonperformance.*[77]

The breaching party bears the burden of proving that losses could have been mitigated.[78] While not an exhaustive list, mitigation options for delayed (or defective) work include: (1) allowing the breaching party to "cure" its own breach, (2) resequencing the work and "working around," (3) accelerating the work to overcome delay, (4) finding substitute work, (5) finding substitute materials for those that are unsuitable or unavailable, and (6) determining when and under what circumstances to substitute other subcontractors or suppliers for those unable or unwilling to perform in conformance with contractual obligations.[79]

Release via Change Order

Owners who include release language in change orders may be able to preclude delay damages through the affirmative defense of accord and satisfaction, unless

---

75. Edward M. Crough, Inc. v. Dep't of Gen. Servs. of D.C., 572 A.2d 457, 466 (D.C. 1990) (citing A. Corbin, 5 Corbin on Contracts § 1039, at 241 (1964)).

76. Shea-S&M Ball v. Massman-Kiewit-Early, 606 F.2d 1245, 1249 (D.C. Cir. 1979).

77. *Shea-S&M Ball*, 606 F.2d 1245, 1249 (internal citations omitted, emphasis added) (citing Parker v. Harris Pine Mills, 206 Or. 187, 291 P.2d 709 (1955)).

78. Phillip L. Bruner & Patrick J. O'Connor, Jr., Limitation on Contract Damages—Duty of Damage Avoidance and Mitigation- "Reasonableness" of Motivation Effort § 19:21; *Edward M. Crough, Inc. v. Dep't of Gen. Servs. of D.C.*, 572 A.2d 457, 466 (D.C. 1990) (citing 5 Corbin on Contracts § 1039, at 251).

79. *Id.*

such release is ambiguous or limited in scope.[80] This principle is illustrated through the case of *Jackson Construction Co. v. United States.* There, the court found that an executed bilateral modification, or change order, which contained the following release provision constituted an accord and satisfaction:[81]

> The contract period of performance remains the same. It is further understood and agreed that this adjustment constitutes compensation in full on behalf of the contractor and his subcontractors and suppliers for all costs and markup directly or indirectly, including extended overhead, attributable to the change order, for all delays related thereto, and for performance of the change within the time frame stated.

Contractors may, however, preserve their right to assert additional claims for work covered by a change order through an explicit reservation provision.[82] Additionally, if the release is ambiguous in scope, courts have permitted the use of parol evidence in order to construe the release in accordance with the parties' intent at the time of execution.[83] Finally, even if the parties have executed a clear and unambiguous release, accord and satisfaction occurs only if certain prerequisites are met, including a proper subject matter, competent parties, meeting of minds, and consideration.[84]

---

80. Jackson Constr. Co. v. United States, 62 Fed. Cl. 84, 91 (2004); *see also* Merritt–Chapman & Scott Corp. v. United States, 198 Ct. Cl. 223, 228–30, 458 F.2d 42 (1972) (finding that where evidence supported findings that both parties tried to fix a firm price on contract price increase attributable to change and delays, additional expenses thereafter incurred were an accord and satisfaction); Brock & Blevins Co. v. United States, 343 F.2d 951 (Ct. Cl. 1965) (where subcontractor made no reservations and certified final payment estimate in amount of award, accord and satisfaction precluded subcontractor from further recovery of delay damages).

81. Jackson Constr. Co. v. United States, 62 Fed. Cl. at 91.

82. *Id.*

83. *Id.* at 93; *see also* Westerhold v. United States, 28 Fed. Cl. 172 (1993) (to prove valid accord and satisfaction defendant must establish proper subject matter, competent minds, meeting of minds, consideration and acceptance of payment or performance in satisfaction of claim).

84. McLain Plumbing & Elec. Serv., Inc. v. United States, 30 Fed. Cl. 70 (1993); Brock & Blevins Co. v. United States, 343 F.2d at 955.

CHAPTER 8

Contractor Delay Damages

Brenda K. Radmacher and Jean M. Terry

It is critical to assess the terms of a contract at the outset of evaluating the scope and extent to which a delay claim can be made by the contractor. "No-damage-for-delay" clauses have become more common and often more explicit in their language, as drafting parties have become more sophisticated. As a general rule, these clauses are enforceable if the language is clear and unambiguous.[1] However, the enforceability of delay damage clauses varies by jurisdiction, and some jurisdictions maintain certain carve-outs for acts of bad faith so as to not preclude a contractor's right to recover.

It is also important to note that recovery in certain jurisdictions may be dependent on whether the contract is a public or private project. For example, in Arizona, no-damages-for-delay clauses are void on public projects.[2] This does not extend to private projects, where Arizona's stance is generally to uphold parties' freedom of contracting, so such clauses are likely enforceable.[3]

Delay Damages or Consequential Damages?

Delay damages, if not carefully drafted as specific provisions in a construction contract, will often fall into the category of "consequential damages." As a general rule, to be recoverable, consequential damages need to be foreseeable at the time of contracting.[4] In construction contracts, this "foreseeability" is often viewed broadly and based on a number of factors, including the sophistication of parties, the detailed nature of definitions in construction contracts, the detailed definition of damages, and the industry appreciation for the consequences of most breaches.

1. Green Intern., Inc. v. Solis, 951 S.W.2d 384, 387 (Tex. 1997).
2. Tech. Constr., Inc. v. City of Kingman, 229 Ariz. 564 (App. 2012); A.R.S. §§ 34-221(F), 41-2617.
3. 1800 Ocotillo, LLC v. WLB Grp., Inc., 219 Ariz. 200, 202 (2008).
4. Keystone Airpark Auth. v. Pipeline Contractors, Inc., 266 So. 3d 1219 (Fla. 1st DCA 2019); 11 Corbin on Contracts § 56.6 (2018); E. Materials Corp. v. Mitsubishi Plastics Composites Am., Inc., 307 F. Supp. 3d 52 (E.D.N.Y. 2018).

Determination of liability for delay damages will often lie with the ability of parties to shift the burden and exposure of the delay to another party. While delays are often unavoidable, the drafting of the contract will have the largest impact on the party responsible for the damages. In the event of a delay, documenting the impact and adjusting the schedule to attempt to make up time on the critical path (mitigation), will also serve to reduce the potential exposure of any delays.

It is notable that a number of commonly used form construction contract documents seek to impose waivers of consequential damages. For example, the American Institute of Architects (AIA) A201-2017 section 15.1.7 contains language (which was first introduced in the 1997 version of the document, A201-1997 section 4.3.10) by which the contractor and the owner waive all rights to make claims for consequential damages arising out of or relating to the contract. Specific damages waived include:

- Damages incurred by the owner for rental expenses; for losses of use, income, profit, financing, business, and reputation; and for loss of management or employee productivity or of the services of such persons, and
- Damages incurred by the contractor for principal office expenses, including for compensation of personnel stationed there; for losses of financing, business, and reputation; and for loss of profit other than anticipated profits arising directly from the work.

A201-2017 Section 15.1.7 provides the waiver is applicable, without limitations, to *all consequential damages* due to either party's termination in accordance with Article 14 (Termination or Suspension of the Contract). Nothing contained in section 15.1.7 precludes an award of liquidated direct damages, when applicable, in accordance with the requirements of the contract documents.

Another commonly used set of form documents, ConsensusDocs, also include a basic consequential damages waiver:

> The Parties agree to waive all claims against each other for any consequential damages that may arise out of or relate to this Agreement . . . Owner agrees to waive damages, including but not limited to the Owner's loss of use of the Project, any rental expenses incurred, loss of income, profit, or financing related to the Project, as well as the loss of business, loss of financing, loss of profits not related to this Project, loss of reputation, or insolvency. [Contractor] agrees to waive damages, including but not limited to loss of business, loss of financing, loss of profits not related to this Project, loss of bonding capacity, loss of reputation, or insolvency.[5]

5. ConsensusDocs 200, Article 6.6.

Despite the prevalence of consequential damages waivers in private contracts, similar provisions are not usually included in public contracts with federal, state, or local government bodies. Moreover, while consequential damages waivers are common, contractors should be wary and carefully examine the contracts for the existence of an express waiver. These provisions usually apply to and protect both parties to a contract, so if the contract does not have a consequential damages waiver, negotiating its addition may be easier than negotiating other liability limitations. In addition, it is very important to clearly define the term "consequential damages" and list in the clause at least some of the consequential damages being waived, as in the preceding example. Lost profits are perhaps the most significant type of consequential damages and should be specifically referenced in the waiver. This is due to the fact that lost profits can quickly outpace the total value of a construction contract.

The Illinois Appellate Court has recognized the ability to recover delay damages based on the terms of the contract. In *Calumet*, the contract provided the contractor could recover delay damages, but only for premiums paid on the contractor's bond and for the wages and salaries of workers needed to maintain the work, the plant, and the equipment during the delay.[6] The court also applied the more modern rule of apportionment of fault for mutual delay between two contracting parties pursuant to a liquidated damages clause.[7]

Some contracts permit the contractor to recover delay damages only after a designated number of days of delay. This avoids the apparent unfairness of the no-damage clause and gives the owner a chance at the float. Even if the contractor surmounts this obstacle, the contractor may be denied recovery if the contractor cannot apportion the delay between that chargeable to the owner and that chargeable to itself.

For federal government contracts, the considerations may be slightly different. Under the Federal Acquisition Regulation (FAR), direct costs are defined as "any cost that is identified specifically with a particular final cost objective."[8] The Federal Circuit defines direct costs as costs "that are directly attributable to the performance of a specific contract and can be traced specifically to that contract."[9] Thus, for a construction delay claim under a government contract, a direct cost must be a dedicated cost. This dedicated cost must be clearly identified and shown to have been incurred specifically for a certain cost objective and to benefit only that cost objective.

6. Calumet Constr. Corp. v. Metro. Sanitary Dist., 222 Ill. App. 3d 374, 581 N.E.2d 206 (1991), *appeal denied*, 143 Ill. 2d 636, 587 N.E.2d 1012 (1992).

7. *Id.* (applying Illinois law).

8. FAR § 2.101; 48 C.F.R. § 2.101.

9. Nicon, Inc. v. United States, 331 F.3d 878, 882 (Fed. Cir. 2003).

Contract Damages Principles: Direct Versus Consequential Damages

The starting point to evaluate what damages may be available to a contractor for project delays is a close review and examination of contract damages principles.

It is generally understood that contract damages seek to place the nonbreaching party in the same position as if the breach had not occurred. Most often, these are considered "expectation damages," which are designed to ensure that the injured party receive what it expected from the bargain. Thus, under standard contract damages principles, the aggrieved party should be placed in the same position as though the contract had been fully performed. However, this often is not as simple as it might appear, particularly in the context of project delays. In the construction setting, the appropriate measure of damages arising from a breach of an enforceable contract is usually "the difference between the value expected from the contract and the value actually received by the non-breaching party."[10]

Actual damages flowing from the breach of contract are either "direct" or "consequential." Thus, the initial assessment must be to distinguish between whether the damages are direct or consequential. Much has been said on this distinction, both in case law and hornbooks across the United States.

Stated at its core, direct damages are those damages that were—at the time of contracting—contemplated by the parties or were reasonably foreseeable at the time of the contract and compensate the plaintiff for the harm proximately (directly) caused by the breach. The Federal Circuit has explained that "direct costs" are those that "arise solely because of and are attributable directly to performance of a specific contract."[11]

With respect to direct delay costs, courts have explained that such costs are "'direct' costs in the sense that they flow directly from the act or omission supporting a claim."[12] For example, the *Merritt-Chapman* court described a holding by the Armed Services Board: "Where the board found that steel was wrongfully rejected, resulting in a constructive change, the contractor was allowed all standby or delay costs which unavoidably followed as a result of the change."[13] Courts have also defined direct delay costs as those that stem from "extended performance due to a change under the changes clause of the contract."[14]

---

10. Tenn. Gas Pipeline Co. v. Technip USA Corp., 2008 WL 3876141, at *5 (Tex. Ct. App. 2008).
11. West v. All State Boiler, 146 F.3d 1368, 1372 (Fed. Cir. 1998).
12. Merritt-Chapman & Scott Corp. v. United States, 429 F.2d 431, 445 (Ct. Cl. 1970).
13. *Id.* citing *Appeal of Hardeman-Monier-Hutcherson*, ASBCA No. 11785, 67-1 B.C.A. (CCH) ¶ 6210 (A.S.B.C.A. Mar. 13, 1967).
14. G.M. Shupe, Inc. v. United States, 5 Cl. Ct. 662, 695–96 (1984).

On the other hand, consequential damages are secondary or indirect consequences or losses. A party may be entitled to recover consequential damages—losses to the nonbreaching party that "result naturally, but not necessarily, from the breach."[15] "Consequential damages are those which arise from the intervention of 'special circumstances' not ordinarily predictable."[16] In other words, consequential damages must be foreseeable and must be directly traceable to the wrongful act in order to be recoverable.[17] Consequential damages are often items such as lost rents, additional labor costs, or lost profits.

Consequential damages are available only if they were either known or foreseeable at the time of contracting. In order to be "known," the special circumstances must have been communicated to or be known by the defendant, and the defendant must have had the ability to voluntarily assume the risk of liability. This is a subjective test, which is not met simply by virtue of entering into the contract. To be "foreseeable," the defendant should have known or contemplated the loss due to the special circumstances as a consequence of the breach.[18] A delay and interference claim is a claim for direct damages if such damages were allegedly to be the extra costs for labor and equipment brought on and thus were a natural and ordinary result of another party's breach.[19]

While interpretations of what constitutes consequential damages vary widely among different jurisdictions, contracts, and circumstances, they are typically described as damages that do not flow directly from the delay, but rather are a secondary or indirect consequence and loss as a result of the construction delay. There is not, however, a bright line test applicable to all contracts and delay circumstances. One way to differentiate between direct and consequential damages is to view direct damages as the actual costs of completing the project (e.g., additional labor and materials), and consequential damages as all other losses and expenses (e.g., loss of profits, increased financial costs, loss of use of completed project, additional supervisory expenses, loss of opportunities, increased overhead expenses, and damages to reputation). In many instances, counsel can pose a valid argument that extended overhead, lost profits, additional financing costs, and loss of use were within the contemplation of the parties and thus should not be considered consequential damages.

---

15. *Tenn. Gas*, 2008 WL 3876141, at *6.

16. Roanoke Hosp. Ass'n v. Doyle & Russell, Inc., 214 S.E.2d 155, 160 (Va. 1975).

17. *See Tenn. Gas*, 2008 WL 3876141, at *6.

18. *Tenn. Gas*, 2008 WL 3876141, at *6; *Roanoke Hosp.*, 214 S.E.2d at 160 (discussing direct damages as those that "arise 'naturally' or 'ordinarily' from a breach of contract; they are damages that, in the ordinary course of human experience, can be expected to result from a breach").

19. *See* Ryan Inc. v. Toll Bros., 43 Fed. Appx 601 (4th Cir. 2002).

One of the key assessments undertaken by courts as to this differentiation is the foreseeability of the damage at the time of contracting. Bruner and O'Connor suggest that "foreseeability" might be viewed more broadly in modern construction contracts than in other commercial contracting relationships for several reasons:

1. The sophistication of the parties;
2. The detail with which construction contracts are prepared;
3. The flexibility built into construction contracts to make changes or to give definition to contract requirements during construction;
4. The frequent practice of giving contractual definition to the type and amount of damages awarded for certain breaches;
5. The recognized "hurly-burly" of the construction process; and
6. The common industry appreciation for the likely consequences of most breaches.[20]

Proof of damages must be demonstrated to a reasonable degree of certainty. The delay damages must be clearly ascertainable; proof of actual harm and its cause must be established and most often must be done through expert testimony. However, a contractor should proceed with caution to ensure that the delay damages, which may seem obvious to it, are carefully documented such that both the actual harm and the cause of the harm can be easily followed after the fact.

Direct Delay Costs

"The term 'delay' implies a stopping or hindrance for some period; "delay damages" are obviously those which flow from that increment in time."[21] In essence, direct delay costs are just the "direct costs" that result from a delay, as opposed to a changed design or a breach of a contractual provision.[22]

Direct delay costs can impact a variety of different expense categories on a construction project, including labor, equipment, and overhead. These categories and the necessary proof to support a claim for increased expenses are discussed herein. In order to recover such damages, however, a contracting party must show, among other things, that there was "a prolongation of performance beyond the anticipated date of completion."[23]

---

20. 6 Philip L. Bruner & Patrick J. O'Connor, Jr., Bruner & O'Connor Construction Law § 19:18 (Aug. 2023).

21. Paul Hardeman, Inc. v. United States, 406 F.2d 1357, 1361 (Ct. Cl. 1969).

22. West v. All State Boiler, 146 F.3d 1368, 1372 (Fed. Cir. 1998).

23. *Paul Hardeman, Inc.*, 406 F.2d at 1361.

Labor Kept on Standby

It is axiomatic that a delayed project will necessarily increase the labor costs for that project. People expect to be paid for showing up to work, whether the work is ready for them or not. Accordingly, if labor is placed on standby while a project attempts to recover from a delay, that labor will expect to be paid, regardless of whether there is actual work for them to perform. The costs of standby labor may include wages, taxes, overtime, wage escalation/inflation, insurance, and fringe benefits.[24]

In order to prove standby labor damages, a contractor must show that its labor force was actually idle. Courts have recognized, however, that there does not need to be a complete cessation of work. Labor will be considered to be on standby if there were "total or partial suspensions, delays or disruptions that unreasonably delayed and disrupted the contractor such that it was never able to man the job as planned."[25]

A contractor must also prove the amount spent on labor as well as that such costs were caused by a delay not within the contractor's control. In *A. S. Schulman Electric Co. v. United States*,[26] the court denied standby labor costs because the claimant had not shown that the labor was "in fact idle" or that it had expended any amounts on standby labor.

Added Mobilizations and Demobilizations

A delay on the project could also cause increased costs in the form of added mobilizations and demobilizations of different workforces. "Mobilization is defined . . . as work consisting of 'moving personnel, equipment, material, and incidentals to the project and performing all work necessary before beginning work at the project site.'"[27] Mobilization costs can include additional equipment rental costs, additional labor costs (including costs to retrain a new labor force if the original labor force is lost), as well as costs to perform work out of sequence. In the *CEMS* case for instance, the plaintiff was awarded its mobilization costs in the form of trucking costs after providing "make and model of vehicle, hourly vehicle rate, and hours and dates of usage."[28]

Parties pursuing mobilization costs as a result of a delay, however, must be careful to show a causal link. For instance, courts denied recovery of mobilization costs when it appeared that the choice to re-mobilize was a business decision,

---

24. *See* BRUNER & O'CONNOR, *supra* note 20, at § 19:98-100.

25. Redondo Constr. Corp. v. P.R. Highway & Transp. Auth. (*In re* Redondo Constr. Corp.), 505 B.R. 388, 408 (Bankr. D.P.R. 2014), *rev'd on other grounds*, 820 F.3d 460 (1st Cir. 2016).

26. 145 Ct. Cl. 399, 422 (1959).

27. CEMS, Inc. v. United States, 59 Fed. Cl. 168, 225 (2003).

28. *Id.*

rather than a direct result of the delay itself. In *American Line Builders, Inc. v. United States*, when the government delayed the project, the plaintiff opted to move its equipment to other projects while it waited for the delay to be resolved. Although plaintiff presented expert witness testimony that its decision was the "cheapest alternative," the court still found that it was a business decision that was not compensable.[29]

Thus, while mobilization costs can be recovered when there is a project delay, a claimant must be careful to present accurate cost data and a clear causal link in order to recover.

Idle Construction Equipment

The next category of direct delay damages is the cost "of equipment . . . in 'standing by' in periods of compensable delay."[30] "Even when a piece of equipment is not operating, its owner incurs costs due to its ongoing depreciation, its care and maintenance, the time value of the owner's investment, and the typically escalating cost of purchasing replacement equipment."[31]

When calculating the costs of such idled equipment, there is a distinction between equipment owned by the contractor and equipment rented from a third party.[32] "'Cost' of equipment rented from a third party under a written equipment lease negotiated at 'arm's length' ordinarily is the agreed rental rate."[33] Contractor-owned equipment, however, is a hornet's nest of controversy as to accepted methodology, with the industry divided as to whether attempting to calculate the actual cost of ownership or reliance on an accepted manual rate[34] is the better approach.

For idle claims involving contractor-owned equipment, federal courts will "allow the proved rental value [provided by an accepted manual], discounted by one-half because of the absence of actual use with its resulting wear and tear."[35]

---

29. Am. Line Builders, Inc. v. United States, 26 Cl. Ct. 1155, 1218 (1992).

30. *See* BRUNER & O'CONNOR, *supra* note 20, at § 19:104.

31. Douglas S. Oles, *Elements of Damages, in* CONSTRUCTION DAMAGES AND REMEDIES 37, 43 (2d ed. 2013).

32. *Id.*

33. *Id.*

34. The U.S. Army Corps of Engineers publishes its "Construction Equipment Ownership and Operating Expense Schedule"; Associated General Contractors of America has its "Contractor's Equipment Ownership Expense Manual" and the "Contractor's Equipment Cost Guide"; there is the "Caterpillar Performance Handbook" and the "Associated Equipment Distributors Manual of Rental Rates for Construction Equipment"; and Data Quest Inc.'s "Rental Rate Blue Book." (*See* BRUNER & O'CONNOR, *supra* note 20, at § 19:104.)

35. Brand Inv. Co. v. United States, 102 Ct. Cl. 40, 44–45, 58 F. Supp. 749, 751 (1944); *see also* Luria Bros. & Co. v. United States, 369 F.2d 701, 714 (Ct. Cl. 1966).

Regardless of whether the parties use a manual rate or actual costs, "proof of the delay period including accurate records of the impact on equipment usage will be a necessary component of demonstrating entitlement to equipment costs."[36] For example, the U.S. District Court for the District of Columbia declined to award costs for idle equipment when the claimant failed to present evidence of "when each piece of equipment arrived and left the site . . . [and] that these items were used solely for the [delayed portion of the work]."[37] Further, the claimant must show that it was required "to have standby equipment available for work" in order to recover for idle equipment.[38]

The Louisiana Court of Appeals denied recovery for "idle equipment charges" when the claimant failed to present evidence of "*when* the delays occurred. . . . [and] did not prove what equipment was at the job site when the actual delays occurred."[39]

Alternatively, the parties can agree in their contract or in subsequent change orders the amount that is compensable for idle equipment. In *R&D Contracting, L.L.C. v. Jenkins Construction, Inc.*, the court enforced an oral agreement between the parties whereby the prime contractor agreed to pay the subcontractor "for eight hours per day for each item of equipment listed on the [subcontractor's] invoice . . . at the hourly rates listed on that invoice, for each day of the stand-down."[40] In the *Sullivan* case, the court noted that the Department of Transportation and Development issued an Engineering Directives and Standards Manual that proscribed the formula for calculating idle equipment damages.[41]

Extended General Conditions

Extended general conditions is another term for direct overhead costs that a claimant incurs when a project extends past its planned completion date.[42] These costs can include "field supervision, field engineering, materials handling, timekeeping, office, storage and trailers, temporary power and water, sanitary facilities, and

---

36. W. Stephen Dale & Robert M. D'Onofrio, Construction Schedule Delays 237 (2019).

37. Williams Enters., Inc. v. Strait Mfg. & Welding, Inc., 728 F. Supp. 12, 20 (D.D.C. 1990), *superseded on other grounds by statute*, Fed. R. Evid. 701, *as recognized in* Certain Underwriters at Lloyds v. Inlet Fisheries, Inc., 389 F. Supp. 2d 1145, 1155 (D. Alaska 2005).

38. Peru Assocs., Inc. v. State, 334 N.Y.S.2d 772, 775 (Ct. Cl. 1971).

39. Sullivan v. City of Baton Rouge, 170 So. 3d 186, 197 (La. Ct. App. 2015).

40. R&D Contracting, L.L.C. v. Jenkins Constr., Inc. (*In re* R&D Contracting, L.L.C.), 383 B.R. 890, 897 (Bankr. E.D. Mich. 2008).

41. *Sullivan*, 170 So. 3d at 201.

42. John Marshall Cook, W. Stephen Dale & Richard F. Smith, *Overhead Costs*, *in* Federal Government Construction Contracts, 664 n.4 (3d ed. 2017).

other costs incurred in field support of labor, materials and equipment."[43] "The ordinary charges of maintaining the establishment for the carrying on of business are referred to as overhead."[44]

There is a distinction between overhead costs that are directly charged against the project versus those indirect overhead costs that are spread across all projects. Federal regulations allow for the recovery of both direct and indirect overhead.[45] "It is well known that extended field costs incurred after the scheduled completion date of a project are recoverable as additional and direct expenses to the injured party."[46]

There are two methods of pricing extended general conditions: (1) "a percentage markup that approximates the additional costs incurred"; or (2) "divide the pool of time-related project overhead costs incurred by the number of days of project performance."[47]

An example of issues that can arise when using the percentage markup method is *Guy James Construction Co. v. Trinity Industries, Inc.*, where the Fifth Circuit affirmed an award of "19 percent" of the field overhead costs sought by a prime contractor when a steel fabricator failed to deliver satisfactory materials on time.[48] The court reasoned that "because [the prime contractor] was performing work on several construction contracts at [the same project site] . . . the total job-site overhead could be allocated" among all the projects.[49]

As to the second method, claimants should take care to present evidence of actual damage. In *North American Mechanical, Inc. v. Walsh Construction Co. II, LLC*,[50] the claimant's bid included general conditions as a line item. When the claimant was delayed by the prime contractor, it divided the bid line item "by the number of days . . . the Project was initially expected to last" to get a daily general conditions rate.[51] The claimant then multiplied the daily rate by the num-

43. *See* BRUNER & O'CONNOR, *supra* note 20, at § 19:106; *see also* S. Leo Harmonay, Inc. v. Binks Mfg. Co., 597 F. Supp. 1014, 1034 (S.D.N.Y. 1984) (claimant was awarded its actual costs for extended field supervision caused by the opposing party's delay).

44. *Peru Assocs., Inc.* 334 N.Y.S.2d at 775.

45. FAR § 31.105(d)(3), 48 C.F.R. § 31.105(d)(3) ("Costs incurred at the job site incident to performing the work, such as the cost of superintendence, time keeping and clerical work, engineering, utility costs, supplies, material handling, restoration and cleanup, etc., are allowable **as direct or indirect costs**, provided the accounting practice used is in accordance with the contractor's established and consistently followed cost accounting practices for all work.").

46. *S. Leo Harmonay*, 597 F. Supp. at 1034.

47. DALE & D'ONOFRIO, *supra* note 36, at 238–39.

48. Guy James Constr. Co. v. Trinity Indus., Inc., 644 F.2d 525, 533 (5th Cir. 1981).

49. *Id.*

50. N. Am. Mech., Inc. v. Walsh Constr. Co. II, LLC, 132 F. Supp. 3d 1064, 1081 (E.D. Wis. 2015).

51. *Id.* at 1082.

ber of days it was delayed to get a total claim amount for general conditions. The court rejected the claim because the claimant "provided no evidence of the actual additional general conditions costs, if any, that [the claimant] actually incurred as a result of this Project taking longer than initially expected."[52] Similarly, "the fact that [general conditions costs] are incurred after the scheduled completion date is not dispositive; a court should ascertain whether the items are duplicative, exaggerated, or partially included in allowed claims for extra work."[53]

Indirect Delay Costs

Escalation of Wage Rates (Labor Escalation)

Typically, the contractor assumes the risk of fluctuations in labor, equipment, and materials. However, if the contractor or project is delayed, the contractor may be entitled to recover some or all of the additional costs incurred. Thus, wage rates are often one of the elements of delay damages. When seeking to claim escalation of wage rates, contractors must take several items into consideration to determine the strength of the claim. Again, as with many other categories of damages for delay, the terms of the contract will be controlling. In addition, documenting the impact and adjusting the schedule to attempt to make up time on the critical path (mitigation), will also serve to reduce the potential exposure of any delays.

The wage period is the period within which wages are payable to an employee for work done under the terms of the contract and subcontracts. Delays will often extend the wage period, including into time periods where the wage rate is increased. Performing the work during a higher-than-expected wage period is relatively easy to recover. The contractor is entitled to recovery for the excess labor escalation costs incurred in light of the delay. These costs are recoverable because they are consequential to the delay—in other words, they are the exact type of delay contemplated by courts when discussing "consequential damages."[54]

As delays occur, expenses for wages can increase both in (1) the additional time required to complete the project (including any time standing down or standing up), and (2) changes in the labor market resulting in higher wage rates. It is important to remember that certain wage damages are liquidated damages, while others are relatively easy to calculate and determine. Damages for wages during a higher-than-expected wage period are calculated by multiplying the additional/extended period by the wage rate. The contractor seeking damages must prove

52. *Id.*

53. *S. Leo Harmonay*, 597 F. Supp. at 1034.

54. Gardner Displays Co. v. United States, 346 F.2d 585 (Ct. Cl. 1965); Am. Bridge Div., U.S. Steel Corp. v. Int'l Union of Operating Eng. Local 487, 772 F.2d at 1554 (11th Cir. 1985).

that the rates paid were reasonable for the labor.[55] However, for wage damages where the market has changed, extensive expert testimony will be required to parse out the impact from the changes in the market and what the contractor may be able to recover.

Escalation of Materials Costs

When a project is delayed, another possible component of damages is material costs. "Material costs include the costs of such items as raw materials, parts, subassemblies, components, and manufacturing supplies, whether purchased or manufactured by the contractor, and may include such collateral items as inbound transportation and in-transit insurance."[56] "When delay becomes foreseeable, contractors are placed on the horns of a dilemma—either purchasing materials at current prices and then arranging for their storage, or delaying purchase and risking that price escalation will not exceed the saved costs of storage."[57]

In order to recoup escalation of materials cost a claimant must show: "(1) the claimant based its bid on lower prices that were available at an earlier point in time; (2) it was impossible or impractical for the claimant to purchase the materials prior to the price escalation; and (3) the claimant actually paid more for the materials than it anticipated."[58] For example, a claimant was successful in recovering increased materials costs when it "produced a quote from its supplier . . . ; price lists before and after [the period of delay]; purchase orders . . . and . . . . trial testimony supporting and recapitulating these figures."[59] "Proof of the actual costs incurred, presented with the actual . . . quotes showing what the claimant anticipated it would pay for the materials, is the best proof of material escalation costs. If actual cost records are not available, industry-wide averages may be accepted as proof of percentage material escalations."[60]

Likewise, in *Levering & Garrigues Co. v. United States*, the government took four months to approve the brick sample supplied by the contractor. During those four months, the contractor "repeatedly called the defendant's attention to the fact

55. First Atl. Bldg. Corp. v. Neubauer Constr. Co., 352 So. 2d 103 (Fla. 4th DCA 1977).

56. FAR § 31.205-26(a), 48 C.F.R. § 31.205-26(a).

57. *See* Bruner & O'Connor, *supra* note 20, at § 19:103.

58. Stephen B. Shapiro & Dirk D. Haire, *Pricing of Claims, in* Federal Government Construction Contracts 657 (3d ed. 2017) (citing to *George Hyman Constr. Co.*, ENG BCA 4541, 85-1, BCA ¶ 17,847).

59. *S. Leo Harmonay*, 597 F. Supp. at 1034.

60. Shapiro & Haire, *supra* note 58, at 659.

that the market price of bricks was advancing."[61] The contractor was awarded "the increased cost" of the bricks that resulted from the government's delay.[62]

As stated, delays can also force a contractor to incur additional storage costs and additional costs to repair or maintain materials that were stored. Courts have found that these costs are recoverable.[63] However, claimants should examine their contracts closely as courts have also enforced provisions which limit recovery for delays.[64]

Additional Insurance Premiums

Another indirect delay damage may be additional insurance premiums incurred by the contractor for extended time on a project. Most contractors obtain insurance for a particular project, and the insurance coverage may be for a set period of time under the contract terms. However, when there is a delay, the contractor may be required to obtain additional insurance or extend the coverage, in particular builder's risk coverage (if carried by the contractor) and worker's compensation coverage and thus incur additional and often substantial premium fees.

In some cases, insurance premiums are based on the dollar amount of the contract. Thus, one key to the evaluation of the recoverability of insurance premiums is careful review of the contract requirements as well as the cause of the delay that required further insurance coverage.

If there is an owner-directed change that increases the amount of the contract, it will necessarily result in increased insurance premiums. Owner-caused delay may require existing insurance policies to be renewed for the extended period of performance. The actions or inactions of the owner will need to be evaluated to determine if they resulted in increased insurance premiums. When owner-directed changes increase the amount of the premium, the contractor is entitled to recover the difference between the original premium price and the increased premium price. No further calculation is required to establish the increased cost of the insurance premiums. When the contractor incurs increased insurance costs due to delay, the entire cost of the extended or new policy is often recoverable.[65] It

61. Levering & Garrigues Co. v. United States, 73 Ct. Cl. 566, 576 (Ct. Cl. 1932).

62. *Id.*

63. *See* Am. Bridge Co. v. State, 283 N.Y.S. 577, 584 (3d Dep't 1935).

64. *See, e.g.*, Elec. Contractors, Inc. v. Fid. & Deposit Co., No. 3:13-cv-00514 (MPS), 2015 U.S. Dist. LEXIS 39860 (D. Conn. Mar. 30, 2015) (subcontractor's claims for increased costs of copper wire denied because contract allowed prime contractor "to change schedules and require[d] [subcontractor] to absorb the effects of those changes").

65. *Luria Bros.*, 369 F.2d 701.

is a fact-based analysis. For example, in *Luria Brothers*, the U.S. Court of Claims permitted the contractor to recover the entire amount of the increased insurance premium and stated:

> [t]he trial commissioner has determined that the plaintiff suffered delay damages and additional expenditures directly attributable to the defendant's breaches . . . [including] wage and material price increases plus 100 percent of an insurance premium plaintiff was required to pay.[66]

In federal government contracts, contractors may also be able to recover self-insurance costs in addition to the costs of purchased insurance as long as those costs are approved and required by the FAR.[67]

Sufficient documentation must be presented to ensure recovery of insurance premiums resulting from a delay. It should first be shown that the insurance premium is a result of the owner's delay. In addition, the contractor is advised to keep clear records of the additional insurance premiums that are being required and, if possible, segregate the costs with both accounting measures and statements from brokers about the additional premiums being paid. Maintaining the records of the extended policy coverage and payment of the additional premiums will also aid in the recoverability of the additional insurance premiums as part of the contractor's delay claim.

In addition to proper documentation of the insurance premiums, a contractor should ensure that the contract terms support such a claim as well. For example, language in the contract that "time is of the essence" will be beneficial. If a contractor can negotiate an express provision regarding insurance premiums and/or a delay provision, this will be helpful to specifically preserve recovery of increased insurance premiums resulting from delay.

Unabsorbed/Extended Home Office Overhead

Contractors are often quick to press for recovery of extended home office overhead when a project is delayed. This category of potential damages includes "[t]hat portion of the contractor's cost which cannot properly and accurately be allocated to a specific operation on any project."[68]

Again, the documentation of the claim is critical, as is ensuring that clear delineation of what is "home office" versus "field office" overhead. Record keeping

---

66. *Id.* at 709.

67. *See* FAR § 31.205(19); 48 C.F.R. § 31.205(19).

68. Construction Dictionary, 8th Edition, The National Association of Women in Construction, 1991.

is also important for proving up total billings for the contract, total project overhead, the days of contract performance, the daily contract overhead rate, and the days of compensable pay.

Formulas and Approaches

If a project is delayed or suffers a setback, a contractor may incur other indirect costs to support its home or other extended office operations. For example, a contractor may not be able to absorb additional costs such as rent, payroll, insurance premiums, or utilities due to lack of project revenue that it would have otherwise been entitled to if not for the delay caused by a third party.

In the event of unabsorbed or extended home office overhead costs due to delays from a third party, courts will generally use a formula to determine the amounts attributable to home office overhead for awardable damages.

The Eichleay Formula

The *Eichleay* formula was born out of a decision by the Armed Services Board of Contract Appeals (ASBCA) in 1960. The qualitative formula adopted in *Eichleay Corp.*[69] is the *exclusive* method of calculating unabsorbed overhead for both federal government construction contracts[70] and federal government manufacturing contracts.[71]

To be entitled to unabsorbed overhead recovery under the *Eichleay* formula, the following three elements must be established:

1. A government-caused or government-imposed delay;
2. The contractor was required to be on "standby" during the delay; and
3. While "standing by," the contractor was unable to take on additional work.[72]

Once the first two elements have been proven by the contractor, the burden of proof then shifts to the government to show that the contractor did not suffer or should not have suffered any loss because it was able to either reduce its overhead or take on other work during the delay.[73]

---

69. *Eichleay Corp.*, ASBCA No. 5183, 60-2 BCA ¶ 2688, *aff'd on recons.*, 61-1 BCA ¶ 2894.

70. Wickham Contracting Co. v. Fischer, 12 F.3d 1574 (Fed. Cir. 1994).

71. West v. All State Boiler, Inc., 146 F.3d 1368 (Fed. Cir. 1998); *Genisco Tech. Corp.*, ASBCA No. 49664, 99-1 BCA ¶ 30,145, *mot. for recons. den.*, 99-1 BCA ¶ 30,324; *Libby Corp.*, ASBCA No. 40765, 96-1 BCA ¶ 28,255.

72. Melka Marine, Inc. v. United States, 187 F.3d 1370 (Fed. Cir. 1999).

73. Satellite Elec. Co. v. Dalton, 105 F.3d 1418 (Fed. Cir. 1997).

The *Eichleay* formula involves a complicated three-step calculation that can be summarized as follows:

- Step One

(Total Contract Billings/Total Billings)
× Total Overhead for Performance Period
= Overhead Allocable to Contract

- Step Two

Overhead Allocable to Contract/Actual Days of Performance
= Daily Contract Overhead Rate

- Step Three

Daily Contract Overhead Rate × No. of Days of Delay
= ***Amount Recoverable***

A contractor is not entitled to profit on an unabsorbed overhead claim under the *Eichleay* formula.

State courts also frequently refer to the *Eichleay* formula as the method for calculating unabsorbed home office damages.[74]

HOOP

While the *Eichleay* formula is widely adopted, some states and municipalities have adopted their own measure of unabsorbed home office damages in the event of a project delay without a corresponding increase in revenue. These formulas generally rely on the same principles used in the *Eichleay* formula but may vary in their complexity or overall allowance.

The Ohio Department of Transportation has specified a contractor is entitled to a "Home Office Overhead Payment" (HOOP) in the event of a project delay as a result of the Department. In *Wood Electric, Inc. v. Ohio Facilities Construction Commission*,[75] an electrical contractor on a multi-prime school construction project run by a construction manager brought suit against the owner for damages suffered by the electrical contractor as a result of delays in the construction allegedly caused by the owner and other contractors. The Court of Appeals held the electrical contractor's election to use the HOOP formula for its unabsorbed home

74. JMR Constr. Corp. v. Env'l Assessment & Remediation Mgmt., Inc., 244 Cal. App. 4th 75 (2016).

75. Wood Elec., Inc. v. Ohio Facilities Constr. Comm'n, 90 N.E.3d 371 (10th Dist. 2017).

office overhead claim was acceptable, and *Eichleay* is not the exclusive manner by which to prove these damages.[76]

HOOP damages are calculated by finding the "Daily HOOP Payment," which is equal to the Original Contract Amount multiplied by the Overhead Rate, divided by the Original Contract Duration in Calendar Days. Using this formula requires reference to the current Ohio Department of Transportation's Overhead Rate specification, which may give some certainty as to the amount of potential damages as opposed to the variable rates used under the *Eichleay* formula.

Subcontractor Delay Costs

The contractor may be liable for the negligent acts of its subcontractors, which may impact the contractor's ability to recover delay damages. If the negligent subcontractor is in the chain of privity with the contractor, the contractor cannot recover delay damages from the owner as those delays are the responsibility of the contractor. However, if the subcontractor has a direct contractual relationship with the owner of the project, the contractor most likely will be able to recover damages as it was not in a position to prevent the delay.

Subcontractors, like general contractors, are frequently impacted by events and actions beyond their control. In addition to the typical risks involved in construction (such as scope changes, differing site conditions, work stoppages, delays, material and labor shortages, adverse weather, and other similar issues), subcontractors face circumstances that may be caused by the general contractor, the owner, other subcontractors, third parties, or force majeure events.

Contractor-Caused Impacts

In order for a subcontractor to recover delay damages, it will have to demonstrate not only a right to the damages based on contractual terms but also that the damages were caused by others and not the subcontractor. The impacts to subcontractors may be contractor-caused impacts such as poor administration of the project, including inadequate coordination or scheduling, problems in the delivery and processing of subcontractor submittals, and failure or refusal to pass subcontractor delay or cost impact notices to the owner. In addition, the subcontractor may experience inefficiencies due to the means and methods allowed by the contractor. For example, contractors may impose restrictions on elevator and crane use, restrictions to the layout space available, and restrictions impacting access to the subcontractor's work. Lack of direction from the contractor or a failure to communicate

76. *Id.* at 381.

clearly regarding work coordination may cause stacking of trades that leads to inefficiencies for the subcontractor. A change in the scope of work generated by the contractor or contractor-directed means and methods could also create an impact.

Owner-Caused Impacts

Owners may cause impact to subcontractors due to many of the similar issues with the contractor, including poor or inadequate contract administration, slow decision-making regarding submittals, RFIs or substitutions, and burdensome inspection methods. The owner's processing legitimate change orders and time extensions can also impact subcontractors, including creating issues with cash flow and labor and materials.

Impacts by Others

Subcontractors can also be impacted by the actions or inactions of other subcontractors and third parties. For example, if a lead framing subcontractor is running behind schedule due to lumber not arriving on site timely, then follow-on plumbing and electrical subcontractors may be unable to rough-in their work as planned in a timely manner. If other subcontractors are terminated or have issues in their work requiring rework, this will impact the subcontractor as well. Government agencies, utility companies, railroads, and owner-supplied vendors may also impact a subcontractor and create delays that may be compensable.

Again, just as for the contractor's claims, a subcontractor's ability to recover on a delay or inefficiency claim will depend in large part on the contract verbiage and other related documents. If there is a no-damages-for-delay clause in the subcontract agreement, however, the subcontractor may be limited and unable to recover for delays caused by the contractor.[77] In *Howard Contracting, Inc. v. G.A. MacDonald Construction Co., Inc.*, the California Appellate Court held that a subcontractor can recover damages for cost overruns caused by delays and disruption even though the city's prime contract barred the recovery of such claims. This case arose out of a public works contract relating to a construction project to rehabilitate the Venice Canals located in Los Angeles. The project was owned and designed by the City of Los Angeles, which awarded the general contract to G.A. MacDonald Construction Co., Inc. The contract between the City and MacDonald contained a limited no-damage-for-delay clause, which stated that a contractor was entitled to

77. Michel & Pfeffer v. Oceanside Props., Inc., 61 Cal. App. 3d (1976); Harper/Nielsen-Dillingham Builders, Inc. v. United States, 81 Fed. Cl. 667 (2008) (enforcing "no damages for delay" clauses in subcontracts even where such clauses are expressly disallowed by statute).

an extension of time to complete work delayed by unforeseen events but was not entitled to collect damages attributable to the delay.[78]

In addition to subcontract terms and conditions, subcontractor delay claims may be affected by terms in the change orders, which may contain exculpatory language eliminating future claims for delays. In *NAFCO Electrical Contractors, Inc. v. Turner Construction Co.*,[79] for example, the court found that in a subcontract change order that contained such waiver language, the subcontractor gave up all rights to raise claims of delay damages.

Subcontractors also need to be careful in signing lien releases. Some lien release forms are specifically designed as *partial* lien releases that are intended to release the general contractor from liability for anything paid for to date. Other lien release forms are much more broadly designed and are *full* lien releases, which may be interpreted as having the effect of releasing the subcontractor for any and all issues arising on the project up to the date of the lien release. Some courts have interpreted broad lien release language to deny subcontractor recovery of damages related to any of the work performed during the period covered by a lien release, and further released the general contractor from the obligation of paying costs arising out of a change order.[80]

Contractors must be aware of the potential for a subcontractor delay claim, and all involved must carefully review and consider the potential for subcontractor delay claims.

Claim Preparation Costs and Attorneys' Fees

As part of the analysis and determination of the efficacy of seeking delay damages, several issues should be considered in careful claim preparation. One of those elements to assess is whether the cost to prepare the claim as well as attorneys' fees for making the delay claim will be recoverable.

The availability of attorneys' fees awards in civil litigation is governed by the so-called American Rule. Under this doctrine, each party to litigation is generally responsible for its own attorneys' fees.[81] Many jurisdictions apply the American Rule in the recovery of attorneys' fees. In California, each party to a lawsuit must

78. Howard Contracting, Inc. v. G.A. Macdonald Constr. Co., Inc., 71 Cal. App. 4th 38 (1998).

79. NAFCO Elec. Contractors, Inc. v. Turner Constr. Co., U.S. Court of Appeals, 2d Cir., No. 09-1369-CV, Dec. 21, 2009.

80. Sauer, Inc. v. Honeywell Bldg. Solutions SES Corp., --- F. Supp. 2d ---, 2010 WL 3824228 (W.D. Pa. Sep. 21, 2010) (NO.CIV.A. 08-92J0); Martin Bros. Constr., Inc. v. Thompson Pac. Constr., Inc., 179 Cal. App. 4th, 102 Cal. Rptr. 3d 419 (2009).

81. *See* F.D. Rich Co., Inc. v. U.S. for Industrial Lumber Co., Inc., 417 U.S. 116, 126 (1974).

ordinarily pay its own fees.[82] Similarly, Florida also follows the American Rule where attorneys' fees may only be awarded by a court pursuant to an entitling statute or an agreement between the parties.[83]

First and foremost is getting a solid handle on the terms of the contract. While many contracts have specific provisions laid out regarding recoverability of claim preparation costs and attorney fees, many contracts are not as precise. Following are two examples of the attorneys' fees provision that may appear in the contract:

- *Attorneys' Fees.* In the event that litigation is brought by any party in connection with this Agreement, the prevailing party shall be entitled to recover from the opposing party all costs and expenses, including reasonable attorneys' fees, incurred by the prevailing party in the exercise of any of its rights or remedies hereunder or the enforcement of any of the terms, conditions, or provisions hereof.
- *Attorney's Fees.* If either Party employs an attorney in conjunction with a Dispute related to this Contract, a Party who successfully defends or prosecutes any such claim, or portion of a claim is entitled to reimbursement from the other Party for necessary and reasonable attorneys' fees, arbitration fees, court costs, expert witness fees, and expenses related to the specific claims successfully defended and/or prosecuted.

As noted earlier, attorneys' fees are generally not recoverable unless there is an applicable attorneys' fees provision. In the absence of a contractual agreement pertaining to attorneys' fees, in some situations, a plaintiff in a construction delay claim may be entitled to attorneys' fees if provided by an applicable statute. Even if the contract does not provide clearly for attorney's fees for bringing a delay damages case, there may be alternative means such as specific statutory bases.

While the contract interpretation for recovery of fees and costs for the claim may present jurisdictional and choice of law issues, there are also key differences depending on the trier of fact. In an arbitration proceeding, there may be alternative issues to consider regarding recovery of costs and attorneys' fees. For the various form construction documents, it is notable that the template, unaltered AIA and Engineers Joint Contract Documents Committee (EJCDC) documents do *not* provide for attorneys' fees to the prevailing party of a dispute. Unaltered ConsensusDocs *do* provide that the prevailing party may recover attorneys' fees.

82. Trope v. Katz, 11 Cal. 4th 274 (1995).
83. Dade Cnty. v. Pena, 664 So. 2d 959, 960 (Fla. 1995).

Profit

The recovery of profit as a result of a delay is more controversial than the other areas of damage we have examined in this chapter. On federal projects, claimants are explicitly forbidden from recovering profit when there is a delay by the government.[84] On private projects, in order to recover profits a claimant must prove (1) foreseeability, (2) amount of damages to a reasonable certainty, and (3) that the lost profits were a proximate consequence.

An exemplary case is that of *Downey, Inc. v. Bradley Center Corp.*,[85] which involved the construction of the arena for the Milwaukee Bucks, the Milwaukee Admirals, and the Marquette Warriors and resulted in an award of lost profits to the claimant. The court noted that the other party "caused numerous delays, placed numerous 'holds' on [the subcontractor's] work, refused to grant extensions and demanded timely performance."[86] The season openers for the teams were already scheduled and thus the subcontractor:

> [W]as told to "do whatever it had to do" to get the job completed. . . . [The subcontractor] pulled workers and resources off other independent contracts to comply with the completion date. [The other party] was informed that the only way to meet the completion date was to pull resources off other independent projects. There was no objection from [the other party].[87]

The court found that the subcontractor had sufficiently notified the other party of the "impact" the delays were having on the subcontractor's other projects, thus making the profits the subcontractor lost on those other projects "reasonably foreseeable" and thus recoverable.[88]

In addition to foreseeability, courts also require that "loss of profits . . . be established with reasonable certainty[.]"[89] However, "uncertainty merely as to the amount of profits that would have been made does not prevent a recovery," given the fact that lost profits are a prospective estimation.[90] But if evidence of the lost profit is "completely speculative," recovery will be denied.[91]

---

84. FAR § 52.242-14(b); 48 C.F.R. § 52.242-14(b); *see also* Mai Steel Serv., Inc. v. Blake Constr. Co., 981 F.2d 414 (9th Cir. 1992) (Miller Act does not allow for recovery of lost profits.).

85. Downey, Inc. v. Bradley Ctr. Corp., 188 Wis. 2d 435 (Ct. App. 1994).

86. *Id.* at 445.

87. *Id.* at 446.

88. *Id.*

89. Gen. Sprinkler Corp. v. Loris Indus. Developers, Inc., 271 F. Supp. 551, 561 (D.S.C. 1967); *see also* Peru Assocs., Inc. v. State, 334 N.Y.S.2d at 775 ("The profit claimed approximating 10% of the bid is fair, reasonable and readily ascertainable and is allowed[.]").

90. *Gen. Sprinkler.*, 271 F. Supp. at 561.

91. ADC Fairways Corp. v. Johnmark Constr., Inc., 343 S.E.2d 90 (Va. 1986) ("The [lost profit] figure was nothing more than the profit Johnmark hoped to make at the time of the bid. There was

Finally, a claimant must show that "[l]ost profits . . . were a proximate consequence of the breach."[92]

Conclusion

The ability of a contractor to recover delay damages starts with an analysis of the terms of the contract and requires a diligent evaluation of the circumstances and careful preparation of the claims to ensure that the damages can be recovered. The best chance for recovery will be for those direct damages, such as increased labor and equipment, standby time, mobilization, and general conditions. However, for the more remote or consequential damages, a contractor will be wise to take efforts to document and detail the potential claims and seek to negotiate contract terms that will allow for recovery of those consequential damages from delay that are not the fault of the contractor. Ultimately, the cause of the delay will need to be established along with the foreseeability and certainty of the damages for delay that the contractor seeks to recover, an often much more complex endeavor than what might appear.

---

no evidence to establish that this is the profit what would have been made had Johnmark completed the project.").

92. River Rd. Dev. Corp. v. Carlson Corp., Civil Action Nos. 89-7037, 90-2386 (consolidated), 1992 U.S. Dist. LEXIS 13103 (E.D. Pa. Aug. 27, 1992); *see also* Dupont Flooring Sys. v. Discovery Zone, Inc., 98 Civ. 5101 (SHS), 2004 U.S. Dist. LEXIS 13149, at *19 (S.D.N.Y. July 13, 2004) ("New York courts have refused to award damages for lost profits due to a defendant's delay in completing construction where a plaintiff was unable to prove that the delay in construction caused the lost profits.").

CHAPTER 9

Liquidated Damages for Delay

Sunu Pillai

Introduction

Liquidated damages are a sum agreed to by the parties at the time of contract formation, "as being payable to satisfy any loss or injury flowing from a breach of their contract," and represent "the parties' best guess of the amount of injury that would be sustained in a contractual breach."[1] Liquidated damages clauses attempt to limit the damages incurred due to delay in construction projects by setting a predetermined damage amount, in lieu of actual damages. Providing for liquidated damages in a construction contract could benefit both contractors and owners. Liquidated damages clauses help contractors quantify risks at the time of contract formation, thereby managing them better. At the same time, these clauses help owners by eliminating the need for proving actual damages, which may be uncertain, and could be difficult and expensive to determine.[2]

Over the years, courts have reached varying conclusions regarding the validity of liquidated damages clauses. "While some state courts are hostile to liquidated damages clauses, federal law does not look with disfavor upon 'liquidated damages' provisions in contracts."[3] Federal courts have upheld liquidated damages clauses in cases where the amount of prospective damages are difficult to determine at the time of formation of the contract, and the parties agree on payment of a fixed amount in the event of a breach as liquidated damages, thereby bypassing litigation to determine the damages at issue.[4] A liquidated damages clause "is an appropriate

1. VICI Racing, LLC v. T-Mobile USA, Inc., 763 F.3d 273, 291 (3d Cir. 2014).
2. Fred A. Arnold, Inc. v. United States, 979 F.2d 217 (Fed. Cir. 1992).
3. DJ Mfg. Corp. v. United States, 86 F.3d 1130, 1134 (Fed. Cir. 1996).
4. *Id.*

means of inducing due performance, or of giving compensation, in case of failure to perform; and courts give it effect in accordance with its terms."[5]

The tension between the freedom of contract and the traditional damages for breach based on the interests it protects is at the heart of the diverging opinions regarding liquidated damages clauses. Each of these concepts is discussed herein.

Interests Protected by Damages

There are three interests protected by damages provisions in a contract:[6]

1. Expectation interest protects "the expectation that the injured party had when he made the contract . . . by attempting to put him in as good a position as he would have been in had the contract been performed," aimed at giving "the injured party the benefit of the bargain."[7]
2. Reliance interest recognizes that the injured party "may have changed his position in reliance on the contract by, for example, incurring expenses in preparing to perform, in performing, or in foregoing opportunities to make other contracts."[8] Damages based on reliance attempts to put the injured party "back in the position in which he would have been had the contract not been made."[9] Damages based on reliance interest are generally smaller than those based on expectation interest, "because it does not include the injured party's lost profit."[10]
3. Restitution interest is granted "if a party has not only changed his own position in reliance on the contract but has also conferred a benefit on the other party by, for example, making a part payment or furnishing services under the contract."[11] Damages based on restitution interest require the breaching party "to disgorge the benefit that he has received by returning it to the party who conferred it," and generally result in the least damages "because it includes neither the injured party's lost profit nor that part of his expenditures in reliance that resulted in no benefit to the other party."[12]

5. Robinson v. United States, 261 U.S. 486, 488 (1923).
6. *See* Restatement (Second) of Contracts § 344 (1981).
7. *Id.*
8. *Id.*
9. *Id.*
10. *Id.*
11. *Id.*
12. *Id.*

In the absence of a valid liquidated damages clause, damages are "ordinarily based on the injured party's expectation interest."[13] This preference for expectation damages is the reason many courts look at the reasonableness of liquidated damages at the time the contract was made.

Parties' Freedom to Contract

Parties' freedom to contract forms the basis for the validity of liquidated damages clauses. Freedom of contract to pre-determine damages prior to a breach is especially important in the construction industry, where projects involve multiple parties.

The tendency of the courts at one time was to construe the language as a penalty, so that nothing but actual damages sustained by the nonbreaching party could be recovered.[14] Starting in the early 1900s, the courts became more tolerant of liquidated damages provisions and are now generally inclined to allow parties to make their own contracts.[15] As the Supreme Court stated in 1902:

> [T]he business of the court . . . is to inquire after the meaning and intent of the parties; and when that is clearly ascertained from the terms and language used, it must be carried into effect. A court of law possesses no dispensing powers; it cannot inquire whether the parties have acted wisely or rashly, in respect to any stipulation they may have thought proper to introduce into their agreements. If they are competent to contract within the prudential rules the law has fixed as to parties, and there has been no fraud, circumvention, or illegality in the case, the court is bound to enforce the agreement. Men may enter into improvident contracts where the advantage is knowingly and strikingly against them; they may also expend their property upon idle or worthless objects, or give it away if they please without an equivalent, in spite of the powers or interference of the court; and it is difficult to see why they may not fix for themselves by agreement in advance, a measure of compensation, however extravagant it may be, for a violation of their covenant (they surely may after it has accrued), without the intervention of a court or jury. Can it be an exception to their power to bind themselves by

---

13. *See id.* § 347. The Restatement's recitation of the three interests and its preference for expectation interest has its origin in the seminal article authored by Fuller and Perdue in 1936. *See* L.L. Fuller & William R. Perdue, Jr., *The Reliance Interest in Contract Damages* (pts. 1 & 2), 46 YALE L.J. 52, 373 (1936–37). However, its conclusions have been disputed in recent years. *See* Richard Craswell, *Against Fuller and Perdue*, 67(1) UNIV. OF CHI. L. REV. Art. 3 (2000).

14. *See* United States v. Bethlehem Steel Co., 205 U.S. 105, 119 (1907).

15. *See* United States v. Bethlehem Steel Co., 205 U.S. 105, 119 (1907), which states: "The question always is, What did the parties intend by the language used? When such intention is ascertained, it is ordinarily the duty of the court to carry it out."

> lawful contract? We suppose not; and regarding the intent of the parties, it is not to be doubted but that the [liquidated damages] was fixed upon by them "mutually and expressly," as they say, "as the measure of damages for the violation of the covenant, or any of its terms or conditions." If it be said that the measure is a hard one, it may be replied that the defendants should not have stipulated for it; or, having been thus indiscreet, they should have sought the only exemption, which was still within their power; namely, the faithful fulfilment of their agreement.[16]

Courts now acknowledge that "there is no sound reason" why competent parties may not agree on liquidated damages, "or why their agreement, when fairly and understandingly entered into with a view to just compensation for the anticipated loss, should not be enforced."[17] Instead, the focus is on whether the liquidated damages clause unambiguously[18] demonstrates the parties' intention to set a fixed amount to be paid in the event of breach, and whether the amount "is reasonable in the light of the anticipated or actual loss caused by the breach and the difficulties of proof of loss."[19] However, there is still considerable tension between the respect accorded the parties' freedom to contract and the prohibition against enforcing a penalty.

Validity of Liquidated Damages Clauses

While courts acknowledge the parties' freedom of contract, they often review these clauses for the reasonableness of the bargain, and will review whether the amount stipulated is "extravagant, or disproportionate" and "that compensation was not the object aimed at or as to imply fraud, mistake, circumvention or oppression."[20] Thus the determination of the validity of a liquidated damages clause is always a factual enquiry to determine reasonableness.

Jurisdictions differ regarding the temporal perspective from which to evaluate the reasonableness of the liquidated-damages provision.[21] Some jurisdictions only

16. Sun Printing & Publ'g Ass'n v. Moore, 183 U.S. 642, 669–70 (1902).

17. K-Con Bldg. Sys., Inc. v. United States, 778 F.3d 1000, 1008 (Fed. Cir. 2015).

18. *See* VICI Racing, LLC v. T-Mobile USA, Inc., 763 F.3d 273, 291 (3d Cir. 2014) ("A term is ambiguous when the provision is reasonably or fairly susceptible of different interpretations or may have two or more different meanings."); Weitz Co. LLC v. MacKenzie House, LLC, 665 F.3d 970, 976 (8th Cir. 2012) (Where, however, the contract is ambiguous, the meaning of its terms is to be determined by the jury in the light of the evidence of the surrounding circumstances and the practical construction of the parties.).

19. Space Master Int'l, Inc. v. City of Worcester, 940 F.2d 16, 17 (1st Cir. 1991), citing Restatement (Second) of Contracts § 356(1) (1979).

20. K-Con Bldg. Sys., Inc. v. United States, 778 F.3d 1000, 1008 (Fed. Cir. 2015).

21. Hutton Contracting Co. v. City of Coffeyville, 487 F.3d 772, 781 (10th Cir. 2007).

review the reasonableness of liquidated damages prospectively—that is, they consider only the reasonableness of the estimated damages at the time of contract formation.[22] This matches with the preference for expectation damages in cases where liquidated damages are not specified. Others perform an additional retrospective analysis[23]—that is, they also compare the actual amount of liquidated damages with the actual damages suffered by the nonbreaching party.[24] Jurisdictions that also review the reasonableness of the liquidated damages retrospectively cite to the Restatement of Contracts for the position that the reasonableness of the liquidated damages clause should be reviewed as of the time of contracting and at the time of actual breach.[25] These jurisdictions enforce the liquidated damages clause if it is reasonable at either time.

In cases involving construction contracts, courts usually assume the occurrence of loss, as "it can seldom be shown that no use would in fact have been made, had completion been on time, or that no profit would have been made from such use."[26] In determining whether the liquidated damages provision is reasonable, courts generally consider two factors provided in the Restatement (Second) of Contracts: (1) the difficulty in either proving that loss has occurred or in establishing its amount of loss with the requisite certainty; and (2) the anticipated or actual loss caused by the breach.[27]

---

22. PYCA Indus., Inc. v. Harrison Cty. Waste Water Mgmt. Dist., 177 F.3d 351, 367 (5th Cir. 1999) ("Whether a sum stipulated is a penalty [a disfavored approach] or liquidated damages [an acceptable approach] is a question of construction to be decided upon the terms and inherent circumstances of each particular contract, judged at the time of the making of the contract, not as at the time of the breach." (under Mississippi law)).

23. See Kelly v. Marx, 44 Mass. App. Ct. 825, 832, 694 N.E.2d 869, 873 (1998), for a listing of jurisdictions that follow a prospective (single look) approach, and those that require a retrospective (second look) approach.

24. Yockey v. Horn, 880 F.2d 945, 953 (7th Cir. 1989). ("The reasonableness of the amount set in a liquidated damages clause is to be looked at as of the time of contracting and at the time of actual breach. If at either time the estimate is reasonable, the clause will be enforced." (citing to RESTATEMENT (SECOND) OF CONTRACTS § 356 cmt. b; decision under Illinois law)).

25. 880 F.2d at 953.

26. Space Master Int'l, Inc. v. City of Worcester, 940 F.2d 16, 18 (1st Cir. 1991).

27. Leaman v. Wolfe, 629 F. App'x 280, 283 (3d Cir. 2015); Sw. Eng'g Co. v. United States, 341 F.2d 998, 1001 (8th Cir. 1965) ("Two requirements must be considered to determine whether the provision included in the contract fixing the amount of damages payable on breach will be interpreted as an enforceable liquidated damage clause rather than an un[en]forceable penalty clause: First, the amount so fixed must be a reasonable forecast of just compensation for the harm that is caused by the breach, and second, the harm that is caused by the breach must be one that is incapable or very difficult of accurate estimation.").

Difficulty of Proving Anticipated or Actual Loss

The underlying reason to provide for liquidated damages in a contract is that the actual damages cannot be calculated at the time the contract is made. As such, "the inherent difficulty of affixing actual damages flowing from a potential breach is a factor favoring the use of liquidated damages clauses."[28] The greater the difficulty to calculate actual damages at the time of contract, the easier it is to show that the liquidated damages are not a penalty, and are valid. As discussed earlier, in evaluating the validity of a liquidated damages provision, most courts review the difficulty of calculating actual damages at the time of the contract (i.e., anticipated actual losses), not whether the actual losses could be calculated after the fact.

Amount of Actual Loss

If the liquidated damages approximate the anticipated or actual loss resulting from the breach, it will likely be held that it is not a penalty.[29] The amount needs to be only a reasonable approximation, not an accurate estimate. "The mere fact that the amount of damages ultimately suffered by a party was less than the amount payable under the liquidated-damages clause does not, standing alone, permit courts to recharacterize a liquidated damages provision as a penalty."[30] This is because the reason parties are including a liquidated damages clause in the contract is that actual damages are difficult to estimate. As such, the parties' reasonable agreement on the amount of liquidated damages is provided considerable deference where losses are difficult to quantify.[31]

At the same time, courts have held that the liquidated damages cannot be so disproportionate as to constitute a penalty. If "the damages flowing from a breach of a contract are easily ascertainable, or the damages fixed are plainly disproportionate to the contemplated injury," the stipulated liquidated damages "will be treated as a penalty and disallowed."[32] Where the liquidated damages are "unreasonably large," courts have held them to be "unenforceable on grounds of public policy as

---

28. PYCA Indus., Inc. v. Harrison Cnty. Waste Water Mgmt. Dist., 177 F.3d 351, 368 (5th Cir. 1999).

29. Leaman v. Wolfe, 629 F. App'x 280, 283 (3d Cir. 2015).

30. PYCA Indus., Inc. v. Harrison Cnty. Waste Water Mgmt. Dist., 177 F.3d 351, 368 (5th Cir. 1999).

31. Space Master Int'l, Inc. v. City of Worcester, 940 F.2d 16, 18 (1st Cir. 1991).

32. U.S. Fid. & Guar. Co. v. Braspetro Oil Servs. Co., 369 F.3d 34, 71 (2d Cir. 2004); Space Master Int'l, Inc. v. City of Worcester, 940 F.2d 16, 17–18 (1st Cir. 1991) (Courts generally look at two factors while assessing reasonableness: (1) whether the amount approximates either the actual loss or the loss anticipated at the time the contract was executed; and (2) the difficulty either of proving that loss has occurred or of establishing the amount of loss with the requisite certainty.).

a penalty."[33] Since the liquidated damages must approximate the anticipated actual damages, courts sometimes hold that the same damages cannot be specified for all breaches, reasoning that if the contract specifies "a single sum in damages for any and all breaches even though it is apparent that all are not of the same gravity," then the liquidated damages provision "is not a reasonable effort to estimate damages."[34]

Evaluating the reasonableness of a contractual provision must always be balanced against the parties' freedom to contract. Courts should take care not to rewrite the risk allocations in the contract after the fact, in the name of "reasonableness." If the damages are considered "unreasonable," "it may be replied that the defendants should not have stipulated for it; or, having been thus indiscreet, they should have sought the only exemption, which was still within their power; namely, the faithful fulfilment of their agreement."[35]

Liquidated Damages as a Penalty

Liquidated damages are not enforceable if they are considered a penalty—that is, if the liquidated damages are "unreasonably large" considering "the anticipated or actual loss caused by the breach."[36] The "burden of proving that a liquidated damages clause constitutes an unenforceable penalty rests with the party challenging the provision."[37] "Whether the sum stipulated represents a liquidation of the anticipated damages or a penalty is a question of law, with due consideration for the nature of the contract and the attendant circumstances."[38]

Liquidated damages clauses will not be regarded as penalties if they are found to be reasonable.[39] Thus, in most cases, the question of whether a liquidated damages clause is a penalty will lead to the analysis discussed in the prior section as to whether the clause is reasonable. Liquidated damages clauses are "deemed unenforceable penalties generally only in limited cases where (1) the actual damage

33. Yockey v. Horn, 880 F.2d 945, 952 (7th Cir. 1989).
34. Lake River Corp. v. Carborundum Co., 769 F.2d 1284, 1290 (7th Cir. 1985).
35. *Id.*
36. Restatement (Second) of Contracts § 356.
37. Hutton Contracting Co. v. City of Coffeyville, 487 F.3d 772, 781 (10th Cir. 2007) (citing Kansas law).
38. U.S. Fid. & Guar. Co. v. Braspetro Oil Servs. Co., 369 F.3d 34, 71 (2d Cir. 2004).
39. United States v. United Eng'g & Constr. Co., 234 U.S. 236, 241 (1914); Sun Printing & Publ'g Ass'n v. Moore, 183 U.S. 642, 669 (1902) (Discussing various cases from the English Courts – "The following are the leading cases: *Astley v. Weldon*, 2 Bos. & P. 346; *Barton v. Glover*, Holt, N. P. 43, and note; *Reilly v. Jones*, 1 Bing. 302; *Davies v. Penton*, 6 Barn. & C. 216; *Crisdee v. Bolton*, 3 Car. & P. 240; *Randall v. Everest*, 2 Car. & P. 577; *Kemble v. Farren*, 6 Bing. 141. In our court are the following: *Dennis v. Cummins*, 3 Johns. Cas. 297, 2 Am. Dec. 160; *Slosson v. Beadle*, 7 Johns. 72; *Spencer v. Tilden*, 5 Cow. 144, and note, p. 150; *Nobles v. Bates*, 7 Cow. 307; *Knapp v. Maltby*, 13 Wend. 587.").

resulting from the breach may be readily ascertained, or (2) the contract discloses no intention to fix the sum as liquidated damages or leaves the intention in this regard in doubt."[40]

Lack of Actual Damages

Where no actual loss was sustained as a result of the breach, courts have held liquidated damages to be an unenforceable penalty.[41] This is because "liquidated damages must compensate for loss rather than punish for breach."[42] "An exaction of punishment for a breach which could produce no possible damage has long been deemed oppressive and unjust."[43] The only function for a liquidated damages clause when there is no actual damage is to secure performance and to deter default. Such clauses will be held to be an unenforceable penalty. As the Restatement of Contracts states, the parties to a contract are not free to provide a penalty for its breach as "the central objective behind the system of contract remedies is compensatory, not punitive."[44] "Punishment of a promisor for having broken his promise has no justification on either economic or other grounds and a term providing such a penalty is unenforceable on grounds of public policy."[45]

Optional Liquidated Damages

An optional liquidated damages provision provides for liquidated damages but, in addition, provides the owner the option to prove actual damages. Such a clause may state that the owner may elect to recover its actual damages resulting from the contractor's default as an alternate measure of damages, and in lieu of the liquidated damages. There is no agreed-upon measure of damages, since the contractor is always at risk of damages greater than the liquidated damages. On the other hand, the owner may choose to assess liquidated damages only if it is more than the actual damages, in which case it could be considered an unenforceable penalty. Some courts have held that such optional liquidated damage clauses are unenforceable, since they do not involve a reasonable attempt to estimate the loss, with the

40. PYCA Indus., Inc. v. Harrison Cnty. Waste Water Mgmt. Dist., 177 F.3d 351, 367 (5th Cir. 1999).

41. Space Master Int'l, Inc. v. City of Worcester, 940 F.2d 16, 18 (1st Cir. 1991).

42. *Id.*

43. Priebe & Sons, Inc. v. United States, 332 U.S. 407, 413 (1947).

44. Restatement (Second) of Contracts § 356, cmt. (a).

45. *Id.*

result that only actual damages due to the breach are recoverable.[46] Other courts have enforced such provisions based on the freedom of contract.[47]

Liquidated Damages in Addition to Actual Damages

Recovery of actual damages for delay in addition to those liquidated by the contract is typically prohibited. One reason is that liquidated and actual damages are mutually exclusive remedies.[48] Hence a liquidated damages clause precludes any recovery of actual damages. Further, liquidated damages could be considered a penalty in such cases. "Where a contract provides that the breaching party must pay all damages caused by the breach as well as a specified sum in addition thereto, the sum so specified can be nothing but a security for performance which constitutes an unenforceable penalty."[49] Where a damages clause provides for more than actual damages, then it "is not a reasonable effort to estimate damages, and is a penalty."[50]

Liquidated Damages in Cases of Delay by Both Parties

Construction disputes may involve delay by both parties. As a general rule, a party asserting that liquidated damages were improperly assessed bears the burden of showing the extent of the excusable delay to which it is entitled.[51] However, in the context of assessing liquidated damages, the owner has the "initial burden of showing that the contract performance requirements were not substantially completed by the contract completion date and that the period for which the assessment was made was proper."[52] Once it has met that burden, "the burden then shifts to the contractor to show that any delays were excusable and that it should be relieved of all or part of the assessment."[53]

If the contractor meets the burden to show that excusable delays exist, then the question will turn to whether the delays are concurrent or sequential. If both parties are responsible for the same period of delay, that is, concurrent delay, then

46. Grossinger Motorcorp, Inc. v. Am. Nat'l Bank & Tr. Co., 607 N.E.2d 1337, 1347 (1992); Lefemine v. Baron, 573 So. 2d 326, 330 (Fla. 1991).

47. Ravenstar, LLC v. One Ski Hill Place, LLC, 401 P.3d 552, 558.

48. U.S. Fid. & Guar. Co. v. Braspetro Oil Servs. Co., 369 F.3d 34, 71 (2d Cir. 2004).

49. Telenois, Inc. v. Vill. of Schaumburg, 628 N.E.2d 581, 585 (1993).

50. Raffel v. Medallion Kitchens, 139 F.3d 1142, 1146 (7th Cir. 1998).

51. Sauer Inc. v. Danzig, 224 F.3d 1340, 1347 (Fed. Cir. 2000).

52. E. Coast Repair & Fabrication, LLC v. United States, 199 F. Supp. 3d 1006, 1030 (E.D. Va. 2016).

53. *Id.*

courts are generally in agreement that the contract receives additional time, and that it precludes the recovery of delay damages.[54] However, courts have varied in their treatment when one party and then the other cause different delays intermittently, that is, sequential delay.

One set of cases "follows the so-called 'rule against apportionment,' and holds that where delays are caused by both parties to the contract the court will not attempt to apportion them, but will simply hold that the provisions of the contract with reference to liquidated damages will be annulled."[55] These courts follow the principle that "if the non-breaching party somehow prevented the performance of the contract within the stipulated time, then even if the work is delayed by the fault of the breaching party, the rule of the original contract cannot be insisted upon, and liquidated damages measured thereby are waived."[56] As the Tenth Circuit noted, this rule against apportionment reflected "a hostility to liquidated damages that arose from an outdated view that while parties could determine their own contractual obligations, damages were the province of the courts" and relied on the "axiom that once a party has violated the terms of a contract, it has abrogated all terms in the same contract and cannot then enforce rights under it."[57]

Other courts, relying on the Supreme Court's opinion in *Robinson*, hold that delays by the owner "presents no legal ground for denying it compensation for loss suffered wholly through the fault of the contractor," since the intention is that the contractor should pay for delay at a certain specified rate, even if it were relieved from that obligation for some of the delay due to the owner's action.[58] These courts require apportionment of liquidated damages due to delay and limit *United Engineering* to its facts, holding that it "only requires annulment where, due to [owner] delay, the contract documents in question no longer provide a valid reference date from which to calculate liquidated damages."[59]

Over time, courts have generally moved away from the rule against apportionment, and hold that "damages for delay should be imposed for those delays, and only those delays, for which the contractor is responsible."[60] Courts have justified this shift on the basis that "apportionment of damages based on fault comports with modern notions of fairness" (similar to "near-universal adoption of comparative responsibility in tort actions"), and that "such apportionment can encourage

54. R.P. Wallace, Inc. v. United States, 63 Fed. Cl. 402, 410 (2004).

55. *Id. See also* Airline Constr. Inc. v. Barr, 807 S.W.2d 247, 262 (Tenn. Ct. App. 1990) (Liquidated damages will not be awarded to one that has contributed to or mutually caused the delay or breach.).

56. United States v. United Eng'g & Constr. Co., 234 U.S. 236, 242 (1914).

57. Hutton Contracting Co. v. City of Coffeyville, 487 F.3d 772, 783–84 (10th Cir. 2007).

58. Robinson v. United States, 261 U.S. 486, 488 (1923).

59. R.P. Wallace, Inc. v. United States, 63 Fed. Cl. 402, 411 (2004).

60. Hutton Contracting Co. v. City of Coffeyville, 487 F.3d 772, 784 (10th Cir. 2007).

efficient behavior."[61] Even in states that still follow the nonapportionment rule, it is unclear whether the rule will be maintained in light of the modern view on apportionment.[62]

Waiver of Liquidated Damages

Liquidated damages clauses may be waived by conduct. The "purpose of the waiver doctrine is to protect contractors who are led to believe that time is no longer of the essence and undertake substantial efforts after the performance date specified in the contract has passed."[63] Whether waiver exists is a factual question to be determined by the fact finder. To prevent waiver, it is important to clearly communicate the assessment of liquidated damages.

Parties often argue that liquidated damages were waived because the deadline triggering the assessment of those damages was waived. This could occur when the nonbreaching party signs change orders after the planned substantial completion date, or if the nonbreaching party was otherwise led to believe that it will not be held to the contractual substantial completion date.

For example, in a case where the owner "repeatedly assured [the contractor] that the substantial completion deadline would be extended" and the owner "uninterruptedly issued hundreds of change orders and construction change directives," the court concluded that the owner waived "its right to liquidated damages":

> [The owner's] conduct in issuing hundreds of change orders and construction change directives after expiration of the substantial completion date . . . constituted waiver of the "time is of the essence" provision of the contract. In addition, [the owner] failed to set a new substantial completion date, thus it failed to reserve its right to enforce the liquidated damages provision for any date after [the original substantial completion date].[64]

Even when the change orders specifically stated that there will be no time extensions, but were signed after the scheduled substantial completion date, courts have held those statements to be ambiguous, since the execution of the change orders after the substantial completion date was considered inconsistent with the

---

61. *Id.*

62. Great Am. Ins. Co. v. E.L. Bailey & Co., Inc., 841 F.3d 439, 448–49 (6th Cir. 2016) ("It is unclear, however, whether the Michigan Supreme Court, if faced with the issue today, would maintain the strict non-apportionment rule in light of the modern view documented by the Tenth Circuit.").

63. State of Fla., Dep't of Ins. v. United States, 81 F.3d 1093, 1096–97 (Fed. Cir. 1996) (discussing waiver doctrine in the context of termination for default).

64. RDP Royal Palm Hotel, L.P. *ex rel.* PADC Hosp. Corp. I v. Clark Constr. Grp., Inc., 168 F. App'x 348, 354 (11th Cir. 2006).

alleged intent to hold the contractor to the strict requirements of the time provision.[65] Liquidated damages could be considered waived in those circumstances.

Courts have also held that where the owner and the contractor worked together to complete the project after the scheduled substantial completion date, the "time is of essence" provision, and the right to assess liquidated damages, was waived.[66] If the owner's intent is to assess liquidated damages in accordance with the contract, it must either clarify that liquidated damages will be assessed, or it should "set a new deadline for performance so that the parties will understand when performance is required."[67]

Some contracts specify that any waiver has to be in writing. But such provisions are unlikely to be effective. "Neither the parol evidence rule, the Statute of Frauds, nor express provision in the written contract against waiver by subsequent oral agreement or conduct, prevent the introduction of evidence that a party to the contract by subsequent conduct or agreement—oral or written—waived a condition to his performance of the contract."[68] Thus, a party may prevail on an oral waiver argument despite a contractual provision that such waiver must be in writing.

Liquidated Damages for Interim Milestone Dates

Liquidated damages could be specified for interim milestones, especially when the delay of such milestones will result in additional costs. For example, damages may be tied to an interim milestone for making a building weather tight. Any delay to this milestone could result in delays to the project or in additional costs (e.g., temporary heat), especially in regions experiencing cold weather. Any liquidated damages should approximate the anticipated actual costs due to the delay. The clause should also provide for reduction in liquidated damages if the contractor is able to mitigate the delay later in the project.

---

65. Rockwell v. Mountain View Elec. Ass'n, Inc., 521 P.2d 1272, 1274 (Colo. App. 1974).

66. Banks Bldg. Co., LLC v. Malanga Family Real Estate Holding, LLC, 926 A.2d 1, 7 (2007).

67. State of Fla., Dep't of Ins. v. United States, 81 F.3d 1093, 1096–97.

68. Searoad Shipping Co. v. E. I. duPont de Nemours & Co., 361 F.2d 833, 838 (5th Cir. 1966) (citing Corbin 3A id. § 763, at 531, which states: "A provision that an express condition of a promise or promises in the contract cannot be eliminated by waiver, or by conduct constituting an estoppel, is wholly ineffective. The promisor still has the power to waive the condition, or by his conduct to estop himself from insisting upon it, to the same extent that he would have had this power if there had been no such provision.").

Liquidated Damages After Substantial Completion

Historically, courts have held that a finding of substantial completion tolls the assessment of liquidated damages, thus refusing to impose liquidated damages after the date of substantial completion.[69] The rationale behind this policy was that liquidated damages otherwise would become a penalty because those damages are designed to approximate an owner's loss before occupancy, and an owner is able to use the project upon substantial completion. However, this is not true in the case of many construction projects. Hotel projects, for example, cannot be used until final completion, or at least until all internal punch list items are completed.

While there are not many decisions on this topic, courts have stated that assessment of liquidated damages for final completion could be acceptable. For example, the Sixth Circuit stated in a case where the contract had "two separate liquidated damages provisions: one for failure to achieve substantial completion on time, and another for failure to achieve final completion on time," if the contractor was responsible for delays after substantial completion, the contractor "would remain liable for ongoing liquidated damages for each day that [it] did not settle."[70] While the assessment of liquidated damages based on final completion has a logical basis for some projects and could be justified based on the parties' freedom to contract, this could result in a potential risk for contractors, as final completion could be delayed much more than substantial completion due to disputes.

The liquidated damages for final completion, in most cases, will have to be lower than that for substantial completion. This is because of the requirement that liquidated damages approximate actual damages. In most cases, actual damages will be reduced once the project achieves substantial completion. Both ConsensusDocs and Engineers Joint Contract Documents Committee (EJCDC) contract documents allow for the assessment of liquidated damages based on final completion.[71]

Considerations While Specifying Liquidated Damages

While the trend is toward upholding liquidated damages clauses, the ease of enforceability will vary by jurisdiction. Care should be exercised in (1) drafting the provision, (2) negotiations on the use of a liquidated damage clause, and (3) the

---

69. Stone v. City of Arcola, 536 N.E.2d 1329 (Ill. 1989) (holding that liquidated damages can only be awarded until the substantial completion date).

70. Great Am. Ins. Co. v. E.L. Bailey & Co., 841 F.3d 439, 449 (6th Cir. 2016).

71. ConsensusDocs 6.5.2 and EJCDC 1910-8-A-1 4.03.

process of arriving at a reasonable estimate of damages and preserving for the record the documentation that supports the amount. Some best practices include:

- Including preamble language that the parties would be damaged by delay, that the exact calculation of damages is difficult or impossible, and that the actual delay is reasonably approximated by the liquidated damages provision.
- Keeping records that demonstrate best efforts in arriving at an accurate anticipated damages amount. This will include a reasonable and comprehensive estimate of the probable loss in the event of delay, accurate records of the parties' negotiations, and industry source records or financial projections used to develop the estimate and arrive at the liquidated amount.
- Describing the elements of anticipated damages that would or might be sustained on a particular project and why they would be difficult to calculate if the contractor does not achieve substantial completion by the scheduled date. The damages that liquidated damages provisions are intended to cover typically include the owner's additional daily construction costs, daily overheads, and daily profits lost as a result of the contractor's failure to achieve substantial completion by the agreed-upon date.
- If liquidated damages are imposed for interim milestones before substantial completion, giving credit to the contractor if recovery is made and substantial completion is still achieved according to the schedule.
- Triggering liquidated damages by a specific event might be more justifiable than merely imposing a daily amount. For example, if a school project is delayed and, therefore, unavailable for use at the start of the school year, a substantial liquidated damage amount on a certain date might be a more reasonable estimate of actual damages than a smaller per diem amount.

CHAPTER 10

Owner Actual Damages for Delay

Brian J. Schoolman and Stephen R. Dowd

Introduction

An axiom of construction is that it can be seen as a form of legalized gambling due to the range of risks that parties take. One of the most common of these risks is delay. Delays can have devastating economic impacts on any affected party, but perhaps the greatest delay risk falls on the owner. Typically, the owner is taking a financial risk on the front end to build something, and on the back end because of the need for the completed project to generate revenue or to add capacity.

In today's construction practice, most parties immediately associate owner damages with liquidated damages. Chapter 9 discusses liquidated damages in greater detail, and there will be only passing discussion of that subject here. The purpose of this chapter is to examine the owner's "actual" damages that are caused by contractor delays.

"Actual damages" are defined as those "awarded to a complainant to compensate for a proven injury or loss; damages that repay actual losses."[1] As a threshold matter, an owner and its attorney are often going to have to determine whether to seek actual damages or liquidated damages. However, as discussed herein, in some jurisdictions, an owner may recover both actual and liquidated damages, which obviates the need for that decision. But if an owner can only have one or the other, then an evaluation of what actual damages are recoverable needs to be undertaken, so the owner knows which path to recovery makes the most financial sense.

Recovering Both Liquidated Damages and Actual Damages

The rule in a number of jurisdictions is that, when the contract contains a liquidated damages provision, the owner is barred from recovering both the liquidated

1. *Actual Damages*, Black's Law Dictionary (11th ed. 2019).

damages and actual damages, in order to avoid allowing double recovery. The rationale behind this general rule is that liquidated damages are intended to be a substitute for actual damages. Additionally, a provision that allows the owner to choose between liquidated damages and actual damages, or that permits the owner to pursue them both for the same delay, is void.[2]

A century ago, the U.S. Supreme Court stated that, in relation to a claim against the United States, "there is no reason why parties competent to contract may not agree that certain elements of damage difficult to estimate shall be covered by a provision for liquidated damages and that other elements shall be ascertained in the usual manner."[3] Following the same rationale as *J.E. Hathaway*, some states, including Minnesota and Florida,[4] have held that a liquidated damages clause that does not specify the types of delay damages intended to be included within the clause does not preclude recovery of additional delay-related damages under various other provisions within the contract.[5]

For example, in *Northern Petrochemical Co. v. Thorsen Thorshov, Inc.*,[6] the Minnesota Supreme Court held that a liquidated damages provision "was intended to apply only to 'normal' delays in the rate of construction, not to the extraordinary 8-month delay resulting from defective construction and design and necessary reconstruction of the building." Thus, under the specific circumstances shown by the owner in claims against the contractor and designer, the fact of the *per diem* liquidated damages provision did not preclude the owner from also recovering damages for loss of use of the building in question.

In Arizona, both actual and liquidated damages may be awarded as long as they are awarded for different injuries.[7] In *Miner Contracting, Inc. v. Toho-Tolani County Improvement District*, the court allowed an award of actual damages related to the cost of completion, in addition to the contractually stipulated liquidated damages. The court found that the actual damages were recoverable on top of the liquidated damages because the damages in question, including engineering, construction administration, maintenance, and out-of-pocket payments to other

---

2. MCA Television Ltd. v. Pub. Interest Corp., 171 F.3d 1265, 1272–76 (11th Cir. 1999).

3. J. E. Hathaway & Co. v. United States, 249 U.S. 460, 464 (1919).

4. *See* Hillsborough Cnty. Aviation Auth. v. Cone Bros. Contracting Co., 285 So. 2d 619, 621–22 (Fla. 2d D.C.A. 1973) (owner suing contractor could seek both liquidated damages for delayed completion of entire project and actual damages paid to subcontractors due to delayed completion of certain phases of the work).

5. *But see* Edward Kraemer & Sons v. City of Kansas City, 1995 U.S. Dist. LEXIS 9523, at *15 (D. Kan. June 19, 1995) ("If KDOT intended to provide for indemnification of claims paid to contractors for the delay of another contractor, it could have provided for it specifically in the contract.").

6. 297 Minn. 118, 126 N.W.2d 159, 166 (1973).

7. A. Miner Contracting, Inc. v. Toho-Tolani Cnty. Improvement Dist., 233 Ariz. 249, 311 P.3d 1062, 1071 (Ariz. App. 2013).

third parties, were separate and distinct from the delay damages captured by the liquidated damages.[8]

A key element for certain courts that considered allowing owners to recover both liquidated damages and additional actual damages is how clearly and specifically the liquidated damages provision is drafted,[9] and whether it adequately distinguishes the liquidated damages from the actual damages also being sought.

Liquidated Damages Clause Precludes Actual Damages

States, including Illinois and New Jersey, preclude an owner from recovering actual damages when a contract has a liquidated damages clause, as long as "the fixed sum is a reasonable forecast of just compensation that is incapable of or difficult to assess accurately, liquidated damage clauses are both enforceable and favored in the law."[10]

Other states, including New York, view liquidated damages provisions as a contract's "exclusive remedy" in the sense that such a provision "precludes any recovery of actual damages."[11] This ensures that parties do not have an option after the breach to choose between liquidated or actual damages, based on the conclusion that allowing the party to choose which method was more valuable would ultimately defeat the certainty that liquidating provisions were intended to provide.[12] A majority of states do not allow parties to elect the remedy of actual delay damages in lieu of liquidated damages simply because the actual damages are greater.[13]

For example, in *Brower Co. v. Garrison*,[14] the Washington Court of Appeals refused to allow the owner to recover actual damages in excess of those covered

8. *Id.* at 249, 311 P.3d 1062.

9. *See, e.g.*, Metro. Dade Cnty. v. Frank J. Rooney, Inc., 627 So. 2d 1248 (Fla. 3d DCA 1993); Hall Constr. Co. v. Beynon, 1507 So. 2d 1225 (Fla. 5th DCA 1987).

10. People *ex rel.* Hammer v. Lumbermens Mut. Cas. Co. (*In re* Liquidation of Lumbermens Mut. Cas. Co.), 2018 IL App (1st) 171613, ¶ 63, 431 Ill. Dec. 186, 206, 127 N.E.3d 719, 739 (citing Monsen Eng'g Co. v. Tami-Githens, Inc., 219 N.J. Super. 241, 530 A.2d 313, 318 (N.J. Super. Ct. App. Div. 1987)).

11. GFI Brokers, LLC v. Santana, 2008 U.S. Dist. LEXIS 59219, at *33–34 (S.D.N.Y. Aug. 6, 2008) (citing Federal Realty Ltd. Partnership v. Choices Women's Medical Center, Inc., 289 A.D.2d 439, 735 N.Y.S.2d 159, 161 (N.Y. App. Div. 2d 2001)).

12. X.L.O. Concrete Corp. v. John T. Brady and Co., 482 N.Y.S.2d 476, 479 (N.Y. App. Div. 1st 1984) (denying plaintiff right to choose to recover actual instead of liquidated damages).

13. *See* Metro. Dade Cnty. v. Frank J. Rooney, Inc., 627 So. 2d 1248 (Fla. Dist. Ct. App. 1993) ("Liquidated damages are in lieu of actual delay damages and an owner cannot elect to seek actual delay damages simply because the actual damages are greater than the liquidated damages."); Burns v. Hanover Ins. Co., 454 A.2d 325 (D.C. 1982) (finding that a contract clause that did not delineate to which potential damages it applied could serve to substitute for all actual damages and should be enforced as written).

14. 468 P.2d 469 (Wash. App. 1970).

under the liquidated damages provision, reasoning that the owner is the party who drafted the contract and is the party who benefited from the liquidated damages provision.[15] Similarly, Mississippi's highest court has held that if the contract provides for liquidated damages, then such damages are the owner's sole remedy and the owner cannot claim actual damages following the delay by the contractor, simply because at that point it appears that the liquidated damages assessed will not fully compensate the owner.[16]

Proof Requirements for Recovery of Delay Damages

Notice

Each time a party faces a delay or potential obstacle, it is usually required by contract to give notice to the other parties of the delayed work. When it comes to delays encountered by the contractor, the notice requirement provides the owner with the ability to control its liabilities,[17] and conduct its own investigation into the cause and consequences of the delay. It also gives the owner the opportunity to mitigate the cause or grant timely relief to the contractor.[18]

Most construction contracts require the claimant to give notice before a delay claim can be recognized. In the American Institute of Architects (AIA) general conditions, notice is required to be provided to both the other party and the Initial Decision Maker (who is frequently the project architect).[19] The ConsensusDocs owner-constructor standard agreement requires the party claiming a delay to give notice of such claim to the other party.[20]

Judicial enforcement of notice requirements varies among jurisdictions. However, ultimately the court's decision is likely to turn on the contract's express terms. Just as a contractor's failure to provide timely notice may be deemed a waiver of future damages, an owner's right to timely notice may be waived if the owner was in fact aware of the event or condition that caused the delay.[21]

In *Brinderson Corp. v. Hampton Rds. Sanitation Dist.*,[22] the Fourth Circuit held that compliance with the contract's notice provisions is ultimately determined

---

15. *Id.* at 477.
16. *E.g.*, Cheatham v. Kem Mfg. Corp., 372 So. 2d 1085 (Miss. 1979).
17. *See, e.g.*, Seaboard Lumber Co. v. United States, 45 Fed. Cl. 404, 406–07 (Fed. Cl. 1999).
18. *Id.*
19. AIA A210-2017, ¶ 15.1.3.1.
20. ConsensusDocs 200, ¶ 6.4 (2018 ed.).
21. 6 Philip L. Bruner & Patrick J. O'Connor, Jr., Bruner & O'Connor Construction Law § 15:71 (2020).
22. 825 F.2d 41 (4th Cir. 1987).

by (1) whether the owner had actual and constructive notice of the conditions underlying the claim, and (2) whether the owner had a sufficient opportunity to investigate the noticed claim.[23] Strict adherence to the contractual notice requirements is not necessary if the contracting entity has actual or constructive notice of the cause of the delay.

Government Contracts

In the public construction context, there are statutory notice requirements that mandate strict compliance. When a public entity is involved, the contractor is required to provide written notice to the government owner.[24] Notice requirements for public construction projects are codified in the applicable statute and are incorporated in a majority of contracts involving a government entity as an owner. Generally, compliance with the relevant statute is mandatory to maintain a claim for delay damages against the government. However, there have been cases where the government owner clearly knew the facts that were giving rise to the delays and the court found that this was sufficient to informally satisfy the notice requirements.[25]

For example, in *Ernest Bock & Sons, Inc. v. City of Philadelphia*,[26] the contractor did not strictly comply with the notice provisions, but the court held that Pennsylvania law applies a more lenient approach to interpreting notice provisions in construction contracts. "[T]he spirit of the provision rather than the strict terms" dictates whether there has been compliance.[27] This particular finding was affirmed by the appellate court, because "the City 'clearly knew the operative facts giving rise to the construction delays and [the contractor's] claims for accelerated work.'"[28]

However, when it comes to federal government projects, compliance with notice requirements is more stringent. As mentioned before, there are typically two types of compensable delays when it comes to federal government contracts. Under each, the Federal Acquisition Regulation (FAR) requires the contractor to put the government on notice that the government's conduct has suspended the work,

23. Brinderson Corp. v. Hampton Rds. Sanitation Dist., 825 F.2d 41, 44 (4th Cir. 1987).

24. *See* Huff Enterprises, Inc. v. Triborough Bridge & Tunnel Authority, 191 A.D.2d 314, 595 N.Y.S.2d 178 (1st Dep't 1993).

25. These courts have held that such notice provisions should "not be applied too technically and illiberally where the Government is quite aware of the operative facts." Hoel-Steffen Constr. Co. v. United States, 456 F.2d 760, 768, 197 Ct. Cl. 561 (Ct. Cl. 1972); *see also* Copco Steel & Eng'g Co. v. United States, 341 F.2d 590, 598, 169 Ct. Cl. 601 (Ct. Cl. 1965); Miller Elevator Co., Inc. v. United States, 30 Fed. Cl. 662, 699 (1994).

26. 2018 Phila. Ct. Com. Pl. LEXIS 26 (C.P. May 8, 2018).

27. *Id.* at 6.

28. 2020 Pa. Commw. Unpub. LEXIS 418 (Commw. Ct. Aug. 12, 2020).

especially for constructive suspension.[29] Additionally, for excusable delays, the contractor has only ten days from the beginning of any such excusable delay to notify the government owner's contracting officer in writing of the cause for delay.[30]

Burden of Proof

Generally, the party claiming delay damages must demonstrate to the trier of fact (1) what delays occurred, (2) whether the delays are compensable, (3) who caused the delays, (4) whether the delay was offset by concurrent delays, and (5) the relationship between the delay and damages claimed.[31]

The Delay Occurred

In order to recover delay damages, an owner must prove that there was a delay. Generally, this means demonstrating that the completion of work extended beyond the completion date specified within the contract. However, because construction projects involve dynamic project conditions, the greatest challenge can be locating the alteration in the critical path:

> There very well may be more than one critical path on a project and the critical path may change during the life of the project, i.e., activities that were not on the original critical path subsequently may be added. It is also true that delay of a critical path item may not result in a per se delay in completion because the critical path is only an educated estimate of the impact of delay; lost time in one phase may be made up in later phases.
>
> Theoretically, if an activity on the critical path is delayed by one day, and no compensating changes made by rescheduling or some form of acceleration, the entire project will be delayed by one day. Running parallel to the construction events on the critical path, there will probably be other activities, which should easily keep pace with the critical construction events. Because these events have more time available to them on the schedule than is necessary to complete these events, they are said to have "float time," i.e., an amount of time in excess of the minimum reasonable amount of time required to complete that item of work.

---

29. Aron C. Beezley & Sarah Sutton Osborne, *A Gov't Contractor's Guide to Excusable, Compensable Delays,* LAW360 (Apr. 7, 2020), https://www.bradley.com/-/media/files/insights/publications/2020/04/articlelaw360a-govt-contractors-guide-to-excusable-compensable-delay-abeezley-sosborne-april-2020.pdf.

30. 48 C.F.R. § 52.249-10(b)(2).

31. 67 AM. JUR. PROOF OF FACTS 3d 339 (originally published in 2002). *See, e.g.*, Fieldcrest Builders, Inc. v. Antonucci, 311 Ill. App. 3d 597, 243 Ill. Dec. 740, 724 N.E.2d 49 (1st Dist. 1999); Premier Elec. Constr. Co. v. American Nat'l Bank of Chicago, 276 Ill. App. 3d 816, 213 Ill. Dec. 128, 658 N.E.2d 877 (1st Dist. 1995); Pathman Constr. Co. v. Hi-way Elec. Co., 65 Ill. App. 3d 480, 22 Ill. Dec. 133, 382 N.E.2d 453 (1st Dist. 1978).

While every construction event can eventually become "critical" by having its cushion or float time used up, this is not anticipated in the initial scheduling.[32]

The Delay Is Not Compensable or Excused

After the owner establishes that there was a delay in project completion, the burden is then on the contractor to prove that the delay was an excusable or compensable project delay.[33] In these cases, the contractor must demonstrate that the cause of the delay was beyond the contractor's control and occurred without the fault or negligence of the contractor.[34] The contractor must further prove that it took reasonable action to perform the contract notwithstanding the occurrence of such excuse.[35] Lastly, the unforeseeable cause must specifically delay the critical path.[36] It is not enough for an activity to be delayed; the activity delay must increase the time necessary for total performance of the work.[37]

The Contractor Caused the Delays

To establish liability for the contractor delay, the owner must prove that the delay was caused by the contractor. This requirement and the following requirement regarding concurrent delays go hand in hand, but before the owner can prove that they did not contribute to the delay, the owner must first establish that the contractor caused the delay.

The owner must prove with reasonable certainty the cause of the damages, meaning the owner must demonstrate with reasonable certainty that the contractor caused the damages.[38]

The Delay Was Not Offset by Concurrent Delays

In order to recover delay damages, an owner could not have contributed to the delay in such a manner that it would create a concurrent delay. For concurrent delays, the contractor has the additional burden of proving a clear apportionment

32. Sterling Millwrights, Inc. v. United States, 26 Cl. Ct. 49, 85–86 (1992).

33. *See* Fru-Con Constr. Corp. v. United States, 43 Fed. Cl. 306 (1999), *on reconsid. in part*, 44 Fed. Cl. 298 (1999).

34. *See* Cherokee Gen. Corp. v. United States, 150 Fed. Cl. 270, 278 (2020).

35. Sauer Inc. v. Danzig, 224 F.3d 1340, 1345 (Fed. Cir. 2000).

36. *See* RIF Contract § 01311, pt. 2.4; Mel Williamson, Inc. v. United States, 229 Ct. Cl. 846, 850–51 (1982) (contractor failed to establish that the unforeseeable event "caused delay in the overall contract performance"); Sauer Inc. v. Danzig, 224 F.3d 1340, 1345 (Fed. Cir. 2000).

37. Mega Constr. Co., Inc. v. United States, 29 Fed. Cl. 396, 425 (1993).

38. *See* Restatement Second, Contracts § 352 ("Damages are not recoverable for loss beyond an amount that the evidence permits to be established with reasonable certainty.").

of the delay, and any expenses attributable to each party.[39] In jurisdictions that recognize this apportionment of damages for concurrent delays, the contractor has the burden of separating its delays from those chargeable to the owner.[40]

There Is a Relationship Between the Delay and the Damages

Once causation has been proven to a reasonable certainty, the focus then shifts to the amount of damages. To determine the amount attributable to the contractor-caused delay, an owner must be able to quantify these damages with "reasonable certainty." Though the standards of causation and amount appear to be the same, the burden of proof in the amount of damages is a lower burden than the reasonable certainty requirement for the proof of causation of damages.[41] Additionally, some jurisdictions apply different standards of proof for direct versus consequential damages. In New York, a court discussed that "general" damages "merely requir[e] a 'reasonable estimate' of damages before an award can be made" while consequential damages require proof "with a reasonable certainty."[42]

To satisfy the standard of reasonable certainty, the owner must demonstrate that its damages are not "speculative" or "hypothetical,"[43] but rather are "capable of being ascertained by reference to some definite standard, such as market value, established experience, or direct inference from known circumstances."[44] Additionally, an owner must prove that its claimed damages were foreseeable. The analysis of the foreseeability of the construction owner's delay damages begins with the determination of whether the damages sought are "direct" or "consequential."[45]

---

39. Blinderman Constr. Co. v. United States, 695 F.2d 552, 559 (Fed. Cir. 1982).

40. Issues in Construction Law: New Perspectives on Liability and Contracts A.B.A. Sec. Real Property, Probate, And Trust Law 64 (1988) [at 89].

41. *See In re* Roberts Constr. Co., 172 Neb. 819, 111 N.W.2d 767, 770 (1961) ("When it is established that a party has suffered damage, uncertainty as to the exact amount does not justify a denial of all recovery. The fact that the amount of damages may not be susceptible of exact proof or may be in a degree uncertain or difficult of ascertainment should not be a bar to any recovery."); Walter Kidde Constructors, Inc. v. State, 37 Conn. Supp. 50, 434 A.2d 962, 976 (Super. Ct. 1981) ("It is incumbent upon a plaintiff in a contract action to prove his damages with all the certainty which is reasonably possible, but where exactness is not possible he is not therefore to be precluded from a recovery, and the best approximation to certainty is all that is required.").

42. Compania Embotelladora Del Pacifico, S.A. v. Pepsi Cola Co., 650 F. Supp. 2d 314, 322 (S.D.N.Y. 2009) (addressing whether the breach of contract damages sought by the plaintiff "are general, thus merely requiring a 'reasonable estimate' of damages before an award can be made, or instead consequential, thus requiring CEPSA to prove such damages 'with reasonable certainty'").

43. *See* JTE Constructors of N.C., Inc. v. United States Fid. & Guar. Co., 2003 U.S. Dist. LEXIS 22301, at *21 (M.D. N.C. Nov. 25, 2003).

44. *See* Michael J. Cook, Richard F. Bero & Bret R. Gunnell, *Claims for Lost Profit*, *in* Proving and Pricing Construction Claims 14.14 (Cushman, Jacobsen, Trimble eds., 1996).

45. *Damages; Time Is Money: Recovery of Liquidated Damages by the Owner*, 24 Constr. Lawyer 28 (2004).

Quantum of Evidence

The owner must quantify delay damages resulting from the contractor-caused delay with reasonable certainty. The key to supporting the quantum of damages claimed ultimately comes down to the quality and quantity of the owner's record keeping.[46]

The most significant document in a delay claim is the project schedule. This "as-planned" project schedule serves as a key piece of evidence in showing the parties' original intent as to the time in which the project was anticipated to be completed. The ability to compare the "as-planned" schedule to the "as-built" schedule provides the basic method by which delays and the events and factors that caused them can be identified.[47] This method is known as critical path methodology, which allows an analysis of the legal requirement that a delay must affect the overall completion of the project.[48]

A critical path method (CPM) analysis must be completed in order to establish whether the delay impacted the critical path.[49] However, in order to properly demonstrate delay to a project, the CPM schedule must be kept current to reflect delays as they occur.[50] "The required nexus between the [owner's] delay and a contractor's failure to complete performance at some unspecified earlier date cannot be shown merely by hypothetical, after-the-fact projection."[51]

Due to the complexities and the technical knowledge that occurs in the construction industry, expert testimony is frequently required to support the quantum of damages. Field and supervisory personnel may testify about the job progression and the different problems encountered, such as the various delays. However, they may not have the necessary qualifications or judgment to make conclusions about which party is responsible for which action or nonaction that affected the progression of the project.[52]

---

46. Dennis C. Cavanaugh, *Chapter 7 Damages*, *in* ABA Model Jury Instructions for Surety Cases (Robert C. Niesley ed., 2000).

47. Issues in Construction Law: New Perspectives on Liability and Contracts A.B.A. Sec. Real Property, Probate, And Trust Law 64 (1988) [at 90].

48. Morrison Knudsen Corp. v. Fireman's Fund Ins. Co., 175 F.3d 1221, 1233 (10th Cir. 1999).

49. Mega Constr. Co. v. United States, 29 Fed. Cl. 396, 435 (Fed. Cl. 1993).

50. Fortec Constructors v. United States, 8 Cl. Ct. 490, 505 (1985), *aff'd,* 804 F.2d 141 (Fed. Cir. 1986).

51. Interstate Gen. Gov't Contractors, Inc. v. West, 12 F.3d 1053, 1060 (Fed. Cir. 1993).

52. Cavanaugh, *supra* note 46.

Concept of Direct Damages

In circumstances in which liquidated damages are not provided for by contract or by law, an owner may seek to recover its actual damages from the party responsible (e.g., contractor, designer, architect) if the actual damages were foreseeable and can be proven with reasonable certainty. Actual delay damages include both direct damages and consequential damages. Direct damages flow directly from a breach of the contract itself and include harm that can be tied back to the immediate scope of the contract.[53] For example, the Supreme Court of Texas defined direct damages as losses that, "clearly flow naturally and necessarily" from the wrongdoing and "compensate the plaintiff for the loss that is conclusively presumed to have been foreseen by the defendants from his wrongful act."[54] Other collateral impacts incurred as a result of a breach that are not part of what the owner was supposed to receive as part of the contract are typically considered indirect or consequential damages.[55]

The ultimate determination as to whether a loss claim constitutes a direct or consequential damage often falls upon the specific contract limitations and the facts, circumstances, and jurisdiction of each individual case.

Examples of Direct Damages

The impacts to an owner resulting from delayed completion of a project can go well beyond the additional cost to complete or repair the project through replacement contractors and/or change orders. If the owner has direct involvement in a project, it often incurs other costs associated with replacing the performance that the contractor failed to render.[56] Examples of additional owner costs that have been recognized by courts as direct damages due to delay are provided in the following subsections.

---

53. "Direct damages refer to those which the party lost from the contract itself—in other words, the benefit of the bargain—while consequential damages refer to economic harm beyond the immediate scope of the contract." Penncro Assocs., Inc. v. Sprint Spectrum, L.P., 499 F.3d 1151, 1156 (10th Cir. 2007).

54. *See Arthur Andersen & Co.*, 945 S.W.2d at 816.

55. "[T]he difference between direct and consequential damages depends on whether the damages represent (1) a loss in value of the other party's performance, in which case the damages are direct, or (2) collateral losses following the breach, in which case the damages are consequential." Atl. City Associates, LLC, v. Carter & Burgess Consultants, Inc., 453 Fed. Appx 174, 179 (3d Cir. 2011).

56. Jay Jala, LLC v. DDG Constr., Inc., 2016 WL 6442074, at *2 (E.D. Pa. 2016).

Jobsite or Field Overhead Costs

Like contractors, owners are frequently required to provide project specific site costs necessary to support work in the field. Sometimes referred to as field or jobsite overhead, these types of costs often increase when a project's duration is extended. Examples of extended or additional jobsite or field overhead costs absorbed by owners following a breach include:

- Office/trailer rental;
- Jobsite supervision, management, inspection or commissioning;
- Architect and engineering fees;
- Supply or rental of project equipment and maintenance;
- Temporary facilities;
- Site utilities or consumables;
- Material or equipment storage;[57]
- Permits; and
- Insurance.

In the event of a compensable delay, the owner will often seek to recover time-dependent field overhead costs that it is expressly responsible for under the contract, as direct damages. For example, in *Tennessee Gas Pipeline Co. v. Technip USA Corp.*, the owner's damage claim included additional expenditures for "permits; construction and permanent power; incoming high power transmission lines; storage and lay down areas at the Sites; space at the Sites for construction trailers; water; potable water; fire water; hydrotest media; and operation personnel for commissioning." In this case, the court found that the continuation of "Owner Responsibilities" constitutes direct damages as "the parties clearly contemplated that TGP would incur these costs throughout the Project and a breach of the Contract by delay naturally and necessarily would cause these costs to be extended over a longer period of time."[58]

Administrative or Office Overhead Costs

In addition to job site overhead, owners can also incur additional office overhead expenses to continue with administration of the project during the delay period. General overhead costs that are not fully attributable to only one project can include project management, rental of office facilities, administrative personnel,

57. Plaisance v. Dutton, 336 So. 2d 1034 (La. Ct. App. 1976).

58. Tennessee Gas Pipeline Co. v Technip USA Corp., No. 01-06-00535-CV, 2008 WL 3876141 (Tex. App.—Houston [1st Dist.] Aug. 21, 2008, *pet. denied*) (mem. op.) at 20–21.

bookkeeping expenses, supplies, and travel. Office overhead also may include certain taxes as an element therein.

It is well settled that a plaintiff may recover his overhead and supervisory costs notwithstanding that he makes the repairs himself.[59] For example, in *Jay Jala*, the court held that reimbursement of the owner's overhead costs, including project management/staff time, for the time period during which it served as its own contractor was a direct damage. The court's reasoning was as follows:

> Defendant's performance under the contract was to construct the motel, but Defendant did not complete that performance. Plaintiff is straightforwardly entitled to recover the cost of finding substitute performance, and if it had hired a replacement general contractor, that company may well have charged an overhead fee just as Defendant did (or it might be otherwise built into the price). The fact that Defendant arranged substitute performance by managing the project on its own does not mean it is not entitled to the same costs as any other contractor, provided the cost is reasonable.[60]

However, an owner may be denied recovery of additional administrative costs if not properly supported. In the case of *White Buffalo Construction Inc. v. United States*, the government's assessment of excess administrative costs against a defaulting contractor was found to be improper because the support for the claim was lacking.[61]

Further, an owner's recovery of increased administrative overhead may be prohibited for the period the owner is recovering lost profits. In *Guntert v. City of Stockton*,[62] the court held that "to award the plaintiff not only lost profit but also the cost of producing the profit causes a double recovery."[63]

Construction Financing

Construction contracts often require an owner to borrow external funds to finance projects. Courts have held that additional financing charges, such as interest carrying charges, incurred as a result of delays in construction constitute compensable direct damages when it is determined that the carrying charges flow naturally from the delay. Examples of such cases include:

---

59. Reliable Elec. Co. v. Clinton Campbell Contractor, Inc., 459 P.2d 98, 103 (Ariz. App. 1st Div. 1969); Baltimore & Ohio Railroad Co. v. Commercial Transport, Inc., 273 F.2d 447 (7th Cir. 1960); Ford Motor Co. v. Bradley Transp. Co., 174 F.2d 192 (6th Cir. 1949).

60. *Jay Jala*, 2016 WL 6442074, at *2 (E.D. Pa. 2016) at 6–8.

61. AGBCA No. 93-113-1 (Aug. 30, 1994).

62. 55 Cal. App. 3d 131, 148–49 (1976).

63. *See also* Burnett & Doty Dev. Co. v. C.S. Phillips, 84 Cal. App. 3d 384, 148 Cal. Rptr. 569 (1978).

- ***Roanoke Hospital Ass'n v. Doyle & Russell, Inc.*, 215 Va. 796, 214 S.E.2d 155, 160–61 (1975).** Case involved an owner against a general contractor arising out of a contract for the construction of a building. The court found that interest costs to carry a construction loan during a period of delay in construction were direct damages. The court's reasoning was as follows:

  > Customarily, construction contracts, particularly large contracts, require third-party financing. Ordinarily, delay in completion requires an extension of the term of construction financing. The interest costs incurred and the interest revenue lost during such an extended term are predictable results of the delay and are, therefore, compensable direct damages.[64]

- ***Elar Investments, Inc. v. Southwest Culvert Co., Inc.*, 139 Ariz. 25, 676 P.2d 659, 662–63 (Ariz. Ct. App. 1983).** Case involved a developer against a supplier of prefabricated steel for the construction of townhouses. The court found that extended financing charges resulting from delay in delivery were direct damages.
- ***Havens Steel Co. v. Randolph Engineering Co.*, 613 F. Supp. 514, 541 (W.D. Mo. 1985).** Case involved a contractor against a subcontractor for defective work. The court found that interest charges on monies borrowed to finance additional work were recoverable as ordinary, direct, or foreseeable damages.[65]
- ***Chestnut Hill Development Corp. v. Otis Elevator Co.*, 739 F. Supp. 692, 702 (D. Mass. 1990).** Case involved an alleged delayed installation and defective functioning of five elevators in a condominium complex. The court found that extended financing costs due to construction delay are direct damages.
- ***The Bartram, LLC v. C.B. Contractors, LLC*, 2011 U.S. Dist. LEXIS 34972, at *9–10 n.3 (N.D. Fla. Mar. 31, 2011).** Case involved construction of an apartment building, which suffered from water damage allegedly caused by construction defects. The court held that the waiver of consequential damages applied to post-construction disputes as well as termination claims, and encompassed increased financing costs, but distinguished "extended financing costs that flow from construction delay" as direct damages, following *Chestnut Hill.*
- ***Jay Jala, LLC v. DDG Construction, Inc.*, 2016 WL 6442074, at *2 (E.D. Pa. 2016).** Case involved an owner against a contractor for breach of

---

64. *Roanoke*, 214 S.E.2d at 160–61.
65. Havens Steel Co. v. Randolph Eng'g Co., 613 F. Supp. 514, 541 (W.D. Mo. 1985), *aff'd*, 813 F.2d 186, 188 (8th Cir. 1987).

contract for the construction of a motel. The owner sought to recover interest paid on a construction loan prior to the loan converting to a permanent loan. The court found that extended financing costs that flow from construction delay are direct damages:

> But Plaintiff did have to take out and incur interest on a loan to construct the building, and pay additional interest during the delay: clearly, it is an integral cost of completing Defendant's performance, which was construction of the building. The loan interest costs are not much different in this respect than any other necessary construction input. If Defendant agreed to build the motel using no more than a certain amount of concrete, used up the full amount, and left the job incomplete, Plaintiff could certainly recover as direct damages the cost of additional necessary concrete. Here, Defendant agreed to build the motel using no more than a certain amount of time and therefore, necessarily, a certain amount of loan interest. Defendant used up all the time and left the building unfinished, so Plaintiff can recover as direct damages the cost of additional time necessary to finish construction. In this way, Defendant's obligation to complete the project on time, and the contract's allowance of delay damages, are naturally integrated into interest charges, and thus direct rather than consequential damages.[66]

Instances where construction financing is treated as a consequential damage are discussed next.

Concept of Consequential Damages

There is no uniform definition of consequential damages because "no two courts or treatises define consequential damages in the same way."[67] However, the most common conceptualization of consequential damages dates back to an 1854 English case studied by every law student, *Hadley v. Baxendale.*

---

66. Jay Jala, LLC v. DDG Constr., Inc., 2016 WL 6442074, *2 (E.D. Pa. 2016) at 12–13.

67. Axelroth, *Mutual Waiver of Consequential Damages—The Owner's Perspective* § 18:1 The Constr. Law. 11 (Jan. 1998); *see* Heckman & Edwards, *Time Is Money: Recovery of Liquidated Damages by the Owner*, 24:4 The Constr. Law. 28, 29 (Fall 2004) ("It would seem that a comprehensive list of direct and consequential delay damages in the construction context would have been developed by now. Unfortunately, however, deciding whether construction delay damages are direct or consequential has proven to be exceedingly difficult for parties and the courts alike.").

History of Consequential Damages

Hadley v. Baxendale[68] is the landmark case that first attempted to define what consequential damages are and how they are distinct from direct damages. The case involved a broken mill shaft that resulted in the mill being shut down until the shaft could be replaced. To replace the broken shaft, the mill owner had to mail off the broken shaft to another town. The mill owner contracted with a local carrier to transport the shaft to the manufacturer. However, the carrier was delayed in its transportation of the shaft, resulting in the mill being closed for several days beyond what was anticipated. The mill owner filed suit against the carrier to recover his lost profits. In his opinion, Baron Sir Edward Hall Alderson, speaking on behalf of the Court of Exchequer formulated the foreseeability limitation on damages:

> Where two parties have made a contract which one of them has broken, the damages which the other party ought to receive in respect of such breach of contract should be such as may fairly and reasonably be considered either arising naturally, i.e., according to the usual course of things, from such breach of contract itself, or such as may reasonably be supposed to have been in the contemplation of both parties at the time they made the contract, as the probable result of the breach of it. Now, if the special circumstances under which the contract was actually made were communicated by the plaintiffs to the defendants, and thus known to both parties, the damages resulting from the breach of such a contract, which they would reasonably contemplate, would be the amount of injury which would ordinarily follow from a breach of contract under these special circumstances so known and communicated.[69]

The *Hadley* court ultimately defined three distinct damage types: direct, consequential, and special. The court defines: (1) direct (general) damages as those that "may fairly and reasonably be considered either arising naturally, i.e., according to the usual course of things, from such breach of contract itself"[70] despite whether or not it was foreseeable; (2) consequential damages as beyond arising naturally from the contract but are still "as the probable result of the breach of it" as long as they "may reasonably be supposed to have been in the contemplation of both parties at the time they made the contract"; and (3) special damages as those arising from "the special circumstances under which the contract was actually made" and they

68. Hadley v. Baxendale, 1854 WL 7208 (U.K. Ex Ct 1854).
69. Hadley v. Baxendale, 9 Exch. 341 (1854).
70. *Id.*

are recoverable as long as they "were communicated by the plaintiffs to the defendants, and thus known to both parties."[71]

Modern Conceptualization of Consequential Damages

The foreseeability principle established in *Hadley* is no longer as applicable in the construction context to preclude the recovery of consequential damages resulting in project delays because parties are more understanding of the results following delays[72] and construction delays are clearly foreseeable to someone "knowledgeable about the customs and practices of the construction industry."[73] The modern availability of information,[74] along with the sophistication of the parties, detail in which the construction contracts are prepared, flexibility of the construction contracts to make changes and the common industry standard for understanding delays[75] leaves only the most unusual and bizarre events uncontemplated.

Today's Definition

Today, the definition of consequential damages varies from jurisdiction to jurisdiction. One common assumption about consequential damages is that the concept equates to the term "indirect." Courts across the nation contend that consequential damages do not flow directly from the delay/event itself but are an indirect source of loss. While this definition is not exactly wrong, the rule has also been stated as follows:

> The distinction between general [or direct] and special [or consequential] damages is not that one is and the other is not the direct and proximate consequence of the breach complained of, but that general [or direct] damages are such as

71. *See* Dunn, Recovery of Damages for Lost Profits § 1.9 (5th ed.), which recognizes the three distinct damage elements. *See* 6 Philip L. Bruner & Patrick J. O'Connor, Jr., Bruner & O'Connor Construction Law § 19:16 (2020).

72. *See* Wise v. U.S., 249 U.S. 361, 367, 39 S. Ct. 303, 63 L. Ed. 647 (1919) ("The parties to a contract, with full understanding of the results of delay and, before the differences of interested views had arisen between them, were much more competent to determine what the amount of damages would be[.]").

73. Spang Indus., Inc., Ft. Pitt Bridge Div. v. Aetna Casualty & Surety Co., 512 F.2d 365 (2d Cir. 1975) (holding construction delay damages to be clearly foreseeable to someone knowledgeable about the customs and practices of the construction industry).

74. Such as local site conditions—weather records, soils reports, building material qualities, manufacturers data, industry experience. 6 Philip L. Bruner & Patrick J. O'Connor, Jr., Bruner & O'Connor Construction Law § 19:18 (2020).

75. *See* Travelers Cas. & Sur. Co. v. Dormitory Authority-State of New York, 735 F. Supp. 2d 42 (S.D.N.Y. 2010) ("The fact the design modifications, delays or other difficulties could arise on such a project would not surprise a prudent bidder.").

> naturally and ordinarily follow the breach, whereas special [or consequential] damages are those that ensue, not necessarily or ordinarily, but because of special circumstances.[76]

Thus, consequential damages are often equated with the term "indirect," in that they do not flow directly from the delay itself but are an indirect source of loss.[77]

Special Versus Consequential Damages

As already mentioned, the *Hadley* court distinguished between three types of damages: (1) direct damages, (2) consequential damages, and (3) special damages. The distinction between consequential damages and special damages, generally, is no longer followed. Most jurisdictions use the terms synonymously. The Restatement Second of Contracts even points out that "it is not necessary to distinguish between 'general' and 'special' or 'consequential' damages"[78] for the purposes of defining foreseeability.[79] The Restatement Second, Contracts § 351(2)(b) actually merges consequential and special damages into a "special circumstances" test for damages of which the "party in breach had reason to know," thus creating a "new or should have known" basis for objectively judging foreseeability.[80]

While some jurisdictions use "consequential" as the umbrella term, other jurisdictions use "special damages" as such. California courts, for example, use the term "special damages" to include consequential damages. In *Lewis Jorge Construction Management, Inc. v. Pomona Unified School District*, the court stated, "Contractual damages are of two types—general damages (sometimes called direct damages) and special damages (sometimes called consequential damages)."[81]

General Requirements

An owner must prove the consequential damages sought were (1) reasonably foreseeable or within the contemplation at the time of contracting and (2) are the

76. Applied Data Processing, Inc. v. Burroughs Corp., 394 F. Supp. 504, 509 (D. Conn. 1975) (citing 5 A. Corbin, Corbin on Contracts § 1011 (1974)).

77. Thomas J. Kelleher, Jr., John M. Mastin, Jr. & Rondald G. Robey, Common Sense Construction Law 560 (5th ed. 2015).

78. *See* Restatement Second, Contracts § 351, cmt. b ("Loss of results from a breach in the ordinary course of events is foreseeable as the probable result of the breach. . . . the damages recoverable for loss that results other than in the ordinary course of events are sometimes called "special" or "consequential" damages. These terms are often misleading, however, it is not necessary to distinguish between "general" and "special" or "consequential" damages for the purpose of the rules stated in [§ 351].").

79. *See* Restatement Second, Contracts § 351.

80. Restatement Second, Contracts § 351(2)(b).

81. Lewis Jorge Constr. Mgmt., Inc. v. Pomona Unified Sch. Dist., 102 P.3d 257, 261 (Cal. 2004).

proximate consequence of the delay.[82] As discussed, the first element of foreseeability originated from *Hadley*.

Reasonably Foreseeable or Within the Contemplation at the Time

The owner has the burden of proving that the damages are not only the proximate consequence of the breach, but that they were also "reasonably foreseeable" or within the "contemplation of the parties" at the time the parties entered into the contract."[83]

Courts tend to presume that sophisticated and experienced parties can anticipate the consequences resulting from a breach or delay. In *Travelers Casualty & Surety Co. v. Dormitory Authority—State of New York*,[84] the district court, while considering whether a construction delay was "uncontemplated," stated that "ordinary, garden variety poor performance by the contractee is within the contemplation of the parties." The court went further to note that "particularly where sophisticated, high dollar contracts are at issue, courts are skeptical of claims that certain risks were uncontemplated at the time of the contracting."

Proximate Consequence of the Delay

Once the nonbreaching party establishes the consequential damages it seeks should have been in the contemplation of the breaching party at the time the contract was formed, "it must then prove the amount in damages actually caused by the breach of contract, sometimes with 'reasonable certainty.'"[85]

Foreseeability

Some jurisdictions still consider the foreseeability of the damages when making the distinction between direct and consequential damages. This requires the court to consider the "degree of foreseeability"[86] in each particular case.

Determining whether consequential damages are recoverable depends on the damage's foreseeability. However, there is no uniform rule when it comes to how

---

82. Spang Indus., Inc., Ft. Pitt Bridge Div. v. Aetna Cas. & Sur. Co., 512 F.2d 365, 368 (2d Cir. 1975); Schonfield v. Milliard, 218 F.3d 164, 172 (2d Cir. 2000).

83. *Spang Indus.*, 512 F.2d at 368.

84. 735 F. Supp. 2d 42 (S.D.N.Y. 2010).

85. Charles B. Jimerson & Kayla Haines, *What Are Consequential Damages on a Construction Contract*, Lexology (Oct. 24, 2016), https://www.lexology.com/library/detail.aspx?g=1af81a9e-1358-428b-99f8-0644d4258515. *See* Compania Embotelladora Del Pacifico, S.A. v. Pepsi Cola Co., 650 F. Supp. 2d 314, 322 (S.D.N.Y. 2009); Gilmore v. Cohen, 95 Ariz. 34, 36, 386 P.2d 81, 82 (1963).

86. *See* Tate & Lyle Americas LLC v. Glatt Air Techniques, Inc., 2016 WL 7422289 (C.D. Ill. May 20, 2016) ("To determine whether lost profits are direct damages in a particular case, the court generally looks to the degree of foreseeability, Direct damages are 'utterly foreseeable, indeed certain' to stem from a breach of contract.").

courts will make this evaluation. Foreseeability can be evaluated on a subjective, actual knowledge standard or on an objective, reasonably foreseeable standard.[87] However, this determination of foreseeability is based on whether the damages were foreseeable at the time of contracting, rather than at the time of the delay.

The rationale for proving foreseeability is that a party who can reasonably foresee the consequences of a breach of contract can adjust the contract price accordingly to compensate for the risk that is being assumed. Some states like Arizona and California view delay damages as a subset of consequential damages. In *Chinese Hospital Association v. Jacobs Engineering Group, Inc.*, this general view of delay damages as consequential precluded the owner from recovering all delayed construction costs under the consequential damages waiver within the contract.[88] As a category of consequential damages, delay damages have to be foreseeable in order to be recoverable.[89]

Not Using Foreseeability

Although some jurisdictions use foreseeability as a determination of the difference between direct and consequential damages, others do not. In a case out of the Eastern District of Pennsylvania, the court opined that rather than turning on foreseeability, the difference between direct and consequential damages depends on whether the damages represent "(1) a loss in value of the other party's performance, in which case the damages are direct, or (2) collateral losses following the breach, in which case the damages are consequential."[90] The court continued by stating that consequential damages "refer to the economic harm beyond the immediate scope of the contract."[91]

"Special Circumstances" but "Not Ordinarily Predictable"

Nationally, courts have held that consequential damages are those that arise from the intervention of special circumstances not ordinarily predictable.[92]

---

87. Will W. Allensworth & Allenworth & Porter, LLP, 30th Annual Construction Law Conference: A Question of Consequence (2017).

88. "Thus, while Plaintiff's delayed construction costs might be recoverable as consequential damages, they are barred here by the parties' consequential damages waiver." Chinese Hosp. Ass'n v. Jacobs Eng'g Grp., Inc., 18-CV-05403-JSC, 2019 WL 6050758, at *5 (N.D. Cal. Nov. 15, 2019).

89. *See* Tech. Constr., Inc. v. City of Kingman, 229 Ariz. 564, 569, 278 P.3d 906, 911 (Ct. App. 2012).

90. Jay Jala, LLC v. DDG Constr., Inc., 2016 WL 6442074, at *2 (E.D. Pa. 2016).

91. *Id.*

92. Bramble & Callahan, Construction Delay Claims § 12.19[B], at 12-128 to 12-129 (3d ed.).

In *Roanoke Hospital Ass'n v. Doyle & Russell, Inc.*,[93] the court distinguishes the difference between direct and consequential by defining consequential damages as "those which arise from the intervention of 'special circumstances' not ordinarily predictable."[94] Only consequential damages are recoverable if it is determined that these special circumstances were within "contemplation" of both contracting parties.[95]

Challenges of Proof: Difficult to Evidence, and Speculative

The degree of proof required to recover consequential damages is higher than for direct damages, thus requiring it to be pled with greater specificity.[96] The most frequently sought types of consequential damages in connection with delay claims are lost profits, interest on tied up capital, and damage to business reputation.[97] However, these are also some of the most difficult damages to prove. The causal link between consequential damages and the delay events may be tenuous and uncertain since these losses are only related indirectly to the delay.[98]

Questions and issues of the "remote and speculative" nature of claimed damages frequently arise when a claimant seeks to recover consequential damages.[99] As mentioned before, one of the elements required to recover consequential damages is the ability to reasonably ascertain the amount of loss. Generally, state statutes have codified this requirement. Although these statutes may require "exact computation," most courts have taken a somewhat less stringent approach.[100] For example, in Florida, courts have "long specified that reasonable certainty as to the facts of injury and causation is more critical than reasonable certainty as to the computation of the resultant losses."[101]

In seeking consequential damages, the owner or the claimant assumes a much heavier burden of proof as compared to direct damages. Additionally, many contracts and, in particular, public construction contracts, exclude claims for

93. 214 S.E.2d 155 (Va. 1975).

94. *Id.* at 160.

95. *Id.*

96. Wheatley & Canche, *Navigating the Labyrinth of Consequential Damages in the Construction Industry: A History of and Legal Approaches to Living with Them*, 33 Const. Law. 6 (Summer 2013).

97. Thomas J. Kelleher, Jr., John M. Mastin, Jr. & Rondald G. Robey, Common Sense Construction Law 560 (5th ed. 2015).

98. *Id.*

99. *Id.*

100. *Id.* at 561.

101. Gonzalez v. Barrenechea, 170 So. 3d 13, 16 (Fla. App. 2015) (quoting Maggolc, Inc. v. Roberson, 116 So. 3d 556, 558 (Fla. App. 2013).

consequential damages.[102] However, consequential damages, though they may not need to be exact, must be determined with a degree of certainty based on the evidence presented. The evidence presented cannot be merely speculative but rather requires "proof with a reasonable degree of certainty."[103]

Additionally, since consequential damages are considered "special" damages, Rule 9(g) of the Federal Rules of Civil Procedure, as well as several state counterparts, requires parties to "specifically plead" consequential damages.[104] Therefore, when attempting to prove consequential damages, if a party does not specifically plead those damages, the evidence of those damages would be inadmissible.[105]

Distinguishing Consequential Damages from Direct Damages

As a general matter, the distinction between direct and consequential damages is a question of fact.[106] However, there is an exception to this. Courts have held that when the parties have "gone a long way in defining the scope of consequential damages in the contract itself" then the court may find as a matter of law that the damages sought constitute consequential damages rather than direct.[107]

In *Jay Jala*, the court noted: "Direct damages are the costs of a plaintiff getting what the defendant was supposed to give—the costs of replacing the defendant's performance. Other costs that the plaintiff may not have incurred if the defendant had not breached, but that are not part of what the plaintiff was supposed to get from the defendant, are consequential."[108] Similarly, the Third Circuit explained in *Atlantic City Associates, LLC v. Carter & Burgress Consultants, Inc.*,[109] that "the difference between direct and consequential damages depends on whether the damages represent (1) a loss in value of the other party's performance, in which case

---

102. ConsensusDocs 200, § 6.6 (© 2007, Revised 2014), AIA A201, § 4.3.10 (1997 ed.), and AIA A201, § 15.1.6 (2007 ed.) are all examples of express waiver of consequential damages language.

103. Suitt Constr. Co. v. Ripley's Aquarium, LLC, 108 Fed. Appx 309, 314 (6th Cir. 2004) (citing Moore Constr. Co. v. Clarksville Dep't of Elec., 707 S.W.2d 1, 15 (Tenn. App. 1985)).

104. Charles B. Jimerson & Kayla Haines, *What Are Consequential Damages on a Construction Contract*, Lexology (Oct. 24, 2016), https://www.lexology.com/library/detail.aspx?g=1af81a9e-1358-428b-99f8-0644d4258515.

105. *Id.*

106. "[T]he precise demarcation between direct and consequential damages is a question of fact ... [which] must be left for resolution at trial." Roneker v. Kenworth Truck Co., 944 F. Supp. 179, 186 (W.D.N.Y. 1996) (quoting American Elec. Power Co. v. Westinghouse Elec. Corp., 418 F. Supp. 435, 459 (S.D.N.Y. 1976)).

107. Roneker v. Kenworth Truck Co., 977 F. Supp. 237, 239–40 (W.D.N.Y. 1997).

108. *Jay Jala*, 2016 U.S. Dist. LEXIS 150969, at *5.

109. Atlantic City Assocs, LLC v. Carter & Burgess Consultants, Inc., 453 Fed. Appx 174, 180 (3d Cir. 2011).

the damages are direct, or (2) or collateral losses following the breach, in which case the damages are consequential."

Examples of Consequential Damages

"Time is money." For this reason, identification of the period of expected performance is a critical component of construction contracts that is often relied upon by owners in operational planning and financial decision-making. In fact, the time-dependent collateral impacts due to delayed performance can be substantial and go well beyond the direct damages associated with simply completing the project.

Consequential losses incurred by owners due to delay can take various forms due to the unique nature of each project and project owner. As a result, there is no definitive listing of the type of consequential losses as they are only limited by what an owner can prove to a reasonable degree of certainty. Some examples of more common types of consequential damages include the following:

- Lost revenues/profits;
- Loss of use;
- Loss of goodwill or damage to business reputation; and
- Diminished value of property.

Lost Revenues/Profits

Most if not all construction projects are performed with the expectation that they will realize profit. For commercial owners, lost benefits due to delay often take the form of decreased revenues, higher operating costs, or lower productivity, all of which ultimately lead to reduced profits.

The general rule regarding establishing a claim for lost profits is summarized by the Court of Appeals of the State of New York in *Kenford Co. Inc. v. County of Erie*. This case involved an appeal from a contract dispute between the county and a contractor for the construction and operation of a domed stadium for the Buffalo Bills football team. The contract called for construction of the stadium to commence within 12 months, and to negotiate an acceptable 40-year lease within three months after preliminary plans and cost estimates were submitted. The parties never agreed on the lease, no construction ever occurred, the Bills spent another 50-plus years playing outdoors, and the dispute led to over ten years of protracted litigation. On the specific issue of lost profits, the court held:

> Loss of future profits as damages for breach of contract have been permitted in New York under long-established and precise rules of law. First, it must be demonstrated with certainty that such damages have been caused by the breach and,

second, the alleged loss must be capable of proof with reasonable certainty. In other words, the damages may not be merely speculative, possible or imaginary, but must be reasonably certain and directly traceable to the breach, not remote or the result of other intervening causes. In addition, there must be a showing that the particular damages were fairly within the contemplation of the parties to the contract at the time it was made. If it is a new business seeking to recover for loss of future profits, a stricter standard is imposed for the obvious reason that there does not exist a reasonable basis of experience upon which to estimate lost profits with the requisite degree of reasonable certainty.[110]

Where damages consist of lost profits, a proper award of lost profits must be confined to lost net profits rather than simply lost revenue or gross losses.[111] For example, take the case of an owner who enters into leases with prospective tenants based on the contractual completion date of a commercial development. Construction delays could result in lost rental payments during the delay or the loss of tenants entirely. Gross losses would include lost revenues (e.g., rental payments, management fees, parking fees) plus any fixed costs incurred by the owner that would have been passed onto tenants during the delay period (e.g., property taxes, occupancy fees, and utilities). In this case, net lost profits are calculated by reducing the calculated gross losses by any expenses that the owner avoids (e.g., employee costs, commissions, utilities) by not operating during the delay period.

Examples of courts awarding lost profit damages to commercial owners as a result of delays include the following:

- ***Uebelhack Equipment, Inc. v. Garrett Bros.*, 408 N.E.2d 136 (Ind. App. 1980).** Case involves a contract to renovate and upgrade a grain elevator and storage facility. The trial court awarded the owner lost profits due to nonperformance and schedule delays. In affirming the verdict, the appeals court provided the following summary:

  > Here, it is clear from the trial court's findings that Uebelhack was aware of Garrett's need to have the elevator operating by certain dates or that Garrett would lose money by not moving grain through the elevator during harvest season. Much of the loss of profits awarded by the trial court was not based on the loss of use of expanded capacity, but rather the inability to use the elevator at all effectively. The volumes that were used for measuring damages were based on the previous year. The profit margins were standard; that is: Garrett got a certain price per bushel for moving the grain through the elevator at certain times of the year. It

110. Kenford Co. Inc. v. Cnty. of Erie, 67 N.Y.2d 257, 261 (1986) (internal citations omitted).
111. Ashland Pipeline Co. v. Ind. Bell Tel. Co., Inc., 505 N.E.2d 483, 490 (Ind. App. 1987).

> would buy a certain price below market and then immediately resell at market. We especially note that none of the damages awarded were based on anticipated profits from speculation in the grain market; in other words, expected profits from a rise or fall in the market price. Rather, the damages were awarded on the typical profit for a grain elevator acting as a "middleman." It is true that the profit margin changed based on the season and the amount of grain available; however, these margins were fairly predictable. We also note there was sufficient evidence to support the conclusion that at least the same volume levels could have been met in summer of 1977 due to a larger crop than the year before.

The only loss of profits based on new capacity was also based on previous year volumes. This loss was due to failure to buy at harvest time and take advantage of lower prices. The bin in question was filled at higher cost as soon as it was put in operation.[112]

- ***Naegeli Transportation v. Gulf Electroquip Inc.*, 853 S.W.2d 737, 739 (Tex. App. 1993).** Case involves a contract for the hauling storage and delivery of an electrical transformer. The court held that plaintiff was entitled to consequential damages in the form of lost profits resulting from the nondelivery and scrapping of an electricity transformer that the plaintiff intended to repair and resell.
- ***Clark's Pork Farms v. Sand Livestock Systems, Inc.*, 563 N.E.2d 1292, 1298 (Ind. App. 1990).** Case involves a contract for the design and construction of a new building to be used in a production operation. The court held that the plaintiff may receive damages for the lost profits during the period required to bring the structure into accordance with contract.

Loss of Use

Loss of use is a type of consequential damage stemming from not being able to access or utilize property. Actual damages flowing from the loss of use should be measured based on the nature of the loss experienced and could include the cost of substitute property, the fair rental value of the structure during the period of delay, operating inefficiencies caused by the delay, or even lost profits. For example, in the case of *Northern Petrochemical Co. v. Thorsen Thorshov, Inc.*, the plaintiff sought to recover losses arising out of the faulty construction and subsequent reconstruction of an industrial building. Upon appeal, the Supreme Court of Minnesota held that the "[l]oss of use is a proper subject of damages where the loss is a direct and proximate result of the injury and such damages are within the contemplation of

112. *Uebelhack Equipment*, 408 N.E.2d at 140.

the parties at the time of making the contract. Under the facts of this case, plaintiff was entitled to recover its full damages for loss of use, including both lost profits and excess operating costs for the period in which its promised occupancy was delayed."[113]

Loss of Goodwill or Damage to Business Reputation

Goodwill is an intangible asset that represents the portion of a business's assets that are not separately identifiable. Although intangible (and not easy to prove), goodwill is nonetheless real and attaches to a business on account of name, location, reputation for competency, and the imponderables that cause buyers to return.[114] Consequential damages arising out of injury to goodwill including the loss of reputation, alienation of customers, or harm to business reputations, provided the plaintiff offers sufficient proof connecting the breach to the damages.[115]

To succeed on a claim for consequential damages in the form of loss of goodwill, a claimant must show (1) that in fact there was a loss of goodwill, (2) objective proof of the amount of that loss, and (3) that the loss was caused by the opposing party's breach.[116]

Diminished Value of Completed Facility

Under the right market circumstances, an owner may be able to recover damages for the loss of value during the delay period. For example, in the case of *Oliver B. Cannon & Son, Inc. v. Dorr-Oliver, Inc.*, the Supreme Court of Delaware concluded the owner of a commercial facility was entitled to recover for any actual loss caused by a contractor's breach, including any actual decline in value or actual "depreciation" of the buildings and equipment during the four months in which the plant was shut down.[117]

Similarly, delaying the completion of a project during a falling real estate market could reduce the ultimate sale proceeds realized by an owner. In such cases, the owner's claim may be quantified as the difference between the fair market value on the actual date of completion and the date specified in the contract.[118] However,

---

113. Northern Petrochemical Co. v. Thorsen Thorshov, Inc., 211 N.W.2d 159 (Minn. 1973).

114. Westric Battery Co. v. Standard Elec. Co., Inc., 522 F.2d 986, 987–88 (10th Cir. 1975).

115. Robert T. Donaldson, Inc. v. Aggregate Surfacing Corp., 47 A.D.2d 852, 853, 366 N.Y.S.2d 194, 196 (2d Dep't) (mem.); General Riveters, Inc. v. Morse Chain Co., 15 A.D.2d 859, 860, 224 N.Y.S.2d 746, 748 (1962); Moran v. Standard Oil Co., 211 N.Y. 187, 195, 105 N.E. 217 (1914).

116. Hangzhou Silk Imp. & Exp. Corp. v. P.C.B. Int'l Indus., 2002 U.S. Dist. LEXIS 16578 24 (S.D.N.Y. 2002), and Toltec Fabrics, Inc. v. August, Inc., 29 F.3d 778, 780 (2d Cir. 1994).

117. Oliver B. Cannon & Son, Inc. v. Dorr-Oliver, Inc., 394 A.2d 834 (D.C. 1980).

118. Cates Constr., Inc. v. Talbot Partners, 980 P.2d 407, 412 (Cal. 1999).

owners seeking to recover loss of resale profits as a result of "missing the market" due to delay will need to show lost profits resulting from its inability to sell were within reasonable contemplation of the parties at the time of contracting.[119]

Things the Owner Can't Typically Recover

Emotional Distress

Generally, courts have been reluctant to allow owners to recover damages for emotional distress or mental suffering.[120] For example, in Pennsylvania, the courts have followed the Restatement Second of Contracts, by prohibiting the recovery of emotional distress or mental suffering "unless the breach of contract was wanton or reckless and caused bodily harm or the breach is of such a nature that serious emotional disturbance was a *particularly* likely result."[121] And in *Swanson v. First National Bank*, the court stated, "In actions for breach of contract, it is only in exceptional cases that damages for injury to reputation or for mental suffering can be recovered."[122]

Impact to Credit Rating

In Texas, the rule is that while loss of credit may be a factor in assessing exemplary damages in a proper case, it is never an item of compensatory damages.[123] On the subject of loss of business credit as an item of damages, Corpus Juris Secundum states: "Loss of business credit and reputation due to the wrongful act of another may afford a proper element of damages. It has been held, however, that loss of commercial credit cannot be assessed as an element of damages for breach of a contract, unless it immediately connects itself with some tangible pecuniary loss of which it was the cause."[124]

Construction Loan Interest: Direct or Consequential?

Additional or increased interest rates are a major concern, especially in the private construction context. A majority of private owners finance their projects with high interest rate construction loans, with the goal of converting those loans to

119. Elar Invest. Inc. v. Southwest Culvert Co, Inc., 676 P.2d 659, 665 (Ariz. App. 1983).

120. *See* Sanders v. Zeagler, 96-C-1170 C/W96-C-1270 (La. 1996).

121. Gallagher v. Upper Darby Tp., 539 A.2d 463, 467 (Pa. Commw. Ct. 1988) (citing Rodgers v. Nationwide Mutual Ins. Co., 344 Pa. Sup. Ct. 311, 496 A.2d 811 (1985)) (citing RESTATEMENT (SECOND) OF CONTRACTS § 353 (1981)).

122. Swanson v. First Nat'l Bank, 185 Minn. 89, 92 (1931).

123. State Nat'l Bank of Iowa Park, Tex. v. Rogers, 89 S.W.2d 825, 827 (Tex. App. 1935).

124. 25 C.J.S. Damages § 55, at 807. *See also* Raymond Le Chase, Inc. v. Vincent Buick, Inc., 353 N.Y.S.2d 151, 152 (N.Y. Sup. Ct. 1974).

lower-rate permanent loans once construction is complete.[125] Yet, in the event of a construction delay, the owner may be forced into suffering the higher interest rates of the construction loan longer than anticipated or budgeted, or may even be forced into accepting an interest rate on its permanent financing that is substantially higher than it would have been able to negotiate absent the delay.[126]

Additional interest costs incurred by the owner as a result of a contractor-caused delay may be recovered as either direct or consequential, depending on the jurisdiction and the nature of the interest costs. Earlier, we discussed instances where financing has been recognized as a direct damage. Here, we will examine how courts have distinguished financing as a consequential damage.

Additional Construction Loan Interest

While additional loan interest may constitute direct damages, that does not always mean that these damages are recoverable. For instance, whether construction loan costs and lost rents will be recoverable may depend on whether awarding those damages will result in double recovery. Louisiana courts have issued contradicting decisions on whether recovery of both damages will result in double recovery. In *Hemenway Co. v. Bartex, Inc.*, the court awarded both the rent and interest on interim financing as a result of the delay, since "both of these sums would be needed to place plaintiff in the same position it would have been in had the construction been completed timely."[127] Yet, in *Brewhouse, Ltd. v. New Orleans Public Service, Inc.*, the owners were unable to recover both extended interest on the construction loan and lost rents as damages, the court finding that awarding both construction loan interest and lost rents constituted double recovery.[128]

Higher Interest on Permanent Loan

Unlike extended interest rates, damages resulting from an increased interest rate are generally not direct damages, but rather consequential. Courts have held that an increase in interest rates do not flow naturally from the delay but rather are caused by variable pressures and counter-pressures affecting the supply and demand in the money market.[129] In the aftermath of the COVID-19 pandemic, interest rates shot up faster than at any time in decades, which exposed countless owners to higher than expected borrowing costs. However, just because these damages are deemed

125. Kenneth M. Block, *Construction Law; Time Is Money; News; Contractual Treatments of Delay Damages*, N.Y.L.J. (Aug. 29, 2007).

126. *Id.*

127. Hemenway Co. v. Bartex, of Texas, Inc., 373 So. 2d 1272 (La. App. 1979).

128. Brewhouse, Ltd. v. New Orleans Pub. Serv., Inc., 614 So. 2d 118 (La. App. 1993).

129. Roanoke Hosp. Ass'n v. Doyle & Russell, Inc., 215 Va. 796, 214 S.E.2d 155 (1975).

consequential, does not guarantee that the state laws or jurisdiction will allow for recovery of these damages.

As mentioned before, construction delays may force owners into accepting an interest rate on its permanent financing that is substantially higher than it would have been able to negotiate had no delay occur.[130] In states like New York, these additional expenses are recoverable under state law, but only as consequential damages.[131]

Louisiana allows for recovery of the net difference in the costs of the construction and permanent financing for the period of delay rather than the gross amount of construction loan interest.[132] However, this still requires owners to show that the permanent financing commencing following the completion of the project was cheaper than the construction financing.[133]

Waiver of Consequential Damages Clause

When liquidated damages provisions are not included within a contract, the contractor may be exposed to liability for all delay damages incurred by an owner, absent a waiver of consequential damages. In an informal 2007 study surveying New York construction lawyers, the participants reported that the majority of the contracts included some form of a waiver of consequential damages, and a significant number of their contracts had partial waivers limiting the contractor's exposure to only specific types of damages.[134] However, waivers of consequential damages have not always been as widespread. The case that triggered the widespread use of waivers of consequential damages is the New Jersey Supreme Court's decision in *Perini Corp. v. Greate Bay Hotel & Casino.*[135]

Perini Corporation v. Greate Bay Hotel and Casino

In *Perini*, the Sands Hotel and Casino undertook major renovations of the Brighton Hotel, along the Boardwalk in Atlantic City.[136] As a part of these renovations, Sands hired Perini Corporation as the construction manager for elements of the renovation, with a $16.8 million guaranteed maximum price contract and a $600,000

---

130. Block, *supra* note 125.
131. Cooperstein v. Patrician Estates, 117 A.D.2d 774 (N.Y. S. Ct. 1986).
132. Brewhouse, Ltd. v. New Orleans Pub. Serv., Inc., 614 So. 2d 118 (La. App. 1993).
133. *Id.*
134. Block, *supra* note 125.
135. 610 A.2d 364 (N.J. 1992).
136. *Perini*, 610 A.2d at 367.

fee.[137] Sands terminated Perini after the project incurred three months of delays in two elements of the project.[138]

Pursuant to their contract, Perini and Sands submitted three issues to an arbitration panel: (1) lost profit damages alleged by Sands, (2) contract balances due Perini, and (3) wrongful termination of the contract by Sands.[139] The arbitrator awarded Sands over $14.5 million in damages for lost profits.[140] Perini sought to vacate the award on the basis that the lost profits were not contemplated by the parties at the time of the contract and had they contemplated such damages, it would have been included within a provision in the contract.[141] Additionally, Perini argued that they would not have accepted such an outsized risk for the $600,000 fee. The New Jersey Supreme Court rejected Perini's arguments and upheld the award, finding that the arbitrators' holding was not "such an egregious mistake that it amount[ed] to an arbitrary remaking of the contract between the parties."[142]

AIA's Waiver of Consequential Damages

The outcome in *Perini* triggered nationwide fear within the construction industry, directed at the fact that a construction manager was found to have assumed a $14.5 million liability on the basis of a $600,000 fee.[143] This disproportionate risk of recoverable damages led to the inclusion of a waiver of consequential damages clause in the next edition of the AIA A201 general conditions.[144] Following the AIA's lead, the Associated General Contractors of America followed suit by incorporating its own waiver of consequential damages provision.[145] Today, waiver of consequential damages is the norm.

137. *Id.*

138. *Id.* at 367–68.

139. *Id.* at 368.

140. *Id.*

141. *Id.* at 374.

142. *Id.* at 387.

143. Will W. Allensworth & Allenworth & Porter, LLP, 30th Annual Construction Law Conference: A Question of Consequence (2017).

144. *See* AIA Document A201-1997, General Conditions of Contract ¶ 4.3.10 (Providing for a waiver by both the contractor and owner for "consequential damages arising out of or relating to this contract," including "damages incurred by the owner for rental expenses, for loss of use, income, profit, finance, business and reputation, and for loss of management or employee productivity or of the services of such persons" and "damages incurred by the contractor for principal office expenses including the compensation of personnel stationed there, for losses of financing, business and reputation, and for loss of profit except anticipated profit arising directly from the work.").

145. *See, e.g.*, AGC Document 200 (2000), Standard Form of Agreement and General Conditions Between Owner and Contractor (Where the Contract Price is a Lump Sum), § 10.2.

AIA's waiver did not, and does not, define consequential damages. Rather, the clause gives examples of consequential damages, including "rental expenses, . . . losses of use, income, profit, financing, business and reputation,[.]"[146] However, as noted earlier, owner's financing may not automatically be excluded by the standard AIA waiver clause, depending on both the type of financing being contemplated and the jurisdiction.

Sufficiency of Waivers

Generally, waivers of consequential damages are enforceable. However, certain states, including Kentucky,[147] have held that a waiver may be stricken if it is severely one-sided, oppressive, or unfairly surprising.

Additionally, the list of consequential damages within a waiver may prove to be "nonexhaustive."[148] In *The Bartram, LLC v. C.B. Contractors*, the owner argued that the waiver applied only to "losses of financing" as opposed to the increased costs of financing.[149] The court found that the waiver does not limit its applicability to the examples specifically listed and that under generally recognized canons of construction,[150] "increased financing costs are included in the waiver because they are substantially similar to losses of financing."[151]

On the other hand, states including Wyoming have held that the contract must clearly state what "sole and exclusive" remedies for a delay will be available.[152] If the contract is not specific, then other contract remedies will be available, including contract damages.[153] The Wyoming Supreme Court recognized that parties may contract out of delay damages, but the contract must include specific language to achieve that result.[154]

---

146. AIA A201 § 15.1.6.1.

147. *See* Conseco Fin. Servicing Corp. v. Wilder, 47 S.W.3d 335, 341 (Ky. App. 2001).

148. *See* Wal-Mart Stores, Inc. v. S.C. Nestel, Inc., 2010 WL 1190534 (S.D. Ind. Mar. 23, 2010).

149. The Bartram, LLC v. C.B. Contractors, LLC, 2011 WL 1299856, at *3 (N.D. Fla. Mar. 31, 2011).

150. "The principle of *ejusdem generis* provides that where general words follow an enumeration of specific words, the general words are construed as applying to the same kind or class as those that are specifically mentioned."

151. *The Bartram, LLC*, 2011 WL 1299856, at *3.

152. City of Gillette v. Hladky Constr, Inc., 2008 WY 134, ¶ 50 (2008).

153. *Id.*

154. *Id.*

Other Potential Delay Damages

Recovery of Attorneys' Fees

The majority of states[155] follow the American Rule when it comes to recovering attorneys' fees. Under the "American Rule," absent a statute or contractual provision, courts generally will not allow for the recovery of attorneys' fees.[156] Absent some agreement or stipulation specially authorizing the allowance of attorneys' fees and ordinary expenses and burdens of litigation, they are generally not recoverable.[157] Few statutes provide for the recovery of attorneys' fees in specific construction situations outside of contract. An exception, in Kentucky, where under the "strict liability" statute, an owner may recover attorneys' fees in a cause of action for violating a building code.[158]

However, there are exceptions to this rule. If a contractor's conduct in causing the delay is more than a mere breach of contract, such a party "acting in bad faith, vexatiously, wantonly, or for oppressive reasons," then a court may have an inherent power to depart from the American Rule.[159] This exception has also been codified in several state statutes, including Tennessee.[160]

In Oregon, attorney fees may be recoverable if the party's breach caused the nonbreaching party to become involved in litigation with a third party.[161] Similarly, Washington courts may award fees and costs under a theory of equitable indemnity, or the "ABC" rule.[162] Equitable indemnity provides that "when the natural and proximate consequences of a wrongful act by defendant involve plaintiff in litigation with others, there may, as a general rule, be a recovery of damages for the reasonable costs incurred in the litigation, including compensation for attorney's fees."[163]

---

155. *E.g.*, Historic Charleston Holdings, LLC v. Mallon, 381 S.C. 417, 673 S.E.2d 448 (2009).

156. Austin v. Parker, 672 F.2d 508, 518–19 (5th Cir. 1982). *See* St. Joseph Hosp. v. Corbetta Constr. Co., 21 Ill. App. 3d 925, 316 N.E.2d 51, 76 (1974) ("Attorneys' fees and the ordinary expenses and burdens of litigation are not allowable to the successful party in the absence of some agreement or stipulation specially authorizing the allowance thereof, and this rule applies equally in courts of law and in courts of equity.").

157. 21 Ill. App. 3d 925, 316 N.E.2d 51, 76.

158. KRS 198B.130.

159. Alyeska Pipeline Serv. Co. v. Wilderness Soc'y, 421 U.S. 240, 258–59 (1975) (quoting F.D. Rich Co., Inc. v. United States, 417 U.S. 116, 129 (1974)).

160. In cases of malicious harassment or frivolous appeals, a plaintiff may recover attorney's fees. TENN. CODE. ANN. § 4-21-701 (1996), § 27-1-122 (1975).

161. Raymond v. Feldmann, 124 Or. App. 543, 546, 863 P.2d 1269 (1993).

162. Jacob's Meadow Owners Ass'n v. Plateau 44 II, LLC, 139 Wn. App. 743, 759, 162 P.3d 1153 (2007).

163. *Id.*

Interest on Damage Award

An owner may be entitled to pre- and post-judgment interest on the amount of delay damages. Similar to the recovery of attorneys' fees, the owner must rely either on specific contractual provisions or on applicable statutes for the recovery of interest.[164] In some circumstances, pre-judgement interest may be imposed by equity; however, these circumstances only focus on the unjust enrichment behind the lost profits and not on the additional costs. This makes pre-judgement interest only recoverable on liquidated damage amounts that can be calculated with reasonable certainty.

Withholding Payments

The goal of recovering damages is to put the nonbreaching party in the position that they would have been had the breach not occurred. By awarding a party with more money than would be needed to put them in the same position as before, would be to unjustly enrich them. A party may not be unjustly enriched by recovering interest from the date of the breach/event without accounting for and crediting interest that would be earned on contract funds as security for the breach.[165]

One of the best examples of this is from an illustration in the Restatement Second of Contracts. Illustration 5 of section 347 of the Restatement Second states:

> A contract to build a hotel for B for $500,000 and to have it ready for occupancy by May 1. B's occupancy of the hotel is delayed for a month because of a breach by A. The cost avoided by B as a result of not having to operate the hotel during May is subtracted from the May rent lost in determining damages.[166]

Mitigation of Delay Damages by Owner

Pursuant to the doctrine of mitigation, the owner is obligated to take reasonable actions to limit damages caused by contractor delays. Damages that may have been otherwise recoverable as direct or consequential damages are limited to those costs that reasonably could not have been avoided by the nonbreaching party and must be reduced by costs or losses that could have been reasonably avoided.[167]

---

164. Newbert v. Foxworthy, 71 Ill. App. 3d 438, 389 N.E.2d 898 (1979); Plant Planners, Inc. v. Pollock, 91 A.D.2d 1017, 457 N.Y.S.2d 890 (1983), *aff'd*, 60 N.Y.2d 779, 457 N.E.2d 781, 469 N.Y.S.2d 675 (1983).

165. 6 Philip L. Bruner & Patrick J. O'Connor, Jr., Bruner & O'Connor Construction Law § 19:120 (2020).

166. Restatement Second, Contracts § 347, illus. 5.

167. 6 Philip L. Bruner & Patrick J. O'Connor, Jr., Bruner & O'Connor Construction Law § 19:20 (2020).

When a delay occurs, an owner cannot simply stand by and permit the delay to continue unabated.[168] Among the potential mitigation options available to the owner include revising the project's scope, budget, schedule, or quality. In order to be considered mitigation, though, the required activity or activities may need to be at no additional cost to the owner.

Often, mitigation efforts are applied to activities that are not on the critical path. By adjusting activities that are off the critical path, the owner can help clear the field so that when the critical path activities are completed, the remainder of the work is on or even ahead of schedule.[169] Thus the owner, by expediting the project, minimizes its lost profits.[170]

Westec Construction Management Co. v. Postle Enterprises I, Inc. held that although a party is not required to accept a change order addressing the delay if it results in the owner waiving their rights to seek damages for a prior breach, the contractor can assert the defense that the owner has failed to mitigate its damages when it refuses to sign a change order that would have remedied the defect and fails to communicate any objection to the release contained in the change order.[171]

While the owner bears the burden of proving the apportionment of damages when it comes to separating the causes for the delay, courts have held that the mitigation defense should not operate to shift this burden of proof.[172] Additionally, the defending contractor must show that the damages could have been mitigated at the time of the breach; "hindsight" is not sufficient.[173]

---

168. Reynolds Metals Co. v. Westinghouse Elec. Corp., 758 F.2d 1073, 1075–77 (5th Cir. 1985) (recovery for repair damages as delay component denied due to untimely warranty claim by owner).

169. 5 Philip L. Bruner & Patrick J. O'Connor, Jr., Bruner & O'Connor Construction Law § 15:27 (2020).

170. O'Brien (Newark) Cogeneration, Inc. v. Automatic Sprinkler Corp. of America, 361 N.J. Super. 264, 825 A.2d 524 (App. Div. 2003).

171. *Westec Constr. Mgmt. Co.*, 68 P.3d at 533.

172. *See* City of Westminster v. Centric-Jones Constructors, 100 P.3d 472, 476 (Colo. App. 2003).

173. *See, e.g.*, W. G. Cornell Company of Washington, D.C. v. Ceramic Coating Co., 626 F.2d 990, 993–94 (D.C. Cir. 1980); Tennessee Valley Sand & Gravel Co. v. M/V Delta, 598 F.2d 930 (5th Cir. 1979), *modified* 604 F.2d 13.

CHAPTER 11

Termination for Actual or Prospective Delayed Completion

Buck S. Beltzer

Introduction

Although construction delays can result in financial consequences for owners and contractors,[1] sometimes a significant delay results in one of the parties resorting to the nuclear remedy of termination. Because termination (for any reason) is a drastic sanction reserved only for when solid evidence shows termination is justified, a party must overcome significant hurdles when it seeks to terminate another because a project is delayed.[2] Indeed, a party "should not lightly resort" to termination.[3] The consequences for failing to properly establish grounds for termination are high, and a party who terminates for delay "takes a substantial financial risk."[4] This chapter outlines circumstances where delay could constitute a material default, the steps a party would take after default to terminate the other, and whether termination is legally defensible under various factual scenarios.

---

1. This chapter is drafted using owner and contractor as the interested parties, but its contents apply equally to the contractor and subcontractor relationship.

2. CJP Contractors, Inc. v. United States, 45 Fed. Cl. 343, 379 n.58 (1999); J.D. Hedin Constr. Co., Inc. v. United States, 187 Ct. Cl. 45, 57 (1969).

3. PCL Constr. Servs., Inc. v. United States, 47 Fed. Cl. 745, 808 (2000); *see also* McDonnell Douglas Corp. v. United States, 323 F.3d 1006, 1015 (Fed. Cir. 2003) (citing a "judicial aversion to default termination").

4. DeVito v. United States, 188 Ct. Cl. 979, 990 (1969); *cf. Wolfe Constr. Co.*, 1984 Eng. BCA LEXIS 64, at *122 (1984) ("It is a grave responsibility to cause a man to be summarily dismissed from his employment.").

Material Delay as Default

As a threshold issue, when a contractor breaches a contract by causing delays, the owner's remedies turn on whether the delay is a minor breach or material default.[5] If delay is minor, and allows the owner to "receive the substantial benefit of its bargain," then it may only recover damages from the contractor.[6] Material delays, however, may result in default and justify the owner in terminating the contract, ordering the contractor off the job, and seeking redress.[7] Delays may become material because of a contractor's (1) prospective, or (2) actual failure to meet a completion date, or (3) concession that it will not complete the work on time.

Default for Prospective Failure to Meet a Completion Date

A contractor may be in default for prospective failure to meet a completion date when the delay is substantial, and the contract includes a term making timely performance essential.[8] It is typical for a contract to include a term making timely performance essential, such as noting "time is of the essence."[9] However, not all delays

---

5. United States v. SAMCO Constr. Co., 39 F. Supp. 2d 661, 670 (E.D. Va. 1999).

6. *Id.* at 670–71 (E.D. Va. 1999); *see* Mega Constr. Co. v. United States, 29 Fed. Cl. 396, 445 (1993) (finding minor delay entitled a nonbreaching party to "recover damages or a set-off against the breaching party, but it does not excuse that aggrieved party from performing" and, "[e]ven when no contract clause permits the withholding of payments [a party] has the implied right to protects its interests by this means" and for the party "to exercise its common law right to offset [damages for minor delays], the claim need not be reduced to judgment; the offset may be effected pending resolution of the controversy"); *see also* N. Helex Co. v. United States, 197 Ct. Cl. 118, 125 n.3 (1972) ("[W]here one of the parties decides to continue performance after a default which was not material it can still sue for damages.").

7. *SAMCO*, 39 F. Supp. 2d at 673; Mustang Pipeline Co., Inc. v. Driver Pipeline Co., Inc., 134 S.W.3d 195, 196 (Tex. 2004) ("It is a fundamental principle of contract law that when one party to a contract commits a material breach of that contract, the other party is discharged or excused from further performance."); Unified Contractor, Inc. v. Albuquerque Hous. Auth., 400 P.3d 290, 300 (N.M. App. 2017); Marshall Constr., Ltd. v. Coastal Sheet Metal & Roofing, Inc., 569 So. 2d 845, 848 (Fla. App. 1990).

8. *SAMCO*, 39 F. Supp. 2d at 672; *but see Cosmos Eng'rs, Inc.*, 1977 ASBCA LEXIS 307, at *73 (1977) ("Whether time is of the essence is a factor in substantial performance but even where present it does not demand that performance be measured in terms of strict conformity."). *See also* Ripple Resort Media, Inc. v. SkiView Corp., 2008 U.S. Dist. LEXIS 84929, at *8–9 (D. Colo. Oct. 20, 2008) (finding a material breach is one that "goes to the root of the . . . contract and renders substantial performance under the contract impossible" such that it "defeat[s] an essential purpose of the contract"); *see also* Restatement of Contracts (Second, 1980) § 241 (describing factors considered in determining whether a breach is material).

9. *See, e.g.*, *DeVito*, 188 Ct. Cl. at 991 ("Time is of the essence in any contract containing fixed dates for performance."); Empire Energy Mgmt. Sys., Inc. v. Roche, 362 F.3d 1343, 1354 (5th Cir. 2004) (finding "the existence of a contract itself establishes that time is of the essence" where the contract liquidates damages for delay); Lake Steel Erection, Inc. v. Egan, 61 A.D.2d 1125, 1126 (N.Y. Sup.

are substantial. To the contrary, a contractor's untimely performance according to interim schedule milestones is ordinarily not grounds for default.[10] Only when an owner is "justifiably insecure" about a contractor's ability to timely complete the work according to the final date of completion is the delay substantial.[11]

Whether an owner is justifiably insecure about a contractor's delayed performance requires comparing the remaining work to the correct completion date.[12] An owner's subjective beliefs are irrelevant.[13] Unsurprisingly, an owner may be justifiably insecure about delays where it is "mathematically impossible" for a contractor to complete the remaining work by the completion date.[14] But even if not mathematically impossible, an owner may be justifiably insecure where there is "no reasonable likelihood" of timely completion.[15] An owner may consider a contractor's past delays, missed interim milestones, and whether it "reasonably appears" further delay will adversely affect its ability to make substitute arrangements, such as reprocuring work, materials, or equipment.[16]

Default for Actual Failure to Meet a Completion Date

In contracts containing a date certain for requiring completion, a contractor "is properly considered in default the day after it fail[s] to meet the contract

Ct. 1978) (finding even "[w]here there is no express provision in a contract relating to time of performance, a reasonable time will be implied" and delays beyond that reasonable time are material).

10. *SAMCO*, 39 F. Supp. 2d at 672; *McDonnell Douglas*, 323 F.3d at 1014, 1016 (finding owner does not satisfy default termination for prospective failure to meet completion by "merely showing that the contractor was behind schedule").

11. *McDonnell Douglas*, 323 F.3d at 1016–17.

12. *CJP*, 45 Fed. Cl. at 371, 378 (holding default "must be based on a correct understanding of the remaining work and time left for completion"); *PCL*, 47 Fed. Cl. at 808 (finding a contractor's performance should be analyzed "with an eye to fundamental elements of performance").

13. *McDonnell Douglas*, 323 F.3d at 1014, 1016–17.

14. *Empire*, 362 F.3d at 1349, 1351–52, 56–57 (finding default where even, if certain delays were excused, contractor "still would not have been able to complete the project in a timely fashion"); *Unified*, 400 P.3d at 300; *Mustang*, 134 S.W.3d at 200 (finding default where "[e]ven the most ambitious of construction schedules would have great difficulty meeting" deadlines and "there was virtually no chance that [the contractor] would be able to cure its breach and complete the construction on time").

15. *McDonnell Douglas*, 323 F.3d at 1014, 1016–17 (finding an owner must make objective inquiry into "the events, actions, and communications leading to the delay"); *SAMCO*, 39 F. Supp. 2d at 671 (finding most courts do not rely on percentages of completion alone to discern whether an owner is justifiably insecure about a contractor's timely performance).

16. *Mustang*, 134 S.W.3d at 199 (quoting Restatement of Contracts (Second, 1980) § 242); Decker & Co. v. West, 76 F.3d 1573, 1582 (Fed. Cir. 1996) (finding an owner may take contractor's "performance history into account" because "past lack of progress indicates a pattern of nonperformance and delay which should not be ignored").

performance date."[17] While it is not the topic of this chapter, declaring a contractor in default on the day after the completion date is likely not appropriate if the contractor is entitled to or has justifiable claims for additional contract time from the owner.

Default Due to Express Disclaimer of Ability to Timely Perform

Under the anticipatory repudiation doctrine, a contractor may be in default for delay if it repudiates its intention to make adequate progress or follow an approved schedule before the time fixed for its performance arrives.[18] The prevailing rule is that a definite and unconditional communication repudiating (or rejecting) a party's contractual obligations constitutes a breach of contract entitling the other party to take immediate action, despite the possibility that the communication "takes place long before the time prescribed for the promised performance."[19]

Repudiation can occur, for example, when a contractor "clearly and unmistakably" informs the owner that it could not resume operations without an immediate time extension or "infusion of cash."[20] Thus, a contractor should be cautious when discussing its progress with an owner, lest its statements be construed as admission of the operative conditions to contract termination—that is, default due to the contractor's acknowledged inability to timely perform.

Procedural Steps Required for Termination Due to Delay

Most standard-form industry contracts contain required procedural steps before a party can terminate another for delay. Each of the Federal Acquisition Regulations (FAR),[21] American Institute of Architects (AIA),[22] ConsensusDocs,[23] Design Build

17. State Corps v. United States, 142 Fed. Cl. 21, 31 (2019); *but see McDonnell Douglas*, 323 F.3d at 1014 (finding first unmet schedule milestone is "insufficient to sustain a default termination").

18. *Composites Horizons*, 1985 ASBCA LEXIS 707, at *48 (1985); Roehm v. Horst, 178 U.S. 1, 19–20 (1899); Kennedy v. United States, 164 Ct. Cl. 507, 514 (1964) (finding "when a contract upon which [a party] is relying cannot or will not be brought to fruition" it "may take immediate action to safeguard its interests"); *PCL*, 47 Fed. Cl. at 809 ("When one party to a contract absolutely refuses to perform his contract, and before the time arrives for performance distinctly and unqualifiedly communicates that refusal to the other party, that other party can, if he choose, treat that refusal as a breach and commence an action at once therefor."); Esplendido Apartments v. Olson, 697 P.2d 1105, 1110 (Ariz. App. 1984).

19. Holiday Inns of Am., Inc. v. Peck, 520 P.2d 87, 89 n.3 (Alaska 1974).

20. *Kennedy*, 164 Ct. Cl. at 514.

21. FAR § 52.249-6 Termination (Cost-Reimbursement) (May 2004); *id.* § 52.249-8 Default (Fixed-Price Supply and Service) (Apr. 1984); *id.* § 52.249-10 Default (Fixed-Price Construction) (Apr. 1984).

22. AIA Document A201–2017, General Conditions of the Contract for Construction, § 14.2.1.1, .4; *id.* § 14.2.2.

23. ConsensusDocs 205–Standard Agreement and General Conditions Between Owner and Constructor (Short Form) Article 18 (2011, Revised May 2017).

Institute of America (DBIA),[24] and Engineer Joint Contract Documents Committee (EJCDC)[25] forms specify a pre-termination process. While each form approaches the problem slightly differently, there are substantial commonalities, which include: owner's obligation to give notice and an opportunity to cure; contractor's obligation to cure or begin to implement a cure, sometimes under an express recovery plan; and a mutual obligation to mitigate damages.

First Breach Rule

Under the "first breach" rule, "a party to a contract cannot claim its benefit where [it] is the first to violate its terms."[26] Thus, an owner who is itself in default of the contract before termination—for example, by causing delay, failing to give valid notice or sufficient time to cure the delay, or making a cure impossible by barring the contractor from the site or wrongfully withholding payments—takes a substantial risk of exposure to wrongful termination claims.[27]

Strict Compliance as Condition Precedent to Termination

Independent of the first breach rule, proper termination cannot take place until the contractual termination process is exhausted.[28] Courts may forgive minor deviations from the contract's required process, but because termination is a drastic forfeiture, an owner's compliance with the contract's termination process is typically a condition precedent to termination.[29]

---

24. DBIA Contract Document #535, Standard Form of General Conditions of Contract Between Owner and Design-Builder, § 11.2 (3d ed., 2022).

25. EJCDC J-700, Standard General Conditions of the Construction Contract § 16.02 (2018).

26. *See* Serenity Painting & Decorating, LLC v. Hall-Irwin Corp., 2020 Colo. Dist. LEXIS 2765, at *27 (Oct. 13, 2020) (citing Coors v. Sec. Life of Denver Ins. Co., 112 P.3d 59, 64 (Colo. 2005)).

27. *Ripple*, 2008 U.S. Dist. LEXIS 84929, at *8–9 (finding default by owner where "termination of Agreement was without just cause" due to failure to give proper notice and opportunity to cure); *DeVito*, 188 Ct. Cl. at 990 (finding wrongful termination where owner "terminates prior to the expiration" of the cure period); Ranta Constr. Inc. v. Anderson, 190 P.3d 835, 838, 840, 841–42 (Colo. App. 2008) (finding wrongful termination by owner who "barred . . . contractor from the property and withheld all progress payments due to the contractor"); Cuddy Mountain Concrete, Inc. v. Citadel Constr., Inc., 824 P.2d 151, 158–61 (Idaho 1992) (upholding assessment of liquidated damages against contractor who wrongfully terminated subcontractor for delay without giving cure notice and opportunity when such termination was "conceived in frustration and consummated in anger" without "any thought to the consequences" of the termination).

28. New Design Constr. Co., Inc. v. Hamon Contractors, Inc., 215 P.3d 1172, 1181 (Colo. App. 2008).

29. Florida Dep't of Ins. v. United States, 81 F.3d 1093, 1098 (Fed. Cir. 1996); *see Decker*, 76 F.3d 1573 ("various minor or technical defects in a default termination notice d[o] not invalidate the termination"); *see also* Philadelphia Regent Builders v. United States, 634 F.2d 569, 573 (Ct. Cl. 1980) ("To nullify this termination for default solely on the ground of these harmless technical defects would grant plaintiff an entirely unwarranted windfall."); Acme Process Equip. Co. v. United States, 171 Ct. Cl. 324, 343 (1965), *rev'd on other grounds*, 385 U.S. 138 (1966); *DeVito*, 188 Ct. Cl. at 990; *see* J.F. Kane Contracting Co., Inc., GSBCA 2005, 66-2 BCA ¶5992, at *9 (1966) (holding a party's actions

Notice

Construction contracts often require an owner to give some sort of notice before declaring the contractor in default and terminating the contract. Some industry documents require only one notice,[30] others require multiple,[31] and some contracts require no notice.[32] But even in the absence of an express provision requiring notice, some courts may, as a matter of equity, impose a requirement for notice prior to declaring default.[33] Further, notice may be critical to making a claim against a contractor's surety.[34]

Notice is intended as a warning of possible termination.[35] It must describe the issue "with enough particularity of the performance failures which have placed the contract in danger of termination."[36] Provided proper notice is given, however, it is usually not necessary for an owner to give repeat notice directed at related concerns.[37] This could be the case, in certain circumstances, even when the original notice does not "specify the particular failure for which" the contract is ultimately terminated.[38]

---

relating to purported termination must be "taken in strict accordance with the pertinent contractual provision[s]"); *Unified*, 400 P.3d at300 (finding courts will "strictly construe default clause" which does "not require that a contractor be afforded a period in which to cure defects before a contract is terminated for default"); N.W. Water Corp. v. Westminster, 432 P.2d 757, 759 (Colo. 1967) (holding 30-day notice requirement at issue "was a condition precedent to termination"); *Composites Horizons*, 1985 ASBCA LEXIS 707, at *60.

30. *E.g.*, AIA Document A201–2017, General Conditions of the Contract for Construction, § 14.2.1.1, .4; *id.* § 14.2.2. (allowing owner to terminate on one-weeks' notice if contractor commits substantial delay).

31. *E.g.*, ConsensusDocs–410 Standard Design-Build Agreement with General Conditions Between Owner and Design-Builder – 2011, Revised October 2017 § 12.2, .1, .2; *id.* § 12.3, .1 (allowing owner to terminate after one-weeks' notice and subsequent half-weeks' notice after contractor's failure to cure).

32. For example, it is not unusual for a subcontract to be silent on notice and an opportunity to cure.

33. Pro. Servs. Supplier, Inc. v. United States, 45 Fed. Cl. 808, 811 (2000) (requiring "some notice before a contract is placed in default").

34. Surety claims are outside of the scope of this chapter, but if the contractor has a performance bond, the owner is advised to investigate whether the bond requires notice before triggering the bond's benefit.

35. Danzig v. AEC Corp., 224 F.3d 1333, 1337 (Fed. Cir. 2000); Hannon Elec. Co. v. United States, 31 Fed. Cl. 135, 148 (1994).

36. *Hannon*, 31 Fed. Cl. at 148.

37. *Empire*, 362 F.3d at 1356.

38. Am. Marine Upholstery Co. v. United States, 170 Ct. Cl. 564, 571–72 (1965); *see Empire*, 362 F.3d at 1356 (finding original cure notice "directed more specifically" does not require terminating party to "provide another formal cure notice" for subsequent related default).

Opportunity to Cure

In addition to requiring notice, some construction contracts require an owner to afford the contractor an opportunity to cure a default before the contract is terminated.[39] Unlike notice provisions, however, it is unlikely a court would impose an equitable requirement to afford a contractor the opportunity to cure if not required by contract.[40] Thus, when a contractor agrees to a contract which lacks an express opportunity to cure, it effectively "abrogate[s] any common law rights it might have had to" a right to cure.[41] For example, a contractor who enters into a contract with the government containing FAR section 52.249.10, which is silent as to a right to cure,[42] is not "afforded a period in which to cure [default] before [the] contract is terminated."[43]

What exactly constitutes a cure and whether the cure must be completed (or just commenced) may be addressed in the contract but is usually left silent. In most cases, "assurances that progress is being made toward a timely completion" may be enough to stave off termination.[44] Thus, when a contract requires only commencement of a cure and a contractor "possessed the intent or the ability to cure its [delayed] performance in the time remaining" then cure commencement may be sufficient.[45] In other cases, however, a contractor must exceed minimal performance efforts to eliminate delays to "levels reasonably commensurate with contract requirements."[46] In any event, it is important for a curing party to communicate its progress to the other, as a failure to give reasonable assurances of performance could lead to a conclusion that the party was not adequately curing and justify termination.[47] And, of course, when the contract requires an opportunity to cure, the nondefaulting party must allow and not interfere with the other's cure efforts.[48]

---

39. AIA Document A201–2017 § 14.2.1.1, .4; *id.* § 14.2.2; ConsensusDocs – 410 § 12.2 – 12.2.2; *id.* § 12.3 – 12.3.1.

40. *Pro. Servs. Supplier*, 45 Fed. Cl. at 811 ("there is no indication that [a default] notice must be one offering an ability to cure").

41. *Pro. Servs. Supplier*, 45 Fed. Cl. at 812; *but see Unified*, 400 P.3d at 298–99 (finding "[a]t common law, the concept of cure is deeply engrained as an implied condition in every contract").

42. FAR § 52.249-10 Default (Fixed-Price Construction) (Apr. 1984) ("If the Contractor refuses or fails to prosecute the work or any separable part, with the diligence that will insure its completion within the time specified in this contract including any extension, or fails to complete the work within this time, *the Government may, by written notice to the Contractor, terminate the right to proceed with the work* . . . that has been delayed.") (emphasis added).

43. *Pro. Servs. Supplier*, 45 Fed. Cl. at 811.

44. *Danzig*, 224 F.3d at 1337.

45. *Hannon*, 31 Fed. Cl. at 143.

46. *Danzig*, 224 F.3d at 1337.

47. *Id.* at 1337–38, 40 (finding a lack of communication could lead to "a branch of" anticipatory reputation which may justify termination).

48. *See, e.g.*, *DeVito*, 188 Ct. Cl. at 990; *Ranta*, 190 P.3d at 838, 840, 841–42 (finding owner materially breaches a contract where contractor remains "willing and able" to cure defaulted work

Cure Under Recovery Plan

As a more nuanced approach to the notice and cure process, some complex construction contracts, including infrastructure, public works, and EPC (Engineering Procurement and Construction) agreements, require a contractor to submit a recovery plan for the owner's consideration and, if accepted, the recovery plan becomes the contractor's new standard of performance.[49] Again, the owner must adhere to its notice obligations and not interfere with the contractor's recovery efforts.[50]

A contractor's recovery plan typically must include a schedule and describe how it will eliminate delays, mitigate losses, and complete the project on time. An owner may properly terminate the contractor if it fails to submit or submits an unacceptable recovery plan.[51] Owners have broad discretion to reject plans inconsistent with the parties' existing contract.[52] For example, an owner may reject a contractor's plan when it seeks time and cost relief for accelerated work made necessary by risks borne by the contractor under the parties' contract.[53]

---

performed but the owner inhibits cure performance by barring contractor from the property); Richard Joseph & Co. v. Solaris Prop. Owner, LLC, 2014 Colo. Dist. LEXIS 2228 (Oct. 6, 2014); *Ripple*, 2008 U.S. Dist. LEXIS 84929, at *8–9 (finding that, even if an owner gives proper default notice to a contractor for delayed work, an owner who terminates the contract before the expiration of a prescribed cure period commits a material breach by "not giving [the contractor] sufficient time to cure the alleged default").

49. *E.g.*, FAR § 52.236-15(b)–(c) (Schedules for Construction Contracts) (Apr. 1984) ("If, in the opinion of the Contracting Officer, the Contractor falls behind the approved schedule," then, "without additional cost to the Government . . . the Contracting Officer may require the Contractor to . . . submit for approval any supplementary schedule . . . as the Contracting Officer deems necessary to demonstrate how the approved rate of progress will be regained" and, if Contractor fails to do so, then it may be terminated for default.); 2019 New Mexico Department of Transportation Standard Specifications for Highway and Bridge Construction § 108.3.3.2 ("If it becomes apparent or should have become apparent to the Contractor that the Contractor cannot complete the Work within the Contract Time, the Contractor shall provide a . . . recovery Plan to the" Owner.).

50. *E.g.*, Boldt Co. v. Black & Veatch Constr., Inc., 2023 U.S. Dist. LEXIS 55750, at *53–54 (N.D. Ill. 2023) (finding an EPC contractor properly terminates its subcontractor for material delays where the contractor complies with "procedures to effect a termination for cause under the Subcontract" by giving two notices of default, affording the subcontractor options to perform work, but subcontractor "remained in schedule default at all times" until termination).

51. *Id.* at *7–8, 10, 50–54 (a subcontractor is properly terminated if it fails or refuses to issue a recovery plan "to recover the Construction Schedule" as required by the subcontract).

52. *Id.* at *9 (N.D. Ill. 2023) (it is insufficient for a subcontractor to merely assert it is "ready and willing to exhaust all schedule acceleration options").

53. *Id.* at *9, 11, 49, 50–53 (a recovery plan based on the contractor's demonstrated delays as to the owner is not sufficient when the subcontractor lacked entitlement under "any provision in the Subcontract governing its relationship with [the contractor] that would allow it to piggy back on a schedule extension granted to" the contractor).

If, however, an owner accepts a contractor's recovery plan, it becomes the benchmark against which the contractor's performance is measured.[54] Should a contractor fail to properly perform the work under the accepted recovery plan or the owner become justifiably insecure about a contractor's ability to do so, then the owner may properly terminate the contract.[55]

Damage Mitigation

The "duty to mitigate losses applies to contracts."[56] The parties' contract may describe specific actions required to mitigate damages caused by delay. In the absence of express terms, each party must generally use "reasonable commercial judgment" to mitigate losses either party may suffer because of delay.[57] The duty to mitigate is, however, limited and balanced, particularly when an owner is in the position of having to hire a replacement contractor.[58]

An owner cannot be "lackadaisical" in making its selection, but is afforded a reasonable time to select a new contractor without "rush[ing] into a procurement."[59] Unless limited by contract, however, an owner may have broad discretion in hiring a replacement contractor and is generally not obligated to utilize competitive bidding.[60] The owner is also not required to throw good money after bad by releasing proper withholdings, exerting unreasonable effort, or undertaking substantial expense pending termination.[61]

---

54. *Id.* at *53 (termination is proper when the subcontractor "show[s] no improvement (and arguably worsen[s])" while performing under its proposed but unaccepted recovery plan).

55. *Id.* at *53 (an "initial notice of default stayed operative" throughout the recovery period); *McDonnell Douglas*, 323 F.3d at 16–17; *State Corps*, 142 Fed. Cl. at 31.

56. *Hughes v. Oconee Cnty.*, 2007 S.C. App. Unpub. LEXIS 438, at *13 (Oct. 11, 2007); Newman v. Brown, 90 S.E.2d 649, 653 (S.C. 1955) ("It is the undoubted general rule that it is the duty of the owner of the property, which is injured by the negligence of another, to use reasonable means to minimize the damages."); *N. Helex*, 197 Ct. Cl. at 129; Lisbon Contractors, Inc. v. United States, 828 F.2d 759, 768 (Fed. Cir. 1987) ("The principle of mitigation of damages pervades the" FAR.).

57. United States v. U.S. Fid. & Guar. Co., 236 U.S. 512, 526 (1915); *N. Helex*, 197 Ct. Cl. at 129; *Lisbon*, 828 F.2d at 768 ("The principle of mitigation of damages pervades the" FAR.).

58. *Hughes*, 2007 S.C. App. Unpub. LEXIS 438, at *13; *Mega*, 29 Fed. Cl. at 484.

59. *Mega*, 29 Fed. Cl. at 484; *see also Roehm*, 178 U.S. at 19–20 (finding an owner must timely "act on . . . repudiation" by a contractor").

60. *Roehm*, 178 U.S. at 19–20 (finding "if the contracting officer reasonably believes that the contract must be completed quickly, even though there may be several potential contractors capable of completing the contract, the contracting officer may negotiate with a single source"); *see AAR Corp.*, 1974 ASBCA LEXIS 370, at *36 (1974) (finding when an owner "reasonably believes the desired items are in critical short supply, even where there are several potential producers, the [owner] may negotiate with a single source, *e.g.*, the only proven reliable supplier").

61. T. Ferguson Constr., Inc. v. Sealaska Corp., 820 P.2d 1058, 1061 (Alaska 1991); *see Fid. & Guar.*, 236 U.S. at 536 (holding the general rule that a party must mitigate its losses does not apply to a "fixed loss that cannot be mitigated," e.g., by withholding "progress payments" that "remained as

Finally, an owner's failure to mitigate is an affirmative defense; it cannot reverse a termination.[62] The contractor must show a lack of diligence by the owner to minimize damages when it was possible and reasonable to do so.[63] A contractor's successful defense for failure to mitigate "will not bar [an owner] *entirely* from recovery" for the delay, "but will only prevent the recovery of such damages as might have been avoided by reasonable efforts."[64]

Wrongful Default Termination for Delay

Whether termination is proper depends on the facts.[65] Each party bears the burden of proof for its own claims by a preponderance of the evidence.[66] The owner "bears the initial burden of proof to show that the contractor was in default at the time of termination" and "the correctness of its actions in terminating a contractor."[67] In turn, a contractor may assert a breach of contract claim against the owner for wrongful termination.[68] To succeed, the contractor must show: the parties had a valid contract; the contractor substantially performed up to the termination (or was excused from doing so); the owner failed to follow the contract in terminating the contractor; and the wrongful termination caused the contractor damages.[69] The most often litigated elements are whether the contractor

part of the loss, in addition to the cost of" operations under a replacement contractor); Genovese v. Bergeron, 490 S.E.2d 608, 611 (S.C. Ct. App. 1997).

62. Rapid Indus., Inc. v. Indus. Serv. Works, Inc., 2007 S.C. App. Unpub. LEXIS 157, at *3 (Jan. 1, 2007).

63. *Rapid*, 2007 S.C. App. Unpub. LEXIS 157, at *3; *Hughes*, 2007 S.C. App. Unpub. LEXIS 438, at *16–17.

64. *Id.* (emphasis in original).

65. Olson Plumbing & Heating Co. v. United States, 221 Ct. Cl. 197, 204 (1979).

66. *Lisbon*, 828 F.2d at 763–65 ("The order of presentation of evidence by the parties is a matter of trial management [and] the procedural requirements of the court for one party and then the other to come forward with evidence does not shift the ultimate burden of proof or persuasion on an issue back and forth. In other words, the [owner] d[oes] not . . . satisfy its burden by merely showing that the contractor was behind schedule. Rather, on the entirety of the record, the trial court must determine if the party bearing the burden of proof has proved its side of the issue by at least the weight of the evidence. If the evidence on the issue is evenly balanced, the party with the burden loses.") (finding a "default termination order is . . . a decision by the contracting officer on a government 'claim' against the contractor").

67. Abcon Assocs. v. United States, 49 Fed. Cl. 678, 686 (2001); *Mega*, 29 Fed. Cl. at 414; *Lisbon*, 828 F.2d at 763–65.

68. 211 Eighth, LLC v. Town of Carbondale, 922 F. Supp. 2d 1174, 1183 (D. Colo. 2013) (applying Colorado law) ("a wrongful termination of contract may be fully remedied by a common law breach of contract action").

69. *Abcon*, 49 Fed. Cl. at 687 (finding if a contractor is alleged to be in default "it must next be determined if the default is excusable"); *CJP*, 45 Fed. Cl. at 371–72 (finding that "to recover under the [FAR] excusable delay clause, the contractor has the burden of proving that the delay was excusable");

substantially performed and whether the owner followed the contract in terminating, and they often overlap.

Substantial or Excused Performance

An owner's right to timely completion is "tempered somewhat" by the substantial completion doctrine.[70] Under this rule, an owner forgoes its right to terminate and must, instead, accept "slightly" delayed performance (sometimes in exchange for a price reduction), when a contractor's performance, albeit late, affords the owner the substantial benefit of the contract.[71] This occurs when a contractor causes minor delays curable "within a reasonable time" after a completion date.[72]

For example, a contractor substantially completes its work when the only items remaining to be performed after the completion date are "punch list" items.[73] Relatedly, where a contractor achieves a substantial completion milestone, the owner loses its right to terminate for default with respect to the substantially completed work.[74] A contractor does not, however, substantially perform where it must make

---

Ripple, 2008 U.S. Dist. LEXIS 84929, at *10 (holding that if contractor "is in substantial compliance with the terms of the Agreement" then it "carrie[s] its burden of proving [the owner] breached the Agreement . . . when it wrongfully terminated the Agreement").

70. *Hannon*, 31 Fed. Cl. at 149; *Cosmos*, 1977 ASBCA LEXIS 307, at *73 (finding even where "time is of the essence . . . it does not demand that performance be measured in terms of strict conformity").

71. *Hannon*, 31 Fed. Cl. at 149 (finding "[t]he rationale underlying the equitable doctrine of substantial completion is the avoidance of economic waste"); *but see PCL*, 47 Fed. Cl. at 810 (finding the substantial completion doctrine is not "carried to the point where the [owner] is compelled to accept" less than "all benefits which [it] reasonably anticipated receiving under the contract"); *Kinney Aluminum Co.*, 78 F. Supp. 565 (S.D. Cal. 1948) (finding the equitable substantial performance substantial performance doctrine "is never properly involved unless the [owner] has obtained to all intents and purposes all benefits for which [its] reasonably anticipated receiving under the contract").

72. *Cosmos*, 1977 ASBCA LEXIS 307, at *73 (finding substantial performance occurs where "a party's contract performance departs in minor respects from that which has been promised"); *see* Radiation Tech., Inc. v. United States, 177 Ct. Cl. 227, 232 (1966) (defining substantial performance it terms of "the right to cure . . . defects . . . minor in nature and extent and are susceptible to correction within a reasonable time").

73. *Good*, 1966 ASBCA LEXIS 421, at *2, 8-99 (1966) (finding, even if there is "no question that [contractor] did not complete the contract 100 percent," it "substantially performed [its] contract and the [owner's] right of default termination no longer existed" where "a total of less than 1% of the" work remained at termination); *but see Cosmos*, 1977 ASBCA LEXIS 307, at *73 (finding that a tribunal may "ignore[] the parties' percentage [of completion] estimates as being arbitrary or self-serving" and, instead, "concentrate[] on the specific tasks remaining the time required to get them done").

74. *Metzger Towing, Inc.*, 1993 Eng. BCA LEXIS 31, at *46–47 (1994) (finding substantial completion doctrine applicable where, although behind schedule, contractor could and did complete remaining work "within a few days" after scheduled substantial completion date); *Cosmos*, 1977 ASBCA LEXIS 307, at *71 (finding "the fact that all work is not finished by the completion date will not sustain a termination for default if the contract has been substantially performed").

"extensive repair or readjustment" to timely complete its work.[75] But even a contractor who does not timely or substantially perform its work may succeed on a wrongful termination claim by showing its failure to timely perform was justified or excused.

Thus, a contractor may avoid default termination by showing it was not responsible for the delays. When undefined, excusable delays are generally those that a contractor has no cause to suspect would occur when using usual and established methods of project management.[76] Far more often, the parties' agreement specifies which delays are excusable.[77] For example, a contract may entitle a contractor to day-for-day extensions to the project time for each day it encounters unforeseeable events beyond its control, not caused by its fault or negligence, which delay activities on the critical path, such as material shortages, weather, or delays caused by the owner.[78] In any event, if the aggregate amount of excusable delay would take the contractor out of default, then the contractor satisfies the performance elements of its wrongful termination claim.[79]

Another way for a contractor to justify its nonperformance is to prove the owner made a first material breach. Unsurprisingly, an owner's refusal to acknowledge excusable delays or grant justified time extensions which would avoid default may amount to a material breach that excuses the delayed performance.[80] And

75. *Cosmos*, 1977 ASBCA LEXIS 307, at *73.

76. *J.D. Hedin*, 187 Ct. Cl. at 54.

77. *E.g.* AIA Document A201–2017, General Conditions of the Contract for Construction, § 8.3.1 (Contractor is entitled to more time to perform for each day it encounters excusable delays caused by, among other things, owner's negligence and certain events the contractor cannot control.).

78. *J.D. Hedin*, 187 Ct. Cl. at 53 (finding contractor "entitled to both a time-extension and freedom from liability to a default-termination" where the parties' contract excuses contractor from responsibility for delays caused by unforeseeable events beyond the contractor's control or negligence and the contractor encounters cement shortages and "scour[s] the areas from which it would have been reasonable or practical to obtain cement"); *CJP*, 45 Fed. Cl. at 373–74 (finding contractor may recover additional time under certain FAR provisions for excusable delays caused by owner's issuing a stop-work notice).

79. *Id.* (finding a contractor was wrongfully terminated where the amount of excusable delay was more than the number remaining until the scheduled completion date and, in accordance with its contract with an owner, the contractor continued "to prosecute the work with such diligence as will insure its completion within the time specified in the contract, or *any extension thereof*") (emphasis in original).

80. *Id.* at 58–59 (finding contractor not in default and termination wrongful when owner terminates without "fail[ing] to take into account time-extensions due the contractor for unforeseeable delays, if such an extension would have taken the contractor out of default"); Chaney Bldg. Co. v. Tucson, 716 P.2d 28, 31 (Ariz. 1973) (finding contractor's performance excused where owner terminates an agreement without accounting for delays caused by its failure to furnish adequate and timely designs); *see* United States v. Spearin, 248 U.S. 132, 136 (1918) (finding "if the contractor is bound to build according to plans and specifications prepared by the owner, the contractor will not be responsible for the consequences of defects in the plans and specifications").

while a contractor's financial difficulties are not ordinarily a legitimate excuse, if nonpayment by the owner prevents the contractor from paying its subcontractors, suppliers, or equipment rentals, then nonperformance may be excused.[81] Indeed, an owner's failure to make proper payments "in accordance with the terms of the contract is a material breach."[82] Thus, if a delay is the result of a failure to make proper payment, including wrongful withholdings, nonperformance is justified.[83]

Defect in Termination Process

To prevail on a wrongful termination claim, a contractor must show the termination was a material breach. A material breach in the termination process may occur if the owner fails to strictly comply with contractual conditions precedent to termination, such as giving notice and the opportunity to cure.[84]

There must also "be a nexus between" an owner's decision to terminate and a contractor's delayed performance.[85] For termination due to delay, the alleged delay is typically understood at the times the owner decides to declare default and terminate.[86] Nevertheless, the owner must use "reasonable discretion" in making those decisions, and may materially breach the contract if it uses default as a pretext for

81. 224 F.3d at 1339 (finding a party's financial difficulties not ordinarily a legitimate excuse for nonperformance); *Wolfe*, 1984 Eng. BCA LEXIS 64, at *131–32 (finding it "well established . . . that cessation of performance by reason of non-payment which renders performance financially impossible is not abandonment or default" and "this principle extends to inability to perform one Government contract on account of failure to pay on another"); Discount Co., Inc. v. United States, 213 Ct. Cl. 567, 576–77 (1977) (holding "that financial difficulties create excusable delays only if precipitated by Government actions"); *Wolfe*, 1984 Eng. BCA LEXIS 64, at *135 (holding owner responsible when its non-payment causes a contractor to be unable to pay for its equipment or supplies).

82. *Wolfe*, 1984 Eng. BCA LEXIS 64, at *119–20 (finding if the government fails to pay in contractor in accordance with contract by effecting "unnecessary withholdings" the "contractor may, at its election, discontinue performance and take action to recover monies so withheld in addition to damages for breach").

83. *T. Ferguson*, 820 P.2d at 1061 (finding the "right to withhold progress payments is limited to circumstances which clearly warrant it"); *but see N. Helex*, 197 Ct. Cl. at 125 (finding "mere delay in payment, for a while, would not be a material breach but there is a clear distinction between delay of that kind and a total failure to pay over many months" and "the latter sort of breach by the [owner] is material"); *Wolfe*, 1984 Eng. BCA LEXIS 64, at *119–20, 25 (finding the "Government cannot lightly withhold funds the contractor may need" to "properly finance the contract").

84. *E.g.*, Cuddy Mountain Concrete, Inc. v. Citadel Constr., Inc., 824 P.2d 151 (Idaho 1992).

85. *PCL*, 47 Fed. Cl. at 808–09; *McDonnell Douglas*, 323 F.3d at 1013 (finding termination for default "barred . . . where there is no nexus between the default termination and the Contractor's performance under the contract").

86. *CJP*, 45 Fed. Cl. at 379 (finding when making decision to terminate for default an owner may consider "any valid grounds existing at the time of termination, regardless of whether the [owner] originally removed the [contractor] for another reason"); *Mega*, 29 Fed. Cl. at 421 (finding any "extant reasons for supporting a default termination are sufficient to sustain the default, even if not known or discovered until after the decision to terminate for default is made"); Pots Unlimited, Ltd. v. United

a termination unrelated to contractor's performance, such as owner's convenience or minor delays.[87]

Wrongful Termination Damages

When a contractor is wrongfully terminated for default, "the goal is to put [it] in as good a position as [it] would have" been had the owner not breached the parties' contract.[88] When the contract delineates damages available to a wrongfully terminated contractor, courts enforce the contract as written.[89] In the absence of such terms, a contractor may recover its direct (or general) damages, but recovery of consequential (or special) damages is less certain. Direct damages are a "natural result" of wrongful termination.[90] Consequential damages "are secondary or derivative losses" due to a contractor's particular circumstances.[91] Consequential damages are subject to heightened scrutiny. A contractor must show the owner was subjectively aware of the special circumstances underlying its consequential damages and should reasonably have been aware of the damages when it entered the contract.[92] "[M]athematical" certainty is unnecessary, but a contractor must show consequential damages to a "reasonable degree" using historical data if possible.[93]

States, 220 Ct. Cl. 405, 410 (1979) (finding "it is well settled law that a party can justify a termination if there existed at the time an adequate cause, even if then unknown").

87. McDonnell Douglas Corp. v. United States, 182 F.3d 1319, 1326 (Fed. Cir. 1999) (finding no proper nexus between owner's decision to terminate for default and contractor's performance when the decision was made solely to "rid the [owner] of having to deal with [contractor]"); *PCL*, 47 Fed. Cl. at 808–09; *McDonnell Douglas*, 323 F.3d at 1013 (finding termination for default "barred . . . where there is no nexus between the default termination and the Contractor's performance under the contract").

88. *Lewis Jorge Constr. Mgmt., Inc.*, 102 P.3d 257, 261 (Cal. 2004).

89. Team Contractors, L.L.C. v. Waypoint NOLA, L.L.C., 2017 U.S. Dist. LEXIS 160763, at *8 (E.D. La. Sep. 29, 2017) ("when the words of a contract are clear and explicit and lead to no absurd consequences, no further interpretation is required to determine the parties' intent" regarding a waiver of the right to receive lost profits); Airport Mart., Inc. v. Dunkin' Donuts Franchising LLC, 2019 U.S. Dist. LEXIS 162131, at *24 (S.D.N.Y. Sep. 16, 2019) ("[L]imitation on liability provisions [and e]xplicit waivers of . . . lost profits . . . are routinely upheld by courts.").

90. Med Plus Props. v. Colcock Constr. Grp., Inc., 628 So. 2d 370, 377 (Ala. 1993); Chinese Hosp. Assoc. v. Jacobs Eng'g Grp., Inc., 2019 U.S. Dist. LEXIS 198635, at *4 (N.D. Cal. Nov. 15, 2019).

91. Chinese Hosp. Assoc., 2019 U.S. Dist. LEXIS 198635, at *4–5.

92. *Lewis Jorge Constr. Mgmt., Inc.*, 102 P.3d 257, 261–62 (Cal. 2004) ("Alternatively, the nature of the contract or circumstances in which it is made may compel the inference that the [owner] should have contemplated the fact that such loss would be the probable result of [owner's] breach."); *Chinese Hosp. Assoc.*, 2019 U.S. Dist. LEXIS 198635, at *4; Abrogio v. Beaver Rd. Assocs, 836 A.2d 1183, 1189 n.7 (Conn. 2003) (finding that where a contractor is wrongfully terminated it may recover direct damages, and "consequential or special damages may also be recovered when they were foreseeable when the contract was made"); Med Plus Props. v. Colcock Constr. Grp., Inc., 628 So. 2d 370, 376–77 (Ala. 1993).

93. Med Plus Props. v. Colcock Constr. Grp., Inc., 628 So. 2d 370, 375–77 (Ala. 1993) (finding the requirements that a contractor prove "loss of profits . . . with reasonably, or sufficient certainty"

Whereas direct damages represent "loss in [contract] value" due to wrongful termination, consequential damages are "collateral losses following" termination.[94] Lost profit from under a wrongfully terminated construction contract itself is generally recoverable as a direct damage.[95] Conversely, a contractor's right to recover consequential lost profits, for example, because of a decrease in bonding capacity, loss of subsequent business, or loss of a competitive opportunity, is reserved for situations where "anticipated" profits are neither "vague and speculative" nor unknown to the owner.[96] Consequential lost profit claims are "frequently denied as too speculative" unless "the sum certain and flowing from a particular project that the contractor would likely have won as the low bidder."[97]

---

without "absolute certainty . . . appl[ies] only to consequential, loss-of-profit damages"); *Ripple*, 2008 U.S. Dist. LEXIS 84929, at *10–15.

94. *Chinese Hosp. Assoc.*, 2019 U.S. Dist. LEXIS 198635, at *10.

95. *Lewis Jorge Constr. Mgmt., Inc.*, 102 P.3d 257, 263 (Cal. 2004) (finding that "profits unearned on the very contract that was breached" by an owner who wrongfully terminated a contractor for default due to delay may be "used as the measure of generally damages for breach of contract," for example when the owner repudiates a contract or prevents a contractor from performing); Med Plus Props. v. Colcock Constr. Grp., Inc., 628 So. 2d 370, 375–77 (Ala. 1993) (finding in cases where the "owner has breached a construction contract after partial performance, the proper measure of damages is the difference between the price agreed upon in the contract and the cost of performance, or, in other words, the contractor's 'lost profits'"); *Ripple*, 2008 U.S. Dist. LEXIS 84929, at *10–14 (finding if a wrongful termination deprives a contractor from profit it would have otherwise received had it been allowed to perform, then the contractor may recover such lost profits when the contract is silent on the matter); Berkel & Co. Contractors, Inc. v. Palm & Assocs., Inc., 814 N.E.2d 649 (Ind. App. 2004) (finding that where a "contractor is prevented from completing a project by the owner, the contractor, as a part of its measure of damages, is entitled to its lost profit").

96. *Lewis Jorge Constr. Mgmt., Inc.*, 102 P.3d 257, 263–67 (Cal. 2004) (finding "[l]ost profits from collateral transactions as a measure of general damages for breach of contract typically arises when the contract involves crops, goods intended or resale, or an agreement creating an exclusive sales agency" where "[t]he likelihood of lost profits from related or derivative transactions is so obvious . . . that the breaching party must be deemed to have contemplated them at the inception of the contract").

97. *Lewis Jorge Constr. Mgmt., Inc.*, 102 P.3d 257, 266 (Cal. 2004) (finding "even in a common-law suit there would be no recovery for general loss of business, the claimed cost of the contractor's entire net worth, and losses on the non-federal work—such damages are all deemed to remote"); Med Plus Props. v. Colcock Constr. Grp., Inc., 628 So. 2d 370, 376–77 (Ala. 1993) (finding "the phrase 'lost profit' has been used either to designate an item of what is often called [direct] damages, or to designate a form of "consequential damages" and "[m]any claims for consequential damages are claims for loss of profits" which "is sometimes used loosely to refer to any gain the [contractor] would have made but for the contract breach," but some gains, "such as gains in a simple market transaction, are not profits in the sense that income from business operations are profits" and if the owner's wrongful termination "causes the [contractor] to lose a market gain, the claim is merely one for general damages as to which no special proof requirements attach").

Alternatives to Termination for Default

"Even if a contractor is technically in default, [the owner] may not automatically terminate the contract": It must first consider whether termination "is in [its] best interest."[98] The owner may consider, for example, how urgently the work is truly needed, the contractor's ability to perform, and "the period of time required to obtain the work from other sources, in comparison with the time needed by the delinquent contractor."[99] Thorough consideration of these matters is essential when the contractor makes "palpable progress."[100] After weighing its options, an owner may elect to avoid the risk of wrongful default termination altogether, and instead terminate the contractor for convenience or allow the contractor to complete its work late and seek damages.

Termination for Convenience

As an alternative to terminating a contractor for default, many industry contracts allow an owner to terminate a contract for convenience.[101] An owner who terminates for convenience forgoes certain rights, for example, the ability to recover damages caused by the delay.[102] For this reason, and assuming the contractor does not hold a performance bond, termination for convenience may be appropriate when an owner doubts a contractor's performance ability but delay has not yet occurred, or when the contractor may be unable to pay a damages award and the owner wants to stop incurring damages.[103]

98. *Hannon*, 31 Fed. Cl. at 148.

99. *Metzger*, 1993 Eng. BCA LEXIS 31, at *49.

100. *Id.*

101. *E.g.*, DBIA Contract Document #535, Standard Form of General Conditions of Contract Between Owner and Design-Builder, Third Edition, 2022 § 11.6); ConsensusDocs 230—Standard Agreement and General Conditions Between Owner and Constructor (Cost of the Work Plus a Fee with GMP) - October 2017, § 12.4); *Metzger*, 1993 Eng. BCA LEXIS 31, at *57 ("Most contracts issued under the FAR contain a 'Default' General Provision that provides for a conversion of the default into a termination for convenience of the Government if the default action is determined to be invalid.").

102. *E.g.*, Rogerson Aircraft Corp. v. Fairchild Indus., Inc., 632 F. Supp. 1494, 1499 (C.D. Cal. 1986) (finding a typical contract containing termination for default and convenience terms (but no conversion term *infra*) "force[s Owner] to elect either to terminate . . . for its convenience" and make "payment of [Contractor's] termination costs . . . or to terminate the contract for default . . . without having to pay a termination settlement").

103. Handi-Van, Inc. v. Broward Cnty., 116 So. 3d 530, 535 (Fla. App. 2013) ("Termination for convenience clauses are contractual provisions which permit one party to terminate a contract, even in the absence of fault or breach by the other party, without suffering the usual financial consequences of a breach of contract.").

Under some contracts, a wrongful default termination is converted to one for convenience.[104] Such terms are enforced as written.[105] If a contract does not contain a conversion clause, however, an owner "cannot invoke the termination for convenience provision to cure its improper default termination" to limit its liability after the fact.[106]

Continued Performance and Assessment of Damages

The duty to mitigate damages dictates the most prudent path for an owner is often to let a defaulting contractor complete the work and recover damages, even when delay seems unbearable. Delay damages are frequently liquidated in commercial contracting by stipulating an amount of damages accruing each day the contractor fails to complete the work past a specified date.[107] If the contract includes liquidated damages for delay, then "[p]roof of actual damages [for delay] is rendered unnecessary."[108] Liquidated damages terms are generally enforceable provided the prospective actual amount of delay damages is difficult to ascertain when the contract is made, but the liquidated damages amount nevertheless represents "a reasonable estimate of the presumed actual damages" delay will cause.[109] But if a contract fixes "unreasonably large liquidated damages," it may be void on public policy grounds "because it goes beyond compensation into punishment."[110]

The parties' contract may provide that liquidated damages are the owner's sole remedy for delay, regardless of whether the contractor continues performance or is terminated.[111] Or it may allow the owner to recover liquidated damages if the

---

104. *E.g.*, DBIA Contract Document #535, Standard Form of General Conditions of Contract Between Owner and Design-Builder, Third Edition, 2022 § 11.2.4 (converting a wrongful termination for default into one for convenience).

105. *Rogerson*, 632 F. Supp. at 1499 ("It is fundamental that where the parties to a contract have agreed to termination provisions for that contract, those provisions are binding upon the parties and must be enforced as written.").

106. *Id.* (finding an owner who elects to terminate for default "cannot now reverse that decision and avoid liability" and "payment to [Contractor] of what would have been a substantial termination settlement" because of the owner's "groundless default termination by alleging that it should have terminated the . . . contract for its convenience and paid [contractor's] termination and settlement costs at the time of termination"); United States v. K.O.O. Constrs., Inc., 2021 U.S. Dist. LEXIS 253434, at *12 (S.D. Cal. Nov. 30, 2021) (finding an owner's contention that a wrongful termination be changed to one for convenience in absence of conversion clause "would, in effect, retroactively give a different legal effect to what was originally intended by changing the label which has been expressly and purposely attached to it when the termination occurred").

107. United States v. Am. Surety Co., 322 U.S. 96, 98 (1944).

108. *Id.*

109. Ravenstar, LLC v. One Ski Hill Place, LLC, 401 P.3d 552, 555 (Colo. 2017).

110. Nearburg v. Yates Petroleum Corp., 943 P.2d 560, 566 (N.M. 1997).

111. *E.g.*, ConsensusDocs 230—Standard Agreement and General Conditions Between Owner and Constructor (Cost of the Work Plus a Fee with GMP) – October 2017, § 6.5 (liquidated damages are owner's sole remedy for contractor's failure to timely achieve completion).

contractor continues performance, actual damages if the contractor is terminated, or some variation thereof.[112]

In the alternative, some contracts contain a cumulative remedies term providing the owner with the right to recover liquidated damages for the delay, and actual damages for other items, such as cover costs if the contract is terminated. Cumulative remedies provisions are generally enforced as written.[113] But notably, "[t]here is no common-law right to recover actual damages in addition to liquidated damages."[114] Thus, an owner may waive its right to recover actual damages for delay if it "does not preserve the right" in contracts specifying liquidated damages.[115] Further, some jurisdictions void cumulative "double damage" for delay provisions in favor of actual damages, reasoning recovery of both makes liquidated damages punitive.[116]

Waiver of Right to Terminate for Delay

Each party may insist on compliance with contract terms and is "under no obligation to accept" delayed performance.[117] An owner may, however, waive its right

112. *Am. Surety*, 322 U.S. at 100–01 (finding an owner "waive[s] its right to liquidated damages" for delay by terminating a contractor and electing to hire replacement contractor when the parties agreement states if the owner elects to allow the contractor to continue delayed performance it may assess liquidated damages but if the contractor is terminated the owner may only recover actual damages).

113. *E.g.*, *Appeal of Wells Constr.*, 1969 IBCA LEXIS 20, at *7–8 (1969) (finding an owner may recover actual and liquidated damages from contractor where the parties' agreement states after default termination for delay owner may recover "liquidated damages until such reasonable time as may be required for final completion for the work together with any increased costs occasioned [by the owner] in completing the work").

114. *In re* Lumbermens Mut. Cas. Co., 127 N.E.3d 719, 740 (Ill. App. 2018).

115. *Id.*

116. *E.g.*, Arctic Contractors, Inc. v. Alaska, 564 P.2d 30, 49–51 (Alaska 1977) ("It has been repeatedly held in construing standard construction contracts" that when a party terminates a contract for default due to delay "it may let the unfinished portion to a new contractor and collect the excess costs, but it may not also collect liquidated damages.") (finding if the owner elects to terminate for default due to delay, then the option to assess liquidated damages "disappear[s] from the picture" and is "thereafter mere surplusage") (also finding that even where a contract contains a liquidated damages clause "which standing alone appears valid," the assessment of liquidated damages "operates as a penalty when viewed in conjunction" with the recovery of actual damages); Indus. Indem. Co. v. Wick Constr. Co., 680 P.2d 1100, 1104 n.2 (Alaska 1984) (finding owner could not recover actual and liquidated damages after terminating a contractor for default due to delay where the contract "quite specifically directs a result contrary to the general rule" by stating the owner may recover actual delay costs plus liquidated damages after termination).

117. *Mega*, 29 Fed. Cl. at 420; *see Marshall*, 569 So. 2d at 848 ("It is a well-settled contract principle that unexpected difficulty, expense, or hardship does not excuse a party from performance of its obligations under a contract."); *but see DeVito*, 188 Ct. Cl. at 990 (finding the "Government is

to insist on timely performance by intentionally relinquishing its known right to terminate a contractor for delay.[118]

Whether waiver occurs is more complex than whether a contractor continues working.[119] The contractor must show (1) the owner had notice of and accepted contractor's delayed performance; (2) the contractor continued performing in reliance on the owner's perceived approval of the delayed performance; and (3) it would be unfair for the owner to retract its waiver.[120] Waiver may occur when an owner does not terminate the contractor within a reasonable amount of time after the right to do so arises.[121] An owner's intent to accept the contractor's performance may be determined by the owner's words or inferred from its conduct.[122] When waiver occurs, the owner cannot terminate the contract until a new completion date is set and the contractor defaults with respect to the new date.[123] These factors are discussed next.

Owner's Acceptance of Delayed Performance

An owner must commence the termination process within a "reasonable time after" the contractor commits a default.[124] The reasonableness of the period "depends

---

habitually lenient in granting reasonable extensions of time for contract performance, for it is more interested in production than in litigation").

118. *Arctic*, 564 P.2d at 40; *State Corps*, 142 Fed. Cl. at 32.

119. *N. Helex*, 197 Ct. Cl. at 129 (finding the inquiry into waiver "a more complex inquiry than . . . merely 'did performance continue?'"); *Arctic*, 564 P.2d at 40.

120. *CJP*, 45 Fed. Cl. at 376.

121. *DeVito*, 188 Ct. Cl. at 990–91 ("This is popularly if inaccurately referred to as 'waiver' of the right to terminate."); *see Florida Dep't of Ins.*, 81 F.3d at 1096 ("The purpose of the waiver doctrine is to protect contractors who are led to believe that time is no longer of the essence and undertake substantial efforts after the performance date specified in the contract has passed."); *cf. Olson*, 221 Ct. Cl. at 204–05 (finding a party "cannot allow an *unwary* contractor to continue performance and thus incur *large expenses*, all of which the Government will refuse to reimburse if and when it decides to cancel the contractor on ground of the violation") (emphasis in original); *see N. Helex*, 197 Ct. Cl. at 125 n.3 (noting "waiver" of the right to terminate and "materiality of breach" by contractor are "separate issues" that should not be "intermixed").

122. *Arctic*, 564 P.2d at 40 (finding a waiver "turns upon an examination of [owner's] intent as expressed by words"); *Composites Horizons*, 1985 ASBCA LEXIS 707, at *49–50 (finding a waiver "inferred from [owner's] conduct"); *see CJP*, 45 Fed. Cl. 343 ("[A] contractor can use the government's unprotesting observation or acceptance of noncontractual performance to demonstrate the government has waived a contract requirement.").

123. Panoramic Studios, Inc. v. United States, 188 Ct. Cl. 1092, 1103 (1969).

124. *Acme*, 171 Ct. Cl. at 335–36, *rev'd on other grounds*, 385 U.S. 138 (1966) ("sanction of contract cancellation is too drastic to permit a delay" in termination and "To avert extreme hardship, we think that the Government is obliged to take such a course within a reasonable time after it has discovered the breach."); *S.T. Research Corp.*, 1992 ASBCA LEXIS 145, at *25 (1992); *see State Corps*, 142 Fed. Cl. at 33 (finding the government "should not have to immediately terminate a contract, after a contractor's failure to meet a delivery date, on pain of waiving the right to do so").

on the circumstances of each case" and requires balancing the advantages to an owner, versus the disadvantages to a contractor, should it continue performing after a default.[125] For example, an owner has more time to terminate after default when a contractor abandons the project or performance is rendered "impossible or unlikely," than when a contractor continues performing "in reliance on the lack of termination."[126] The period is even shorter when a contractor "has no reason to know that a decision to terminate has already been privately made" and is only pending owner's executive approval.[127] Further, when an owner encourages the contractor to continue performing despite delay, the owner must make its decision to terminate "expeditiously" when delays become material.[128]

Nevertheless, an owner's "election to allow work to continue does not automatically equate to a waiver."[129] Nor does waiver necessarily occur when an owner acknowledges delay or the parties negotiate but do not agree on a new performance time.[130] And an owner's mere silence and inaction, by itself, also does not constitute waiver.[131] Instead, waiver occurs when the owner acts in a way which reasonably demonstrates its intent to allow the contractor to continue performing after default.[132] This generally occurs when an owner administers the contract in a way giving a "reasonably intelligent and alert" contractor the impression its default is

125. *DeVito*, 188 Ct. Cl. at 991; *but see Acme*, 171 Ct. Cl. at 337 n.7, *rev'd on other grounds*, 385 U.S. 138 (1966) (finding there may be "situations in which the Government can cancel a contract notwithstanding the amount of time elapsing between discovery of the violation and termination of the contract" but such cases "involve more than a plain material breach of the contract"); *Olson*, 221 Ct. Cl. at 205; Ling-Temco-Vought, Inc. v. United States, 201 Ct. Cl. 135, 149 (1973) (finding owner's failure to reserve rights to claim unsuspected breach was basis of denying recovery because it denied contractor option of choosing "whether to terminate the contract entirely at that time . . . or to continue at the risk of having to pay greater damages and incurring additional costs").

126. *Id.*

127. *Id.*

128. *S.T.*, 1992 ASBCA LEXIS 145, at *25.

129. *State Corps*, 142 Fed. Cl. at 33; *Empire*, 362 F.3d at 1355 (finding in the construction industry, encouragement of timely completion before the date on which a party believes it is entitled to terminate "cannot result in a waiver and [is] entirely permissible").

130. *McDonnell Douglas*, 323 F.3d at 1020.

131. *S.T.*, 1992 ASBCA LEXIS 145, at *25; *but see State Corps*, 142 Fed. Cl. 21 ("When a contractor defaults on a contract, that default may be waived by the contracting agency—expressly or *through inaction*.") (emphasis added).

132. *Composites Horizons*, 1985 ASBCA LEXIS 707, at *62 (finding owner's action must "lead a reasonable contractor to believe that time was not of the essence"); Panoramic Studios, Inc. v. United States, 188 Ct. Cl. 1092, 1103 (1969) (requiring action "reasonably indicat[ing] a manifestation of intention to permit continuation of performance"); *S.T.*, 1992 ASBCA LEXIS 145, at *26 (requiring "affirmative actions"); *Florida Dep't of Ins.*, 81 F.3d at 1096 (finding owner's action must "justify a conclusion that the default has been excused").

waived or suspended.[133] Thus, a contractor may struggle showing an owner waived its right to terminate for delay if the owner expressly reserves its right to terminate or assess liquidated damages.[134] On the other hand, waiver may occur when the owner's acts after default deny the contractor "options then lawfully available" to it, such as terminating for convenience under the parties' contract or suspending subcontractors' work.[135]

Contractor's Continued Performance

Traditionally, a contractor would have to prove the owner expressly approved a contractor's continued performance, but the modern rule is an owner's express "assent is not a prerequisite."[136] In any event, a contractor must, naturally, continue performing to reap the benefits of the waiver doctrine.[137] Specifically, the contractor must perform substantive work as if it expected the contract would not be terminated.[138] For example, waiver is less likely to occur where the only expenditures made by a contractor after a missed completion milestone are "[h]ousekeeping

---

133. *CJP*, 45 Fed. Cl. at 376; *but see* Panoramic Studios, Inc. v. United States, 188 Ct. Cl. 1092, 1110 (1969) (finding that mere "poor administrative practice did not excuse [contractor] from complying with the contract by producing within the prescribed period").

134. *Olson*, 221 Ct. Cl. at 204–05 (finding assessment of liquidated damages "is evidence of the intent to hold the defaulting party liable for its delayed performance"); *see N. Helex*, 197 Ct. Cl. at 128 (finding a "party who with explicit reservation of rights . . . assents to performance in a manner . . . offered by the other party does not thereby prejudice the rights reserved" and words such as "without prejudice, under protest, or the like are sufficient" to accomplish that result).

135. *Id.* at 205; *see also e.g., DeVito*, 188 Ct. Cl. at 993 (finding termination for default by government improper where contractor did not renounce contract and was capable of, willing to perform, and diligently continues performance of work "with a fair likelihood of reasonable success" and government makes no reservation of rights); *see* Acme Process Equip. Co. v. United States, 171 Ct. Cl. 324, 336 (1965), *rev'd on other grounds*, 385 U.S. 138 (1966) (finding when termination is unreasonably delayed "it would be a great wrong to permit the Government to awaken such a 'sleeper' to justify its cancellation").

136. *N. Helex*, 197 Ct. Cl. at 129–30.

137. *Id.* at 131 n.8; Panoramic Studios, Inc. v. United States, 188 Ct. Cl. 1092, 1103 (1969); Olson Plumbing & Heating Co. v. United States, 221 Ct. Cl. 197, 206 (1979) (finding government "cannot be said to have waived due date or have elected to continue performance if the contractor has abandoned performance"); Acme Process Equip. Co. v. United States, 171 Ct. Cl. 324, 335 (1965), *rev'd on other grounds*, 385 U.S. 138 (1966) ("Where a contract is breached in the course of its performance, the injured party has the choice presented to him of continuing the contract or of refusing to go on. If he chooses to continue performance he has doubtless lost his right to stop performance.").

138. Discount Co., Inc. v. United States, 213 Ct. Cl. 567, 572–73 (1977) (requiring "more-than-piddling construction activities" and finding a party does not waive its right to terminate where the other party makes "little progress," does "practically nothing toward" completing the project, and does not provide adequate assurances of timely completion); *McDonnell Douglas*, 323 F.3d at 1020 (finding a contractor must do more than what it "would have done regardless of whether" the contract was terminated).

costs which merely attempt to preserve the status quo," than where a contractor incurs costs which significantly "contribute to performance," for example, by placing material orders and securing labor commitments.[139]

Inequity of Retracting Waiver of Right to Terminate

An owner's waiver of the right to terminate for a contractor's untimely performance infers time is no longer of the essence and further delays are not material.[140] To reestablish the essence of time, the owner must communicate and set a new performance period to serve as the basis for default.[141] The new period may be established by mutual agreement or unilaterally by owner.[142] If unilateral, owner's schedule must be reasonable in light of its obligation to mitigate damages and circumstances existing at the time the new schedule is imposed, such as availability of materials and labor, contractor's capabilities, and amount of remaining work.[143] Should the contractor fail to properly perform the work under the new schedule or the owner becomes justifiably insecure about the contractor's ability to do so, then the owner may commence default termination proceedings under the contract.[144]

Conclusion

Terminating a contractor for delay is a path fraught with landmines. Owners who wish to do so must first thoroughly consider the contract's requirements, and the facts, prior to taking such actions. And while it is difficult to be terminated, contractors who have caused delay remain subject to damages and should avoid the situation altogether by timely performing and following the contract's requirements for extensions of time when appropriate. Termination is a drastic sanction that will undoubtedly result in litigation and parties are well served to avoid it when possible.

---

139. *Olson*, 221 Ct. Cl. at 205.

140. *DeVito*, 188 Ct. Cl. at 986, 991–92 (finding the inference that time is no longer of the essence is "not subsequently cut off by a cure notice"); *Olson*, 221 Ct. Cl. at 208 (finding a party's duty to reestablish a reasonable time for performance after default "does not arise . . . until the facts and circumstances show the due date has been waived").

141. *DeVito*, 188 Ct. Cl. at 992; *McDonnell Douglas*, 323 F.3d at 1019; *Florida Dep't of Ins.*, 81 F.3d at 1096–97 (finding a newly established performance period allows "the parties [to] understand when performance is required"); *Composites Horizons*, 1985 ASBCA LEXIS 707, at *62 (finding owner failed to reestablish the essence of time by not "putting [its] foot down and stating plainly and unequivocally that [it] was not going to continue to permit the period of performance to be enlarged *ad infinitum*") (emphasis in original).

142. *Composites Horizons*, 1985 ASBCA LEXIS 707, at *64; *McDonnell Douglas*, 323 F.3d at 1019.

143. *McDonnell Douglas*, 323 F.3d at 1018–19.

144. *Composites Horizons*, 1985 ASBCA LEXIS 707, at *48; *DeVito*, 188 Ct. Cl. at 992.

CHAPTER 12

Early Completion Schedules and Claims

John M. Neary and Daniel R. Miktus

"Finish early" is a mantra that should remain front and center on a construction project. Many contractors consider early completion to be central to submitting winning bids, minimizing risk, and increasing profits. Some owners do not believe that early completion benefits them, and perceive, instead, that early completion schedules pose an increased risk of claims for compensable delay. This tension, although not the only issue presented by early completion schedules, is why this chapter exists.

What Is Early Completion?

The typical construction project has a deadline by which the owner wants to complete the work. The bid documents may express this and can either take the form of a hard date for project completion or a number of days after commencement of the work.

The American Institute of Architects (AIA) form A101, for example, provides:

> **§ 3.3** The Contractor shall achieve Substantial Completion of the entire Work not later than « » (« ») days from the date of commencement, or as follows:
>
> *(Insert number of calendar days. Alternatively, a calendar date may be used when coordinated with the date of commencement. If appropriate, insert requirements for earlier Substantial Completion of certain portions of the Work.)*[1]

An early completion schedule is merely one by which the contractor plans to complete the work before that deadline or within fewer days from the start of the project.

1. *See* American Institute of Architects A101-2017, Standard Form of Agreement Between Owner and Contractor, where the basis of payment is a Stipulated Sum, at section 3.3.

How parties establish the contractual completion deadlines may have consequences for how likely it is that a contractor may achieve early completion of a project. The project engineer or architect of record may originate the deadlines based on the engineer's or architect's estimate of how long construction ought to take.[2] Alternatively, the owner may establish the schedule to meet its needs, such as where a university building must be complete before the beginning of the next semester. Sometimes legal or regulatory requirements set deadlines, where, for example, a thermal power plant must install environmental air or water control equipment in advance of a date set through a federal regulation, or where litigation forced a municipality to improve its wastewater treatment plant and a settlement or judgment imposed a deadline for compliance.

Given how circumstances establish these completion deadlines, it should not be any surprise that it may be possible to complete the project in less time. The contractor may have superior information to that of the owner, architect, or engineer who estimated the project duration. Perhaps material fabrication and delivery may take place more quickly, or the contractor may perform some scopes of work in parallel, rather than sequentially, or take less time to perform than initially thought by the engineer or architect. It might even be that the financial benefits to the contractor of finishing early exceed the costs of paying overtime and accelerating the schedule, so the contractor will accelerate the work.

Why Does the Contractor Want to Finish Early?

Case law from federal courts, administrative boards, and state courts increasingly makes it clear that the contractor has the right to finish early, manage the schedule, deviate from the original plan by resequencing, compress performance time, and react to changing conditions.[3] With this in mind, the contractor can leverage an early completion schedule to its benefit. For example, even if the work requires the same number of man-hours despite the shorter duration, the contractor can save on general conditions, general requirements, insurance, bond costs, and other items by finishing the job earlier. General conditions are the costs to the contractor of managing a project, such as project supervision, the job trailer and field office, and office supplies. These are nonmanagement indirect costs, including costs to deal with jobsite conditions, and energy/utility costs.

---

2. Or, perhaps, a "guesstimate." James G. Zack, Jr., *Early Completion Schedules: A Form of Contingency Bidding – Revisited*, Navigant Construction Forum (2015).

3. Jon M. Wickwire et al., Construction Scheduling: Preparation, Liability, and Claims 5-63 (Michael Tuller & Ellen Ros eds., 4th ed. 2019).

The contractor may realize other financial benefits by finishing early. If, for example, the contractor called on a line of credit to manage its cash flow, it can save on interest payments by paying off the line of credit sooner with an earlier final payment. Of course, there is always the time value of money—money received now is worth more than money received later—so there is tangible benefit to the contractor to get paid earlier even if there are no financing costs. Moreover, with an early completion, the contractor increases its capacity for additional work by freeing resources for another project or bidding on other work.

Finally, planning to finish early reduces the contractor's risk of finishing late. Since every contractor must anticipate the risk that it or its subcontractors or suppliers will cause an inexcusable delay, or that an owner will not grant a schedule extension to which the contractor believes it is entitled, the difference between the planned completion date and the contractual deadline for completion is float to protect the contractor from contractual breach and potentially suffering the imposition of actual or liquidated damages.

The benefits of an early completion may inure to the benefit of the owner as well. The owner could begin using the project, and, thus, begin receiving revenues, rents, or other benefits of the project earlier. The owner, too, incurs time-related costs, like the fees paid to the architect or construction manager to oversee the project as well as additional insurance or bond premiums, which costs are reduced if the project takes less time to construct. The float built into the project by virtue of the contractor's plan to finish early, by introducing a margin for error, also reduces the risk to the owner that the project will not finish on time.

Why Would an Owner Not Want the Contractor to Finish Early?

There certainly are situations in which it is disadvantageous for the owner to receive delivery of the project too early. At the most basic level, early completion means that the contractor is paid more rapidly than the owner anticipated based on the contractual completion date. One possibility is that the owner's cash flow or sources of financing cannot accelerate to match the faster rate of payment. This could lead to a situation where the owner could be caught short, unable to pay the contractor's bills on time, or is able to pay, but not without impact to the owner's other business ventures.

The owner may also not be ready for certain responsibilities that commence upon project completion. For example, upon project completion, responsibility for insurance, cleaning, maintenance, and payment of utilities transfers from the contractor to the owner, and the owner may not be ready to assume those costs.

This would be especially true where the owner's tenant is not prepared to move in earlier than planned or is not obligated to begin paying rent upon early occupancy. The owner or the tenant may not be ready for installation of furniture, fixtures, and equipment, meaning the owner cannot utilize the building despite an early completion. Similarly, the obligation to procure permanent property insurance shifts to the owner upon completion. Thus, early completion could actually add to the owner's carrying costs for the project between the early completion date and the date the owner or the tenant can make use of the project.

The owner may believe that the contractor's plan for early completion increases other risks. The owner may have concerns that, in its haste to complete the project early, the contractor may compromise safety or quality. It is possible that, by compressing all the margin for error out of the schedule to create one that calls for completion of the work early, the contractor actually increases the probability of running into scheduling problems that result in delays of the project to beyond the contractual completion date.

One of the most common concerns of owners is that the contractor's plan to finish early increases the risk that the contractor will ask for an adjustment of the schedule or increase in price due to delays. That is, if completion of the work is delayed beyond the completion date shown on the early completion schedule and not caused by the contractor, the contractor will want to be compensated for the general conditions and other costs that it incurred during that delay.

The owner's concern is that the early completion schedule is not legitimate, and that it is a "claims trap."[4] In this scenario, the contractor's early completion schedule is not one that it can actually accomplish, or, at least, one that has a high risk of failure. The contractor might create such a high-risk early completion schedule by including minimal durations for all activities, such that the risk of delayed completion is very high. Then, when it cannot complete the activity within the time shown on the schedule, the contractor would attempt to find some reason to blame the owner. For example, the contractor may base the claims-oriented schedule on an unrealistically fast turnaround of requests for information (RFIs), approvals of submittals, issuances of permits, or governmental inspections or other actions.

Owners can protect themselves against unrealistic early completion schedules by reviewing the contractor's proposed schedule carefully at the outset, and refusing to approve if unrealistic. The owner can also insert into the contract minimum time periods for turnarounds of RFIs and submittal approvals, or provide for prior approval of a submittal schedule. One potential solution is to indicate in the contract that the contractor is not entitled to additional compensation—whether

---

4. Zack, *supra* note 2.

additional general conditions and requirements or otherwise—unless the impact to the critical path of the construction schedule exceeds the overall duration for the project. Another suggestion is to provide that, if the contractor submits a schedule showing early completion, the contractual deadline for completion—and the trigger for liquidated damages for unexcused delay—is moved back to the early completion date shown on the contractor's schedule. This permits the contractor and the owner to enjoy the benefits of a legitimate early completion schedule but would punish a contractor with an illegitimate early completion schedule by increasing the risk of incurring liquidated damages.

Owners can also expressly prohibit exploitation of early completion schedules with specific contract language. An example developed by the authors of this chapter follows.

1.02 *GENERAL*

A. Progress Schedule shall be based on and incorporate all constraints, milestone and completion dates specified in Contract Documents.

B. Overall time of completion and time of completion for each milestone shown on Progress Schedule shall adhere to times in the Contract Documents , unless an earlier time of completion is requested by Contractor and agreed to by Owner. A Change Order shall formalize any such agreement.

   1. Owner is not required to accept an earlier schedule, i.e., one that shows early completion date(s) for the Contract Time.
   2. Contractor is not entitled to extra compensation in event agreement is reached on an earlier schedule and Contractor completes its Work, for whatever reason, beyond completion date shown in earlier schedule but within the Contract Time.
   3. A schedule showing the Work completed in less than the Contract Time, which has been accepted by Owner, shall be considered to have Project Float. The Project Float is the time between the scheduled completion of the Work and Contract Substantial Completion. Project Float is a resource available to both Owner and Contractor.
   4. Float Ownership: Neither Owner nor Contractor owns float. The Project owns the float. As such, liability for delay of any Substantial Completion or Final Completion date rests with the party whose actions, last in time, actually cause delay to a Substantial Completion or Final Completion date.
      a. For example, in the event of unexcused delay by Party A and Party B, and if Party A uses some, but not all of the float and Party B later uses remainder of the float as well as additional time beyond the float, Party B shall be liable for the time that represents a delay to the Substantial Completion date.

b. Under this scenario, Party A would not be responsible for the time since it did not consume all of the float and additional float remained; therefore, the Substantial Completion Date was unaffected.

This provision would, in some respects, penalize the contractor for planning to finish early, or, at least, for disclosing to the owner its plan to finish early. That is, if the contractor provides the owner with a schedule showing early completion, then the contractor is, essentially, giving the owner the right to use the float as a buffer against having to pay for compensable delays. If the contractor keeps its intent to finish early a secret from the owner by providing the owner with a schedule that shows completion at the contractual deadline date, then the contractor gets to keep the float hidden in the schedule all to itself. Under either scenario, the owner can deprive the contractor of the benefits of early completion without any cost to the owner.

Another example of a contractual provision developed by the authors of this chapter, which prohibits a contractor's claim for compensable delays in early completion is:

> If the Contractor's schedule shows a shorter construction period than provided in the Contract Documents, the Contractor's schedule shall be prepared in sufficient detail to demonstrate the feasibility of early completion and shall be submitted within thirty (30) days after beginning construction. This CPM schedule shall show all required submittals and dates for ordering, shipping and receiving critical materials and equipment. Contractor's submittals shall be submitted with sufficient time to permit thirty (30) days for a response and not impact Contractor's schedule.
>
> It is agreed that the Contract Price includes the Contractor's office and field overhead, profit and related charges for the full Contract Time. The Contractor may, at its option, complete the work in a shorter period than the Contract Time but the Contractor may not make a claim for extended overhead or other charges for: (1) delays that extended completion beyond the date planned by the Contractor but not beyond the Contract Time, and (2) delays contemplated by the Contractor and the Owner. All float in the schedule shall first be for the benefit of the Owner, the Engineer, the Design Engineer, and then for the benefit of the Contractor. To the fullest extent permitted by law, the Contractor on behalf of itself and its subcontractors, waive any and all claims for damages attributable to delays, interference, or acceleration caused by the Owner, the Engineer, the Design Engineer and each of their officers, employees, agents and consultants, and the Contractor and its subcontractors shall be entitled to an extension of the Contract Time as their exclusive remedy.

The first paragraph of the quoted provision is an attempt to prevent an early completion schedule from compressing the owner's time to respond to submittals and to force the contractor to schedule realistic dates for delivery of materials and equipment. The second paragraph, however, goes further to punish the contractor for showing an early completion schedule by depriving it of the benefit of float.

There may be legal limitations on the ability of the owner to contractually disclaim any liability to the contractor for damages for delays in early completion that are the fault of the owner. In California, for example, Public Contract Code section 7102 states:

> Contract provisions in construction contracts of public agencies and subcontracts thereunder which limit the contractee's liability to an extension of time for delay for which the contractee is responsible and which delay is unreasonable under the circumstances involved, and not within the contemplation of the parties, shall not be construed to preclude the recovery of damages by the contractor or subcontractor.
>
> No public agency may require the waiver, alteration, or limitation of the applicability of this section. Any such waiver, alteration, or limitation is void. This section shall not be construed to void any provision in a construction contract which requires notice of delays, provides for arbitration or other procedure for settlement, or provides for liquidated damages.[5]

This statute at least arguably prohibits a public entity in California from disclaiming responsibility for delays for which the public entity is responsible and which delay is "unreasonable under the circumstances involved," including delays in early completion.

Another example is California's Public Contract Code section 1104, which says:

> No local public entity, charter city, or charter county shall require a bidder to assume responsibility for the completeness and accuracy of architectural or engineering plans and specifications on public works projects, except on clearly designated design build projects. Nothing in this section shall be construed to prohibit a local public entity, charter city, or charter county from requiring a bidder to review architectural or engineering plans and specifications prior to submission of a bid, and report any errors and omissions noted by the contractor to the architect or owner. The review by the contractor shall be confined to the contractor's capacity as a contractor, and not as a licensed design professional.[6]

---

5. Cal. Pub. Cont. Code § 7102.
6. *Id.* § 1104.

This statute would arguably prohibit a public entity from disclaiming liability for delays caused by defects in the plans and specifications prepared by the public entity's architects or engineers, including delays in early completion.

Other authority, too, may impose limitations on the ability of an owner to disclaim liability for delays in early completion schedules. In *John E. Green Plumbing & Heating Co. v. Turner Construction Co.*,[7] a case involving a "no damages for delay clause" (and in which the claim was not for delays in early completion), the court stated, "No-damage-for-delay clauses 'are commonly used in the construction industry and generally recognized as valid and enforceable.' However, because of their harsh effects, these clauses are to be strictly construed."[8]

This principle was applied in *Maron Construction v. GSA*.[9] The General Services Administration (GSA) hired Maron Construction to renovate a post office. The contractor made a claim for government-caused delays for a period between the date the contractor said it would have completed the project early and the actual completion date, which was after the contractual deadline. The government denied the portion of the claim for the period between the contractor's alleged early completion date and the contract deadline for completion, relying on a provision in the contract that required the contractor to prepare a critical path method (CPM) schedule showing the contract completion deadline as the date of completion on the schedule, and on a provision that stated that the contractor is entitled to schedule extensions only if the government-caused delay exceeds the "total float" in the schedule. The government argued these provisions:

> precluded early completion delay damages because they required Maron to prepare and to update a CPM schedule using April 20, 1995 as the contract completion date, and if Maron had anticipated finishing the contract work before that date, the CPM scheduler would have simply built in more float, which would have been available to absorb any GSA-caused delays. In other words, GSA says there was no such thing as early completion of this contract. Either Maron would finish work on April 20, 1995, or Maron's CPM scheduler would build in float time before that date which would absorb any GSA-caused delays until that date.[10]

The Board rejected the government's arguments, noting that, although "the Government can draft a contract clause that limits or eliminates its liability for delay damages," "such a clause must specifically and expressly exempt the Government from liability."[11] The contract provisions cited by the government neither

7. 742 F.2d 965 (6th Cir. 1984).
8. *Id.* at 966 (citations omitted).
9. 98-1 BCA ¶ 29685, GSBCA No. 13625 (1998).
10. *Id.* at 147,109.
11. *Id.* at 147,109–10.

specifically prohibited early completion delay damages nor early completion. The contractual provisions cited by the government "address the mechanics of constructing a CPM schedule and do not specifically and expressly tell Maron either that GSA would not be responsible for any claim for early completion delay damages before April 20, 1995, or that it was not possible for Maron to complete the project early."[12]

In general, any argument available to a contractor to oppose a "no-damages-for-delay" provision in a contract will most likely be available to oppose a "no-damages-for-delay in early completion" provision.

The Cause of Action for Damages for Delay in Early Completion

The generally recognized case as the landmark federal decision on the right to finish early is *Metropolitan Paving Company v. United States.*[13] The U.S. Air Force hired Metropolitan to pave an airfield and gave Metropolitan 300 days within which to complete the work. Metropolitan completed the work within 300 days, but Metropolitan nevertheless alleged that the government deliberately harassed it and engaged in dilatory tactics to delay performance:

> Plaintiff now claims that but for "failure of defendant's employees to give plaintiff a reasonable measure of cooperation in the performance of essential inspections and tests," plus the "deliberate harassment and dilatory tactics" of defendant's employees and "the absence of adequate supervision by the contracting officer," plaintiff could have and would have completed the work some 94 days earlier.[14]

The court noted that the three elements of the cause of action were: (1) the government's employees did cause delay, (2) the delay constituted a breach of contract, and (3) the plaintiff suffered damage. It is to the third element that the court addressed itself, asking the question, "whether as a matter of law a plaintiff can recover damages when delay has not prevented completion of the contract *within the specified time.*"[15]

The government relied on *United States v. Blair,*[16] arguing that *Blair* held there is "no obligation or duty on the part of defendant to aid a contractor towards early

12. *Id.* at 147,110.

13. 163 Ct. Cl. 420, 325 F.2d 241 (1963). While *Metropolitan Paving* is the seminal case, the principle was articulated well before, in *Haley v. Brady*, 17 Wash. 2d 775, 137 P.2d 505 (1943).

14. *Metro. Paving Co.*, 325 F.2d at 421–22.

15. *Id.* at 422 (emphasis in original).

16. 321 U.S. 730 (1944).

completion."[17] The Court acknowledged the holding in *Blair* but drew a distinction between an obligation to assist the contractor in finishing early and a duty to avoid hindering early completion. The Court stated:

> While it is true that there is not an "obligation" or "duty" of defendant to aid a contractor to complete prior to completion date, from this it does not follow that defendant may hinder and prevent a contractor's early completion without incurring liability. It would seem to make little difference whether or not the parties contemplated an early completion, or even whether or not the contractor contemplated an early completion. Where defendant is guilty of "deliberate harassment and dilatory tactics" and a contractor suffers damages as a result of such action, we think that defendant is liable.[18]

The Court eventually found that *Metropolitan* did not actually prove the government caused any delay, and thus ruled for the government. Nevertheless, the *Metropolitan* opinion established, fairly universally, that an owner who prevents a contractor from finishing early may be liable to the contractor for damages.[19] Many states have followed this federal precedent and also recognized such a cause of action.[20] Boards of contract appeals also have held the government can be liable for delay even if the contract is completed early.[21]

Courts considering such claims acknowledge the following principles:

1. The covenant of good faith and fair dealing.
2. The duty of one party to cooperate with the other in performing its contractual obligations.
3. The implied warranty of the correctness and completeness of detailed design documents.

"Every contract, including one with the federal government, imposes upon each party an implied duty of good faith and fair dealing in its performance and enforcement."[22] On that principle, courts have concluded it is neither good faith

17. *Id.*

18. *Metro. Paving Co.*, 325 F.2d at 423.

19. As stated in *Sun Shipbuilding & Dry Dock Co. v. United States Lines, Inc.*, 439 F. Supp. 671, 682 (E.D. Pa. 1977), "Costs due to delay are no less damaging merely because they occur fortuitously before a contract deadline rather than after."

20. *See, e.g.*, Castle Constr. Company/Tuskegee Lumber Co. v. Owens & Woods P'ship, 590 So. 2d 186 (Ala. 1991); Hous. Auth. of Texarkana v. E. W. Johnson Constr. Co., 264 Ark. 523, 573 S.W.2d 316 (1978).

21. *See, e.g.*, Barton & Sons Co., ASBCA Nos. 9477, 9764, 65-2 BCA ¶ 4874 (1965); Kemmons-Wilson. Inc. (Florida) & South Patton, Inc., A Joint Venture, ASBCA No. 16,167, 72-2 BCA ¶ 9689 (1972); Canon Constr. Corp., ASBCA No. 16,142, 72-1 BCA ¶ 9404 (1972); Sydney Constr. Co., ASBCA No. 21,377, 77-2 BCA ¶ 12,719 (1977).

22. Metcalf Constr. Co. v. United States, 742 F.3d 984, 990 (Fed. Cir. 2014).

nor fair for one party to delay the performance by the other party and not pay the other party for the expenses incurred as a result of the delay.

The duty of cooperation is sometimes expressed in negative terms, as the "obligation implied in every contract that the Government shall not hinder the contractor in his performance[.]"[23] There is in every contract an implied duty on the part of both parties to cooperate and not to interfere negligently or willfully with the performance of the other party.[24]

The implied warranty of the correctness and completeness of design documents is relevant only where the delay was caused by errors or omissions in the design documents.[25]

In *Interstate General Contractors, Inc. v. West*,[26] the Federal Circuit held that to recover damages for delayed early completion, a contractor must show it:

1. Intended to complete the contract early;
2. Had the capability to do so; and
3. Actually would have completed early, but for the acts or omissions of the government or owner.[27]

This formula has been widely cited as the standard,[28] although some courts also require that the owner be given advance notice of the contractor's intent to finish early, while others do not require the contractor to have an intent to finish early at the outset of the work.[29]

Intent to Finish Early

The meaning of this element of the cause of action and whether it is actually required are uncertain. Does this requirement mean that the contractor must have had the subjective intent to finish early at or before the outset of the work? Or is it sufficient that the contractor developed that subjective intent at some time during the prosecution of the work? *Interstate General* appears to hold that the contractor must have had the subjective intent to finish early at the outset of the project,[30] but

23. Gardner Displays Co. v. United States, 171 Ct. Cl. 497, 503, 346 F.2d 585 (1965).

24. *See* C. Sanchez & Son, Inc. v. United States, 6 F.3d 1539, 1542 (Fed. Cir. 1993).

25. *See* Blake Constr. Co., Inc., 70-1 BCA ¶ 8128, GSBCA No. 2807 (1970).

26. 12 F.3d 1053 (Fed. Cir. 1993).

27. *Id.* at 1058–59.

28. *See, e.g.*, Howard Contracting, Inc. v. G.A. MacDonald Constr. Co., 71 Cal. App. 4th 39, 55–54, 83 Cal. Rptr. 2d 590 (Cal. Ct. App. 1998).

29. *See, e.g.*, Eickhof Constr. Co., ASBCA No. 20049, 77-1 BCA ¶ 12,398.

30. *See also* Maron Constr. v. GSA, 98-1 BCA ¶ 29685, GSBCA No. 13625 (1998), where the GSBCA denied the contractor's motion for summary judgment in part because, "[t]he most persuasive piece of evidence offered by Maron to support its position is the original schedule that it

also suggests that it would be sufficient if the subjective intent was manifest before the delay occurred:

> First, IGGC provided virtually no evidence to establish IGGC's intent to complete early. Indeed, there is no direct evidence whatsoever. The fact that IGGC actually completed the contract 13 days early is not probative that in bidding for the contract IGGC planned to complete performance prior to the 472 day contract performance period. In fact, Mr. Christiansen testified to the contrary. He said that following the delay in issuance of the [notice to proceed], "we also put additional staff of [sic] personnel on site, more than what I had anticipated when I first estimated the job, and using this new work schedule we accomplished this job at a much faster rate than the government thought possible." Instead of indicating that when Christiansen "first estimated the job" IGGC intended to complete the contract early, this testimony suggests that IGGC did not intend to complete early, but after the delay invoked significant acceleration methods not contemplated at the time of signing the contract. *Moreover, the record contains no contemporaneous evidence, such as internal or external documentation, that even before the government delay IGGC had intended to complete the contract early.* Nor does Christiansen assert that he so informed the government. Therefore, there is no legally sufficient evidence to support a finding that IGGC planned from the outset to complete early.[31]

Despite *Interstate General*, whether subjective intent to finish early is a required element of the cause of action is subject to some doubt. That is, there are cases that hold it is unnecessary for the contractor to possess the intent to finish early at the outset of the project; the only issue is whether the contractor would have finished early but for the acts or omissions of the owner, regardless of whether the contractor had developed the subjective intent to do so. These questions arose in the context of litigation over the issue of whether the contractor was required to provide the owner with notice of its intent to finish early to make a claim for delayed early completion.

In *Weaver-Bailey Contractors, Inc. v. United States*,[32] the U.S. Army Corps of Engineers (USACE) hired the contractor to construct improvements in recreational facilities around a lake in Oklahoma. The specifications underestimated the amount of excavation. USACE paid the contractor for the costs of the extra excavation, but not for the delay caused by the need to perform that extra excavation. USACE argued that the contractor was not entitled to any delay damages because

---

submitted to GSA, but that schedule was developed months after contract award and so does not shed any light upon what Maron intended *from the outset of the contract*." (emphasis added). *Id.* at 147,113.

31. 12 F.3d at 1059 (emphasis added).

32. 19 Cl. Ct. 474 (1990).

the work was completed within the contractual time. USACE also argued that there was no delay because the contractor's schedule showed that it would use the entire contract time. The Court of Claims rejected the government's argument, stating:

> "It would seem to make little difference whether or not the parties contemplated an early completion, or even whether or not the contractor contemplated an early completion." . . . Thus, even if Weaver-Bailey failed to rebut the government's evidence relating to its intended completion date, the government's point carries little weight. The proper focus is not whether Weaver-Bailey informed the government, at the inception of the contract, that it *intended* to complete the project before winter; rather, the focus should be on whether Weaver-Bailey *would have* completed the project early, but for the government-caused delay.[33]

Following the *Weaver-Bailey* holding, one of the predecessor boards to the Civilian Board of Contract Appeals, in *Rampart Waterblast, Inc.*,[34] questioned the "vitality" of this element of the cause of action. Rampart was hired to repair the parking structure at the John F. Kennedy Center for the Performing Arts. After the work was complete, Rampart filed a claim for "delays, disruptions, and loss of labor productivity caused by the Government." The government moved for summary judgment on the grounds that:

> Rampart, when it entered the contract, did not intend to better the contract's completion date. In its motion, the Government asserts that Rampart, in order to recover on its delay claims, must prove the fact of its early notification to the Government of its intent to better the contract schedule, and that the record presents no genuinely material factual issue on this subject. In other words, the Government contends that there is no credible evidence that Rampart, when it first took on the contract obligation, intended to complete the required work before the completion date specified in the contract. Thus, the Government avers that it is entitled to the Board's summary disposition of Appellant's delay claims.[35]

Citing *Weaver-Bailey* and quoting the preceding passage, the Board in *Rampart* denied the government's motion for summary judgment, stating:

> Therefore, the law applicable to delay claims focuses primarily on facts related to the actual performance of the contract. Examination and evaluation of the evidence concerning whether Rampart would have completed the project early but for any proven Government caused delay, will require a hearing, and in the course of a hearing evidence of Rampart's intent concerning an early finish, the feasibility of Rampart's plans concerning an early finish and, the timing,

33. *Id.* at 479.

34. IBCA Nos. 3658-96 to 3662-96, 98-2 BCA ¶ 29,894.

35. Appeals of Rampart Waterblast, Inc., 98-2 BCA ¶ 29,894, IBCA 3660-96 (1998).

> the number and the completeness of Rampart's communications concerning the plans for an early finish will be relevant. We do not read the law as making a contractor's early disclosure of a plan to finish early the *sine qua non* for recovery of a delay claim.[36]

In a footnote, the Board said:

> The Federal Circuit's decision in *Interstate General Government Contractors, Inc. v. United States,* 12 F.3d 1053, 1058-1059 (Fed. Cir. 1993), which concerned the recovery of unabsorbed overhead in a delay claim, and upheld an Armed Services Board of Contract Appeals (ASBCA) decision denying a contractor's delay claim, adopted what the Federal Circuit characterized as a three part test that had been earlier enunciated by the ASBCA in *Appeal of Frazier-Fleming Co.,* ASBCA No. 34537, 1990 ASBCA LEXIS 367, 91-1 BCA P23,378, at 117,287-88. Proof of the contractor's intention to finish early is the first part of the three part test, *and this Board would consider the vitality of that element at hearing.* Nothing we say here in response to the Government's [motion for summary judgment] forecloses or prejudges either parties' evidentiary presentation during a hearing.[37]

More explicitly, in *Eickhof Construction Co.,*[38] the Armed Services Board of Contract Appeals permitted a contractor to recover damages for a government caused delay in early completion despite the fact that the contractor's CPM schedule did not show early completion, ruling that the schedule did not "preclude a contractor from bettering its progress in accordance with the circumstances and its capabilities." This would indicate at the very least that the contractor need not have subjective intent at the outset of the project to finish early in order to maintain a cause of action for damages for owner-caused delay, and could go so far as to hold that there is no requirement for the contractor to have ever had subjective intent to finish early.

In *E. R. Mitchell Construction Co. v. Danzig,*[39] the prime contractor, who completed the project within the contract time, brought a claim for unabsorbed overhead on behalf of a subcontractor whose work had been delayed due to faulty plans and specifications. The Court of Appeals for the Federal Circuit reversed the ruling of the Armed Services Board of Contract Appeals rejecting the claim, finding no difference between the prime contractor's claim for the subcontractor's direct costs, which the government had already paid, and the prime contractor's claim for the subcontractor's unabsorbed overhead. The court also noted that the govern-

36. *Id.* at 147,984.
37. *Id.* at 147,985 (emphasis added).
38. ASBCA No. 20049, 77-1 BCA ¶ 12398.
39. 175 F.3d 1369 (Fed. Cir. 1999).

ment had actual knowledge of the subcontractor's schedule, which was delayed by the faulty plans and specifications, but said, "[w]hether the result in this case will obtain in a case in which the government has no knowledge of the performance obligations of the subcontractor awaits the presentation of that case for decision."[40]

In *Blinderman Construction Co. v. United States*,[41] the contractor claimed that delays caused by the discovery of unanticipated underground conditions delayed the contractor's early completion. The court rejected that claim citing the three-part test from *Interstate General*, but analyzed it as a four-part test, ruling that the fact that the government had no prior notice of the contractor's intent to finish early was a factor in denying the contractor's claim. Given that the court found that the contractor had proved none of the parts of the *Interstate General* three-part test, it is questionable whether this opinion stands authoritatively for the proposition that prior notice to the owner is required, but it certainly stands for the proposition that the contractor must have had a subjective intent to finish early.

There are reasons why a contractor with the subjective intent to finish a project early might not want to submit to the owner a schedule showing such early completion. As the court explained in *Weaver-Bailey*:

> The government bases its progress payments on the amount of work completed each month, relative to the contractor's proposed progress charts. A contractor which submits proposed progress charts using all of the time in the contract, and which demonstrates that work is moving along ahead of schedule, will receive full and timely progress payments. If such a contractor falls behind its *true* intended schedule, *i.e.*, its accelerated schedule, it will still receive full and timely progress payments, so long as it does not fall behind the progress schedule which it submitted to the government.
>
> On the other hand, if a contractor which intended to finish early reflected such an intention in its proposed progress charts, it would have to meet that accelerated schedule in order to receive full and timely progress payments; any slowdown might deprive the contractor of such payments, even if the contractor is performing efficiently enough to finish within the time allotted in the contract. In short, a contractor cannot lose when it projects that it will use all of the time allowed, but it can be hurt by projecting early completion.[42]

Still, evidence that the contractor intended to finish early is relevant to the issue of whether it would have finished early but for the owner-caused delay. While it may not be necessary that the contractor intended to finish early for the contractor

40. *Id.* at 1374.
41. 39 Fed. Cl. 529 (Fed. Cl. 1997).
42. *Weaver-Bailey Contractors, Inc.*, 19 Cl. Ct. at 479.

to establish it would have finished early but for the owner's delay, evidence that the contractor did intend to finish early supports the contractor's argument that it would have.[43] In *Blinderman*, absence of schedules showing early completion was taken by the trial court as evidence that the contractor *could* and *would* not have finished early.[44] Thus, notice to the owner of intent to finish early, even if not required, might improve the likelihood of success on an early completion claim.

Establishing the Contractor's Intent to Finish Early

If the contractor's subjective intent to finish early is an element of its cause of action for delay damages, then the easiest and best way to prove that intent is for the contractor to have prepared a realistic schedule showing early completion. This could be the schedule provided to the owner, which would likely satisfy the requirement of some courts that the owner has been given advance notice of the contractor's intent to finish early, or it could be an internal schedule that differs from that given to the owner.

Another way to prove that the contractor intended to complete the job early is the contractor's estimate, which ought to show the contractor's accounting for general conditions over the anticipated life of the project. In this respect, however, the bidding contractor should be careful to include such time-related costs only for the time to anticipated early completion, not to the contractual deadline, because the latter would be evidence of lack of intent to finish early.[45]

Conclusory testimony of the contractor of its subjective intent to finish early has been held as insufficient, without documentary support, to establish the truth of that subjective intent. In *Blinderman Construction*,[46] the court said:

> [T]he only evidence of plaintiff's alleged intention to finish the project early is inconclusive. Mr. Pieroni initially asserted that his CPM schedules showed the project being completed 55 days early, but later stated that BCC intended to finish the project 30 days early. This unresolved inconsistency bars any finding regarding plaintiff's *specific* intentions for early completion of the EMIC project.

---

43. *See* Jackson Constr. Co. v. United States, 62 Fed. Cl. 84 (Fed. Cl. 2004).

44. *Blinderman Constr. Co.*, 39 Fed. Cl. at 587.

45. *See* Maron Construction v. GSA, GSBCA No. 13625, 98-1 BCA ¶ 29,685: "GSA relies upon several facts to show that Maron did not have any intent to complete work before April 20, 1995. Maron's vice-president notified GSA's auditor, in writing, that Maron's as-bid anticipated performance period was the full contract performance period. Maron bid a period of seventy-eight weeks for general cleaning and eighteen months for dumpster costs at the project site, which is approximately the entire performance period." *Id.* at 147,112.

46. 39 Fed. Cl. at 587.

The Capability to Finish Early

Whether the contractor actually could finish early is a fact-intensive inquiry. If the contractor had a schedule showing early completion, the question will be whether it was realistic, and whether the contractor could muster the workers, subcontractors, and materials within the timeframes shown on the schedule to accomplish the tasks shown on the schedule.

Some courts have ruled that, where the contractor did not have a schedule showing early completion, the contractor could not have had the ability to finish early because, without a schedule, the contractor could not show a feasible plan to finish early.[47]

That the Contractor Would Have Finished Early but for the Owner's Delay

The contractor must prove not only that it *could* have completed the project early but for the acts or omissions of the owner, but that it also *would* have done so. In *Wickham Contracting Co. v. Fischer*,[48] the contractor's evidence that it would have completed the project early consisted of the government's consultant's CPM schedule showing completion two months before the contractual deadline, and the testimony of the contractor's project manager that the project could have been completed according to that schedule. The Armed Services Board of Contract Appeals ruled, and the Federal Circuit affirmed, that the schedule and the project manager's testimony might have been evidence that the project *could* have been completed two months early but was not evidence that the contractor *would* have done so.

The Board of Contract Appeals, in *Rampart Waterblast*,[49] outlined various facts that would be relevant in a hearing on the issue of whether the contractor would have finished early:

> Therefore, the law applicable to delay claims focuses primarily on facts related to the actual performance of the contract. Examination and evaluation of the evidence concerning whether Rampart would have completed the project early but for any proven Government caused delay, will require a hearing, and in the course of a hearing evidence of Rampart's intent concerning an early finish, the

---

47. *Interstate General Contractors, Inc.*, 12 F.3d at 1059–60; *Blinderman Construction*, 39 Fed. Cl. at 587.

48. 12 F.3d 1574 (Fed. Cir. 1994).

49. IBCA Nos. 3658-96 to 3662-96, CCH Board of Contract Appeal Decisions, Vol. 98, Issue 2, ¶ 29,894 (1998).

> feasibility of Rampart's plans concerning an early finish and, the timing, the number and the completeness of Rampart's communications concerning the plans for an early finish will be relevant.

There is, therefore, in this element, a rather complicated interplay of the other elements. While it might not be necessary to prove subjective intent to finish early to establish a cause of action for damages for delay in early completion, proof of such intent is arguably necessary to prove that the contractor would have finished early but for the owner-caused delay. That is, how can the contractor, itself, claim that it would have finished early if it had never intended that result? Similarly, it may not be expressly required that the contractor prepare a schedule showing early completion, but how can the contractor establish that it would have finished early if it had no plan to accomplish it?

Of course, the contractor must prove not only that it would have finished early, but that the cause of the delay was the act or omission of the owner or government; that "but for" the owner's act or omission, the contractor would have completed its work early. This issue is the same as for any claimed delay, regardless of whether it is for a delay in early completion.

As described in this chapter, claims for delays to early completion involve a complicated analysis that will usually require detailed testimony and documentary evidence. Perhaps most demanding of all, a contractor must show that it *would have* finished early if not for the owner's actions. Such a standard is very high and may prove difficult for most early completion claims. It is vitally important for contractors to be aware of these rules and standards at the outset of a project, to avoid any of the pitfalls inherent in such claims. Similarly, owners should be aware of the relevant law as well, as the need to defend such claims may arise.

CHAPTER 13

Acceleration Claims

John Marshall Cook, Daniel D. Rounds, and Michael J. Maroulis

In construction, time is of the essence. The longer a project takes to complete, the longer the owner must wait to put the project to its intended use, and the more costs the construction contractor will incur to complete the work. Delays on construction projects are commonplace, however, and so are instances where the owner and contractor cannot agree as to source of, or responsibility for, the delay. Sometimes the contractor encounters excusable delays for which the owner refuses to grant a time extension, instead demanding completion by the original contract date. Sometimes the owner insists that the contractor complete the project earlier than the contract requires. Either way, the contractor is faced with completing the project in less time than it had originally scheduled.

Completing the work in less time might require the contractor to re-sequence activities, expedite material and equipment procurement, increase its labor force, or work under less favorable conditions. In turn, multiple subcontractors might have to work simultaneously in the same tight spaces, leading to inefficiencies. This chapter discusses the various circumstances where acceleration can occur, explains the elements of proving claims for acceleration, and reviews methods for proving the costs associated with acceleration claims.

Introduction to Acceleration

Acceleration, or schedule compression, generally means expediting work to complete a project in fewer days than the contract would otherwise demand.[1] Acceleration often results in the contractor incurring additional costs, as the contractor may need to, among other things, pay laborers for overtime, hire additional laborers, expedite the shipment of materials to site, and suffer inefficiency costs. Inefficiency

1. Fraser Constr. Co. v. United States, 384 F.3d 1354, 1360 (Fed. Cir. 2004).

can result from excessive overtime hours, from having multiple different building trades working together in confined spaces (sometimes referred to as "trade stacking"), from having to re-sequence work, or from other disruptions.

Types of Acceleration

There are three types of acceleration: voluntary, directed, and constructive. Voluntary acceleration is when the contractor decides to expedite its performance of its work so as to complete the project earlier than required. Directed and constructive acceleration result from an owner's (or higher-tiered contractor's) actions. Directed acceleration occurs when the owner expressly orders the contractor to finish work in fewer days than originally scheduled. Constructive acceleration occurs when the owner denies a contractor's request for a time extension to which the contractor is entitled under the contract, instead requiring the contractor to complete the work by the existing completion date. Under many circumstances, directed and constructive acceleration are compensable.

Voluntary Acceleration

Voluntary acceleration occurs when a contractor expedites performance of its own volition.[2] Contractors voluntarily accelerate for myriad reasons: to earn contractual early completion bonuses, to reduce project overhead and general conditions, to free up contractor resources to perform other work, to make up for the contractor's own inefficiencies, or to free up bonding capacity.[3] Contractors also have an incentive to overcome their own inexcusable delays to avoid liquidated damages or termination for default. A contractor that voluntarily accelerates generally cannot recover acceleration costs from the owner.[4]

---

2. Atl. Indus., Inc., ASBCA No. 46710, 95-2 BCA ¶ 27,610; Whitesell-Green, Inc., ASBCA No. 53938 et al., 06-2 BCA ¶ 33,323. Contel Advanced Systems, Inc., ASBCA No. 49075, 04-2 BCA ¶ 32,664 (denying constructive acceleration claim, finding that the "[t]he pressure to complete the project timely was . . . driven by [the contractor's] desire to meet its financial commitments, rather than an express or implied order from the government," and explaining that "[t]o the extent [the contractor] actually accelerated, it did so voluntarily"); Atl. Indus., Inc., ASBCA No. 46710, 95-2 BCA ¶ 27,610.

3. Contel Advanced Systems, Inc., ASBCA No. 49075, 04-2 BCA ¶ 32,664; Envirotech Corp. v. Tennessee Valley Authority, 715 F. Supp. 190, 192–93 (W.D. Ky. 1989) (finding contractual early completion bonus evidenced voluntary acceleration).

4. Atl. Indus., Inc., ASBCA No. 46710, 95-2 BCA ¶ 27,610 at 137,609 ("No compensation is due where a contractor voluntarily accelerates performance for its own purposes.") (citations omitted).

Directed Acceleration

Directed acceleration occurs when the owner specifically orders the contractor to complete all or part of the work in less time than originally scheduled. Construction contracts often contain clauses empowering the owner to order a contractor to accelerate. For example, federal government construction contracts contain the Federal Acquisition Regulation (FAR) "Changes" clause.[5] The FAR Changes clause for fixed-price construction contracts states that "the Contracting Officer may . . . make changes in the work within the general scope of the contract, including changes . . . [d]irecting acceleration in the performance of the work."[6] Similarly, contracts for private construction projects sometimes include clauses expressly providing that the owner may direct the contractor to accelerate completion of the work.[7] Private construction contracts might include changes provisions that simply reference the owner's right to unilaterally change the timing of the work.[8]

Directed acceleration often occurs when the owner is attempting to mitigate or eliminate the impact of excusable delays on the project. Examples of directed acceleration include the owner directing the contractor at the outset of the project to complete the project in less time than the contract allowed[9] or when the owner orders the contractor to meet an interim milestone date not required under the contract.[10]

A directive to accelerate is not always compensable. For example, paragraph (b) of the FAR Schedules for Construction Contracts clause[11] permits the government to order the contractor to overcome its own inexcusable delay by accelerating, at no additional cost to the government.[12]

5. FAR 52.243-4.

6. FAR 52.243-4(a)(4).

7. *See, e.g.*, Bovis Lend Lease (LMB), Inc. v. Lower Manhattan Dev. Corp., 108 A.D.3d 135, 147–48 (N.Y. App. Div. 2013) (finding no direction to accelerate where the owner did not provide an acceleration notice or order per the contract's acceleration clause).

8. *See, e.g.*, AIA Document A201-2017 at § 7 Changes in the Work and ConsensusDocs 200 Series at § 8 Changes.

9. Imperial Constr. & Elec., Inc., ASBCA No. 54175, 06-1 BCA ¶ 33,276 at 164,952–953 (owner directed contractor to accelerate by insisting on project completion by a date earlier than the contractual completion date).

10. Hurst Excavating, Inc., ASBCA No. 37351, 93-3 BCA ¶ 25,935. In *Hurst*, the government rejected the contractor's schedule because it included winter work, which was not prohibited by the contract. The government then directed the contractor to complete certain work by mid-October. The Board found that the government had directed acceleration, and on reconsideration, clarified that recovery did not depend on a finding of excusable delay.

11. FAR 52.236-15.

12. FAR 52.236-15(b) ("If, in the opinion of the Contracting Officer, the Contractor falls behind the approved schedule, the Contractor shall take steps necessary to improve its progress, including

The contract's changes clause typically governs a contractor's right to compensation for acceleration-related costs. For example, paragraph (d) of the FAR Changes clause provides:

> If any change under this clause causes an increase or decrease in the Contractor's cost of, or the time required for, the performance of any part of the work under this contract, whether or not changed by any such order, the Contracting Officer shall make an equitable adjustment and modify the contract in writing.[13]

Acceleration orders, which are expressly permitted by paragraph (a) of the FAR Changes clause, represent changes for which a contractor may seek additional compensation.

Although directed acceleration is straightforward in theory, in practice, owners and contractors sometimes dispute whether the owner did in fact order the contractor to accelerate. The clearest example of an acceleration order is when the owner sends the contractor a letter or issues a formal change directive stating that the owner desires the project to be finished by a specific date, instructing the contractor to accelerate its work to meet that deadline, and pledging to pay the contractor for its increased costs incurred due to the acceleration.

Project communication is not always clear, however, and sometimes owner statements or actions falling short of the hypothetical clear letter can be considered a direction to accelerate. The FAR Changes clause requires in paragraph (a) that acceleration orders be issued "by written order designated or indicated to be a change order."[14] This contemplates a situation similar to the hypothetical letter discussed above. But paragraph (b) creates the possibility that other government statements amount to acceleration orders. Paragraph (b) states as follows:

> Any other written or oral order (which, as used in this paragraph (b), includes direction, instruction, interpretation, or determination) from the Contracting Officer that causes a change shall be treated as a change order under this clause; Provided, that the Contractor gives the Contracting Officer written notice stating- (1) The date, circumstances, and source of the order; and (2) That the Contractor regards the order as a change order.[15]

---

those that may be required by the Contracting Officer, without additional cost to the Government."). *See also* David Boland, Inc., ASBCA No. 59,313 et al., 24-1 BCA ¶ 38,680 at 188,040–41 (acknowledging that letter from USACE administrative officer directing contractor to get back on schedule after self-imposed delay fell within FAR 52.236-15).

13. FAR 52.243-4(d).
14. FAR 52.243-4(a)(4).
15. FAR 52.243-4(b).

This can result in a situation where the government issues what the contractor interprets as an acceleration order, the contractor subsequently accelerates, but the government denies that it ordered acceleration and refuses to pay the contractor for the acceleration costs it incurred.

Whether communication by the owner constitutes an acceleration order is fact specific. Not all statements from the owner expressing concern about the contractor's progress or advising that the contractor will need to pick up the pace constitute acceleration orders, particularly if they are not in the context of an owner's rejection of a time extension request.[16] A contractor that accelerates in response to an ambiguous acceleration order might find itself without recourse if a court later finds that the owner did not actually order the contractor to accelerate.

A contractor that believes it has received an acceleration order from the owner should consult their contract's changes clause, particularly the notice provisions. Private construction contracts might include strict notice requirements or short notice time frames.[17] Contractors should therefore have internal procedures in place to help ensure its project management team is in the position to provide timely notice as required by the contract.

Constructive Acceleration

Introduction

Constructive acceleration claims arise when the owner does not expressly order the contractor to complete the project in less time than the contract allows. Rather, these claims involve situations in which the contractor encounters excusable delays, but the owner fails to grant a time extension, instead requiring the contractor to complete the project by the unadjusted completion date.

Where excusable delays entitle the contractor to a time extension, an owner mandate that the contractor complete the project by the original completion date effectively reduces the contract duration. The contractor must then perform the work in less time than it bargained for. Faced with the threat of liquidated damages or termination for default, the contractor may recover the reasonable costs it incurs in its attempt to expedite performance to meet the original deadline.

---

16. David Boland, Inc., ASBCA No. 59,313 et al., 24-1 BCA ¶ 38,680 at 188,041 (citing Fraser Constr. Co. v. United States, 384 F.3d 1354, 1367 (Fed. Cir. 2004)).

17. *See, e.g*, Titan Stone, Tile & Masonry, Inc. v. Hunt Constr. Grp., Inc., 2007 WL 1659056, at *2 (D.N.J. June 5, 2007) (holding that a contractor's constructive acceleration claim was equitably barred because the contractor failed to submit a written claim within 48 hours as required by the contract).

Federal procurement law has long recognized a cause of action for constructive acceleration.[18] As the Western District of Virginia observed, "The majority of cases involving claims for constructive acceleration have been litigated in the federal agency appeals boards and the United States Court of Federal Claims, and have involved construction or procurement contracts with the federal government."[19] As a result, other jurisdictions often look to the Federal Circuit (along with the Court of Federal Claims and the federal Boards of Contract Appeals) for guidance on constructive acceleration. Moreover, the federal common law of government contracts can sometimes govern disputes between prime contractors and subcontractors on a federal project. This most often occurs on subcontracts for federal projects when the subcontract's choice of law clause expressly adopts the law of federal government contracts.[20]

Though widely recognized, not all jurisdictions have adopted a cause of action for constructive acceleration, and several states have not yet addressed the concept in reported decisions. California, for example, has yet to recognize constructive acceleration. In *Kiewit Power Constructors Co. v. City of Los Angeles*, the Central District of California noted the absence of California state or federal appellate authority on constructive acceleration claims.[21] However, the court cited decisions from other jurisdictions and the U.S. Court of Federal Claims as support for its conclusion that "[t]he doctrine of constructive acceleration is commonplace in other jurisdictions."[22] New York courts have not yet adopted a test for constructive acceleration, but have also cast doubt as to whether New York recognizes a cause of action for constructive acceleration. [23]

---

18. *See* John Cibinic Jr. et al., Administration of Government Contracts 402 (5th ed. 2016) (citing *Sanders*, Army BCA 1468, 4 CCF ¶ 60,526 (1948); Samuels et al., Army BCA 1147, 4 CCF ¶ 60,703 (1949)).

19. SNC-Lavalin America, Inc. v. Alliant Techsystems, Inc., 858 F. Supp. 2d 620, 635 (E.D. Va. 2012) (citations omitted).

20. *See, e.g.*, L3Harris Mar. Servs., Inc. v. BAE Sys. Norfolk Ship Repair Inc., No. 2:23CV259, 2023 WL 7095096, at *1 (E.D. Va. Oct. 26, 2023) (slip copy) (applying federal common law to subcontractor's constructive acceleration claim and explaining that "under the General Terms and Conditions, the parties agreed that any provision of the subcontract that is either 'incorporated in full text or by reference from the Federal Acquisition Regulations ('FAR'),' 'incorporated in full or by reference from any agency regulation that implements or supplements the FAR,' and/or 'is substantially based on any such agency regulation or FAR provision,' shall be construed and interpreted according to the U.S. federal common law of government contracts.").

21. Kiewit Power Constructors Co. v. City of Los Angeles, 2018 WL 9868225, at *5–6 (C.D. Cal. Oct. 19, 2018), *aff'd*, 813 F. App'x 261 (9th Cir. 2020).

22. *Id.* at *5 (rejecting the argument that "theory of constructive acceleration is invalid. . . . because there is no California authority on the theory of constructive acceleration[.]").

23. In *Bovis Lend Lease (LMB), Inc. v. Lower Manhattan Dev. Corp.*, 108 A.D.3d 135, 148 (N.Y. App. Div. 2013), the court denied the contractor's constructive acceleration claim "to the extent such a claim even exists."

Elements of Constructive Acceleration

Although the essential elements have remained rather constant through the decades, the Federal Circuit and its predecessor court have made some modest reformulations throughout the years. *Fraser Construction Co. v. United States* provides the most recent formulation.[24] In *Fraser*, the Federal Circuit enumerated the elements of constructive acceleration as follows:

> Although different formulations have been used in setting forth the elements of constructive acceleration, the requirements are generally described to include the following elements, each of which must be proved by the contractor: (1) that the contractor encountered a delay that is excusable under the contract; (2) that the contractor made a timely and sufficient request for an extension of the contract schedule; (3) that the government denied the contractor's request for an extension or failed to act on it within a reasonable time; (4) that the government insisted on completion of the contract within a period shorter than the period to which the contractor would be entitled by taking into account the period of excusable delay, after which the contractor notified the government that it regarded the alleged order to accelerate as a constructive change in the contract; and (5) that the contractor was required to expend extra resources to compensate for the lost time and remain on schedule.[25]

The *Fraser* court cited, *Norair Engineering Corp. v. United States*,[26] as support for its reformulation of the elements in *Fraser*, noting, however, that *Norair* compressed these elements into three essential elements: excusable delay, an order to accelerate, and acceleration with attendant costs.[27]

Fraser amended the *Norair* test by requiring the contractor also show that it made timely and sufficient notice of the underlying excusable delay and that the government either denied the request or failed to grant the time extension within a reasonable time. While *Fraser* listed five elements for a constructive acceleration claim, the fourth *Fraser* element is a compound requirement—the contractor must show that (1) the government insisted on completion of the contract without an extension for the excusable delay, and (2) the contractor notified the government

---

24. *See* Zafer Taahhut Insaat v. Ticaret A.S., 833 F.3d 1356, 1362 (Fed. Cir. 2016) (citing Fraser Constr. Co. v. United States, 384 F.3d 1354, 1360–61 (Fed. Cir. 2004)); LCC-MZT Team IV v. United States, 155 Fed. Cl. 387, 486 (2021) (same). *But see* Nova Grp./Tutor-Saliba v. United States, 159 Fed. Cl. 1, 52 (2022), *aff'd*, 87 F.4th 1375 (Fed. Cir. 2023) (applying the *Norair* elements instead of the *Fraser* elements, because "requiring the contractor to submit a time extension request would not be appropriate here since the evidence established that the Government was insisting on compliance with the original schedule despite the delay caused by the global stability dispute").

25. Fraser Constr. Co. v. United States, 384 F.3d 1354, 1361 (Fed. Cir. 2004).

26. Norair Eng'g Corp. v. United States, 229 Ct. Cl. 160, 666 F.2d 546, 548 (1981).

27. *Id.*

that the contractor considered the government's requirement to be a direction to accelerate.

While the *Fraser* formulation for constructive acceleration has been adopted by some jurisdictions,[28] others have adopted different formulations. For example, some district courts have cited the constructive acceleration test stated in the Bruner & O'Connor treatise, which is essentially the same as the *Fraser* test.[29] Some states, including Pennsylvania, have adopted the *Norair* test.[30] Other states have adopted formulations of constructive acceleration that are similar to *Fraser* but do not require the contractor to notify the owner of its intent to accelerate and submit a change order for the additional costs. In *Murdock & Sons Construction, Inc. v. Goheen General Construction, Inc.*, for example, the Seventh Circuit considered whether constructive acceleration is a viable claim under Indiana law, and, if so, which test to adopt.[31] Despite the lack of Indiana precedent on constructive acceleration, the Seventh Circuit predicted that Indiana would recognize a cause of action for constructive acceleration because constructive acceleration "is recognized in many jurisdictions."[32] Although the Seventh Circuit court mentioned *Fraser*, it ultimately applied the formulation articulated in *Sherman R. Smoot Co. v. Ohio Department of Administrative Service*:

> (1) the contractor experienced an excusable delay entitling it to a time extension, (2) the contractor properly requested the extension, (3) the project owner failed or refused to grant the requested extension, (4) the project owner demanded that the project be completed by the original completion date despite the excusable

28. *See, e.g.*, Matter of Allan Myers MD, Inc., 2022 WL 3645697 (Md. Ct. Sp. App. 2022) (adopting the *Fraser* test for constructive acceleration).

29. 6 Bruner & O'Connor Construction Law § 15:97, "Acceleration: Compression of contract time—'Constructive' Acceleration." *See also* Lunda Constr. Co. v. County of Anoka, 2018 WL 3309037 (Minn. Dist. Ct. 2018), *rev'd on other grounds,* 2019 WL 178511 (Minn. Ct. App. Jan. 14, 2019) (citing Bruner & O'Connor for the requirement that the contractor properly request a time extension for excusable delays and denying contractors constructive acceleration claim for failure to meet that requirement); Boston Ship Repair LLC v. Ocean Ships Inc., 2016 WL 4398677, at *6 (S.D. Tex. Aug. 18, 2016) (adopting the Bruner & O'Connor elements for a contract governed by General Maritime law and thereafter Texas law).

30. D.A. Nolt, Inc. v. Philadelphia Municipal Auth., 2021 WL 6049829 at *54–*56 (E.D. Pa. 2021) (citing Dep't of Transp. v. Anjo Constr. Co., 666 A.2d 753, 757 (Pa. Commw. Ct. 1995)); Nello L. Teer Co. v. Washington Metro. Area Transit Auth., 695 F. Supp. 583, 590 (D.D.C. 1988); Mergentime Corp. v. Washington Metro. Area Transp. Auth., 2006 WL 416177, at *82 (D.D.C. Feb. 22, 2006). *See also* Johnson Controls, Inc. v. Nat'l Valve & Mfg. Co., 569 F. Supp. 758, 760 (E.D. Okla. 1983) (considering the *Norair* test persuasive, but denying recovery for failure to comply with the contract's notice provisions).

31. Murdock & Sons Constr., Inc. v. Goheen Gen. Constr., Inc., 461 F.3d 837, 840 (7th Cir. 2006).

32. *Id.*

delay, and (5) the contractor actually accelerated the work in order to complete the project by the original completion date and incurred added costs as a result.[33]

The *Smoot* formulation is similar to the *Fraser* formulation, but it omits the post-time-extension denial acceleration notice requirement. Both *Fraser* and *Smoot* trace their origins to federal procurement case law. The *Smoot* court cited *Envirotech Corp. v. Tennessee Valley Authority*,[34] a decision in which the Western District of Kentucky derived its formulation from an Armed Services Board of Contract Appeals decision. The Seventh Circuit did not explain in *Murdock* why it adopted *Smoot* over *Fraser*.

In *SNC-Lavalin America, Inc. v. Alliant Techsystems, Inc.*, the Western District of Virginia applied the *Murdock/Smoot* formulation instead of the *Fraser* formulation in a contract dispute between a prime contractor and subcontractor on a public construction project.[35] In doing so, the Western District traced the post-notice requirement in *Fraser* and determined it originated from the specific language of the FAR Changes clause, which, "expressly addresses 'changes . . . [d]irecting acceleration in the performance of the work,' and which expressly requires a contractor to give 'written notice . . . that the Contractor regards [a order to accelerate] as a change order[.]'"[36] This analysis suggests that states without constructive acceleration standards might adopt the *Murdock / Smoot* formulation rather than the *Fraser* formulation, at least in the context of private construction contracts. However, if the contract in question requires notice of acceleration like the FAR Changes clause, then, as suggested by the Western District of Virginia in *SNC-Lavalin*, a court might apply the *Fraser* test and require the contractor to demonstrate that it notified the owner that it intended to accelerate and submit a request for equitable adjustment.

Proving the Elements of Constructive Acceleration

The Contractor Experienced an Excusable Delay Entitling It to a Time Extension

Constructive acceleration claims are in essence derivative claims, with excusable delay being "the first and central element of an acceleration claim."[37] A contractor generally cannot prevail on a constructive acceleration claim without

33. *Id.* (citing Sherman R. Smoot Co. v. Ohio Dept. of Adm. Serv., 136 Ohio App. 3d 166, 178–81 (2000)).

34. Envirotech Corp. v. Tennessee Valley Authority, 715 F. Supp. 190, 192 (W.D. Ky. 1988).

35. SNC-Lavalin America, Inc. v. Alliant Techsystems, Inc., 858 F. Supp. 2d 620 (W.D. Va. 2012).

36. *Id.* at 636–37 (quoting FAR 52.243-4).

37. *See* IAP Worldwide Servs., Inc., ASBCA No. 59397, 17-1 BCA ¶ 36763 at 179,158 (citing Lovering-Johnson, Inc., ASBCA No. 53902, 06-1 BCA ¶ 33,126 at 164,174) (stating "[t]he first and central element of an acceleration claim is proof of an excusable delay").

demonstrating that it encountered an excusable delay for which a time extension should have been granted. If the contractor cannot establish excusable delay, then any acceleration the contractor might have undertaken would likely be deemed voluntary and therefore noncompensable.[38]

The contract generally defines what constitutes an excusable delay. For instance, FAR 52.249-10, Default (Fixed-Price Construction) lists delays due to "causes beyond the control and without the fault or negligence of the Contractor" and includes: "(i) Acts of God or of the public enemy, (ii) Acts of the Government in either its sovereign or contractual capacity, (iii) Acts of another Contractor in the performance of a contract with the Government, (iv) Fires, (v) Floods, (vi) Epidemics, (vii) Quarantine restrictions, (viii) Strikes, (ix) Freight embargoes, (x) Unusually severe weather, or (xi) Delays of subcontractors or suppliers at any tier arising from unforeseeable causes beyond the control and without the fault or negligence of both the Contractor and the subcontractors or suppliers."[39]

Constructive acceleration depends not only on the existence of excusable delays but also on entitlement to a time extension due to excusable delays. Change orders are a common source of excusable delay, but owners sometimes include clauses in change orders stating that the change does not affect the time for performance. A contractor's execution of a bilateral change order with such language might bar a later constructive acceleration claim by waiving or releasing the contractor's right to a time extension for the change.[40] Contractors should carefully read bilateral change orders, lien releases, and other contractual documents before

38. *See* Fraser Constr. Co. v. United States, 384 F.3d 1354, 1364–66 (Fed. Cir. 2004); Sherman R. Smoot Co. v. Ohio Dep't of Adm. Serv., 136 Ohio App. 3d 166, 178–81 (2000) (contractor failed to prove that it suffered an excusable weather delay); Holder Constr. Group v. Georgia Tech Facilities, Inc., 282 Ga. App. 796, 798–99 (2006) (material delay not excusable because contractor bore risk of material delay under the contract); Turner Constr. Co. v. Smithsonian Institution, CBCA 2862, 4085, 4802, 17-1 BCA ¶ 36,739; Murdock & Sons Constr., Inc. v. Goheen General Constr., Inc., 461 F.3d 837, 840–43 (7th. Cir 2006) (contractor failed to provide any evidence that it encountered an excusable performance delay); Holder Constr. Grp. v. Georgia Tech Facilities, Inc., 282 Ga. App. 796, 798, 640 S.E.2d 296, 298 (2006) (denying acceleration claim stemming from material cost escalation and delivery delays caused by steel shortage because the contractor failed to request a time extension and the cause of the delay did not qualify as excusable under the contract).

39. FAR 52.249-10(b)(1).

40. *See, e.g.*, B.L. Harbert Int'l v. United States, 175 Fed. Cl. 513, 519–21 (2025), *appeal filed*, Case No. 25-1724 (Fed. Cir. May 1, 2025); Bart Assocs., Inc., EBCA No. C-9406176, 97-2 BCA ¶ 29,206 (denying contractor's acceleration costs due to delays extending the project into winter months because the contractor executed a bilateral modification extending the completion date without reserving the contractor's rights to claim additional costs); Mcnutt Constr. Co., Inc., ENGBCA No. 4724, 85-3 BCA ¶ 18397 ("A bilateral agreement resolving a particular claim operates as an accord and satisfaction as to that claim, barring any subsequent attempts to recover for that claim.").

signing them to ensure that they do not inadvertently waive or release their right to seek a contract time extension for change work.

The Contractor Properly Requested a Time Extension

The second element of constructive acceleration requires the contractor to show that it properly requested a time extension for excusable delay. What constitutes a proper request for time extension depends on both the language of the contract and on how the jurisdiction interprets contractual notice requirements. Often, the contract requires the contractor to notify the owner in writing that it has encountered excusable delays within a certain period after the delay.[41] A contractor that waits until after it has accelerated to request a time extension might jeopardize its chances to succeed in its constructive acceleration claim.[42]

A contractor that fails to provide timely and sufficient notice in a jurisdiction that requires strict compliance might waive its right to receive a time extension for the delay.[43] Some jurisdictions strictly interpret and enforce contractual notice provisions. Even where the contractor provides notice or the owner is aware of the excusable delay event, courts have denied recovery for constructive acceleration because the contractor failed to follow up the initial notice with a time extension request in the manner required by the contract.[44] If a contractor waives its right to a time extension by failing to comply with contractual time extension request requirements, the contractor could jeopardize its right to acceleration damages stemming from the contractor's efforts to overcome that delay.

Public projects and complex private projects tend to require the contractor to submit a baseline critical path method (CPM) schedule at the outset of the project. The contractor must also update the schedule periodically, generally on a monthly basis. Contracts frequently condition entitlement to a time extension on the submission of a CPM delay analysis, and some contracts specify a certain delay analysis methodology. The owner's failure to grant a time extension may not support a

---

41. *See, e.g.*, Morganti Nat., Inc. v. United States, 49 Fed. Cl. 110, 132 (2001), *aff'd*, 36 F. App'x 452 (Fed. Cir. 2002) (explaining the "well settled" principle that a contractor seeking a time extension must prove "not only the existence of an excusable cause of delay but also the extent to which completion of the contract work as a whole was delayed thereby").

42. *See, e.g.*, Cape & Sons Co. v. State, 52 Ill. Ct. Cl. 322, 365 (2000) (denying the contractor's acceleration claim where the contractor "did not formally seek an extension of the completion date until near the end of the work and after most of the acceleration efforts were completed").

43. *See* Johnson Controls, Inc. v. Nat'l Vale & Mfg. Co., 569 F. Supp 758 (E.D. Okla. 1983) (denying a subcontractor's constructive acceleration claim for failure to provide timely notice of excusable delays).

44. *See* Curry, Contracting Co., ASBCA No. 53716, 06-1 BCA ¶ 33,242; R.J. Lanthier Co., Inc., ASBCA No. 51636, 04–1 BCA ¶ 32481.

constructive acceleration claim where the contractor failed to respond to the owner's reasonable requests for supporting documentation to review the time extension request.[45]

Courts might excuse the contractor's failure to submit a time extension request if the owner indicated to the contractor that it would not entertain a request for additional time or if the circumstances otherwise indicate that a request for time extension would have been futile.[46] Nevertheless, contractors can eliminate any potential issue by complying with contractual notice and time extension request submission requirements even when the owner clearly indicates that it does not intend to grant a time extension.

The Owner Denied the Contractor's Request for an Extension or Failed to Act on It Within a Reasonable Time

The contractor must show that the owner either denied the contractor's request for a time extension or failed to grant it within a reasonable time. This element typically is not difficult to establish in situations in which the owner outright refuses to grant a time extension for a delay. Owner refusals to grant time extensions are often issued in writing and are part of the project record. If an owner does not provide a written denial of a time extension request, the contractor could document the refusal by writing a letter to the owner stating that the contractor understands the owner to have denied the time extension request.[47] The contractor should also raise the issue at project progress meetings and ensure that its concerns are accurately reflected in the meeting minutes.

Constructive acceleration claims can also be premised on an owner's unreasonable delay in granting a time extension request, though constructive acceleration claims based on an owner's failure to act within a reasonable time can be more difficult to establish. The specific facts of the project and the language in the contract concerning the timing of owner responses to contractor time extension

45. *See* Intermax, Ltd., ASBCA No. 43899, 93-2 BCA ¶ 25,699 (denying contractor's acceleration claim and finding that the contractor had failed to provide any supporting documentation for its time extension request prior to substantial completion).

46. *See* James Corp. v. North Allegheny School Dist., 938 A.2d 474, 483–85 (Pa. Commw. Ct. 2007) (A formal request for time extension would have been futile where the owner's construction manager informed the contractor that any time extension request was "non-negotiable."); Todd Pac. Shipyards Corp., ASBCA No. 53674, 04-1 BCA ¶ 32560 (written requests for time extensions would have been "pointless" where the government denied contractor's oral requests for time extension and insisted upon completion by the original completion date despite excusable delay).

47. Alliance Elec., Inc. v. Atlantic City Bd. of Educ., 2004 WL 583211, at *2–4, *8 (N.J. Super. Ct. App. Div. Mar. 2, 2004) (The contractor notified owner of several delays during project relating to weather, design, and site conditions that a jury ultimately determined to be excusable, but the owner refused grant time extensions for those delays during the project.).

requests are relevant considerations for determining whether the owner's failure to act was reasonable. An owner's belated grant of a time extension rarely absolves the owner of liability for constructive acceleration.[48] An owner that waits for months to issue a decision on the time extension request while the contractor scrambles to meet the existing contract completion date may be at risk to be found as having acted unreasonably. Similarly, an owner's acknowledgment of the underlying cause of the excusable delays but failure to issue a decision on the time extension request can support a finding that the owner failed to act within a reasonable time.[49] An owner's direction that the contractor provide additional information or supporting documentation that is reasonably necessary for the owner to evaluate the time extension request on the merits typically is not considered unreasonable delay.[50] But an owner that defers review of a time extension request by requesting additional information it does not need to assess the time extension request risk a court later finding that the owner engaged in unreasonable delay.[51]

Courts have recognized narrow exceptions to an owner's duty to timely grant time extensions where, for instance, the record did not suggest that the owner threatened to impose liquidated damages and "the parties had a verbal understanding that [the contractor] would receive a time extension."[52]

The Owner Insisted on Completion of the Contract in Less Time Than the Contractor Would Be Entitled If Granted a Time Extension for Excusable Delay

The contractor must show that the owner demanded project completion by the original completion date despite excusable delays. This element is most easily satisfied when the owner has sent demand letters to the contractor insisting that it

---

48. *See* Cont'l Heller Corp., GSBCA No. 6812, 84-2 BCA ¶ 17,275 ("As a defense to a claim of constructive acceleration, a belated time extension is worthless.").

49. *See* Azure v. United States, 129 F.3d 136 (1997) (unpublished opinion) (holding that "[T]he contracting officer's decision to delay granting the extension until after completion of the project was unreasonable and that failure to timely issue the extension was tantamount to a refusal thereof").

50. Zafer Taahhut Insaat v. Ticaret A.S., 833 F.3d 1356, 1364 (Fed. Cir. 2016) (denying constructive acceleration claim upon finding that the government never denied a proper time extension request, explaining that "the contracting officer repeatedly asked for more information so that it could make a proper determination, a request that [the contractor] repeatedly failed to comply with" and noting that contractor failed to request a specific number of days of additional time, although not expressly required by contract).

51. *See* Cont'l Heller Corp., GSBCA No. 6812, 84-2 BCA ¶ 17,275 (finding the government's insistence on supporting documentation of heavy rains improper because "[t]he Government could not, by continually insisting on documentation of what was already known, justify its refusal to grant a time extension").

52. Mckenzie Eng'g Co., ASBCA No. 53374, 05-2 BCA ¶ 33,090 (nine months to grant a time extension).

complete the project by the original completion date and threatening liquidated damages or termination if the contractor fails to do so. The contractor need not show that the owner used any specific wording, only that the owner continued to insist upon completion by the original completion date.[53] A recurring feature of successful constructive acceleration claims is that the owner has exerted undue pressure on the contractor to complete the project by the original deadline despite excusable delay.[54]

Courts usually consider the totality of circumstances in deciding whether owner statements or conduct qualify as acceleration orders. Historically, "[c]ircumstances from which [an acceleration] order may be implied include expressions of urgency by the Government, especially if coupled with (i) a threat of default or liquidated damages for not meeting a given accelerated schedule, or (ii) actual assessment of liquidated damages[.]"[55] Owner threats of default termination provide compelling evidence of an acceleration order.[56] Where the owner issues a cure notice after refusing to grant a time extension for excusable delays, the cure notice could be construed as an acceleration order.[57] Other owner conduct that might support a finding that the owner ordered the contractor to accelerate include threatening to issue unsatisfactory performance reports,[58] threats and the withholding of progress payments,[59] and expressions of concern about lagging progress.[60] Courts

53. *See* Alliance Elec., Inc. v. Atlantic City Bd. of Educ., 2004 WL 583211, at *4–5, *8 (N.J. Super. Ct. App. Div. Mar. 2, 2004) (communications from owner's construction manager demanding completion by the original contract date despite excusable delays constituted a constructive acceleration order); Ace Constructors, Inc. v. U.S., 70 Fed.Cl. 253, 280–81 (2006), *aff'd*, 499 F.3d 1357 (Fed. Cir. 2007) (Owner's continued insistence that contractor achieve original contract completion date and imposition of LDs despite contractor's excusable delay was sufficient to establish acceleration order.).

54. *Compare* Norair Eng'g Corp. v. United States, 666 F.2d 546, 547 (Ct. Cl. 1981) ("There was also considerable pressure applied to open the building as quickly as possible.") *with* Intermax, Ltd., ASBCA No. 43899, 93-2 BCA ¶ 25,699 (denying contractor's constructive acceleration claim because, while the government did not act on the contractor's time extension request, the contractor proffered no evidence that the government pressured the contractor to complete within the original project duration, noting that "[a]n affirmative denial of a time extension . . . may be a constructive acceleration order, but a 'mere' failure to grant a claimed extension at the time submitted is not").

55. Titan Pac. Constr. Corp., ASBCA No. 24148, 87-1 BCA ¶ 19,626 (quoting Fermont Division Dynamics Corp. of Am., ASBCA No. 15806, 75-1 BCA ¶ 11,139); *see also* Nova Grp./Tutor-Saliba v. United States, 159 Fed. Cl. 1, 56 (2022), *aff'd*, 87 F.4th 1375 (Fed. Cir. 2023) (finding that "the Government's repeated warnings that [the contractor] maintain the original project schedule despite a critical path work stoppage of over two months constituted an order to accelerate").

56. See IAP Worldwide Servs., Inc., ASBCA No. 59397, 17-1 BCA ¶ 36,763; Hugh Brasington Contracting Co., ASBCA No. 25471, 84-3 BCA ¶ 17,528.

57. *See* Monterey Mech. Co., ASBCA No. 51450, 01-1 BCA ¶ 31,380.

58. *See* Gibbs Shipyard, Inc., ASBCA No. 9809, 67-2 BCA ¶ 6499.

59. Natkin & Co. v. George A. Fuller Co., 347 F. Supp. 17, 35 (W.D. Mo. 1972).

60. Dep't of Transp. v. Anjo Constr. Co., 666 A.2d 753, 757 (Pa. Commw. Ct. 1995).

are more likely to find that owner exhortations amount to an acceleration order where the owner's motivation for wanting the project completed by the original deadline is more readily apparent.[61] However, expressions of concern by the owner to the contractor about the status of the project do not always constitute acceleration orders, particularly if they are made before the contractor has requested a time extension.[62]

Courts can consider the context of the project when deciding whether the threat of liquidated damages imposed sufficient pressure to induce the contractor to accelerate. For example, the Armed Services Board of Contract Appeals has found that withholding $30,000 in liquidated damages on a $7.5 million contract did not amount to an acceleration order.[63] Conversely, the ASBCA reached the opposite conclusion where the owner initially assessed $46,846 in LDs (later reduced to $26,996) on a $2,549,485 contract.[64]

Contractors should carefully review the owner's written directives when determining whether the owner is insisting on completion by the original completion date despite excusable delays. In one case, the owner sent the contractor a letter stating the project completion date but clarifying that this date did not account for a change order.[65] By excluding the change order—and thus any associated excusable delay—the letter did not "unconditionally order" the contractor to meet the unadjusted completion date. Accordingly, there was no order to accelerate. An owner's request for information or an acceleration proposal is unlikely to qualify as an acceleration order without more.[66] Similarly, if the contractor has not yet submitted a time extension request, pressure by the owner to complete the work by the

61. *See* Downey, Inc. v. Bradley Ctr. Corp., 524 N.W.2d 915, 921 (Wis. Ct. App. 1994) (The owner admonished the contractor that meeting the original completion date "was of paramount importance" on a project to renovate a sports stadium where NBA games scheduled shortly thereafter.); James Corp. v. N. Allegheny Sch. Dist., 938 A.2d 474, 486 (Pa. Commw. Ct. 2007) ("over-riding consideration for [School District] . . . was that not a single day of school would be missed") (alteration in original).

62. David Boland, Inc., ASBCA No. 59,313, 24-1 BCA ¶ 38,680 at 188,041 (citing *Fraser*, 384 F.3d at 1367).

63. Phillips Nat'l, Inc., ASBCA No. 53241, 04-1 BCA ¶ 32,567 ([I]nasmuch as the original contract amount was in excess of $7.5 million, we do not believe that withholding $30,000 (0.4 percent of the contract amount) could have placed so much pressure on [the contractor] to cause it to embark on a $600,000 acceleration effort.").

64. Robust Constr., L.L.C., ASBCA No. 54056, 05-2 BCA ¶ 33,019 (remanding for determination of quantum on the contractor's $393,521 acceleration claim).

65. Sherman R. Smoot Corp., ASBCA No. 52173, 03-1 BCA ¶ 32,212.

66. *See* Mergentime Corp. v. Washington Metro. Area Transp. Auth., 400 F. Supp. 2d 145, 247 (D.D.C. 2005), *opinion amended and superseded*, 2006 WL 416177 (D.D.C. Feb. 22, 2006) (citing A. Teichert & Son, Inc., ASBCA Nos. 10265 et al., 68-2 BCA ¶ 7175; John C. Grimberg Co., Inc., ASBCA No. 58791, 18-1 BCA ¶ 37,191 *rev'd on other grounds*, 817 Fed. Appx 960 (Fed. Cir. 2020).

original deadline generally does not amount to an acceleration order.[67] Contractors who are unsure whether the owner is ordering accelerate should seek clarification in writing.[68] Federal government contractors should ensure that any admonitions to complete by the original deadline or communications that it regards as an order to accelerate comes from the contracting officer and not from others unauthorized to give such a direction.[69]

Contractor Notified the Owner That It Regarded the Alleged Order to Accelerate as a Constructive Change in the Contract

Under the *Fraser* formulation of the test for constructive acceleration, the federal government contractor must show that it notified the government that it considered the government's refusal to grant a time extension and insistence upon completion by the original completion date to be an acceleration order, for which the contractor intended to submit a request for equitable adjustment.[70] While the FAR Changes clause expressly grants the government the right to unilaterally modify the contract by "directing acceleration in the performance of the work," it also requires the contractor to satisfy the notice requirements of paragraph (b) in the event the contractor receives a "direction, instruction, interpretation, or determination" from the contracting officer that "causes a change." Thus, under the *Fraser* formulation, the contractor is required to provide notice that it considers an order to be an acceleration order, and a contractor's failure to provide this notice of constructive acceleration could bar recovery. However, depending on the circumstances, federal courts have declined to treat the post-denial acceleration notice as essential for prosecution of a constructive acceleration claim.[71]

---

67. *See* Fraser Constr. Co. v. United States, 384 F.3d 1354, 1366–67 (Fed. Cir. 2004) ("Because there was no reason for the [owner] to believe at that time that [the contractor] had a valid claim for an extension for delays that were not weather-related, it was not unreasonable for the [the owner] to remind [the contractor] of its responsibility to adhere to its contract schedule.").

68. *See, e.g.*, Robust Constr., L.L.C, ASBCA No. 54056, 05-2 BCA ¶ 33,019 (no written acceleration order, but contractor followed up on CO's oral acceleration directive the same day in a letter to the CO).

69. *See* Fluor Intercontinental, Inc., CBCA 490 et al., 12-1 BCA ¶ 34,989 (verbal statements that contractor was running behind schedule and letter expressing disappointment with contractor's performance that did not come from the CO were not acceleration orders); MC II Generator & Elec., ASBCA No. 53389, 04-1 BCA ¶ 32,569 ("To establish that a constructive change occurred, [the contractor] must prove that . . . the person directing the change had contractual authority unilaterally to alter the contractor's duties under the contract[.]").

70. *See* Fraser Constr. Co. v. United States, 384 F.3d 1354, 1361 (Fed. Cir. 2004).

71. Nova Group / Tutor-Saliba v. United States, 159 Fed.Cl. 1, 51–52 (2022) (applying the *Norair* elements instead of the *Fraser* elements, because "requiring the contractor to submit a time extension

Whether post-denial notice is a condition precedent can depend on the contract language, especially the language of the relevant changes clause. The changes clause in a contract between private parties might differ from the FAR Changes clause in keyways that preclude application of the *Fraser* formulation. *SNC-Lavalin America, Inc. v. Alliant Techsystems, Inc.* is instructive. The *SNC* court adopted the *Murdock* test for contracts between private parties, distinguishing *Fraser* because, unlike *Fraser*, the dispute in *SNC* involved a contract between two private parties, and the contract at issue did not include the FAR Changes clause and did not require a post-denial acceleration notification from the contractor.[72]

A contractor performing in a state that has yet to recognize a cause of action for constructive acceleration should consider providing a post-denial acceleration notice to accommodate the risk that a reviewing court adopts the *Fraser* test or interprets the contract at issue to require notice. Additionally, a post-denial acceleration notice could serve to clarify whether the owner is actually insisting on completion by the original deadline.[73] While courts sometimes excuse the lack of timely notice on constructive changes, contractors should be aware that they might face a heightened burden of persuasion if they fail to provide notice.[74] Finally, contractors on state public procurement projects should consider providing post-denial notice even if the state had previously adopted the *Murdock* or *Norair* test for constructive acceleration. State courts tend to track federal procurement law and may adopt the *Fraser* test even if the state had previously adopted the *Murdock* or *Norair* test.[75]

---

request would not be appropriate here since the evidence established that the Government was insisting on compliance with the original schedule despite the delay caused by the global stability dispute").

72. *SNC-Lavalin America, Inc.*, 858 F. Supp. 2d at 637–38.

73. *See* Utley-James, Inc., GSBCA No. 5370, 85-1 BCA ¶ 17,816 *aff'd*, 14 Cl. Ct. 804 (1988) ("Whatever doubt there might have been that the February 28 letter was an acceleration directive is disposed of by [the contractor's letter in response,] in which he stated flatly that he regarded it as an acceleration directive and would comply unless told otherwise. At that point, if [the owner] wanted the point clear, it was obliged to respond and make it clear. Its silence said all that needed saying.").

74. *See T.* Brown Constructors, Inc. v. Pena, 132 F.3d 724, 733 (Fed. Cir. 1997) (quoting Mingus Constructors, Inc. v. United States, 812 F.2d 1387, 1392 (Fed. Cir. 1987)) ("[T]he existence of prejudice resulting from the dilatory notice usually serves to increase the burden of persuasion facing the contractor asserting its claim for equitable adjustment rather than to bar its claim entirely."). *See also* Grumman Aerospace Corp., ASBCA No. 46834, 03-1 BCA ¶ 32,203 (discussing notice requirements and exceptions).

75. *Compare* Hensel Phelps Constr. Co., MSBCA No. 1080, 1167 (1992) (applying *Norair*) *with* Allan Myers MD, Inc., MSBCA No. 3153 (2020) (applying *Fraser* and acknowledging that the Board had previously held that claimants must satisfy the *Norair* test to prevail on a constructive acceleration claim).

The Contractor Actually Accelerated the Work in an Attempt to Complete the Project by the Original Completion Date and Incurred Added Costs as a Result

The final element of constructive acceleration is that the contractor must show it actually accelerated its work on the project to attempt to achieve the original completion date and thereby incurred costs. Failure to prove that the contractor actually accelerated and incurred additional costs is a common reason that courts deny recovery on constructive acceleration claims.[76]

The contractor need not actually achieve the expedited completion date, as depending on the magnitude of the excusable delay achieving the original contract completion date might have been impossible. Rather, the contractor need only establish that it did, in fact, reasonably accelerate its work and incurred additional costs, be it through paying for overtime, hiring more workers, ordering more tools and equipment, paying material expedition fees or other premiums, incurring greater than normal costs due to inefficiencies caused by working out of sequence or by trade stacking, or other attempts to speed up the pace of the work in order to meet the original contract date. Fundamentally, a contractor can only recover acceleration costs actually incurred, and a contractor that cannot demonstrate it accelerated its work and thereby incurred damages will not prevail in a constructive acceleration claim.[77]

A contractor can recover costs only for reasonable acceleration efforts. Reducing the duration of the critical path is necessary to reducing the overall project duration. Accordingly, if a contractor disregards the critical path when performing its alleged acceleration, the costs it incurs unrelated to an effort to progress work on the critical path might be unrecoverable.[78] But a contractor is not necessarily limited to only recovering for costs incurred in accelerating work on the critical path.[79] As work is accelerated, multiple paths may have zero or negative float. Thus,

---

76. *See, e.g.*, Utley-James, Inc., GSBCA No. 5370, 85-1 BCA ¶ 17,816, *aff'd*, 14 Cl. Ct. 804 (1988) ("Even if one of the other five elements of a constructive acceleration can in theory be discarded on occasion, this one is essential. And if a contractor is actually accelerating, there ought to be some evidence of it.").

77. *See, e.g.*, St. Louis Housing Authority ex rel. Jamison Electric, LLC, 2014 WL 7408944, at *8–9, *11–12 (E.D. Mo. Dec. 31, 2014) (subcontractor did not establish additional hours worked were due to contractor-caused delay rather than subcontractor staffing choices or other factors).

78. *See* Lovering-Johnson, Inc., ASBCA No. 53902, 06-1 BCA ¶ 33,126 (finding a lack of actual acceleration and explaining that "appellant appears to have concentrated on activities that were not proven to be on the critical path to completing the phases in order").

79. *See, e.g.*, Clark Constr. Grp., Inc., GAOCAB No. 2003-1 (Nov. 23, 2004) ("[T]he accelerated work during this time frame need not be on the critical path to be compensable acceleration; the record shows that all aspects of the project needed to be accelerated in order for the contract to be substantially complete by August 31.").

it might be possible to further expedite overall project completion only by expediting multiple paths simultaneously.[80]

Acceleration Damages

Types of Acceleration Costs

Acceleration can result in significant additional expense for the contractor. The Court of Appeals of Ohio explained that "[a] contractor who accelerates its work as the result of the denial of a justified time extension is entitled to recover its increased costs for labor, equipment, overhead and efficiency, as well as any lost profits."[81] In order to complete a scope of work in less time than expected, contractors might incur several different types of costs. Contractors will likely incur additional labor costs, potentially including paying for premium and overtime, adding additional laborers and supervision to augment existing crews (as well as paying subcontractors for doing the same), and securing additional tools and equipment so that the expanded workforce can perform its work. Contractors might also incur additional costs related to inefficiencies caused by the acceleration. Out of sequence work, trade stacking, and overtime work is all less efficient than work under normal conditions. A contractor might also need to pay expediting fees and other premiums to ensure that material arrives in time to accommodate the accelerated schedule. Contractors might also recover costs due to adverse weather "if the acceleration order forced [the contractor] to work during expected bad weather which would, absent an acceleration order, have resulted in cessation of the work."[82] Contractors have claimed and recovered all of these costs and more in constructive acceleration actions.[83]

---

80. *Id.*

81. Sherman R. Smoot Co. v. Ohio Dep't of Adm. Serv., 136 Ohio App. 3d 166, 178 (2000).

82. Gibbs Shipyard, Inc., ASBCA No. 9809, 67-2 BCA ¶ 6499 (July 10, 1967). *See* Maint. Engineers, ASBCA No. 23131, 81-2 BCA ¶ 15,168 (contractor entitled to additional costs after being ordered to mow sodden fields despite recent heavy rains); Azure v. United States, 129 F.3d 136 (Fed. Cir. 1997) (unpublished opinion) ("[The Contractor] was induced to work on days where the weather conditions made it impracticable."). *See also* Dick Pacific Constr. Co., ASBCA No. 57675, 16-1 BCA ¶ 36,196 at 176,632–633, 637.

83. Wood Elec., Inc. v. Ohio Facilities Constr. Comm'n, 90 N.E.3d 371, 377–79 (Ohio Ct. App. 2017) (describing trade stacking, other inefficiencies); James Corp. v. North Allegheny School Dist., 938 A.2d 474, 485–86, 494–95 (Pa. Commw. Ct. 2007) (appeals court upheld award of acceleration damages based on a measured-mile analysis by expert witness, describes additional costs of overtime and adding workforce); Ace Constructors, Inc. v. United States, 70 Fed. Cl. 253, 280–81 (2006) (contractor certified payroll records evidence of overtime worked, entitled to recover those costs plus mark-ups for field and home-office overhead, profit, and bond cost); Gilchrist Constr. Co., LLC v. State, Dept. of Transp. and Dev., 166 So. 3d 1045 (2015) (finding contractor entitlement for costs associated with jobsite overhead, idle equipment, and material stockpiling).

How to Prove Acceleration Costs

When establishing its acceleration costs, a contractor generally must prove "the amount of loss with sufficient certainty so that the determination of the amount of damages will be more than mere speculation."[84] Simply applying a 30 percent markup on the contractor's total labor cost, for example, is "wholly speculative."[85]

A contractor can best prove increased acceleration costs by keeping thorough records of its acceleration efforts during the project. Courts usually accord significant weight to contemporaneous project documentation.[86] The contractor should document its acceleration efforts by keeping comprehensive daily logs, by detailing acceleration activities in regular progress meetings with the owner, by letters and emails as appropriate, and by tracking acceleration efforts in the accounting system as closely as reasonably possible. Courts have relied on contractor-certified payrolls as evidence of the contractor's acceleration.[87] Progress meeting minutes are also important because they represent the discussions and contemporaneous understanding of the parties throughout the project. All parties should verify that

---

84. Fireman's Fund Ins. Co. v. United States, 92 Fed. Cl. 598, 698 (2010) (quoting Lisbon Contractors, Inc. v. United States, 828 F.2d 759, 767 (Fed. Cir. 1987)). *See* Amatea/Grimberg JV, ASBCA Nos. 60426 et al., 23-1 BCA ¶ 38,366 (noting that although the contractor claimed acceleration damages for having to assign additional supervisors and bring in additional equipment, "there [wa]s no evidence that the costs of more supervisors for a shorter period of time (via acceleration) was greater than a smaller number of supervisors over a longer period of time would have been. The same goes for the extra equipment."); Edge Constr. Co. v. United States, 95 Fed. Cl. 407, 415 (2010) (quoting Wunderlich Contracting Co. v. United States, 173 Ct. Cl. 180, 351 F.2d 956, 968 (1965)) ("The contractor 'need not prove his damages with absolute certainty or mathematical exactitude. It is sufficient if he furnishes the court with a reasonable basis for computation, even though the result is only approximate.'").

85. J & K Plumbing & Heating Co. Inc. v. State, 235 A.D.2d 751, 753, 652 N.Y.S.2d 369 (1997). *See also* Bat Masonry Co., Inc., v. Pike-Pachen Joint Venture III, 842 F. Supp 174, 182 (1993) (rejecting subcontractors alleged 30–40 percent inefficiency ratios and setting upper limit of 20 percent before remanding to the parties to settle).

86. *See* Park Construction Co., ENGBCA No. 6113, 95-2 BCA ¶ 27,777 (denying contractor's constructive acceleration claim for lack of excusable delay due to unseasonably severe weather where the contractors quality control reports and daily logs failed to indicate any weather-related issues, explaining that "contemporaneous written records are presumed by the Board to represent the actual job site conditions"); Robust Constr., L.L.C., ASBCA No. 54056, 05-2 BCA ¶ 33,019 ("testimony and daily logs more probative than bar chart impact analysis"); E.C. Morris & Son, Inc., ASBCA No. 20697, 77-2 BCA ¶ 12,622 ("[C]ontemporaneous records are more accurate than the imperfect memory of a witness defending his actions three years after occurrence.").

87. Ace Constructors, Inc. v. United States, 70 Fed. Cl. 253, 280–81 (2006) (contractor certified payroll records evidence of overtime worked, entitled to recover those costs plus mark-ups for field and home-office overhead, profit, and bond cost, cost supported by testimony for contractor's expert witness).

the minutes accurately reflect discussions during the meeting, correcting any misstatements in the record.[88]

Contractors will usually need to provide expert analysis to support recovery of inefficiency costs. One option for proving the impact of acceleration is the use of a measured-mile analysis comparing the efficiency of an unaccelerated part of the project against the efficiency of project work during the acceleration period.[89] Courts have recognized several variations to the measured-mile method.[90] Damages for inefficiency should be substantiated by "fact witnesses who actually participated in the work and who can precisely describe the nature and extent of any inefficiencies and impact."[91] Contractors should present testimony from personnel involved in the day-to-day administration of the project.[92]

Industry studies offer another way to quantify loss of productivity. The Mechanical Contractors Association of America, for example, has published a study on "Factors Affecting Labor Productivity," which provides a range of expected inefficiency corresponding to 16 factors: stacking of trades, morale and attitude, reassignment of manpower, crew size inefficiency, concurrent operations, dilution of supervision, learning curve, errors and omissions, beneficial occupancy, joint occupancy, site access, logistics, fatigue, ripple, overtime, and season and weather

88. *See, e.g.*, Imperial Constr. & Elec., Inc., ASBCA No. 54175, 06-1 BCA ¶ 33,276 (May 3, 2006) (noting that owner-prepared meeting minutes observed a lack of sufficient contractor resources to meet the "agreed turnover date" to which the contractor responded by explaining that it had never agree to the expedited date).

89. Wood Elec., Inc. v. Ohio Facilities Constr. Comm'n, 90 N.E.3d 371, 377–79 (Ohio Ct. App. 2017) (expert testimony using measured mile method to identify magnitude of inefficiencies caused by acceleration); James Corp. v. N. Allegheny Sch. Dist., 938 A.2d 474, 485–86, 494–95 (Pa. Commw. Ct. 2007) (appeals court upheld award of acceleration damages based on a measured-mile analysis by expert witness); *see also* Gilchrist Constr. Co., LLC v. State, Dep't of Transp. & Dev., 166 So. 3d 1045, 1064 (2015) (expert testimony supported recovery of inefficiency damages caused by acceleration).

90. *Compare* Clark Concrete Contractors, Inc. v. Gen. Servs. Admin., GSBCA No. 14340, 99-1 BCA ¶ 30,280 *with* Bell BCI Co. v. United States, 81 Fed. Cl. 617 (2008), *aff'd in part and vacated in part*, 570 F.3d 1337 (Fed. Cir. 2009) *and* P.J. Dick Inc., VABCA No. 5597 et al., 01-2 BCA ¶ 31,647, *aff'd in part and vacated in part*, 324 F.3d 1364, 1376 (Fed. Cir. 2003) *and* James Corp. v. N. Allegheny Sch. Dist., et al., 938 A.2d 474 (Pa. Commw. Ct. 2007).

91. R.W. Contracting Inc., ASBCA No. 24627, 84-2 BCA ¶ 17,302.

92. *See* Wilner Constr. Co., ASBCA No. 32449, 88-2 BCA ¶ 20,614 ("It would normally be expected that appellant would call the author of the daily reports since it intended to rely upon them. It did not do so and offered no explanation for not doing so. Under those circumstances, we can and do, draw the inference that the testimony of that person would not support appellant's present position."); McCarthy Bros. Co. v. State, 47 Ill. Ct. Cl. 15, 37 (1995) ("The principle of the [missing witness] rule is that failure of a party to produce evidence available to that party and which testimony could have been produced if that party's position was true, would give rise to a presumption against the party."); Org. for Env'l Growth, Inc., CAB No. D-850 (DCCAB 1994) (drawing an adverse inference against the government for failing to produce a witness with direct knowledge of material facts).

change.[93] But contractors cannot simply cite to an industry study and apply inefficiency markups without an "evidentiary link between the described phenomenon and [the] project."[94] Contractors must "take the next crucial step of analyzing the specific conditions of the Project to assess the extent and impact of any condition to arrive at an appropriate inefficiency rate."[95]

Acceleration Claims and No-Damages-for-Delay Clauses

Delay and acceleration are distinct but related concepts. As demonstrated earlier, there can be no claim for constructive acceleration without excusable delay. And although delay costs, which usually include costs such as extended general conditions, material escalation, and other costs related to the project taking longer than expected, seem to be distinct from the types of costs discussed earlier, which are incurred due to speeding up work in order to complete a project in less time than expected, some courts have lumped them together as delay costs. If acceleration costs are treated as a type of delay cost, then the question arises as to whether the costs are limited by a contractual no-damages-for-delay clause.

Courts have assessed the interaction between no-damages-for-delay clauses and constructive acceleration claims in various ways. As an initial matter, some states prohibit the enforceability of no-damages-for-delay clauses as a matter of law in public construction contracts or in all construction contracts.[96] Moreover, several states have not addressed the enforceability of no-damages-for-delay clauses, and most states have not addressed the applicability of a no-damages-for-delay clause in the context of acceleration.

Some states, like New York, regard delay damages sufficiently similar to acceleration costs so as to bring the latter within the ambit of a no-damages-for-delay

93. Mechanical Contractors Association of America, *Change Orders Productivity Overtime: A Primer for the Construction Industry* (2024) (quoting MCAA Management Methods Bulletin PD2–2020).

94. *See* Danac, Inc., ASBCA No. 33394, 97-2 BCA ¶ 29,184 (denying recovery for "crew overloading" predicated on the Corps of Engineers' Modification Impact Evaluation Guide); Advanced Eng'g & Plan. Corp., Inc., ASBCA No. 53366, 05-1 BCA ¶ 32,806 ("[A]bsent proof of a causal connection between the factors used and impacted event, [industry studies] have not been well received by the Board.").

95. *See* N. Am. Mech., Inc. v. Walsch Constr. Co. II, 132 F. Supp. 3d 1064, 1081 (E.D. Wis. 2015).

96. *See, e.g.*, Howard Contracting, Inc. v. G.A. MacDonald Constr. Co., 71 Cal. App. 4th 38, 51, 83 Cal. Rptr. 2d 590, 596 (1998), *as modified* (Jan. 20, 1999) (citing Cal. Pub. Cont. Code § 7102) (California); VA Code Ann. § 2.2-4335 (Virginia); Wash. Rev. Code Ann. § 4.24.360 (Washington); Kan. Stat. Ann. § 16-1907 (Kansas); Minn. Stat. Ann. § 15.411 subdiv. 2 (Minnesota); Rev. Stat. Mo. § 8.962(2) (Missouri); O.R.S. § 279C.315 (Oregon); R.C. § 4113.62(C)(1)–(2) (Ohio).

clause.[97] Courts in other states have declined to interpret no-damages-for-delay clauses as barring acceleration damages, either because acceleration and delay are distinct concepts or because the facts of a particular case implicated an exception to the general enforceability of a no-damages-for-delay clause.[98] The Supreme Court of Mississippi, for instance, has held that an owner's "refusal to grant extensions on a timely basis can reasonably be interpreted as active interference or bad faith," an exception to the enforceability of a no-damages-for-delay clause.[99] North Carolina courts have likewise explained that a no-damages-for-delay does not necessarily bar a constructive acceleration claim because the source of the contractor's damages is the denial of a time extension, not the delay itself.[100]

The Appeals Court of Massachusetts affirmed an award of acceleration damages to a subcontractor despite a no-damages-for-delay clause in the subcontract where unrebutted evidence established that the prime contractor had indicated that no extensions of time would be granted.[101] The no-damages-for-delay clause was inapplicable for two reasons. First, the court distinguished acceleration damages from delay damages.

> [The subcontractor] was not seeking damages because it had been delayed, but rather, because it had been forced to increase its workforce due to the compression of the schedule occasioned by [the general contractor] breaches of its obligations. . . . [the general contractor's] breaches did not affect [the subcontractor's] ability to complete its work on time . . . but, rather, with its ability to complete its work on budget.[102]

97. *See, e.g.*, Bovis Lend Lease (LMB), Inc. v. Lower Manhattan Dev. Corp., 108 A.D.3d 135, 147–48 (N.Y. App. Div. 2013); Andron Constr. Corp. v. Dormitory Auth. of State of New York, 51 Misc. 3d 1217(A), 38 N.Y.S.3d 830 (N.Y. Sup. 2016).

98. *See, e.g.*, James Corp. v. N. Allegheny Sch. Dist., 938 A.2d 474, 483–87 (Pa. Commw. Ct. 2007); Ernest Bock & Sons, Inc. v. City of Phila., 239 A.3d 1144 (Pa. Commw. Ct. 2020). *See generally* C & H Elec., Inc. v. Town of Bethel, 312 Conn. 843, 847, 96 A.3d 477 (2014) (examining the exceptions to the enforceability of a no damages for delay clause in several jurisdictions).

99. Mississippi Transp. Comm'n v. SCI, Inc., 717 So. 2d 332, 339 (Miss. 1998) ("The Commission's refusal to grant extensions on a timely basis can reasonably be interpreted as active interference or bad faith and would justify a damages award. Therefore, the 'no damages for delay' provision does not preclude a damages award in this case.").

100. *See* Watson Elec. Constr. Co. v. City of Winston-Salem, 109 N.C. App. 194, 199 (1993) ("It does not follow that where the denial of a time extension is the cause in fact of plaintiff's damages, that the exclusive remedy is a time extension. At this point, damages have already been incurred in the form of acceleration costs. Because the contract does not address the issue of remedy for such a breach, the question is not one of law, but must be resolved by the finder of fact interpreting the intent of the parties.").

101. Cent. Ceilings, Inc. v. Suffolk Constr. Co., 91 Mass. App. Ct. 231, 234 (2017).

102. *Id.* at 238.

Second, the court explained that the general contractor had materially breached the contract by depriving the subcontractor of its sole contractual remedy, and under such circumstances, could not escape liability via the no-damages-for-delay clause.[103]

Some contracts contain express "no damages for acceleration" language, which could further jeopardize a contractor's ability to recover for acceleration damages.[104] At least one state has declared no-damages-for-acceleration clauses unenforceable:

> A condition, stipulation or provision in a contract or other agreement for the improvement of property or for the construction, alteration or repair of a work of improvement in this State that attempts to do any of the following is contrary to public policy and is void and unenforceable:
>
> (e) Require a prime contractor or subcontractor to waive, release or extinguish a claim or right that the prime contractor or subcontractor may otherwise possess or acquire for delay, *acceleration*, disruption or impact damages or an extension of time for delays incurred, for any delay, acceleration, disruption or impact event which was unreasonable under the circumstances, not within the contemplation of the parties at the time the contract was entered into, or for which the prime contractor or subcontractor is not responsible.[105]

Ultimately, whether a no-damages-for-delay clause will bar recovery for acceleration costs would turn upon the language of the contract, whether the state strictly construes exculpatory provisions, and the standards for invalidating a no-damages-for-delay clause applicable in the relevant jurisdiction. Contractors should be aware of these pitfalls when reviewing potential contract opportunities.

Concurrent Delay and Pacing

Recovering costs for constructive acceleration becomes more challenging in the face of concurrent delays. "If a period of delay can be attributed simultaneously to the actions of both the Government and the contractor, there are said to be concurrent delays, and the result is an excusable but not a compensable delay."[106] In the face of concurrent delays, federal contractors can recover constructive acceleration

---

103. *Id.* at 236–37.

104. *See* Estep Constr., Inc. v. Seminole Cnty., 2018 WL 7247294 (Fla. Cir. Ct. 2018) (quoting contract language that "It is expressly agreed that CONTRACTOR shall not be entitled to damages for any type of delay whatsoever under any circumstances and the CONTRACTOR expressly waives any increase in Contract Price or damages of any type on account of time impacts to the Project Schedule including, but not limited to, Contract Claims for delay, disruption, suspension, interference, inefficiency and constructive acceleration[.]").

105. Nev. R.S. § 108.2453(2) (emphasis added).

106. Morganti Nat'l, Inc. v. United States, 49 Fed. Cl. 110, 132 (2001), *aff'd*, 36 F. App'x 452 (Fed. Cir. 2002) (quoting Weaver–Bailey Contractors, Inc. v. United States, 19 Cl. Ct. 474, 476 (1990)).

costs under the Changes clause if "the record supports a clear apportionment of the delay and expense attributable to each party." [107] Constructive acceleration claims have failed due to concurrent delays because the contractor was responsible for concurrent delay during the period of acceleration[108] and where the contractor failed to adequately "recognize, account for or segregate" excusable from inexcusable delays.[109] Contractors should therefore attempt to document and apportion concurrent and sequential delays. Additionally, contractors should think twice before slowing down their own work to track owner delays (pacing) and thoroughly document any decisions to pace, lest the owner argue that the contractor concurrently delayed the project.[110]

To Accelerate or Not?

Acceleration efforts can be extremely disruptive and lead to significant costs. The complications of recovering acceleration costs are many, as set forth earlier. Owners are hesitant to direct acceleration because of the significant costs involved. Contractors are similarly hesitant to accelerate absent a direction given the challenges of proving constructive acceleration.

---

107. United Constructors, LLC v. United States, 95 Fed. Cl. 26, 40 (2010) (quoting R.J. Lanthier Co., Inc., ASBCA No. 51636, 04–1 BCA ¶ 32,481); Hemphill Contracting Co., Inc., ENGBCA Nos. 5698 et al., 94-1 BCA ¶ 26,491 at 131,853.

108. LCC-MZT Team IV v. United States, 155 Fed. Cl. 387, 485–88 (2021).

109. *See* Lovering-Johnson, Inc., ASBCA No. 53902, 06-1 BCA ¶ 33,126; John C. Grimberg Co., Inc., ASBCA No. 58791, 18-1 BCA ¶ 37,191. *But see* D.A. Nolt Inc. v. Philadelphia Mun. Auth., No. CV 18-4997, 2021 WL 6049829, at *54 (E.D. Pa. Dec. 21, 2021), *dismissed sub nom.*, No. 22-1120, 2022 WL 18457428 (3d Cir. Oct. 17, 2022) (awarding acceleration damages and observing that "[a]lthough there is reason to believe that Nolt (or its subcontractors) likely contributed in some measure to the need to accelerate, the City did not provide any factual basis on which to parse the responsibility between the City and Nolt. Therefore, the City constructively accelerated the Project and Nolt is entitled to be paid for the overtime and premium costs incurred of $44,887.54.").

110. *See* Alares Constr., Inc., CBCA 6149, 7021, 7597, 2025 WL 1208928 (Mar. 21, 2025) (explaining that contractors may pace non-critical path activities when the owner delays the critical path but "[t]o the extent that [the contractor] is arguing that it also could delay or 'pace' critical path activities when a concurrent critical path activity would have equally caused delay, it cites no support for such a proposition," and indicating the lack of evidence to show that the contractor "was simply pacing its work to account for [owner]-caused delays."); John Driggs Co., Inc., ENGBCA No. 4926, 87-2 BCA ¶ 19,833 ("When a significant owner-caused, construction delay . . . occurs, the contractor is not necessarily required to conduct all of his other construction activities exactly according to his pre-delay schedule, and without regard to the changed circumstances resulting from the delay . . . . The occurrence of a significant delay generally will affect related work, as the contractor's attention turns to overcoming the delay rather than slavishly following its now meaningless schedule."). *But see* Orlosky Inc. v. United States, 64 Fed. Cl. 63, 70 (2005) (explaining that "pacing delay analysis has not been recognized by this circuit as a method of proving causation" in a compensable delay claim).

When faced with an excusable delay and an owner refusing to extend the project completion date, the contractor must make a practical decision. And if the critical path runs through a subcontractor's work the contractor may be faced with having to direct its subcontractor to accelerate (with associated additional costs).[111] But a contractor's direction to its subcontractors to accelerate might expose the contractor to the risk of being jointly liable with the owner to compensate the subcontractor for its costs.[112]

The contractor's first option in response to these difficult conditions is often to push the owner to acknowledge the excusable delay and agree to a time extension. Absent that, the contractor is left to decide whether to accelerate or simply ignore the owner's admonitions about finishing the project on time. Not accelerating has the advantage of not incurred the significant additional costs of acceleration. However, the failure to accelerate comes with the risk of liquidated damages and default termination.

If the contractor decides that accelerating the work is the lesser of two evils, then certain steps should be taken to maximize the chances of recovering the acceleration costs in accordance with the standards set forth in this chapter. The contractor and its counsel must have a clear understanding of the specific requirements for proving constructive acceleration in the jurisdiction. The contractor should communicate clearly with the owner at every stage of the process, even if the owner is not being agreeable or responsive. The contractor should clearly track its costs and separate, where possible, the portions of the costs related to the acceleration effort.

---

111. *Compare* Robust Constr., L.L.C., ASBCA No. 54056, 05-2 BCA ¶ 33,019 (contractor directed five subcontractors to accelerate after the owner orally ordered the contractor to accelerate) *with* Utley-James, Inc., GSBCA No. 5370, 85-1 BCA ¶ 17,816, *aff'd*, 14 Cl. Ct. 804 (1988) ("[The contractor] does not point in its briefs to a single instance when it notified any of its subcontractors, formally or informally, that the Government had ordered an acceleration and that the subcontractor was therefore required to accelerate its own work.").

112. *See* Mobil Chem. Co. v. Blount Bros. Corp., 809 F.2d 1175, 1177 (5th Cir. 1987) (general contractor and owner jointly and severally liable for subcontractor's acceleration costs); Natkin & Co. v. George A. Fuller Co., 347 F. Supp. 17, 19 (W.D. Mo. 1972) (general contractor and owner jointly and severally liable for subcontractor's acceleration costs).

CHAPTER 14

Disruption Claims

Greg Holness

Introduction

Construction projects rarely progress as intended. A multitude of possible issues can derail a project, including design changes, schedule changes, and even the cumulative load of an excessive number of change orders. When one or more disruptions cause a contractor to deviate from its anticipated work plan, the effect is often increased labor and equipment costs. Because these types of expenses are typically a large portion of the overall project budget, recovery of such extra costs that are caused by others is essential in order for contractors to maintain financial viability. Unfortunately, quantifying and proving disruption claims is complicated, fact-specific, and generally requires the use of expert witnesses. Luckily, the courts do not mandate a specific way of calculating the effects of the disruptions. There are a variety of methods available and, as noted in this chapter, some of these methodologies have had more success in the courts and boards of contract appeals than others. One additional hurdle that some contractors must also overcome to recoup disruption costs are contractual provisions that may bar such claims.

Almost all aspects of disruption claims are fraught with difficulties. This chapter provides the legal practitioner with an understanding of the contours of what is required to prove (or defend) requests for additional compensation resulting from disruption.

Definition of Disruption Claim

Disruptions on construction projects result in claims that have many different names, but only minor substantive differences. At a basic level, these claims attempt to recover the cost of increased labor, and sometimes equipment, that result from disruption caused by others. A board of contract appeals succinctly stated, "Impact costs are simply increased labor costs that stem from the disruption to labor productivity resulting from a change in working conditions caused by a contract change."[1] An influential industry group likewise stated:

> Productivity loss . . . is experienced when a contractor is not accomplishing its anticipated achievable or planned rate of production and is best described as a contractor producing less than its planned output per work hour of input. Thus, the contractor is expending more effort per unit of production than originally planned. The result is a loss of money for a contractor.[2]

A proper disruption claim must tie increased labor costs to the change that caused them, and include a reasonable computation to define the quantum of damages.

Distinction from (and Frequent Relationship to) Delay

Although language used by practitioners and judges is often imprecise, there is a difference between delay and disruption on construction projects. As has been explained in the preceding chapters, delay occurs when work cannot proceed as intended and the duration of the project, or a portion of the project, is elongated. Importantly, disruption does not require an extension of the project duration.[3] One court explained the difference as follows:

> Under construction law, delay damages have a technical definition distinct from disruption damages. Delay damages refer to damages arising out of delayed completion, suspension, acceleration or disrupted performance. Disruption damages, on the other hand, are for a project that may be timely completed but nevertheless includes disruption to the contractor and compensates it for a reduction in the expected productivity of labor and equipment—a loss of efficiency measured in reduced production of units of work within a given period of time.[4]

---

1. Centex Bateson Constr. Co., VABCA Nos. 4613, et al., 99-1 BCA ¶ 30,153 at 149,257, *aff'd without opinion*, 250 F.3d 761 (Fed. Cir. 2000) ("Productivity is inversely proportional to the man-hours necessary to produce a given unit of product. As is self-evident, if productivity declines, the number of man-hours of labor to produce a given task will increase. If the number of man-hours increases, labor costs obviously increase.").

2. AACE Recommended Practice No. 25R-03, Estimating Lost Labor Productivity in Construction Claims, at 1 (2004).

3. *See* Sauer Inc. v. Danzig, 224 F.3d 1340, 1348 (Fed. Cir. 2000) (A contractor "need not establish delay to overall contract completion to succeed on its disruption claim."); Cnty. of Galveston v. Triple B Servs., LLP, 498 S.W.3d 176, 182 (Tex. App. 2016) ("A project that finishes on time but at greater expense because of disruptive events or scheduling errors presents a claim for disruption damages."); Southern Comfort Builders, Inc. v. United States, 67 Fed. Cl. 124, 145 (2005) ("[A]n overall delay in the contract is not necessary to recovery for a loss of productivity claim.").

4. Cnty. of Galveston v. Triple B Servs., LLP, 498 S.W.3d 176, 181 (Tex. App. 2016). *See also* Atlantic Coast Mech. v. R.W. Allen Beers Constr., 592 S.E.2d 115, 118 (Ga. Ct. App. 2003), quoting U.S. Indus. v. Blake Constr. Co., 671 F.2d 539, 546 (D.C. Cir. 1982) ("The fundamental distinction

This distinction is confused on projects because both delay and disruption are often experienced simultaneously,[5] and from a practical perspective, those seeking compensation for the resulting increased costs often care more about whether recovery will occur than how the type of recovery is labeled.

Disruption claims attempt to recoup the costs a contractor incurs from its inability to proceed in the manner in which it intended. This typically results in a calculation of relative efficiency of labor and sometimes equipment—a comparison of actual hours to either the contractor's anticipation at the time of bidding or the contractor's actual hours in a similar but undisrupted situation on the same project or a different project.[6]

In contrast, delay claims typically seek to recover additional time-dependent costs resulting from the extended duration of the project. In addition to increased direct costs, examples of these types of delay costs include trailers, utilities, port-o-johns, foremen's vehicles, and other field office expenses; equipment (whether rented or owned); project management and superintendence; escalated labor wages; increased cost of materials; and unabsorbed home office overhead.[7]

Because projects often involve both delay and disruption, it is best practice for the legal practitioner to understand the difference and be precise with the respective labels. Frequently, contracts treat delay claims and disruption claims differently.[8]

---

between the disruption claim and the delay claim is that '[u]nlike the delay claim, the disruption claim is intended not to redress [the subcontractor's] loss from being unable to work, but to compensate [the subcontractor] for the damages it suffered from [the contractor's] actions that made its work more difficult and expensive than [the subcontractor] anticipated and than it should have been.'"); Southwest Elec. Contracting Servs., Ltd. v. Industrial Accessories Co., 2022 WL 1468384, at *14 (W.D. Tex. May 10, 2022) ("Delay damages capture the time and cost of not being able to work whereas disruption damages capture the cost of working less efficiently than planned.").

5. *See* Cnty. of Galveston v. Triple B Servs., LLP, 498 S.W.3d 176, 181 (Tex. App. 2016), quoting Bruner & O'Connor, 5 Construction Law §§ 15:29, 15:102 & 15:103 (2002) ("Disruption damages can also be caused by an 'event [that] both disrupts and delays a critical path activity.'"); Bell BCI Co. v. United States, 72 Fed. Cl. 164, 168 (2006) ("There is a distinction in the law between: (1) a 'delay' claim; and (2) a 'disruption' or 'cumulative impact' claim. Although the two claim types often arise together in the same project, a 'delay' claim captures the time and cost of not being able to work, while a 'disruption' claim captures the cost of working less efficiently than planned.").

6. *See* the section titled "Proving Disruption Claims" later in the chapter.

7. *See* Luria Bros. & Co. v. United States, 369 F.2d 701 (Ct. Cl. 1966); J.D. Hedin Constr. Co. v. United States, 347 F.2d 235 (Ct. Cl. 1965); S. Leo Harmonay, Inc. v. Binks Mfg. Co., 597 F. Supp. 1014, 1031–37 (S.D.N.Y. 1984); Southern New England Contracting Co. v. State, 345 A.2d 550, 558–60 (Conn. 1974); Complete Gen. Constr. Co. v. Ohio Dep't of Transp., 760 N.E.2d 364 (Ohio 2002); Gladwynne Constr. Co. v. Mayor & City Council of Baltimore, 807 A.2d 1141 (Md. Ct. Spec. App. 2002).

8. *See* the section titled "Contract Provisions Regarding Loss of Productivity" later in the chapter.

Causes of Disruption

Like delays, the causes of disruption are numerous. Almost anything can upset the contractor's planned method of execution and induce extra costs. Design changes and schedule changes are the causes most often discussed in case law. Additionally, many disruption claims are premised on the cumulative effect of an excessive number of changes.

Design and Schedule Changes

Design changes and schedule changes often go hand in hand, one leading to the other, and both leading to disruptive financial consequences. In *Luria Brothers & Co. v. United States*, the owner ordered the contractor to stop subsurface foundation work when an apparent design error was suspected.[9] Subsequently, the design was changed significantly and the contractor was directed to excavate in a particular manner under the careful watch of the engineers, which, combined, caused 420 days of delay to the completion of the project.[10] While the plaintiff failed to meet its burden of proof as to damages, the court did not question whether disruption costs were recoverable, stating "when loss of productivity brought about by these conditions results from defendant's breach of contract, the plaintiff is entitled to recover its additional costs occasioned thereby as damages."[11] Similarly, the government owner in *Clark Concrete Contractors, Inc. v. General Services Administration* was found to be responsible for 185 days of delay, caused by "massive" design changes to upgrade the concrete after the work started.[12] The board in that case explained how the numerous changes to the design caused delay and disruption (including altering the planned work sequence, increasing site congestion, and waiting for the procurement of new rebar and the lifting of stop work orders), which caused the contractor to incur compensable labor inefficiency costs.[13]

Sometimes, the scale of the changes is so extreme, the court is brief in its explanation of how it affected the contractor.[14] But just because there were design changes does not mean that a contractor was actually disrupted.[15]

---

9. 369 F.2d 701 (Ct. Cl. 1966).
10. *Id.* at 706–07.
11. *Id.* at 714.
12. GSBCA No. 14340, 99-1 BCA ¶ 30,280.
13. *Id.*
14. *See* G.M. Harston Constr. Co. v. City of Chicago, 371 F. Supp. 2d 949, 952 (N.D. Ill. 2005) (design changes resulted in the project being $300 million over budget and four years late).
15. *See* Flatiron-Lane v. Case Atlantic Co., 121 F. Supp. 3d 515, 543 (M.D.N.C. 2015) (finding contractor's claims of design changes "factually untrue or exaggerated."); Pittman Constr. Co. v. United States, 2 Cl. Ct. 211, 216–17 (1983) (court "unable to find that such errors and omissions as did occur were at all out of the ordinary").

In cases involving subcontractors, the claim is often that the general contractor has not properly managed the other subcontractors, resulting in acceleration and trade stacking for the subcontractor seeking to recover disruption costs.[16] In *Central Ceilings, Inc. v. Suffolk Construction Co.*, the court concluded that the general contractor's failures to manage the work "led to loss of productivity because [the subcontractor] was required to constantly de-mobilize, re-mobilize, and alter the natural sequence of its work."[17] Likewise, in *Hensel Phelps Construction Co. v. King County*,[18] a painting subcontractor's work was accelerated from 45 days on each floor down to 19 days, and the working environment was "chaotic" as a result of trade stacking because the general contractor accelerated other subcontractors too. Not surprisingly, both factors negatively impacted the subcontractor's efficiency, resulting in "huge overruns."[19] Similarly, the court in *Capital Electric Co. v. United States* determined the electrical contractor on a multiple prime project was delayed and disrupted by a separate prime contractor's slow and erratic progress, as well as the government owner's failure to properly administer the submittal process.[20]

Cumulative Impact of Many Change Orders

One of the more difficult claims for a contractor to prove is the cumulative impact of multiple change orders. While all construction projects typically involve change orders to the original scope of work, some jobs involve so many that it becomes an exercise in futility to reasonably tie the resulting disruption costs back to each change order. One court explained as follows:

> Cumulative impact need not be traced to specific causes of increased performance costs, but can arise from changes which, when viewed retrospectively, were so many and had such effect on performance that there is a separately compensable impact claim. We do not require the specificity here that would otherwise be necessary for Appellant to prevail on entitlement. The sheer number of change orders, however, cannot establish the validity of a cumulative impact claim. Impact is not demonstrated solely by showing the number of changes or clarifications to the contract. General unsupported statements that a contractor

16. *See* Hensel Phelps Constr. Co. v. King Cnty., 787 P.2d 58 at n.1 (Wash. Ct. App. 1990) ("Stacking of trades refers to the situation of having more than one trade working in a given work area at the same time."); *see also* Central Ceilings, Inc. v. Suffolk Constr. Co., 2013 WL 8721044, at *10 (Mass. Super. Ct. Dec. 19, 2013), *aff'd*, 75 N.E.3d 40 (Mass. App. Ct. 2017), *appeal denied*, 88 N.E.3d 1167 (Mass. 2017) (referring to stacking of the trades as "the various trades were tripping over each other to complete the work and thus, there was interference with the flow of the work").

17. 2013 WL 8721044, at *6 (Mass. Super. Ct. Dec. 19, 2013).

18. 787 P.2d 58 (Wash. Ct. App. 1990).

19. *Id.* at 60.

20. 729 F.2d 743, 744 (Fed. Cir. 1984).

> suffered impact are not sufficient proof that it did, and the absence of contemporaneous documentary evidence of the disruptive effects to the work may provide reason for rejecting the claim. . . . There must be evidence of the number, timing, and effect of the changes that were issued.[21]

A board of contract appeals stated "[t]he underlying theory is that numerous changes cause a cascading ripple-type of impact on performance time and efficiency which is too uncertain or diffuse to be readily discernable at the time of pricing each individual change."[22]

In determining whether a contractor has proven a cumulative impact claim, courts often consider the number of change orders, the proportionate increase to the original contract value, and the effect on the original contract duration. For example, in *Pittman Construction Co. v. United States*, where 206 change orders were issued, increasing the contract by 12 percent ($3 million added to a $25 million contract) and extending the contract duration by 10 percent (102 days added to the original 1,000 days), the court affirmed the board's conclusion that "no fundamental change in the character of the work had taken place and thus no costs had been experienced whose likelihood had not been foreseeable."[23] The board in *McMillin Brothers Constructors, Inc.* was similarly unpersuaded that a 2.5 percent increase to the contract was sufficient to demonstrate a cumulative impact.[24] In contrast, the board in *Appeal of Ingalls Shipbuilding Division, Litton Systems, Inc.*, found several thousand change orders, and the resulting doubling of the contract value ($113 million to $209 million) that added a four-year increase in duration, to be ample evidence to allow recovery of cumulative impact costs.[25]

There is no mathematical equation or minimum percentage increase required before courts will find support for a cumulative impact claim, but obviously the

---

21. Appeal of Bechtel Nat'l, Inc., NASABCA No. 1186-7, 90–1 BCA ¶ 22,549 at 113,177. *See also* Jackson Constr. Co. v. United States, 62 Fed. Cl. 84, 103 (2004) ("An impact claim—often characterized using other names, such as, 'cumulative impact,' 'ripple effect,' 'loss of labor efficiency,' or 'loss of productivity'—is based upon the theory that individual compensable changes to a Contract, taken as a whole, can have such a disruptive effect on the contractor's performance that the contractor has a compensable claim for costs in addition to the amounts of its individual change orders.").

22. McMillin Bros. Constructors, Inc., EBCA No. 328-10-84, 91–1 BCA ¶ 23,351, citing Appeal of Fruehauf Corp., PODBCA No. 477, 74–1 BCA ¶ 10,596; Appeal of Bechtel Nat'l, Inc., NASABCA No. 1186-7, 90–1 BCA ¶ 22,549.

23. 2 Cl. Ct. 211, 217 (1983).

24. McMillin Bros. Constructors, Inc., EBCA No. 328-10-84, 91–1 BCA ¶ 23,351 ("On the whole, there is nothing in the specific changes which suggests that, despite their facially minor nature, they were capable of causing a cascading ripple effect, with attendant pricing consequences, that is a hallmark of valid cumulative impact claims."). *See also* Appeal of Montgomery-Ross-Fisher, Inc., PSBCA No. 1033, 84-2 BCA ¶ 17,492 (changes amounting to a 5 percent increase in contract found insufficient).

25. ASBCA No. 17579, 78–1 BCA ¶ 13,038.

larger the monetary difference from the original contract value or the longer the project duration is extended, the more likely a court will conclude the contractor's productivity was affected.[26] "In rare circumstances, relief for 'cumulative impact' has been granted because of the sheer number and scope of the changes. However, in the vast majority of cases such claims are routinely denied because there were an insufficient number of changes, contractor-caused concurrent delays, disruptions and inefficiencies and/or a general absence of evidence of causation and impact."[27]

Proving Disruption Claims

Generally

"Loss of productivity claims can be difficult to prove."[28] As with other types of construction litigation, the claimant must prove liability, causation, and resultant injury.[29]

> In order to recover on an impact claim, a contractor must do more than present evidence of the sheer number or scope of changes. Nor is it sufficient to compare the cost of the work, as changed, to the original contract price. A contractor must also present evidence of causation and impact. Cumulative impact claims are fact-intensive and require the contractor to substantiate its claims that its work was delayed or was performed in an inefficient, unproductive, or more costly manner as a result of the individual changes to the Contract. As one board observed, "[t]here must be testimony and contemporaneous documents evidencing the type and extent of disruption to the work, and a showing that the disruption resulted from Government actions."[30]

---

26. *See* Appeal of Montgomery-Ross-Fisher, Inc., PSBCA No. 1033, 84-2 BCA ¶ 17,492 ("There is no fixed rule setting forth the number of changes or percentage of price of changes to establish a cumulative impact due to many changes.").

27. Appeals of J.A. Jones Constr. Co., ENGBCA Nos. 6348, 6386–6391, 00–2 BCA ¶ 31,000. *See also* Jackson Constr. Co. v. United States, 62 Fed. Cl. 84, 103 (2004) (finding contractor's cumulative impact claim "does not merit serious consideration" because of a failure to prove any prerequisite, use of improper calculations, and contractor conceding it made a profit on the project).

28. Southern Comfort Builders, Inc. v. United States, 67 Fed. Cl. 124, 143 (2005).

29. *See* Wayne Knorr, Inc. v. Dep't of Transp., 973 A.2d 1061, 1098 (Pa. Commw. Ct. 2009); Wunderlich Contracting Co. v. United States, 351 F.2d 956, 968 (Ct. Cl. 1965).

30. Jackson Constr. Co. v. United States, 62 Fed. Cl. 84, 103 (2004), quoting McMillin Bros. Constructors, Inc., EBCA No. 328-10-84, 91–1 BCA ¶ 23,351 at 117,105. *See also* Mergentime Corp. v. Washington Metro. Area Transp. Auth., 400 F. Supp. 2d 145, 243 (D.D.C. 2005), *reversed on other grounds* Mergentime Corp. v. Washington Metro. Area Transp. Auth., 2006 WL 416177 (D.D.C. 2006) ("Generalized statements that it suffered an impact is not sufficient proof, and a lack of contemporaneous documents proving the disruptive effects to the work may be reason enough to reject the claim."); Appeal of Montgomery-Ross-Fisher, Inc., PSBCA No. 1033, 84-2 BCA ¶ 17,492 ("[I]mpact

In addition to obstacles with quantifying disruption damages, which are addressed later in this chapter, contractors frequently have difficulty proving the causation prong of their disruption claims because they are unable to link the defendant's actions or inactions with the damages suffered. This lack of connection proved fatal for the contractor in *Net Construction, Inc. v. C&C Rehab & Construction, Inc.* where the court found that although the claimant "established that there were delays in completing the construction project, it failed to demonstrate that its damages for lost productivity were the result of delays for which [defendant] was responsible."[31] Another example involves a road-building contractor in Pennsylvania who was unable to convince the court of a sufficient causal connection.[32]

Exact Mathematical Precision Not Required for Computation of Damages

"The burden on the contractor is not merely to show that disruption resulted from Government actions, but also to establish its extent."[33] Although the plaintiff has the burden of proving the damages resulting from the actions of the defendant, the courts recognize that quantifying this effect is usually a complex and challenging exercise.[34] Therefore, once entitlement is established, the general rule in lost productivity claims cases is that the contractor must provide sufficient evidence to allow the court to make a fair and reasonable approximation of the damages.[35]

---

is not demonstrated solely by showing the number of changes or clarifications to the contract, nor by comparing the cost of the changes to the original contract price.").

31. 256 F. Supp. 2d 350, 355 (E.D. Pa. 2003).

32. Wayne Knorr, Inc. v. Dep't of Transp., 973 A.2d 1061, 1098 (Pa. Commw. Ct. 2009) ("Here, the difficulty with Knorr's claim stems from the lack of evidence establishing a clear causal connection between the 'piecemeal fashion' in which it performed its paving work and an increase in its MPT costs above that contemplated by the Contract."); *see also* Wunderlich Contracting Co. v. United States, 351 F.2d 956, 968–69 (Ct. Cl. 1965.) ("Although we do not doubt that plaintiffs and their subcontractors encountered delays and difficulties in proceeding with the plans provided by defendant, all that plaintiffs have attempted to prove with respect to any of the major claims is the total amount of costs and the total delay experienced on the project. No satisfactory evidence has been presented to differentiate between reasonable and unreasonable government delays, or between delays attributable to defendant and delays unavoidably caused by extraneous circumstances. It is incumbent upon plaintiffs to show the nature and extent of the various delays for which damages are claimed and to connect them to some act of commission or omission on defendant's part.").

33. Appeal of Bechtel Nat'l, Inc., NASABCA No. 1186-7, 90-1 BCA ¶ 22,549 at 113,177.

34. *See* LCC-MZT Team IV v. United States, 155 Fed. Cl. 387, 495 (2021) ("Productivity is, by its very nature, difficult to measure or quantify. The impossibility of proving the amount of loss of productivity with exactitude does not bar recovery for the loss.").

35. *See* Appeal of R.W. Contracting Inc., ASBCA No. 24627, 84-2 BCA ¶ 17,302 ("Assuming causation has been established, the appellant need not prove the amount of costs incurred as a result of a claim event with absolute exactness or mathematical precision but there must be sufficient evidence to make a fair and reasonable approximation."); Electronic & Missile Facilities, Inc. v. United States, 416 F.2d 1345, 1358 (Ct. Cl. 1969), citing Specialty Assembling & Packing Co. v. United States, 355 F.2d 554, 572 (Ct. Cl. 1966) ("The ascertainment of damages, or of an equitable adjustment, is not an

Expert Testimony Generally Required

Although courts like to hear testimony from fact witnesses to understand how the work was disrupted and to what degree those on the job perceived the effects,[36] it is essential that parties asserting disruption costs employ expert testimony. "It is a rare case where loss of productivity can be proven by books and records; almost always it has to be proven by the opinions of expert witnesses."[37] "Experts are generally relied on to develop and document such claim."[38]

Any discussion of expert testimony involves the *Daubert* standard. This topic on how trial courts vet proposed expert testimony is beyond the scope of this publication, but because cases involving disruption and the resulting lost productivity almost always require the use of experts, the topic must be touched upon here to provide the reader a high-level understanding.

The key point is that the courts employ a "gatekeeping" function regarding the admission of expert witness testimony to ensure it is appropriately relevant and reliable, and if a claimant or defendant in a disruption claim case does not meet

---

exact science, and where responsibility for damage is clear, it is not essential that the amount thereof be ascertainable with absolute exactness or mathematical precision: It is enough if the evidence adduced is sufficient to enable a court or jury to make a fair and reasonable approximation."); S. Leo Harmonay, Inc. v. Binks Mfg. Co., 597 F. Supp. 1014, 1030 (S.D.N.Y. 1984), citing Story Parchment Co. v. Paterson Parchment Paper Co., 282 U.S. 555, 562 (1931) ("[T]he general rule barring recovery of uncertain damages is applicable only where damages incurred are not causally connected to the wrong; further, those damages which are definitely attributable to the wrong and only uncertain in respect of their amount are recoverable."); Luria Bros. & Co. v. United States, 369 F.2d 701, 712 (Ct. Cl. 1966) ("That loss of productivity of labor resulting from improper delays caused by defendant is an item of damage for which plaintiff is entitled to recover admits of no doubt; nor does the impossibility of proving the amount with exactitude bar recovery for the item."); James Corp. v. North Allegheny Sch. Dist., 938 A.2d 474, 495 (Pa. Commw. Ct. 2007) ("[T]he law does not require that proof of damages must conform to the standard of mathematical exactness. The law simply requires the claim be supported by a reasonable basis for the calculation."); Wunderlich Contracting Co. v. United States, 351 F.2d 956, 968 (Ct. Cl. 1965) ("A claimant need not prove his damages with absolute certainty or mathematical exactitude. It is sufficient if he furnishes the court with a reasonable basis for computation, even though the result is only approximate.").

36. *See* Mergentime Corp. v. Washington Metro. Area Transp. Auth., 400 F. Supp. 2d 145, 242 (D.D.C. 2005), *reversed on other grounds* Mergentime Corp. v. Washington Metro. Area Transp. Auth., 2006 WL 416177, (D.D.C. 2006) ("A claim of inefficiency must be proven by fact witnesses who participated in the work and can precisely describe the nature and extent of the inefficiencies.").

37. Luria Bros. & Co. v. United States, 369 F.2d 701, 713 (Ct. Cl. 1966).

38. Southern Comfort Builders, Inc. v. United States, 67 Fed. Cl. 124, 144 (2005). *See also* Flatiron-Lane v. Case Atlantic Co., 121 F. Supp. 3d 515, 543 (M.D.N.C. 2015) ("Claims for lost productivity damages, based on the measured mile method or any other method, normally require expert opinion testimony under Rule 702[.]"). *But see* Baker DC, LLC v. Baggette Constr., Inc., 378 F. Supp. 3d 399, 411 (D. Md. 2019) (Defendant "has not identified any cases that held that expert testimony is required as a matter of law. . . . I am unable to state as a matter of law that BDC cannot establish damages without offering expert testimony.").

the court's threshold to allow such testimony, the results will likely be quite grave. Between the U.S. Supreme Court's guidance in *Daubert v. Merrell Dow Pharmaceuticals, Inc.*[39] and *Kumho Tire Co. v. Carmichael*,[40] and the Advisory Committee Notes to the Federal Rules of Evidence,[41] a nonexclusive list of factors has been developed over time to assist the trial courts in administering their gatekeeping role. These factors include whether the theory or technique has been tested or peer reviewed, whether there are standards controlling the technique's operation, whether it enjoys general acceptance within the relevant scientific community, whether the expert's proposed testimony was developed independent of litigation or specifically created for use in the subject litigation, whether the expert has unjustifiably extrapolated from an accepted premise, whether the expert has adequately accounted for alternative explanations, whether the expert is exercising care as he would be outside of his paid litigation consulting, and whether the claimed field of expertise is known for reliable results for the type of opinion the expert would offer.[42]

Methods of Quantifying Lost Productivity

There are a number of methods that have been used by contractors to calculate lost productivity costs resulting from a project disruption. What follows is an explanation of how courts have viewed the most frequently utilized methods.

AACE Recommended Practice No. 25R-03

In 2004, the Association for the Advancement of Cost Engineering International (AACE), a 7,500-member association of estimators, cost control personnel, schedulers, and claims professionals, published what it termed a "recommended practice" for the industry focused on the identification of various methods for estimating

39. 509 U.S. 579, 592–94 (1993).

40. 526 U.S. 137, 147 (1999).

41. FED. R. EVID. 702 Adv. Comm. Notes (The 2023 amendments "clarify and emphasize that expert testimony may not be admitted unless the proponent demonstrates to the court that it is more likely than not that the proffered testimony meets the admissibility requirements set forth in the rule.").

42. *Id.*; *Daubert,* 509 U.S. at 592–94; *Kuhmo,* 526 U.S. at 147. *See also* Trane US Inc. v. Yearout Service, LLC, 2019 WL 2553100, at *6–7 (M.D. Ga. June 20, 2019) ("With no methodology and no factual basis for those claims, Lynn's testimony on shift work inefficiency lacks foundation, relevance, reliable principles and methods, reliable application, and helpfulness to the jury. It is clearly inadmissible. To be clear, the Court does not question Mr. Lynn's qualifications or his experience in the construction industry. His proffered testimony, however, does not pass muster under *Daubert*."); United States for Use & Benefit of Bergelectric Corp. v. Sauer, Inc., 2020 WL 470273, at *1 (N.D. Cal. Jan. 29, 2020) ("Where the matter will proceed by bench trial as in this instance, the importance of the trial court's gatekeeper role is significantly diminished . . . because, there being no jury, there is no risk of tainting the trial by exposing a jury to unreliable evidence.").

lost labor, specifically examining "the issue in terms of claims for cost recovery of lost productivity."[43] It is important to note that the purpose of this publication was not to define how one should properly perform the various analytical methods. Instead, AACE's intent was to identify and discuss the different methodologies and rank them based on reliability, professional acceptance, case law, and construction claims literature.[44]

Prior to publication, draft versions of RP No. 25R-03 were peer reviewed by many of its members. The ultimate product is a concise summary of the available methods for quantifying lost productivity claims. AACE grouped 21 methods for quantifying lost productivity into six categories and organized them into descending order of preference. At the top (most preferred), are the project specific studies including the measured mile study. The next category in preference is the project comparison studies, which include the comparable work study and the comparable project study. AACE found industry studies in the middle, and cost basis methods such as the total cost and modified total cost being preferred only over the productivity impact on schedule analysis.[45]

A substantial factor in AACE's perspective is how prevalent and detailed the contemporaneous project records are. "[W]hen a dispute arises over lost productivity, calculations based upon contemporaneously created project documentation from the project in dispute, supported by personnel who were actually involved in the project and disputed work activities are the most credible."[46] The measured mile method is most preferred—and most accepted by the courts—in large part because it is based on such documents and testimony. On the other end of the spectrum, the total cost method is used only when entitlement and causation have been demonstrated, but the project documentation is insufficient to support more meaningful damages calculations.[47]

While no reference by courts or boards to the AACE recommended practice on methods of quantifying lost productivity could be found,[48] this publication is well written and can educate the legal practitioner, as well as provide solid reasoning to support or attack a particular methodology used in a particular case. In a

43. AACE Recommended Practice No. 25R-03 Estimating Lost Labor Productivity in Construction Claims, at 3 (2004).

44. *Id.*

45. *Id.* at 8–9.

46. *Id.* at 11.

47. *Id.* at 15–16.

48. The reasons for this are not clear to the author.

similar vein, AACE has also published RP No. 130R-23 to provide guidance on the process to demonstrate entitlement to cumulative impact claims.[49]

Measured Mile

The most widely accepted method for quantifying lost labor productivity is what is called the measured mile,[50] which compares impacted periods and unimpacted periods of similar work performed by the contractor on the project.[51] By doing so, the contractor attempts to show that the difference in productivity (i.e., the excess hours) is a result of the impact.

49. AACE Recommended Practice No. 130R-23 Demonstrating Entitlement to Cumulative Impact Claims in Construction, at 2 (2023) ("Due to the complicated nature of construction work, it is not usually well understood by contracting parties and even legal professionals. Cumulative impact, when it occurs on a construction project, is often referred to as an indirect disruption or loss of productivity claim.").

50. *See* Luria Bros. & Co. v. United States, 369 F.2d 701 (Ct. Cl. 1966) ("The use of a 'measured mile' analysis developed by a qualified expert is recognized as the most reliable, though not exact, methodology to quantify labor inefficiency."); United States for Use & Benefit of Southern Site & Underground, Inc. v. McCarthy Improvement Co., 2017 WL 10434414, at *5 (M.D. Fla. Feb. 3, 2017), quoting 5 Philip L. Bruner & Patrick J. O'Connor, Jr., Bruner & O'Connor Construction Law § 15:116 (2016) ("A measured-mile analysis is the measure viewed judicially as most acceptable for proving loss of productivity damages."); James Corp. v. North Allegheny Sch. Dist., 938 A.2d 474, 495 (Pa. Commw. Ct. 2007) ("When a contractor alleges a loss of productivity, the measured mile approach is the preferred method of computing damages."); Wood Elec., Inc. v. Ohio Facilities Constr. Comm'n, 90 N.E.3d 371, 377 (Ohio Ct. App. 2017) (the measured mile analysis "is the industry-preferred method of calculating damages under such circumstances"); Bell BCI Co. v. United States, 81 Fed. Cl. 617, 637 (2006), *aff;d in part, vacated in part, remanded*, 570 F.3d 1337 (Fed. Cir. 2009) (The "'measured mile' approach for measuring productivity is an accepted method to prove a cumulative impact claim.").

51. *See In re* Elec. Machinery Enterprises, Inc., 416 B.R. 801, 853 (Bankr. M.D. Fla. 2009) ("A measured mile analysis, for example, compares an area of work where the trade contractor is able to achieve anticipated or normal productivity, called the 'baseline,' against the areas in which the trade contractor is impacted."); Clark Concrete Contractors, Inc. v. Gen. Servs. Admin., GSBCA No. 14340, 99-1 BCA ¶ 30,280 ("The purpose of a measured mile analysis is to permit a comparison of the labor costs of performing work during different periods of time, so as to show the extent to which costs increased from a standard during periods impacted by certain actions."); James Corp. v. North Allegheny Sch. Dist., 938 A.2d 474, 495 (Pa. Commw. Ct. 2007) ("Stated simply, this approach compares the cost of completing work not subject to delay or acceleration with costs of completing work during a period of impact, the difference representing the measure of damages."); Wood Elec., Inc. v. Ohio Facilities Constr. Comm'n, 90 N.E.3d 371, 377 (Ohio Ct. App. 2017) ("The 'measured mile' is performed by calculating the productivity of the work force on the project at times when they were not impacted by whatever conditions occasioned the claim, comparing that level of productivity to times when they were impacted."); Appeal of Clark Constr. Group, Inc., VABCA No. 5674, 00-1 BCA ¶ 30,870, *reconsideration denied, In re* Appeal of Clark Constr., Inc., VABCA No. 5674R, 00-2 BCA ¶ 30,997 ("A measured mile analysis compares work performed in one period not impacted by events causing a loss of productivity with the same or comparable work performed in another period that was impacted by productivity affecting events.").

The unimpacted period of work is called the baseline. Although the baseline work and the impacted work need not be identical,[52] they must be similar enough to make the comparison of productivity (labor per unit performed) meaningful.[53] One court explained this as follows:

> The measured mile method is a technique where an expert compares unimpacted construction work to work that has been disrupted and measures the difference. The assumption is that the difference between the labor or equipment hours in the unimpacted and impacted work represents the loss to the contractor. It is a recognized and accepted method of calculating loss of productivity. But as a matter of common sense, for the measured mile method to work the impacted and unimpacted activities being compared must be reasonably similar.[54]

Where the two sets of work are not similar enough, the court will reject the measured mile comparison. This occurred in *P.W. Construction, Inc. v. United States*, where the claimant's expert compared an unimpacted period of pipe installation that did not include intensive welding and trenching work with an impacted period that had such work.[55] Similarly, a comparison between a contractor's work and its subcontractor's similar work was found to be "fundamentally flawed."[56]

An important aspect of why the measured mile method is preferred by the courts is that its foundation is based upon project records of labor hours and

---

52. *In re* P.J. Dick Inc., VABCA No. 5597 et al., 01-2 BCA ¶ 31,647, *aff'd in part, vacated in part, rev'd in part*, 324 F.3d 1364 (Fed. Cir. 2003) ("We find no basis to conclude that . . . exactly the same work is a prerequisite for a valid measured mile analysis to establish the amount loss of productivity."); Clark Concrete Contractors, Inc. v. Gen. Servs. Admin., GSBCA No. 14340, 99-1 BCA ¶ 30,280 ("We would be surprised to learn that work performed in periods being compared is ever identical on a construction project, however. And it need not be; the ascertainment of damages for labor inefficiency is not susceptible to absolute exactness.").

53. *See* P.W. Constr., Inc. v. United States, 53 Fed. Appx 555, 557 (Fed. Cir. 2002), quoting Thomas E. Shea, *Proving Productivity Losses in Government Contracts*, 18 Pub. Cont. L.J. 414, 426 (1989) ("The type of work must be equivalent for the pre- and post-disruption periods in order to allow a fair comparison. It would not be valid to compare the rate for the production of large widgets during the pre-disruption (normal) period with the production of smaller widgets during the disruption period."); *In re* P.J. Dick Inc., VABCA No. 5597 et al., 01-2 BCA ¶ 31,647, *aff'd in part, vacated in part, rev'd in part*, 324 F.3d 1364 (Fed. Cir. 2003) ("A measured mile . . . analysis generally presumes that the labor costs or productivity rates being compared are for the same work."); Clark Concrete Contractors, Inc. v. Gen. Servs. Admin., GSBCA No. 14340, 99-1 BCA ¶ 30,280 ("We will accept a comparison if it is between kinds of work which are reasonably alike, such that the approximations it involves will be meaningful."). *See also* James Corp. v. North Allegheny Sch. Dist., 938 A.2d 474, 495 (Pa. Commw. Ct. 2007).

54. JH Kelly, LLC v. AECOM Tech. Servs., Inc., 605 F. Supp. 3d 1295, 1310 (N.D. Cal. 2022), citing United States for the Use of Salinas Constr., Inc. v. W. Sur. Co., 2016 WL 3632487, at *3 (W.D. Wash. July 7, 2016).

55. 53 Fed. Appx 555, 557 (Fed. Cir. 2002).

56. Southern Comfort Builders, Inc. v. United States, 67 Fed. Cl. 124, 150 (2005).

equipment usage. A properly conducted measured mile analysis shows the number of hours expended per unit of production, but in order to do this, the contractor must have sufficient documentation. Often the contractor will have payroll data that can allow an expert to compute the number of hours within the baseline and impacted periods, but if the records do not allow for geographical specificity within the project, or if the records do not demonstrate the correlation between the disrupting impact and the resulting increase in hours, the measured mile analysis will fail. Court opinions sometimes note that the claimant's expert tried to perform this analysis but "the type of detailed records necessary to do so did not exist,"[57] or "he lacked sufficient data to permit him to render a professional opinion that would allow his measured mile analysis to stand on its own,"[58] or even that "it was impossible to do a measured-mile analysis."[59]

Comparison to Similar Projects

A method that is akin to the measured mile involves a study of similar work on a comparable project or projects. This approach may be employed when disruption or another factor has caused there to be no unimpacted period of work to which a comparison can be made. But the projects must be similar enough to make the comparison of value. It is easier to make such a comparison with activities that do not vary considerably from one project to the next. For example, road paving provides an opportunity to meaningfully compare different projects. While there are some differences between paving projects, it is not out of the norm to have very alike paving projects. Another example is comparison of the same project in different locations, such as retail stores or residential developments. In these situations, in addition to the work being very nearly the same, the contractors often have historical records to show repeatedly achieved productivity rates to which divergence can be highlighted.

Comparing the relative productivity of many other activities on different projects proves problematic because of the unique nature of construction that results in dissimilar physical environments, distinct working conditions, or even diverse weather conditions. For example, in *Fireman's Fund Insurance Co. v. United States*, because there was no unimpacted period for the expert to compare, a similar project's concrete finishing productivity was compared without success.[60] The court

57. Central Ceilings, Inc. v. Suffolk Constr. Co., 75 N.E.3d 40, 49 (Mass. App. Ct. 2017), *aff'd*, 75 N.E.3d 40 (Mass. App. Ct. 2017), *appeal denied*, 88 N.E.3d 1167 (Mass. 2017).

58. North American Mech., Inc. v. Walsh Constr. Co. II, 132 F. Supp. 3d 1064, 1080 (E.D. Wis. 2015).

59. City of Cincinnati v. Triton Servs., Inc., 140 N.E.3d 1249, 1257 (Ohio Ct. App. 2019).

60. 92 Fed. Cl. 598 (2010).

noted multiple deficiencies in the analysis including utilizing "projects of questionable comparability."[61]

Industry Studies

Continuing down AACE's list of methods of calculating disruption costs, there are a variety of industry groups that have developed studies of lost productivity. These are less favored by the courts than the measured mile method or comparisons of work between similar projects because these industry studies are not grounded upon the contractor's actual project records, but instead rely upon what a "typical" contractor may experience in a similar situation. Additionally, the source of the data in these studies is not always clearly identified or is based on surveys of association membership (which typically are based upon respondents' generalized perceptions). Further, because the application of the impacted productivity factors in these guides is subjective—whereby using an increased percentage of lost productivity directly increases the contractors' claim amount and is therefore an incentive for unscrupulous claimants to conclude the disruptions' effects are more "severe" than "moderate" or "minor"—how these studies are applied is usually closely scrutinized by the courts.

While caution is utilized to assess the appropriateness of particular construction industry studies in calculating impact claims, courts and boards do employ these to assist with the quantification of lost productivity, often where other means of doing so are not available.[62]

The most well-known lost productivity study is from the Mechanical Contractors Association of America (MCAA). Although its use with claims is not as prevalent, the National Electrical Contractors Association (NECA) also has published its own similar studies.

MCAA's Management Methods Manual

Since 1971, the MCAA periodically publishes its Management Methods Manual, in which it advises its members—generally contractors engaged in heating, air conditioning, refrigeration, plumbing, piping, and mechanical services—on a plethora of topics including the quantification of the effects of a variety of impacts encountered on construction projects.

In the most recent version, the MCAA provides "Factors Affecting Labor Productivity" as a menu of 16 disruptions: stacking of trades, morale and attitude,

---

61. *Id.* at 703.

62. *See* Appeal of Clark Constr. Group, Inc., VABCA No. 5674, 00-1 BCA ¶ 30,870, *reconsideration denied, In re* Appeal of Clark Constr., Inc., VABCA No. 5674R, 00-2 BCA ¶ 30,997; Appeal of Fire Sec. Sys., Inc., VABCA No. 3086, 91-2 BCA ¶ 23,743.

reassignment of manpower, crew size inefficiency, concurrent operations, dilution of supervision, learning curve, errors and omissions, beneficial occupancy, joint occupancy, site access, logistics, fatigue, ripple, overtime, and season and weather change.[63] A contractor implementing the MCAA's guidance decides which of those factors were present on a particular disrupted project, and also to what extent those factors affected the contractor's productivity, choosing from three options: minor, moderate, or severe. For each factor, the MCAA has listed the "percent loss" based on severity. For example, if stacking of trades[64] was present, the percent loss of labor productivity according to MCAA is between 10 percent (minor) and 30 percent (severe). Similarly, if errors and omissions[65] were present, the percent loss is shown as between 1 percent (minor) and 3 percent (severe). The factors are additive, so the presence of multiple factors results in an increased percent lost.

Courts and boards who have considered the MCAA factors in connection with contractors seeking to use them to prove the quantum of their impact claims have come to different conclusions. Where the combination of multiple factors resulted in a purported 340 percent total disruption and the calculation was performed by the contractor's president, the Armed Services Board of Contract Appeals rejected the MCAA methodology and chose a jury verdict perspective to award a substantially decreased amount of lost productivity to the contractor that had proven entitlement to damages.[66] Another board of appeals accepted the application of a 10 percent inefficiency factor for being required to use a less efficient crew size, but was "not persuaded that the severity of the weather has been shown to justify application of the thirty percent factor across the board" and instead found a 25 percent inefficiency should be applied.[67] A Wisconsin court rejected the attempted use of the MCAA factors because the plaintiff's consultant failed to explain why certain disruptive factors were not capable of being anticipated at the time of bid and failed to convince the court he sufficiently analyzed the specific project conditions to

---

63. 2015 MCAA Management Methods Manual, Bulletin PD2 (2011) Revised Factors Affecting Labor Productivity.

64. MCAA defines the Stacking of Trades factor as "Operations take place within physically limited space with other contractors. Results in congestion of personnel, inability to locate tools conveniently, increased loss of tools, additional safety hazards and increased visitors. Optimum crew size cannot be utilized."

65. MCAA defines the Errors and Omissions factor as "Increases in errors and omissions because changes usually performed on crash basis, out of sequence or cause dilution of supervision or any other negative factors."

66. Appeals of States Roofing Corp., ASBCA No. 54860, 10-1 BCA ¶ 34,356 ("We . . . reject the MCCA [sic] analysis here, inasmuch as it was performed not by an expert, but by [the contractor's] president, Mr. DeLauney, making it impossible for us to disregard the inherent subjectivity. Indeed, his analysis produced an impact of such magnitude as to reflect a total lack of reliability.").

67. Stroh Corp. v. Gen. Servs. Admin., GSBCA No. 11029, 96-1 BCA ¶28265 (Mar. 29, 1996).

allow him to appropriately select the extent and impact of the different factors.[68] Other cases involve a philosophical dismissal of the MCAA factor concept, which can be summarized as an objection to the methodology's subjectivity.[69]

The use of the MCAA factors have been approved where the contractor utilized the MCAA factors for pricing change orders and the owner approved this method throughout the project,[70] where no better basis was available to calculate undeniable productivity losses,[71] where a 30 percent MCAA loss factor was sup-

---

68. North American Mech., Inc. v. Walsh Constr. Co. II, 132 F. Supp. 3d 1064, 1081 (E.D. Wis. 2015).

69. *See* Norment Sec. Grp., Inc. v. Ohio Dep't of Rehabilitation & Correction, 2003 WL 22890088, at *7 (Ohio Ct. Cl. Dec. 2, 2003) ("[T]he court finds that plaintiff's calculations that were based upon data contained in the MCA manual are arbitrary and speculative and do not represent a reliable measure of damages. Specifically, plaintiff's estimate of the subjective factors that are quantified in the manual, such as attitude and morale, were not supported by the greater weight of the evidence."); *In re* Elec. Machinery Enterprises, Inc., 416 B.R. 801, 854 (Bankr. M.D. Fla. 2009), *order aff'd in part*, 474 B.R. 778 (M.D. Fla. 2012) ("The problem with the factor analysis method . . . is that in situations like this where there are multiple concurrent impacts, . . . it is extremely difficult to determine what percentage to apply and can be far too subjective. . . . Assigning responsibility when concurrent impacts affect each crew can be highly subjective and impracticable to apply. Accordingly, the Court concludes that it is inappropriate to use the factor analysis method to measure damages in this case."); Trane US Inc. v. Yearout Serv., LLC, 2019 WL 2553100, at *3 (M.D. Ga. June 20, 2019) (finding it "could not conclude that this methodology has any reliability" and noting "MCAA is a trade organization for mechanical contractors. The overarching purpose of the MCAA bulletins is to provide mechanical contractors with negotiating tools: primarily prospectively, to obtain more favorable contract terms, but also retrospectively, to support claims for additional compensation. The bulletins are not, nor do they purport to be, peer-reviewed studies determining whether overtime and shift work 'inefficiencies' exist and, if they do, how these 'costs' can be calculated."); AABCO Sheet Metal Sys. v. City Univ. Constr. Fund, 2022 NY slip op. 30749(U), Index No. 157183/2021, at *13 (rejecting claim based upon MCAA factors in part because "the information contained in the MCAA Factors was gathered anecdotally from a number of highly experienced members of the MCAA's Management Methods Committee. MCAA does not have in its possession any records indicating that a statistical or other type of empirical study was undertaken in order to determine the specific factors or the percentages of loss associated with individual factors."). *See also* Nova Group/Tutor-Saliba v. United States, 159 Fed. Cl. 1, 59 (Fed. Cl. 2022) (Claimant's expert testified that the use of MCAA factors "was a great method for looking forward in time, but because . . . this is after the fact, this is a forensic analysis, we have actual data, a more accurate method would be to use either measured mile or the modified total cost approach."). *But see* JH Kelly, LLC v. AECOM Tech. Servs., Inc., 605 F. Supp. 3d 1295, 1312 (N.D. Cal. 2022) (finding "no basis to conclude that MCAA factors analysis per se fails to satisfy *Daubert* standard").

70. Appeal of Fire Sec. Sys., Inc., VABCA No. 3086, 91-2 BCA ¶ 23,743 ("While the Government's apparent recognition of these factors in negotiating [change orders] does not automatically establish the reasonableness of using the MCA productivity factors in this appeal, it does provide evidence that the MCA factors are a reasonable starting point for the Board's analysis. We also note that the Government has provided no testimony or evidence that the MCAA productivity factors are flawed or unreasonable.").

71. Appeal of Clark Constr. Group, Inc., VABCA No. 5674, 00-1 BCA ¶ 30,870, *reconsideration denied*, *In re* Appeal of Clark Constr., Inc., VABCA No. 5674R, 00-2 BCA ¶ 30,997 ("We will utilize

ported by on-site witness testimony and the contractor's payroll ledger,[72] and where the contractor's use of conservative MCAA factors was pitted against the owner's contention that CPM schedules could adequately compute lost productivity.[73]

NECA's Manual of Labor Units

Like the MCAA, the NECA has published variously named studies since 1983 to guide its membership of electrical contractors on how to price work, and, with regard to lost productivity, the labor associated with electrical work under different conditions.[74] Ostensibly, these guides are for use in pricing future work (bids and change orders) but have on occasion been utilized to support claims for lost productivity. Courts, however, have roundly rejected this after-the-fact use.[75] In *Norment Security Group, Inc. v. Ohio Department of Rehabilitation & Correction*, the court rejected the contractor's use of a NECA guide to price extended overtime inefficiencies and productivity losses, stating the evidence was "insufficient."[76] The board of contract appeals in *Appeals of Hoffman Construction Co.* concluded the NECA manual did not provide a more equitable estimate of the damages than a competing quantification based partially on contemporaneous documents and actual costs.[77]

---

the productivity factors from the MCAA Manual as the best method to arrive at me percentage estimates of PKC's and USM's undeniable productivity losses. We find no other basis in the record on which we could better calculate the amount of PKC's productivity losses.").

72. S. Leo Harmonay, Inc. v. Binks Mfg. Co., 597 F. Supp. 1014 (S.D.N.Y. 1984), *aff'd without opinion*, 762 F.2d 990 (2d Cir. 1985) ("[P]laintiff's Payroll Ledger recorded a disproportionate inefficiency . . . when the work crew had to be increased from 26 people to 98. Furthermore, the 30 percent figure is buttressed by the on-site observations of Leo Harmonay and Klapp, who estimated that percentage of average inefficiency for the full acceleration period.").

73. Hensel Phelps Constr. Co. v. Gen. Servs. Admin., GSBCA No. 14744, 01-1 BCA ¶ 31,249, *aff'd*, 36 Fed. Appx. 649 (Fed. Cir. 2002) ("The data available in a properly maintained and updated CPM schedule may in theory hold great promise as a tool for assessing labor inefficiencies. . . . Instead, we have considerably more confidence, at least in this case, in the use of the MCAA inefficiency factors by appellant's expert—particularly in view of his extensive personal experience in the mechanical construction field.").

74. *Rate of Manpower Consumption in Electrical Construction* published in 1983; *Overtime and Productivity in Electrical Construction* published in 2004 and 2010; NECA Manual of Labor Units.

75. *But see* Appeals of the Fluor Corp., ENGBCA No. 2516 et al., 1968 WL 435, *vacated on other grounds*, ASBCA No. 13166, 69-1 BCA ¶ 7,626 ("[W]e do not consider that the NECA manual, or any other guide, is for automatic application in determining the effect that long work weeks have on a worker's productivity. . . . However, because of all the uncertainties as to loss of productivity due to long work weeks, we accept in principle the formulae which Mr. Cutler has determined represents the loss of efficiency attributable to long work weeks.").

76. 2003 WL 22890088, at *3–4 (Ohio Ct. Cl. Dec. 2, 2003).

77. DOTBCA 94-3 BCA ¶ 27,246, 1994 WL 577236 (noting the "use of the NECA Manual requires the exercise of subjective judgment both in selecting the appropriate column of recommended labor units and in adjusting the recommended labor units to account for particular factors which make the work more difficult than reflected by the recommended labor units.").

Total Cost Method

One of the most straightforward ways of calculating lost productivity costs is the total cost method. It is simply a comparison between the contractor's estimated costs and its actual costs. For good reason, this approach is generally met with significant scrutiny by the courts.[78] The primary objection is that "it blandly *assumes*—that every penny of the plaintiff's costs are prima facie reasonable, that the bid was accurately and reasonably computed, and that the plaintiff is not responsible for any increases in cost."[79] But courts recognize that there are times when a contractor proves entitlement to damages, but is hampered by the lack of a typical method that adequately calculates those damages.[80] As a result, courts generally employ the total cost approach "in those extraordinary circumstances where no other way to compute damages was feasible and where the trial court employed proper safeguards."[81]

---

78. *See* Servidone Constr. Corp. v. United States, 931 F.2d 860, 861 (Fed. Cir. 1991) ("A trial court must use the total cost method with caution and as a last resort."); Delco Electronics Corp. v. United States, 17 Cl. Ct. 302, 327 (1989) ("For good reason, courts and boards view the total cost approach with a jaundiced eye."); John F. Harkins Co. v. Sch. Dist. of Philadelphia, 460 A.2d 260, 263 (Pa. Super. Ct. 1983) ("[B]ecause the total cost method of measuring damages is imprecise it is fraught with danger and must be applied with caution."); U.S. Industries, Inc. v. Blake Constr. Co., 671 F.2d 539, 547 (D.C. Cir. 1982) ("The method is disfavored because it assumes that the defendant's breach was the cause of all the extra cost."); Sunshine Constr. & Eng'g, Inc. v. United States, 64 Fed. Cl. 346, 371 (2005), citing Hi-Shear Tech. Corp. v. United States, 356 F.3d 1372, 1383 (Fed. Cir. 2004) ("A total cost method is not favored and should not be used where another, more reliable, method is available by which to compute a contractor's damages."); Rand Constr. Co. v. Caravan Ingredients, Inc., 662 S.W.3d 44, 53 (Mo. Ct. App. 2022) (noting "case law indicates the total cost method and its 'all-or-nothing' approach lacks the specificity to prove damages with reasonable certainty.").

79. Youngdale & Sons Constr. Co. v. United States, 27 Fed. Cl. 516, 541 (1993). *See also* Penzel Constr. Co. v. Jackson R-2 School Dist., 544 S.W.3d 214, 234 (Mo. Ct. App. 2017) ("This approach presumes that the breaching party is the *sole and exclusive* cause of the non-breaching party's damages, even though the additional costs incurred by the contractor could have actually been caused or contributed to by a myriad of factors.").

80. *See* Scherbenske Excavating, Inc. v. North Dakota State Highway Dep't, 365 N.W.2d 485, 489 (N.D. 1985) ("[T]he total cost theory is premised on the principle that where a contractor is entitled to damages, the governmental body should not be exonerated merely because the contractor cannot prove his increased costs with precision."); Amp-Rite Elec. Co. v. Wheaton Sanitary Dist., 580 N.E.2d 622, 640 (Ill. App. Ct. 1991) ("The total cost method is premised on the principle that, where a contractor is entitled to an adjustment, the contracting entity should not be relieved of its liability for same merely because the contractor is unable to prove its increased costs within a mathematical certainty.").

81. Servidone Constr. Corp. v. United States, 931 F.2d 860, 861–62 (Fed. Cir. 1991), citing Great Lakes Dredge & Dock Co. v. United States, 96 F. Supp. 923, 926 (Ct. Cl. 1951), *cert. denied*, 342 U.S. 953 (1952); Boyajian v. United States, 423 F.2d 1231, 1241 (Ct. Cl. 1970). *See also* WRB Corp. v. United States, 183 Ct. Cl. 409, 426 (1968) ("This theory has never been favored by the court and has been tolerated only when no other mode was available.").

Elements

In order for a contractor to recover under the total cost approach, it must prove (1) it was impossible or highly impracticable to calculate actual damages; (2) the bid estimate was realistic; (3) the actual costs are reasonable; and (4) it was not responsible for the added costs.[82]

Impossible or Highly Impracticable to Calculate Actual Damages

Because of the general distaste for using the total cost method except where absolutely necessary, a contractor must show the impracticability of computing the actual damages by other means.[83] Court opinions often focus on whether it was practical for the contractor to maintain records to allow for a direct correlation between the disrupting event and the resulting costs.[84]

For example, in *Delco Electronics Corp. v. United States*, despite the government insisting the court find the contractor's failure to segregate costs associated with the changes on the job was fatal, the court determined that because "all of the work was changed work," the contractor satisfied the first element, stating:

---

82. *See* JMR Constr. Corp. v. Env'l Assessment & Remediation Mgmt., Inc., 243 Cal. App. 4th 571, 589 (Cal. Ct. App. 2015), quoting Amelco Elec. v. City of Thousand Oaks, 27 Cal. 4th 228, 243, 38 P.3d 1120 (Cal. 2002); Youngdale & Sons Constr. Co. v. United States, 27 Fed. Cl. 516, 541 (1993); WRB Corp. v. United States, 183 Ct. Cl. 409, 426 (1968); Delco Electronics Corp. v. United States, 17 Cl. Ct. 302, 327–28 (1989); Municipality of Anchorage v. Frank Coluccio Constr. Co., 826 P.2d 316, 325 (Alaska 1992); Omaha Public Power Dist. v. Darin & Armstrong, Inc., 288 N.W.2d 467, 476 (Neb. 1980); Jackson Constr. Co. v. United States, 62 Fed. Cl. 84, 104 (2004).

83. *See* U.S. for and on behalf of Delta Metals, Inc. v. R. M. Wells Co., 497 F. Supp. 541, 545 (S.D. Ga. 1980) ("[C]entral to allowance of the total cost method is whether alternative means exist to determine damages with a greater degree of particularity and accuracy."); Certified Power Sys., Inc. v. Dominion Energy Brayton Point, LLC, 2012 WL 384600, at *68 (Mass. Super. Ct. Jan. 3, 2012), citing PHILIP L. BRUNER & PATRICK J. O'CONNOR, BRUNER & O'CONNOR ON CONSTRUCTION LAW § 19:93, at 295 (2002) ("The predicate for use of this measure of damages is a showing that given the nature of the contractor's losses, it is impossible or highly impracticable to determine damages on a segregated basis under the circumstances of the case. The contractor must demonstrate that the costs incurred in performing the original work and the extra work became so inextricably intertwined that segregating damages is impracticable.").

84. *See* Boyajian v. United States, 423 F.2d 1231, 1244 (Ct. Cl. 1970) ("[T]he mere fact that plaintiff's books and records do not, in segregated form, show the amounts of the increased costs attributable to the breaches give it automatic license to use the 'total cost' method. Contractors rarely keep their books in such fashion. Such failure, however, normally does not prevent the submission of reasonably satisfactory proof of increased costs incurred during certain contract periods or flowing from certain events based, for instance, on acceptable cost allocation principles or on expert testimony."); Flatiron-Lane v. Case Atlantic Co., 121 F. Supp. 3d 515, 557 (M.D.N.C. 2015) ("Where a party simply fails to preserve records that with diligence it could have kept, impracticability cannot be shown.").

> To attempt to segregate delay and lost time, set up and breakdown estimates, delay in transit from one location to another on site and loss of efficiency as opposed to normal time would be a wasteful exercise for, in the end, the result should approach the total cost actually experienced. Had we some period of performance free of the dispute we might be better able to judge the damages based on estimates. It is impractical if not impossible to determine with any real degree of accuracy the contract work from the extra work.[85]

Similarly, when presented with a project where "the physical site was like a bomb hit it" due to numerous impacts, another court determined it was impossible or highly impracticable for the contractor to compute its losses with a reasonable degree of accuracy, and therefore allowed the use of the total cost method.[86] In another case where the contractor met its burden on this element, the court commented "[i]n short, . . . it would be easier for plaintiff to identify the items of contract performance that proceeded as planned, rather than the difference in costs between all aspects of the original plan and the work that the deviations occasioned."[87] Other courts finding the contractor has sufficiently addressed this element have done so summarily.[88]

---

85. Delco Electronics Corp. v. United States, 17 Cl. Ct. 302, 328 (1989), quoting Robert McMullan & Sons, Inc., ASBCA No. 19129, 76–2 BCA ¶ 12,072.

86. Amp-Rite Elec. Co. v. Wheaton Sanitary Dist., 580 N.E.2d 622, 641 (Ill. App. Ct. 1991). *See also* State Highway Comm'n of Wyoming v. Brasel & Sims Constr. Co., 688 P.2d 871, 878–79 (Wyo. 1984) ("[W]e know of no precise formula by which the costs of coping with insufficient water and adulterated gravel can be isolated from those costs which [contractor] would have incurred in the absence of the department's breach. The pervasive nature of the problems rendered an exact calculation of losses impossible or highly impracticable."); New Pueblo Constructors, Inc. v. *State*, 696 P.2d 185, 195 (Ariz. 1985) ("Most of the additional expenses were caused by an invisible, rising subterranean water table, so that segregating and precisely recording rework costs and original work costs was impracticable.").

87. Baldi Bros. Constructors v. United States, 50 Fed. Cl. 74, 80 (2001).

88. *See* Servidone Constr. Corp. v. United States, 19 Cl. Ct. 346, 385 (1990) ("The first element is easily satisfied. It would be impossible to isolate the incremental impact of the nature of the changed condition."); J.D. Hedin Constr. Co. v. United States, 347 F.2d 235, 247 (Ct. Cl. 1965) ("The exact amount of additional work which plaintiff had to perform as a result of the foundation problem is difficult, if not impossible, to determine because of the nature of the corrective work which was being performed. . . . There is no precise formula by which these additional costs can be computed and segregated from those costs which plaintiff would have incurred if there had been no government-caused difficulties."); *In re* Elec. Machinery Enterprises, Inc., 416 B.R. 801, 853 (Bankr. M.D. Fla. 2009) ("In a case such as this, where the damage was caused by a continuing failure to coordinate the work of trade contractors, an incident-by-incident approach to damages cannot accurately compensate the aggrieved party. The damages incurred by [contractor] were pervasive throughout the project."); Central Ceilings, Inc. v. Suffolk Constr. Co., 75 N.E.3d 40, 49 (Mass. App. Ct. 2017), *aff'd*, 75 N.E.3d 40 (Mass. App. Ct. 2017), *appeal denied*, 88 N.E.3d 1167 (Mass. 2017) (referencing "the pervasive nature of Suffolk's breaches made it impossible to identify an adequate baseline for assessing damages on an event-by-event basis").

There are times when contractors have simply been unable to prove this prong, and courts have not been generous in describing such a failure.[89] In one case, the Supreme Court of Alaska found the contractor did not satisfy the requirement that the total cost method be the only available way of computing the damages, because although the contractor's expert presented to the court his total cost analysis, he had also put together a separate computation based on actual costs that was not allowed in evidence because it was created after discovery closed. The court there concluded that if such a calculation based on actual costs was performed, then the total cost method necessarily could not be impossible or highly impracticable.[90] Similarly, another court found an expert's testimony that there was no other method available to calculate loss productivity unconvincing because there was clearly an unimpacted period of the project where the contractor stated things "went beautifully," from which the contractor could have performed a measured mile analysis if it wanted.[91]

Bid Estimate Was Realistic

The foundation on which the total cost method is built is that the contractor's bid estimate is realistic.[92] If it is not, then recovery will typically be denied under

89. *See* Youngdale & Sons Constr. Co. v. United States, 27 Fed. Cl. 516, 541 (1993) ("Certainly, it is clear beyond cavil that by 1983 cost accounting had sufficiently advanced to the point where, consistent with Generally Accepted Accounting Practices (GAAP), plaintiff's additional and unanticipated costs stemming from the excess water condition could have been separated out from the original cost estimate with reasonable accuracy."); WRB Corp. v. United States, 183 Ct. Cl. 409, 426 (1968) ("A large measure of our present uncertainty is due to the plaintiff's complete failure to maintain accurate cost records during performance. The only excuse for this lack of diligence was that plaintiff did not expect to become embroiled in litigation over the Fort Hood project. That is feeble justification for taking refuge in the total-cost approach."); Cavalier Clothes, Inc. v. United States, 51 Fed. Cl. 399, 419 (2001) ("[I]n the instant case, it appears impossible for plaintiff to prove the amount of its actual losses directly with reasonable accuracy—but not because of the fleeting or ephemeral nature of those losses, or any theoretical inability to capture or document their magnitude, but simply because plaintiff failed to maintain its records. . . . Given that the total cost method is highly disfavored, this court is disinclined to allow a plaintiff to rely on that method based on a bed of its own making."); AMEC Civil, LLC v. DMJM Harris, Inc., 2009 WL 1883985, at *9 (D.N.J. June 30, 2009) ("When weighing the first prong, where a plaintiff failed to maintain its records, courts are disinclined to allow a plaintiff to rely on this highly disfavored method of recovery based on a bed of its own making.").

90. Municipality of Anchorage v. Frank Coluccio Constr. Co., 826 P.2d 316, 326 (Alaska 1992).

91. Flatiron-Lane v. Case Atlantic Co., 121 F. Supp. 3d 515, 558 (M.D.N.C. 2015) ("It appears that the actual reason that it was 'impracticable' for Case to use the measured mile method is that it would show Case's low production rates were its own fault.").

92. *See* John F. Harkins Co. v. Sch. Dist. of Philadelphia, 460 A.2d 260, 263 (Pa. Super. Ct. 1983) ("The necessity for showing an accurate bid estimate prior to utilization of the total cost method is basic."); Baldi Bros. Constructors v. United States, 50 Fed. Cl. 74, 79–80 (2001) ("Trial courts

the total cost method.[93] In order to make this determination, courts compare a contractor's bid estimate to the estimates from the government and/or other bidders.[94] In *Great Lakes Dredge & Rock Co. v. United States*, the Court of Claims found the government's estimate for impacted items was 11 percent higher, and the average bid of four other contractors was 25 percent higher, and thus concluded that the claimant had underestimated the cost of key work on the project.[95] As a result, the court determined the appropriate starting point for the modified total cost calculation of the contractor's damages was not its actual bid, but instead was the average of the government's estimate and the other contractors' average bid.[96] Similarly, the court in *Servidone Construction Corp. v. United States* noted that the claimant's bid for embankment items was between $1.9 million and $9.2 million less than the other bidders, and $6.2 million less than the government's estimate, and concluded "[i]t is plain that Servidone underbid."[97] Interestingly, the trial court there put significant weight on the fact that one particular bidder's prices were the fifth lowest on the job, and used this as the most realistic and reasonable original estimate of costs upon which to base its calculation of damages.[98]

---

are advised to use this method with caution because bidding inaccuracies can create an unrealistically low estimate of the contractor's costs, and performance inefficiencies can increase the costs incurred.").

93. *See* Servidone Constr. Corp. v. United States, 931 F.2d 860, 861–62 (Fed. Cir. 1991) ("Under this method, bidding inaccuracies can unjustifiably reduce the contractor's estimated costs."); WRB Corp. v. United States, 183 Ct. Cl. 409, 426–27 (1968) ("[W]e would hesitate before concluding that plaintiff sufficiently proved the reasonableness of its estimates or its actual costs. Among other things, it did not produce a reliable breakdown of its overall estimates and the cost of its concrete and carpentry operations."); Youngdale & Sons Constr. Co. v. United States, 27 Fed. Cl. 516, 543 (1993) ("[T]he plaintiff should not get the benefit of increased damages merely because it submitted an unreasonably low bid, thereby increasing the difference between its bid and its actual costs solely by underbidding the project and not by incurring incremental costs caused by the defendant's reprehensible actions."); Tecom, Inc. v. United States, 86 Fed. Cl. 437, 456 (2009), quoting Propellex Corp. v. Brownlee, 342 F.3d 1335, 1338 (Fed. Cir. 2003) ("The danger in using this approach is that it may provide 'a windfall for either the government or the contractor,' depending on whether the contractor underestimated or overestimated the costs of performing the in-scope work under the contract."); AMEC Civil, LLC v. DMJM Harris, Inc., 2009 WL 1883985, at *7 (D.N.J. June 30, 2009) ("This method has always been viewed with disfavor, in part because of concerns about bidding inaccuracies, which can reduce the contractor's estimated costs[.]").

94. *See* Servidone Constr. Corp. v. United States, 19 Cl. Ct. 346, 385–86 (1990), citing Appeal of Ingalls Ship Building Div., Litton Sys., Inc., ASBCA No. 17597, 78-1 BCA ¶ 13,038 at 63,668–72 ("[A] determination of what was a reasonable bid must be made from the bids of others.").

95. Great Lakes Dredge & Rock Co. v. United States, 96 F. Supp. 923, 926 (1951).

96. *Id. See also* Youngdale & Sons Constr. Co. v. United States, 27 Fed. Cl. 516, 543 (1993) ("[B]ecause there is no other testimony in the record as to what would have been a reasonable bid, . . . an average of the government's estimate and the 11 other bids would be the appropriate method for calculating the fairest basis by which to compare the reasonableness of plaintiff's increased costs (bid).").

97. Servidone Constr. Corp. v. United States, 19 Cl. Ct. 346, 385 (1990).

98. *Id.* at 385–86.

Actual Costs Are Reasonable

This requirement to utilize the total cost method requires courts to perform a fact-specific evaluation of the documentary evidence and expert testimony presented. Somewhat surprisingly, it is not an uncommon occurrence for a contractor to present a "dearth of evidence with respect to its actual costs" and therefore fail to prove the reasonableness of its actual costs.[99] Of course, a majority of these cases address this element with little fanfare.[100]

Contractor Not Responsible for the Added Costs

As a final element, the total cost method requires the contractor to show an absence of blame for the claimed extra costs. "[T]he contractor is required to show that it was not the party responsible for the additional costs. . . . It follows that the plaintiff must show how much of its costs were solely the result of the defendant's negligence versus its own."[101]

99. *See* Boyajian v. United States, 423 F.2d 1231, 1239 (Ct. Cl. 1970) ("A schedule of verified costs . . . is not proof of damages but only a starting point . . . Plaintiff's one witness who testified about costs only verified that they were incurred on the job."); Youngdale & Sons Constr. Co. v. United States, 27 Fed. Cl. 516, 544–45 (1993) ("[D]ue to plaintiff's lack of probative evidence as to any of its excess costs, save one significant exception, we would be clearly justified in disallowing all of plaintiff's damages claims irrespective of the method otherwise utilized in the instant case."); WRB Corp. v. United States, 183 Ct. Cl. 409, 426 (1968) ("[W]e would hesitate before concluding that plaintiff sufficiently proved the reasonableness of . . . its actual costs. Among other things, it did not produce a reliable breakdown of its . . . cost of its concrete and carpentry operations."); Propellex Corp. v. Brownlee, 342 F.3d 1335, 1342 (Fed. Cir. 2003) ("Where it is impractical for a contractor to prove its actual costs because it failed to keep accurate records, when such records could have been kept, and where the contractor does not provide a legitimate reason for its failure to keep the records, the total cost method of recovery is not available to the contractor.); G.M. Harston Constr. Co. v. City of Chicago, 371 F. Supp. 2d 949, 953 (N.D. Ill. 2005) ("It is not enough for HSJV to say, 'These are our total costs. Pay them, together with a reasonable profit.' Some proof of reasonableness is required."); Wayne Knorr, Inc. v. Dep't of Transp., 973 A.2d 1061, 1098 (Pa. Commw. Ct. 2009) ("[T]he difficulty with Knorr's claim stems from the lack of evidence establishing a clear causal connection between the "piecemeal fashion" in which it performed its paving work and an increase in its MPT costs above that contemplated by the Contract.").

100. *See* Servidone Constr. Corp. v. United States, 931 F.2d 860 (Fed. Cir. 1991); Penzel Constr. Co. v. Jackson R-2 School Dist., 544 S.W.3d 214 (Mo. Ct. App. 2017); J.D. Hedin Constr. Co. v. United States, 347 F.2d 235 (Ct. Cl. 1965).

101. AMEC Civil, LLC v. DMJM Harris, Inc., 2009 WL 1883985, at *10 (D.N.J. June 30, 2009). *See also* Glasgow, Inc. v. Dep't of Transp., 529 A.2d 576, 579 (Pa. Commw. Ct. 1987) ("When a contractor takes his total cost less his estimated cost under the contract pursuant to the total cost theory, adjustments must be made for various costs incurred which were not a result of the defendant's breach of contract."); City of Gillette v. Hladky Constr., Inc., 196 P.3d 184, 200–01 (Wyo. 2008) (Total cost method "is disfavored primarily because it attributes all responsibility to the owner without

Contractors that cannot establish that they were not responsible for their increased costs will be unable to meet this element. For example, in *Net Construction, Inc. v. C&C Rehab & Construction, Inc.*, the court was unimpressed with the proffered evidence regarding responsibility, concluding the plaintiff "failed to distinguish losses suffered as a result of delays by [defendant] from losses that it might have suffered because of [claimant's] own performance problems, weather, unsuitable soils, or the existence of asbestos at the site."[102] As a result, the contractor's lost productivity claim was denied. Similarly, in *Appeal of Bechtel National Inc.*, although noting that some costs were properly removed from the contractor's inefficiency claim calculation, the NASA Board of Contract Appeals was ultimately unpersuaded that all costs for which the contractor was responsible had been excluded, stating "[t]he Contractor must show freedom from its own inefficiencies as a condition of recovery on this type of claim."[103]

Other contractors have similarly been unable to meet this element. For some, the lack of maintaining project records proved fatal.[104] In one case, the contractor's failure to attend a pre-bid site visit was seen as contributing to its increased costs, and therefore prevented the contractor from meeting its burden.[105] In another case, the claimant's expert's own testimony that the increased hours were "*primarily* caused by" the defendant and that the defendant's actions had caused "the *majority*" of the overrun led the court to find the contractor's proof of its lack of responsibility insufficient.[106]

---

establishing a clear causal connection between the owner's breach and the increased costs."). *But see* Lighting & Power Servs. v. Roberts, 354 F.3d 817, 822 (8th Cir. 2004) ("There are cases that interpret the final factor of the total cost method to require a subcontractor to prove not only that it was not responsible for the added expenses, but also that the defendant was responsible for them. . . . the cases containing such instructions are not Miller Act cases . . . [where] a subcontractor can recover additional expenses incurred because of delay regardless of the fault of the general contractor[.]").

102. Net Constr., Inc. v. C&C Rehab & Constr., Inc., 256 F. Supp. 2d 350, 355 (E.D. Pa. 2003).

103. Appeal of Bechtel Nat'l, Inc., NASABCA No. 1186-7, 90-1 BCA ¶ 22,549. *See also* Amelco Electric v. City of Thousand Oaks, 38 P.3d 1120, 1133 (Cal. 2002) ("Amelco conceded no effort was made during the project to distinguish between those inefficiencies that were Amelco's and those believed to be the responsibility of the City.").

104. *See* Cavalier Clothes, Inc. v. United States, 51 Fed. Cl. 399, 424 (2001) ("Cavalier's inability to distinguish between delays attributable to its own actions and those allegedly attributable to the government again hinges on Cavalier's failure to retain its inspection records, which would have shown how many coats were rejected on account of the modifications."). *See also* WRB Corp. v. United States, 183 Ct. Cl. 409, 426 (1968).

105. Southern Comfort Builders, Inc. v. United States, 67 Fed. Cl. 124, 150 (2005).

106. North American Mech., Inc. v. Walsh Constr. Co. II, 132 F. Supp. 3d 1064, 1079 (E.D. Wis. 2015) ("The court is provided with no means by which to subtract whatever costs were *not* attributable to Walsh (nor even a means of identifying which costs those might be).").

Contractors have, however, met this standard.[107] In *Amp-Rite Electric Co. v. Wheaton Sanitary District*, the owner argued that the contractor's disruption claim included extra hours that were caused by the contractor, but the court noted the owner's granting of a significant time extension "bespeak [contractor's] lack of fault" and found the contractor was seeking only additional costs caused by the owner.[108]

Modified Total Cost Method

It is important to understand that because of judicial criticism, the courts have created a means of addressing the total cost method's downfalls. The *modified* total cost approach uses the same elements but allows the fact finder to adjust or amend certain aspects of those elements in order to deliver a more harmonious quantification of damages once a breach of contract has been proven.[109]

> The theory behind the modified approach is that, in order to prevent the government from obtaining a windfall stemming from the plaintiff's inability to satisfy all of the elements of the total cost method, the court will modify that test, so that the amount that would have been received by the plaintiff under the total cost method, is only the starting point from which the court will adjust the plaintiff's recovery downward to reflect the inability to prove any of the aforementioned four elements.[110]

The difference between the total cost method and the modified total cost method has been described as the former being "an all-or-nothing approach" that can undercompensate or overcompensate the plaintiff, whereas the latter "allows the

---

107. *See* Eagle Supply & Mfg., L.P. v. Bechtel Jacobs Co., 868 F.3d 423, 432 (6th Cir. 2017); JMR Constr. Corp. v. Env'l Assessment & Remediation Mgmt., Inc., 243 Cal. App. 4th 571, 589 (Cal. Ct. App. 2015); Moorhead Constr. Co. v. City of Grand Forks, 508 F.2d 1008, 1017 (8th Cir. 1975).

108. Amp-Rite Elec. Co. v. Wheaton Sanitary Dist., 580 N.E.2d 622, 642 (Ill. App. Ct. 1991).

109. *See* Flatiron-Lane v. Case Atlantic Co., 121 F. Supp. 3d 515, 557 (M.D.N.C. 2015) ("The modified total cost method takes a party's total costs as a starting point rather than an end, and then reduces the damages from there based on three factors: the reasonableness of the contractor's bid, the reasonableness of the contractor's actual costs, and the contractor's lack of responsibility for the added costs."); AMEC Civil, LLC v. DMJM Harris, Inc., 2009 WL 1883985, at *8 (D.N.J. June 30, 2009) ("Under a modified total cost approach, a contractor still has the burden of proving the four elements required for the total cost method, but the burden is not as stringent.").

110. Youngdale & Sons Constr. Co. v. United States, 27 Fed. Cl. 516, 541 (1993), citing Servidone, 931 F.2d 860, 862 (Fed. Cir. 1991). *See also* AMEC Civil, LLC v. DMJM Harris, Inc., 2009 WL 1883985, at *8 (D.N.J. June 30, 2009) ("The modified total cost method addresses some of the objections to the total cost method by adjusting it for a contractor's lack of proof in the requirements of the total cost method.").

fact-finder to calculate damages in a way that more fairly represents the damages actually caused by the defendant-owner."[111]

What is modified is up to the discretion of the court,[112] but the most typical modifications are correction of an unreasonable bid and job costs resulting from the contractor's actions.[113] In some cases, more than one element is revised by the court.[114]

Courts usually discuss the modified total cost method when a contractor is unable to meet the required elements to use the total cost method because it provides the court with an opportunity to craft a quantum of damages that addresses weaknesses with the contractor's presentation of evidence.

Jury Verdict

When none of the preceding methods is deemed acceptable by the court, the jury verdict determination provides one last opportunity to quantify the disruption damages incurred by a claimant that has shown entitlement. In essence, the trier of fact develops a jury verdict by making either suitable adjustments to the parties' proffered calculations, or its own computation of the damages based upon the

---

111. Penzel Constr. Co. v. Jackson R-2 School Dist., 544 S.W.3d 214, 234–35 (Mo. Ct. App. 2017).

112. *See* Neal & Co. v. United States, 36 Fed. Cl. 600, 638 (1996) ("The modified total cost method is simply the total cost method, adjusted for any deficiencies in the plaintiff's proof in satisfying the requirements of the total cost method."); *see* Biemann & Rowell Co. v. Donohoe Cos., 556 S.E.2d 1, 6 (N.C. Ct. App. 2001) (The modified approach assumes the elements of a total cost claim have been established, but permits the court to modify the test so that the amount plaintiff would have received under the total cost method is only the starting point from which the court will adjust the amount downward to reflect the plaintiff's inability to satisfy the test.").

113. *See* Boyajian v. United States, 423 F.2d 1231, 1240–42 (Ct. Cl. 1970); Servidone Constr. Corp. v. United States, 931 F.2d 860, 861 (Fed. Cir. 1991); *In re* Elec. Machinery Enterprises, Inc., 416 B.R. 801, 855 (Bankr. M.D. Fla. 2009); Penzel Constr. Co. v. Jackson R-2 School Dist., 544 S.W.3d 214, 237 (Mo. Ct. App. 2017) (modified total cost method "allows for adjustments to (1) the original contract price (the amount of the contractor's accepted bid), (2) the total cost of performance, or (3) both."); Dillingham-Ray Wilson v. City of Los Angeles, 182 Cal. App. 4th 1396, 1408 (Cal. App. 2010) ("If some of the contractor's costs were unreasonable or caused by its own errors or omissions, then those costs are subtracted from the damages to arrive at a modified total cost."); JMR Constr. Corp. v. Env'l Assessment & Remediation Mgmt., Inc., 243 Cal. App. 4th 571, 589 (Cal. Ct. App. 2015).

114. *See* MacDougald Constr. Co. v. United States, 122 Ct. Cl. 210 (1952) (Court modified the contractor's bid estimate up because it was significantly lower than the other bidders and the government's estimate, and modified the contractor's actual costs down because of its own problems (such as utilizing poor equipment).).

admitted evidence.[115] Obviously, there must be at least sufficient evidence for the court to make a fair approximation of damages.[116]

In *WRB Corp. v. United States*, the court struggled with "paucity of data—both affirmative and rebuttal—on damages."[117] After stating its preference to *not* use the jury verdict method, it concluded that "the age of the case and the great doubt that further proceedings would produce any better foundation for an award, leave us

115. *See* Rustler Constr., Inc. v. Dist. of Columbia, 211 A.3d 187, 196–97 (D.C. 2019), citing Delco Electronics Corp. v. United States, 17 Cl. Ct. 302, 328–33 (1989), Freeman Gen., Inc. v. United States, 918 F.2d 188 (Fed. Cir. 1990) ("There are several cost-calculating techniques that fall under the umbrella of the jury verdict method. . . . calculating damages by awarding a certain percentage of the contractor's claim . . . calculating damages by using the government's cost estimate. The 'most common' technique is for the adjudicating body to make its own detailed computation of the adjustment, based on all of the data provided by the parties."); K&K Recycling, Inc. v. Alaska Gold Co., 80 P.3d 702, 722 (Alaska 2003) ("Courts have also allowed a jury verdict method of calculating damages, a variant on actual cost, that allows the contractor to present evidence of the cost of additional work to the finder of fact, including any actual cost data, accounting records, estimates by law and expert witnesses, and calculations from similar projects. The jury verdict method basically reflects the principle that a contractor need not prove damages with mathematical precision, but may only recover those damages which it proves with reasonable certainty."); WRB Corp. v. United States, 183 Ct. Cl. 409, 425 (1968) ("In the past we have allowed so-called 'jury verdicts' if there was clear proof that the contractor was injured and there was no more reliable method for computing damages—but only where the evidence adduced was sufficient to enable a court or jury to make a fair and reasonable approximation.").

116. Boyajian v. United States, 423 F.2d 1231, 1244 (Ct. Cl. 1970) ("In situations where the court has rejected the 'total cost' method of proving damages, but where the record nevertheless contains reasonably satisfactory evidence of what the damages are, computed on an acceptable basis, the court has adopted such other evidence, or where such other evidence, although not satisfactory in and of itself upon which to base a judgment, has nevertheless been considered at least sufficient upon which to predicate a 'jury verdict' award, it has rendered a judgment based on such a verdict. However, where the record is blank with respect to any such other alternative evidence, the court has been obliged to dismiss the claim for failure of damage proof, regardless of the merits."); Appeals of States Roofing Corp., ASBCA No. 54860, 10-1 BCA ¶ 34,356 ("[I]n evaluating the evidence, we are not precluded from awarding disruption damages on the basis of a jury verdict if: (1) clear proof of injury exists; (2) there is no more reliable method for computing damages; and (3) the evidence is sufficient for us to make a fair and reasonable approximation of the damages."); New Pueblo Constructors, Inc. v. State, 696 P.2d 185, 196 (Ariz. 1985) ("The contractor cannot use the jury verdict method if he can prove only that the state caused part of the damages and cannot make a reasonable approximation of those damages."); North Pac. Erectors, Inc. v. State Dep't of Admin., 337 P.3d 495, 507 (Alaska 2013) ("The jury verdict method permits the contractor to present evidence of the cost of additional work to the finder of fact, including any actual cost data, accounting records, estimates by law and expert witnesses, and calculations from similar projects. But the jury verdict method is only appropriate once the contractor has shown that there was no more reliable method for computing damages."). *See also* Dawco Constr., Inc. v. United States, 930 F.2d 872, 880–82 (Fed. Cir. 1991), *overruled in part on other grounds*, Reflectone, Inc. v. Dalton, 60 F.3d 1572 (Fed. Cir. 1995) (*en banc*); Appeal of Grumman Aerospace Corp., ASBCA No. 50090, 01-1 BCA ¶ 31,316 at 154,646, *aff'd*, 34 Fed. Appx 710 (Fed. Cir. 2003).

117. WRB Corp. v. United States, 183 Ct. Cl. 409, 425 (1968).

with no alternative but to accept that approach" and made numerous adjustments to the parties' damages calculations.[118] The board of contract appeals in *Appeals of States Roofing Corp.* did not have a similar reticence about utilizing a jury verdict before making adjustments to the contractor's (already) modified total cost claim.[119] Other decision-makers have found the evidence submitted did not allow it to use a jury verdict.[120]

Contract Provisions Regarding Loss of Productivity

A good portion of this chapter has addressed how to quantify and recover disruption costs. On many projects, this type of extra expense is contractually recoverable, or at least not explicitly barred. But some construction contracts contain language that prohibits such recovery.

No Damages for Delay

The most prevalent contract provision that may prevent lost productivity is called a no-damages-for-delay clause. While the parties are free to choose whatever language they want, following is an example of the language typically used:

> Notwithstanding anything to the contrary in the Contract Documents, an extension in the Contract Time shall be the sole remedy of the Trade Contractor for any (1) delay in the commencement, prosecution or completion of the work, (2) hindrance or obstruction in the performance of the work, (3) loss of productivity, or (4) other similar claims. . . . In no event shall the Trade Contractor be entitled to any compensation or recovery of any damage in connection with any

118. *Id.*

119. ASBCA No. 54860, 10-1 BCA ¶ 34,356 ("We believe the evidentiary record here fully supports the application of a jury verdict and that we would be remiss if we were to deny SRC recovery for disruption damages under circumstances in which its work was so obviously impacted by the differing site conditions it encountered and the contract changes made by the Navy, a conclusion the Navy itself has conceded. Moreover, our concerns about SRC's adjusted bid price make a jury verdict a more reliable method for computing damages. The evidence is sufficient for us to reach a fair and reasonable approximation of SRC's disruption damages."). *See also* Appeal of Ingalls Shipbuilding Div. Litton Sys., Inc., ASBCA No. 17579, 78-1 BCA ¶ 13,038, *recon. denied*, 78-1 BCA ¶ 13,216 (board had no difficulty employing jury verdict method); Appeal of Bechtel Nat'l, Inc., NASABCA No. 1186-7, 90-1 BCA ¶ 22,549 (board had no difficulty employing jury verdict method).

120. G.M. Shupe, Inc. v. United States, 5 Cl. Ct. 662, 677 (1984) ("[T]he record in this case and the confusion and complexity built into the damage figures presented by plaintiff preclude the court from being able to make a fair and reasonable approximation necessary for resorting to a total award jury verdict remedy, assuming one to be justified."); Boyajian v. United States, 423 F.2d 1231, 1244 (Ct. Cl. 1970).

> Delay, including without limitation, consequential damages, lost opportunity cost, impact damages or other similar remuneration.[121]

Although valid in most jurisdictions,[122] no-damages-for-delay clauses are strictly construed because of their harsh consequences.[123] Courts confronted with this type of contract language review the words carefully in determining the intended meaning. In the case where the language just cited was used, the court found the language unambiguous and precluded the plaintiff's lost productivity claim.[124]

When the language of the no-damages-for-delay clause differs, courts' interpretations change. For example, in a situation where the language forbid damages "should the Contractor be delayed in the commencement, prosecution, or completion" of the project, one court concluded that disruption claims were not barred.[125] The court there drew the distinction between delay and disruption, stating the trade contractor was "not arguing that it suffered damages from delay, but rather that it suffered damages from obstacles created by" the construction manager.[126]

A general line of demarcation in this type of case is whether the clause refers to "delay" only[127] or refers to "delay" and "hindrance" or "disruption."[128] But not all

---

121. C&H Elec., Inc. v. Town of Bethel, 2012 WL 2899314, at *4 (Conn. Super. Ct. June 15, 2012).

122. *See* W.C. James, Inc. v. Phillips Petroleum Co., 485 F.2d 22, 25 (10th Cir. 1973) (No damages for delay clauses "are commonly used in the construction industry and generally recognized as valid and enforceable."); Kiewit Constr. Co. v. Capital Elec. Constr. Co., 2005 WL 2563042, at *8 (D. Neb. Oct. 12, 2005) ("Given that one of the main purposes of construction contracts is to allocate the risks of construction among the parties, no-damages-for-delay clauses are used to assign the risk of delays, for whatever cause, upon one of the contracting parties, with the assumption that the party bearing the risk has bargained for a price that covers the burden of carrying the risk."); Corinno Civetta Constr. Corp. v. City of New York, 493 N.E.2d 905 (N.Y. 1986).

123. Tricon Kent Co. v. Lafarge North America, Inc., 186 P.3d 155 (Colo. Ct. App. 2008) ("[N]o damages for delay clauses are valid and enforceable . . . but they are to be strictly construed against the owner or contractee."); W.C. James, Inc. v. Phillips Petroleum Co., 485 F.2d 22, 25 (10th Cir.1973) ("Such clauses are commonly used in the construction industry and are generally recognized as valid and enforceable."); John E. Green Plumbing & Heating Co. v. Turner Constr. Co., 742 F.2d 965, 966 (6th Cir. 1984); E.C. Ernst, Inc. v. Manhattan Constr. Co. of Texas, 551 F.2d 1026, 1029 (5th Cir. 1977); Cunningham Bros., Inc. v. City of Waterloo, 117 N.W.2d 46, 49 (Iowa 1962).

124. C&H Elec., Inc. v. Town of Bethel, 2012 WL 2899314, at *5 (Conn. Super. Ct. June 15, 2012).

125. John E. Green Plumbing & Heating Co. v. Turner Constr. Co., 742 F.2d 965, 967 (6th Cir. 1984).

126. *Id.*

127. Central Ceilings, Inc. v. Suffolk Constr. Co., 75 N.E.3d 40, 47–48 (Mass. App. Ct. 2017), *appeal denied*, 88 N.E.3d 1167 (Mass. 2017) ("Suffolk's breaches did not affect Central's ability to complete its work on time . . . but, rather, with its ability to complete its work on budget.").

128. *See* North American Mech., Inc. v. Walsh Constr. Co. II, 132 F. Supp. 3d 1064, 1077–78 (E.D. Wis. 2015); Cumberland Farms, Inc. v. Tenacity Constr., Inc., 2016 WL 7735771, at *3–4 (Mass. Super. Ct. Nov. 16, 2016); Cleveland Constr., Inc. v. Ohio Public Emps. Retirement Sys., 2008 WL 885841, at *4 (Ohio Ct. App. Apr. 3, 2008); Quinn Constr., Inc. v. Skanska USA Building, Inc., 730

court opinions follow this distinction.[129] And there are situations where conflicting provisions must be interpreted.[130]

Also, in certain situations courts have found general exceptions to no-damages-for-delay clauses applicable and refused to enforce the exculpatory contract language. For example, a Pennsylvania court found a school district's actions constituted "a failure to act in an essential matter under the contract" (for failing to obtain a permit, not issuing a comprehensive sequencing schedule until months after the project began, and refusing to change the completion date) and therefore the court disregarded a no-damages-for-delay clause in the contract.[131] A Colorado court also chose not to enforce a no-damages-for-delay clause as a result of the contractor engaging in active interference with a subcontractor's ability to perform its work.[132] And many courts have found a no-damages-for-delay clause "does not shield the owner from liability from deliberately and wrongfully interfering with the contractor's work."[133]

Waiver

In addition to no-damages-for-delay clauses in contracts, contractors must also contend with language that may be included in change orders or other agreements made after construction has started that include waiver-type verbiage that could bar recovery of disruption claims.

The case of *Bell BCI Co. v. United States* is instructive on this topic. Early in the job, the contractor and owner signed a modification that included language to the effect that a payment for certain added work would be a "full and equitable adjustment" for the "remaining direct and indirect work" as well as "for all delays

---

F. Supp. 2d 401, 411–12 (E.D. Pa. 2010); Kiewit Constr. Co. v. Capital Elec. Constr. Co., 2005 WL 2563042, at *8 (D. Neb. Oct. 12, 2005).

129. *See* Bates & Rogers Constr. Corp. v. North Shore Sanitary Dist., 414 N.E.2d 1274, 1278 (Ill. App. Ct. 1980) (finding clause referring only to delay excluded cost overruns, excessive labor costs, excessive supervision, etc. "premised on the pleading that plaintiffs were required by the fault of the defendant to perform their work out of sequence, thus ineffectively and less productively. In our view this claim of damages is excluded by the no-damages-for-delay clause.").

130. *See* Atlantic Coast Mech. v. R.W. Allen Beers Constr., 592 S.E.2d 115, 118–19 (Ga. Ct. App. 2003) (broad no-damages-for-delay clause in the contractor's contract with the owner superseded by provision in subcontract stating subcontractor entitled to interference, interruption, and inefficiency).

131. James Corp. v. North Allegheny School Dist., 938 A.2d 474, 485 (Pa. Commw. Ct. 2007).

132. Tricon Kent Co. v. Lafarge North America, Inc., 186 P.3d 155, 160 (Colo. Ct. App. 2008).

133. Zachry Constr. Corp. v. Port of Houston Auth., 449 S.W.3d 98, 101 (Tex. 2014) ("To conclude otherwise would incentivize wrongful conduct and damage contractual relations. This conclusion is supported by lower court decisions in Texas and court decisions in at least 28 American jurisdictions.").

resulting from any and all Government changes" through a certain date. Despite the owner subsequently issuing 113 additional modifications on the project—which the trial court found to have caused the contractor to incur an additional $2 million in labor inefficiencies—the appellate court found that the contractor had released the owner from all liability for equitable adjustment attributable to the modification.[134] In a somewhat similar case, a contractor unsuccessfully urged the court to find that the reason it had signed a modification containing waiver language was economic duress.[135]

Conclusion

Because there are innumerable situations on construction projects that can cause a contractor to incur increased labor and equipment costs as a result of disruptions, there are many court and board opinions explaining the intricate parameters required to entitle a claimant to recovery. A large amount of the verbiage in the case law focuses on the methodology for quantifying the lost productivity costs with an appropriate level of certainty. The method used by the required expert witness to quantify the disruption damages is largely dependent on what contemporaneous records are available. If those documents are readily accessible, accurate, and detailed, then the claim will be more likely to succeed. Where there is little documentation of the effects of disruption, the claimant will have to rely on less-favored methodologies, such as the total cost and jury verdict approaches. In addition to the means of proving entitlement to increased costs, some plaintiffs must also defend exculpatory language in the contract or change orders. All of this must be understood by the practitioner to represent the client adequately and competently in disruption claim cases.

134. Bell BCI Co. v. United States, 570 F.3d 1337, 1340 (Fed. Cir. 2009).
135. Pellerin Constr., Inc. v. Witco Corp., 169 F. Supp. 2d 568, 579–80 (E.D. La. 2001).